YOUR
HEALTH
YOUR
CHOICE

YOUR HEALTH

YOUR CHOICE

Consultant Editor: Simon Mills, MA, MNIMH

PAPERMAC

A Marshall Edition
Edited and designed by
Marshall Editions Ltd,
170 Piccadilly,
London W1V 9DD

Editor
Fran Robinson

Editorial assistant
William Hemsley

Art editor
Roger Kohn

Design assistants
Sarah Lloyd
Vanilla Beer

Managing editor
Ruth Binney

Production
Barry Baker
Janice Storr

Line illustrations
Graham Rosewarne
János Márffy

Consultant editor
Simon Mills MA, MNIMH
Chairman of the Council for
Complementary and Alternative
Medicine.

Acupuncturist
Geoff Wadlow, BA, Dip. Ac. (Nanjing),
MRTCM Co-director of the London
School of Acupuncture, President of the
Register of Traditional Chinese
Medicine, Chairman of the Council for
Acupuncture.

Chiropractor
Susan Moore, DC
President, The British Chiropractic
Association.

Homeopath
Margaret Roy, BA
Principal of the Scottish College of
Homeopathy

Medical herbalist
Mark Evans, MNIMH
Information Officer for the National
Institute of Medical Herbalists.

Osteopath and naturopath
Joseph Goodman, MD, DO, DrAc, FCO,
FBAcA Dean of the College of
Osteopaths, Chairman of the Cranial
Osteopathic Association, Deputy
Chairman of the British Acupuncture
Association and Register, President of
the Council for Acupuncture.

Family doctor
Hilary Graham, BSc, MB, BS
General medical practitioner.

First published in 1988 by Macmillan
London Limited

First published in paperback in 1989 by
PAPERMAC
a division of Macmillan Publishers
Limited
4 Little Essex Street London WC2R 3LF
and Basingstoke

Associated companies in Auckland, Delhi, Dublin,
Gaborone, Hamburg, Harare, Hong Kong,
Johannesburg, Kuala Lumpur, Lagos, Manzini,
Melbourne, Mexico City, Nairobi, New York,
Singapore and Tokyo.

Typeset by MS Filmsetting Limited, Frome, UK
Originated in Hong Kong by Regent Publishing
Services Ltd
Printed in Spain

1   2   3   4   92   91   90   89   88

British Library Cataloguing in Publication Data

Mills, Simon, *1949—*
   Alternatives in healing.
   1. Alternative medicine
   I. Title
   615.5

ISBN 0-333-47340-X

The recommendations included in this book should
not be used as substitutes for consulting a doctor or
alternative medical practitioner.

CONTENTS

INTRODUCTION

As the guardian of your own body, the way you choose to treat it is an intensely personal matter. Just as you are free to decide how to exercise it, and which foods you will eat to fuel it, so you can also choose how your body may best be treated when its smooth working is disrupted by ill health.

Alternatives in Healing is a book about choices in health care, and you should use it to make the decisions that are right for you. It is a uniquely thorough and open-minded appraisal which addresses itself, without prejudice, to this vital contemporary issue, by taking an unbiased look at the effectiveness of both orthodox and non-orthodox medical treatments, and letting the advocates of each speak for themselves. Although these non-orthodox therapies have been termed "alternatives" to orthodox medicine, increasingly they are being seen as "complementary" approaches to healing, working alongside the conventional health care services.

In the search for new ways to treat illness – ways that do not depend on powerful drugs or other drastic interventions such as surgery – many new therapies have been promoted, for which dramatic claims are sometimes made. Without the chance to scrutinize these claims and compare the contrasting therapies, it is difficult, even for those working in the field of health care, to make sound recommendations about them. For the would-be consumer the prospect can be bewildering. Alternatively, you may know a little about one or two therapies but be unsure of the range of their applications and their potential scope for healing.

By offering direct comparisons of six common forms of health care, this book gives you the chance to form your own views and to decide which of the alternatives might best suit your own needs and interests.

The following therapies, five of which complement or serve as alternatives to conventional medicine, have been selected as the most popular representatives of the choices currently available:

Acupuncture offers all the sophistication of an approach to life and health that has developed in China over thousands of years, and is very different from that of Western medicine. Needles are used to stimulate points on the channels of vital energy or *Qi* (pronounced "chee") that flow through the body, and influence the balance of the body's natural health.

Chiropractic therapy specializes in treating muscular and skeletal disorders through manipulation of the spine. Spinal problems can interfere with the nerve supply and blood circulation to the rest of the body. By treating such problems, chiropractic therapy can therefore benefit general health in a variety of ways.

Homeopathy is based on the principle that "like cures like" and regards symptoms of illness as expressions of disharmony within the whole person. Its subtle effectiveness demonstrates the virtues of a system of medicine with energetic rather than material impact on the mind and body. Homeopathic medicines are administered in extremely diluted form and work by influencing the "vital force" or energetic level of the body.

Medical herbalism treats disorders with medicines that are derived exclusively from plant materials. It combines long-standing insights into health and healing with modern pharmacological research, and selects remedies specifically suited to each patient's individual needs, with the object of helping the body heal itself.

Osteopathy with naturopathy, like chiropractic therapy, uses manipulative techniques to adjust structural misalignments of the body. Because the nerves from the spinal cord supply the whole body, spinal problems are often related to other disorders. As a purely physical therapy, it can be effectively combined with a "whole person" therapy such as naturopathy, which seeks to help solve the problems of modern living by reforms of the diet and lifestyle.

Standard Western medicine results from several centuries of scientific pursuit of an understanding of and control over diseases. Doctors practising conventional medicine have access to all the resources of modern medical science and technology. This system of medicine is more clearly orientated toward symptom relief than other therapies and is likely to be most effective in this respect. It may, in some conditions, provide the only realistic option for preserving life.

The book begins with thorough, illustrated introductions to each of the six alternatives, including their principles and philosophy and techniques of diagnosis and treatment.

"Treatments for Health Problems" comprises the major part of the book. Here, the disorders selected for comparison are broadly grouped according to the body parts and systems affected. Although these are conventional medical divisions, they have been chosen for their familiarity – they are not intended to imply any bias toward any one method of treatment.

In the case studies that feature throughout, six practitioners respond to real patients suffering from common medical disorders. Their conclusions are arranged so that immediate comparisons between approaches can be made. A commentary by an independent consultant assures a balanced view. Comparative charts follow each group of case studies and provide a summary of the approaches of the six alternatives to a wide range of other related disorders.

The approach of complementary therapies to two of the dominant health issues of our age – AIDS and cancer – is included separately. Some guidance on the ways the alternatives can be used in accidents and emergencies (which do not lend themselves readily to case studies) is provided in the form of first aid suggestions. A list of contact addresses for the major professional organizations associated with the different alternatives completes the book.

Your body is an everyday miracle, but sometimes the odds are against it. I hope that this book will help guide you in choosing the best method of treatment when things go wrong.

Simon Y. Mills MA, MNIMH

ACUPUNCTURE

Traditional Chinese medicine has existed as a system of health care, and as an academic tradition in its own right, for at least 2,000 years. The first major surviving treatise on Chinese medicine, called *Huangti Neijing* or "Yellow Emperor's Canon of Internal Medicine", was compiled between 400 and 200 BC.

The first Imperial Medical College was founded during the Sui Dynasty (589–618 AD), and since then hundreds of years of experience have been accumulated and recorded from meticulous observation. As a consequence, today's practitioners have a huge body of empirical knowledge that allows them to predict the course of disease and prescribe appropriate remedies for each stage of development.

In Chinese medicine, and therefore in acupuncture, health is determined by a person's ability to maintain a balanced and harmonious internal environment. Disease occurs when the internal environment is disturbed and the normal processes that act to restore balance and harmony are unable to cope. The theory of internal harmony, expressed through the principles of *Yin/Yang* and the *Five Phases*, revolves around maintaining a balance of different and conflicting influences. If one or other of these influences becomes excessive or deficient, this will have the effect of upsetting the internal environment.

Harmony and balance also depend on the smooth and uninterrupted flow of *Qi* (pronounced "chee"), or vitality. *Qi* is responsible for the proper functioning of all spiritual, emotional, mental and physical processes. It circulates along pathways, known as *Jingluo*, or channels, which form a continuous circuit, linking all parts of the body and connecting with the internal organs, or *Zangfu*. The *Zangfu* generate *Qi*, and each has distinct, although closely interrelated, functions.

Traditional Chinese medicine consists of more than just acupuncture. The range of therapeutic methods it draws on includes moxibustion, herbal medicine, massage, osteopathic manipulation, and therapeutic exercise (*Qi Gong*). All are practised according to the basic principles of traditional Chinese medicine.

Acupuncture is not just a tool for the relief of pain. It has wide therapeutic applications, treating diseases that affect both the body as a whole organism, as well as specific functions, although its strength lies in treating functional disorders. It can be used to treat both acute and chronic disease, including infections, in both children and adults.

Yin and *Yang* and the *Five Phases*

Yin/Yang and the *Five Phases* are the two theoretical systems that form the basis of Chinese medical thought. Both are founded on observation of the natural world. Both systems compare natural external conditions and events with the physiology and pathology of humans, as well as describing the effect of environmental forces on them.

The *Yin/Yang* system categorizes phenomena, both in the world in general and the body in particular, under the two headings of *Yin* and *Yang*. *Yin* has connotations of softness, darkness, coldness and wetness, whereas *Yang* has connotations of hardness, brightness, heat and dryness. In a human being, parts of the body are ascribed more *Yin* or more *Yang* qualities, as are all the physiological and pathological processes of the whole person.

Yin and *Yang* are relative terms. All phenomena have a *Yin* and a *Yang* aspect. There is no *Yin* without *Yang*, just as there is no night without day. The *Yin/Yang* system is thus a total system, and its individual parts are meaningless on their own.

In a healthy person, *Yin* and *Yang* are in a state of constant flux. They are also in a state of balance. Daily activity is a more *Yang* state, whereas sleep is a more *Yin* state. Over the weeks and months each state balances the other, yet both are necessary for health. If one or other is indulged to excess, then the *Yin/Yang* balance of the body may be upset and signs and symptoms of this imbalance may appear.

The *Yin/Yang* system provides a means by which illness, its origins and progression from one stage to another, may be understood. A person who is unwell presents a predominance of *Yin* or *Yang* signs and symptoms. Illnesses due to excessive *Cold* penetrating the body, or characterized by signs of coldness – such as pallor or cold hands and feet – are categorized as *Yin* conditions. Conditions due to, or characterized by, signs of *Heat* are categorized as *Yang*. The treatment involves re-establishing a harmonious balance of *Yin* and *Yang* in order to restore health.

The *Five Phases* system also attempts to categorize all natural phenomena. There are five categories: *Wood, Fire, Earth, Metal* and *Water*. The system has its roots in the observation of seasonal changes, and of the natural processes that occur during each season. Each *Phase* represents a stage in the annual progress through the seasons.

The primary characteristic of each *Phase* is determined by what happens in the natural world during each season. One season after another plays its part in the cycle of the year, then smoothly moves on to the next. Plants germinate, grow, produce seed and die back in winter. It is the smooth and harmonious transition from one *Phase* to another that is important, along with the balance between them.

In a human being, the *Zangfu* (internal organs) and their associated activities, the *Jingluo* (channels), the tissues and the parts of the body, all correspond to one or other of the *Five Phases*. The relationship between the *Zangfu* is, like the relationship between the seasons, one of mutual support and restraint.

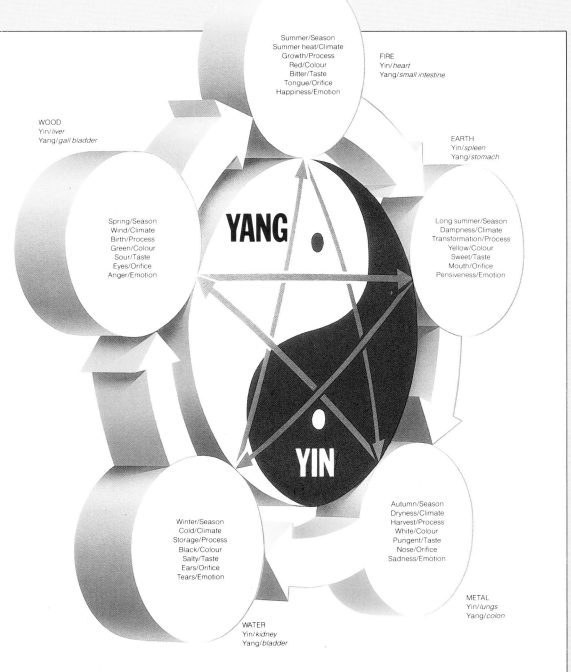

Summer/Season
Summer heat/Climate
Growth/Process
Red/Colour
Bitter/Taste
Tongue/Orifice
Happiness/Emotion

FIRE
Yin/*heart*
Yang/*small intestine*

WOOD
Yin/*liver*
Yang/*gall bladder*

EARTH
Yin/*spleen*
Yang/*stomach*

Spring/Season
Wind/Climate
Birth/Process
Green/Colour
Sour/Taste
Eyes/Orifice
Anger/Emotion

YANG

Long summer/Season
Dampness/Climate
Transformation/Process
Yellow/Colour
Sweet/Taste
Mouth/Orifice
Pensiveness/Emotion

YIN

Autumn/Season
Dryness/Climate
Harvest/Process
White/Colour
Pungent/Taste
Nose/Orifice
Sadness/Emotion

Winter/Season
Cold/Climate
Storage/Process
Black/Colour
Salty/Taste
Ears/Orifice
Tears/Emotion

METAL
Yin/*lungs*
Yang/*colon*

WATER
Yin/*kidney*
Yang/*bladder*

▲ **The relationships between the *Five Phases*** demonstrate the importance of cyclical influence and harmony in Oriental medicine. Each *Phase* nourishes and benefits the following *Phase* (thick arrows), while having a restraining influence on the next *Phase* but one (thin arrows). Thus, balance is maintained.

The concept of *Qi*

The Chinese concept of *Qi* has no English equivalent. It is often translated as "energy", but this does not convey the complexity of its meaning. Broadly, *Qi* is the life-force within the human organism, encompassing all the vital activities – spiritual, emotional, mental and physical. In its narrow sense, *Qi* takes on different forms according to its role in the life process, for example: Constitutional or *Jing Qi*; Nutritive or *Ying Qi*; Defensive or *Wei Qi*.

The health of a person is determined by a sufficient, balanced and uninterrupted flow of *Qi* in the body. *Qi* ensures proper bodily function by keeping *Blood* and *Body Fluids* circulating, by warming the body, fighting disease and protecting the body against incursions by the external environment, such as *Wind, Cold, Damp* and *Heat*. If the circulation of *Qi* is disrupted, blocked, or becomes excessive or deficient, illness may occur.

There are two main ways in which *Qi* becomes disordered. There may be a deficiency, in which case some or all of the functions are not performing properly; or the *Qi* becomes blocked or stagnant, and this usually means that pain results.

Jingluo (channels)

The *Qi* of the body circulates within a network of invisible pathways, or channels, on the body surface. The Chinese term for these is *Jingluo*: *Jing* means "channels" and *Luo* means "collaterals". They are often known as "meridians" in the West.

There are 12 main channels traversing the arms, legs, trunk and head: (*Lung, Large Intestine* or *Colon, Stomach, Spleen, Heart, Small Intestine, Urinary Bladder, Kidney, Pericardium, Sanjiao, Gall Bladder,* and *Liver*). They are connected to each other on a continuous circuit. In addition, two channels traverse the midline of the anterior trunk (*Ren*) and the posterior trunk (*Du*). Secondary channels form interconnections between the main channels, while others are spread in a fine network over the surface of the body, forming the "capillaries" of the channel system.

The connections between the channels ensure there is an even circulation of *Qi*, ensuring a balance of *Yin* and *Yang*. Each of the channels also connects – via internal pathways – with one of the *Zangfu* (internal organs). One of the most important functions of the channels is to connect the internal organs to the surface of the body. In this way the channels carry the *Qi* from the *Zangfu* to all parts of the body. These connections also mean that disorders of *Qi* can be passed from one channel or organ to another. The progression of some degenerative disorders can be explained in this way.

Because the channels are the main conduits of *Qi* in the body, disorders of the *Qi* often manifest themselves along their course. By identifying the exact location of symptoms, the acupuncturist can ascertain the channel involved. Disorders of the internal organs may also manifest themselves along the course of one or more channels, and these may be diagnosed in a similar way. For example, in angina, pain may be felt along the heart channel in the arm.

On each channel there are points that, when stimulated, affect the flow of *Qi* in that and other channels, or in the associated internal organs. By stimulating these points with needles or massage, the *Qi* is activated to correct the imbalances that cause illness. If the correct acupuncture points are to be chosen, and the best results achieved from treatment, an accurate diagnosis must be made according to the principles of traditional Chinese medical theory.

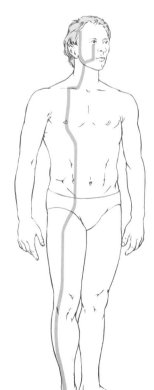

◄ **The *Stomach* channel**
Because the *Stomach* channel runs from the top to the bottom of the body, points on the feet may be used to treat disorders of *Qi* affecting the head.

▶ **The *Kidney* channel**
Channels have both internal and external pathways. The *Kidney* channel, like other channels, connects internal organs with the surface of the body. *Qi* nourishes all parts of the body via the channels.

The other important bodily substances – *Blood, Body Fluids* and *Jing* – are also described as "*Qi*" in various forms or stages of rarification or condensation. *Blood* nourishes the body and supports the functioning of *Qi*. *Body Fluids*, including saliva, sweat, digestive juices and synovial fluid, moisten organs and tissues and lubricate joints. *Jing* (often translated as *Essence*) is similar in many ways to a person's underlying constitution. It is stored in the *Kidney* and acts as a reservoir from which *Qi* may be derived when the channels or organs are weak, or in emergencies.

Recently, a great deal of research has been carried out in China to investigate the phenomenon of "propagation of sensation along the channels" (PSC) – that is, the production of sensation along the length of a channel when acupuncture points on it are needled. This research has shown that the sensation enhances the therapeutic effect of needling. Some researchers and historians in China believe that the pathways and channels were originally discovered in this way.

Internal pathway   **External pathway**

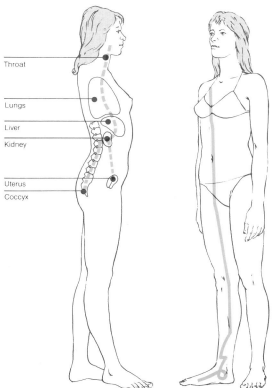

Throat

Lungs

Liver

Kidney

Uterus

Coccyx

Zangfu (internal organs)

The Chinese term for the internal organs is *Zangfu*, which is in fact made up of two words: *Zang*, meaning "viscera" and *Fu*, meaning "bowels". There are five major *Zang*: *Lung, Spleen, Heart, Kidney* and *Liver*. There is also a sixth *Zang*, the *Pericardium*, but its role is minor. There are six *Fu*: *Large Intestine, Stomach, Small Intestine, Sanjiao, Urinary Bladder* and *Gall Bladder*. The *Zang* are "solid" organs which store *Qi*, and are more *Yin* in character.

The *Fu* are seen as hollow organs, through which food and other substances pass. They are more active than the *Zang* and are thus said to be more *Yang* in character. These *Yin* and *Yang* organs are linked in pairs through their channels. They are also paired in terms of function. The *Spleen* and *Stomach*, for example, have a close functional relationship.

Each pair of organs is linked with one of the *Five Phases*. These correspondences are of great importance in diagnosis and form an essential part of the knowledge of traditional Chinese medicine.

The mind and the body are not differentiated in traditional Chinese medicine. The mental and spiritual functioning of a person is inseparable from the physical functioning. Emotional disturbances can both originate in, and be a causative factor in, the development of disorders of the *Qi*. Particular emotions are linked with particular organs.

The *Heart* has a major role in circulating the *Blood*. In traditional Chinese medicine, it also "houses" the Spirit or *Shen*, the consciousness of a person. The *Heart* and the *Shen* are seen as the coordinators of all physiological, spiritual and emotional activities.

The *Lung* is responsible for taking air and transforming it into *Qi*. It has an important role in the circulation of *Qi* and in helping to protect the body from "exterior" diseases.

Along with the *Stomach*, the *Spleen* is mainly responsible for digestion. The *Stomach* receives food, extracting the essential vitality, which the *Spleen* then transforms into *Qi* and distributes to all parts of the body.

Because the *Kidney* is the organ where *Jing* or "essence" is stored, it is the basis of a person's constitution. It is also said to be the source of *Yin* and *Yang* in the body. The *Kidney* has a major role in maintaining the body's water balance and also has a strong relationship with the bones and the lower back.

The role of the *Liver* concerns the free movement of *Qi*. It ensures that there are no obstructions to the circulation of *Qi*, blood and body fluids.

Key Functions of *Zangfu* Organs

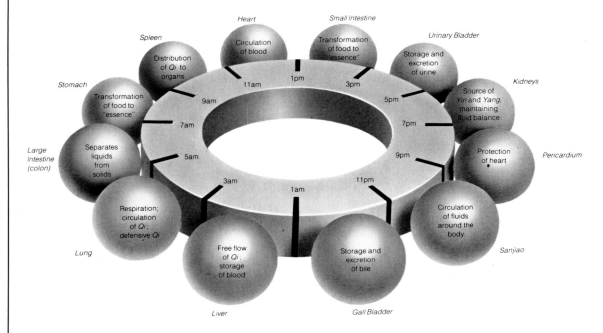

▲ *Zangfu* (internal organs) are responsible for generating, circulating, replenishing and storing *Qi*, *Blood* and *Body fluids*. The activity of each *Zangfu* organ is at its peak for only two hours each day. This peak activity occurs at the same time each day for any one organ, and each organ's activity peaks at a different time from any other organ. Although most of these organs have the same names as organs in Western anatomy, they are not in fact the same anatomical entities, nor do they necessarily have the same functions as ascribed to them in Western medicine. Instead, Chinese medicine – from which acupuncture terminology is derived – describes them and their functions in relation to *Qi*, *Blood,* and *Body fluids*.

Causes of disease

Disease arises because there is an imbalance of *Yin* and *Yang*. As a result, the normal, smooth and harmonious flow of *Qi* becomes disordered. This may occur either because there is not enough vitality to perform the normal bodily functions, or because there is a disruption in, or impediment to, normal circulation.

There are three main reasons why the circulation of *Qi*, blood or body fluids may become disrupted: internal or emotional disturbance; external or climatic factors; imbalances in diet or lifestyle; overwork; or stress.

Emotional disturbance affects the *Qi* as much as physical disturbance. Excessive stimulation of an emotion, or repression of an emotion, may have damaging repercussions on the internal organ with which it is associated.

Climatic factors, such as *Cold, Damp, Heat* and *Dryness*, are also seen as affecting the circulation and balance of *Qi*. The ability of the body to adapt to changes in, or excess of, any of these factors may be undermined if the *Qi* is weak. Although in the West people are less exposed than they are in China to the vagaries of climate, these factors are still important as causes of disease, especially in such conditions as arthritis.

Eating habits, work and rest patterns all play a vital part in determining the origin of disease. Too much or too little food, as well as irregular eating patterns, can damage the *Qi* of the *Stomach* and *Spleen* and may weaken the *Qi* of the whole body. Equally, too little exercise may lead to poor circulation of *Qi*, whereas too much exercise may lead to a weakening of the *Qi*. A strong constitution will not be affected as easily as a weak one.

Principles of treatment

There are three general principles of treatment in traditional Chinese medicine. First there is treatment of the "root" (*Ben*) and the "branch" (*Biao*). Second is regulation of *Yin* and *Yang*. Third is strengthening normal *Qi* and dispelling pathogenic (disease-causing) *Qi*.

Treating the "root" (*Ben*) and "branch" (*Biao*) is the most important principle of treatment in Chinese medicine. This refers to the need to identify the essential core or "root" of the disease in order to administer effective treatment. The "root" is the primary disharmony of *Yin/Yang*, the *Five Phases*, or of *Qi*, from which the "branch", the symptoms of disease or the secondary aspects of an illness, all arise.

A basic principle in Chinese medicine is to restore the balance of *Yin* and *Yang*. The diagnosis identifies whether there is a deficiency or excess of either the *Yin* or the *Yang* of the body and, more specifically, whether this is affecting one or more of the *Zangfu*. The acupuncture points chosen have the effect of strengthening the *Yang* of the body, eliminating excess *Yang* or, alternatively, of strengthening *Yin* or eliminating excess *Yin*.

The normal *Qi* of the body may become weakened for the reasons mentioned above. In addition, and perhaps because of the normal *Qi* being weakened, pathogenic *Qi* may accumulate, inhibiting further the proper functioning of the *Zangfu* and *Jingluo*. It is important for the practitioner to assess the relative strengths of the normal *Qi* and the pathogenic *Qi*.

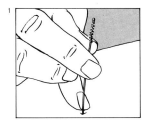

1 A sterilized needle is inserted a little way into an acupuncture point. Generally there is no discomfort but, if there is, it is no worse than a pin-prick.

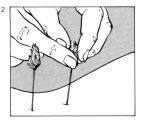

2 Moxibustion is used to warm and tonify the body's *Qi*, particularly in conditions characterized by coldness and dampness. After a needle has been inserted a small cone of moxa is placed around its head.

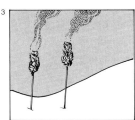

3 The moxa, dried leaves of the herb "common mugwort" that have been processed into a loose woolly material, is ignited and warms the needles, tonifying the *Qi* of the channel concerned.

► **A moxa stick** may be used as an alternative. The glowing tip is held close to an acupuncture point. When the patient finds it too hot, it is withdrawn.

Relationships with other therapies

It is usually confusing for a practitioner of acupuncture if a patient is receiving orthodox drug treatment. This tends to make a tongue diagnosis unreliable, because the drugs may drastically change the appearance of the tongue. Pulse diagnosis may also be affected.

It becomes extremely difficult to understand the "root" disharmony of an illness until the patient has enough relief from his or her symptoms through acupuncture treatment, to reduce or discontinue a drug regime. This is said advisedly, because such action must be undertaken with caution, and always if possible in consultation with the prescribing physician.

Also, there are certain Western drugs that inhibit the progress of treatment of some conditions. For instance, a person who suffers from a chronic digestive problem arising from *Spleen* disharmony may well experience a worsening of symptoms if antibiotics are prescribed, perhaps for a reason unconnected with the digestive disorder.

In China acupuncture is often combined with herbalism, and some Western acupuncturists follow this tradition. However, it is best to avoid having acupuncture treatment simultaneously with any of the other "alternative" disciplines. This is particularly true if the patient consults more than one type of therapist for the same problem. The only exceptions would be if a therapist experienced in more than one discipline decides to apply two or more types of therapy to a single condition, or if two therapists work in close consultation with each other. This is important because it is necessary to be able to monitor the results of treatment in order to know which one is having what effect.

CASE HISTORY

An acupuncturist spends from 15 minutes to one hour talking and listening to a patient as part of the process of reaching a diagnosis, depending on the type of problem concerned. For instance, a superficial problem affecting the *Jingluo* (channels) and involving no internal disharmony usually takes little time. But more complex, long-term problems – particularly if they affect the *Zangfu* (organs) – inevitably take longer, and a second opinion may be sought before treatment begins.

The case history is taken by asking the patient various questions. These focus initially on the history of the problem and the patient's presenting symptoms. Then the acupuncturist asks about the patient's general physical, mental and emotional state of health. This may involve questions about aspects of health which the patient may not think are immediately relevant, such as sleep patterns and preferences for certain types of food. In addition, details about the patient's work, lifestyle and social environment are all taken into account in this analysis.

EXAMINATION

The key parts of an acupuncturist's examination usually involve the patient's tongue and pulse (which is felt at both wrists). The appearance of the tongue can provide an experienced practitioner with much information about the nature, depth, strength and location of any disease process. The colour and shape of the tongue itself, as well as the colour, thickness, moistness and location of any coating, are all relevant to diagnosis.

The radial pulse, at each wrist, gives similar information, although interpretation of the pulses is more difficult and subtle. Initially the acupuncturist notes the strength, speed and overall quality of the pulse. Then three positions on each pulse, which indicate the condition of the *Qi* and *Blood* in each of the *Zangfu*, may be palpated (felt).

The tongue and pulse are less useful diagnostically if the problem is a superficial *Jingluo* disorder, because they concern mainly the internal environment of the body.

If relevant, the practitioner also makes a physical examination. This often concentrates on palpation of parts of the body that are tender or painful; their location can help the acupuncturist to determine the channel or organ that is affected.

DIAGNOSIS

From the information provided by the case history and the examination, the acupuncturist makes his or her diagnosis and explains this to the patient. The number and frequency of treatments is discussed, and at this stage the patient may be given advice about diet, exercise and general lifestyle.

Acupuncturists differentiate diseases according to traditional pathological categories. Depending on the nature of the disorder, these may be *Yin/Yang, Five Phases, Eight Principles, Jingluo* and *Zangfu*. There are also systems for differentiating various types of fever. Some practitioners tend to concentrate exclusively on one system, whereas modern Chinese acupuncturists, and others trained in this approach, tend to use a combination of them, or to select the one best suited to the patient.

TREATMENT

For treatment, the acupuncturist asks the patient to undress sufficiently to expose the areas in which needles are to be inserted, and to lie on the treatment couch. The usual locations for treatment are the forearms, hands, lower legs and feet, although there are, of course, acupuncture points on all parts of the body.

The actual point of insertion depends on the site of the disorder and the way in which the practitioner wishes to influence the *Qi*. This point does not necessarily bear much relation to the disorder presented by the patient. For example, points on the feet may be used to treat conditions affecting the head, as determined by the course of the channel on which they lie.

Acupuncture needles are solid and much finer than hollow hypodermic needles. They range from 12 mm ($\frac{1}{2}$ in) – 10 cm (4 in) in length, and may be inserted to a depth of 6 mm – 7.5 cm ($\frac{1}{4}$ – 3 in), according to the patient's build, the part of the body concerned and whether the disorder affects the exterior or the interior of the body. The needles may be left in place for a few seconds or up to an hour, again depending on the type of disorder and the style of acupuncture being used. The average time is 20 minutes, after which the needles are removed. The patient may then be asked to lie face down, so that other needles may be inserted in the back.

Care is always taken to avoid blood vessels and major organs, and acquiring a thorough knowledge of the anatomy of acupuncture points is an integral part of a practitioner's training. Rarely is blood drawn, and if so it is usually only a small drop. To eliminate any risk of cross-infection, the law usually requires that only sterilized (or pre-sterilized disposable) needles are used.

The insertion of the needles should be painless, particularly if the patient is relaxed. There is a mild pin-prick as the skin is pierced, followed by little or no sensation as the needle goes deeper. The practitioner may induce some sensation around the needle or along the channel, which may be numbing, distending, tingling, "electrical" or possibly soreness.

For some conditions, the acupuncturist may use moxibustion, which involves burning a dried herb (mugwort, *Artemesia vulgaris*) to warm or stimulate certain points on the patient's body. This has a particularly strong effect in tonifying the body's *Qi* in conditions characterized by coldness and deficiency.

It is advisable for the patient to eat something before receiving treatment (but not to have a large meal), to prevent a possible feeling of tiredness, dizziness or weakness. Strenuous exercise should be avoided immediately after treatment.

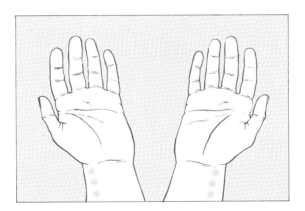

Assessing the quality of the pulses is an essential part of diagnosis and treatment. On each wrist there are three pulse positions which indicate the condition of different organs. Each position has three depths and there are 28 pulse qualities. Together, the position, depth and quality reflect the disposition and balance of *Qi* and *Blood* in the organs and channels.

CHIROPRACTIC THERAPY

Chiropractic therapy is regarded by its practitioners as both a science and an art. Chiropractors specialize in treating a variety of muscle- and joint-related disorders using, in the main, manipulation or adjustment of the spine and joints.

The science element of this therapy relates to diagnostic techniques based on those used in orthodox medicine, involving current scientific and medical knowledge. The manipulation carried out by a skilled practitioner, on the other hand, is an art. It includes not only manipulation itself, but also use of the hands to locate areas of the spine, or joints, that require manipulation. A chiropractor's aim is to treat the fundamental cause of a patient's problem, and not just the symptoms of pain or discomfort that he or she feels.

Chiropractors make an initial diagnosis from a detailed case history and physical examination. As part of the examination, they palpate (feel) the spine or joints, to detect areas where there is an alteration to the normal mobility. Such abnormality suggests an underlying biomechanical problem in the joint or joints which, once corrected, may help to reduce the patient's overall discomfort. Chiropractors may also take X-rays of the area concerned. These provide information about the state of the underlying bone structure, and enable the therapist to rule out any conditions for which manipulation might be inappropriate.

Once a chiropractor has arrived at a diagnosis, treatment can begin. The therapist aims to restore the normal biomechanics to the spine in terms of both position and also of spinal and joint movement, by releasing any muscle spasm or ligamentous strain and adjusting the spinal joints using a quick and precise movement.

Such movement aims to reduce pressure on specific spinal nerves, which is the most common cause of pain. This is usually achieved over a series of treatments. The length of time it takes depends on the type and severity of the condition, how long it has been present, and the general fitness of the patient. In some cases, treatment may be successful only with additional help from the patient with regard to changing diet, losing weight, exercising or taking simple preventive health measures.

As a by-product of treatment for spinal problems, a patient's digestive, respiratory or menstrual disorders may also improve. This is the result of a reduction of pressure on the spinal nerves supplying the organs, and a release of muscle spasm in the vicinity of the organs concerned.

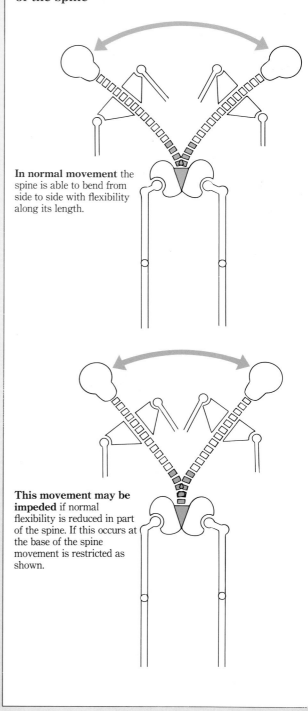

Normal and restricted movement of the spine

In normal movement the spine is able to bend from side to side with flexibility along its length.

This movement may be impeded if normal flexibility is reduced in part of the spine. If this occurs at the base of the spine movement is restricted as shown.

The spine and other bones of the trunk – from the neck and the shoulders to the hips – form a complex interlocking structure. The bones are held together by ligaments, tendons and muscles, which both support the bones and move them in relation to each other. The bones of the trunk also serve to protect the organs and soft tissues within the body.

The most delicate of internal tissues are nerves, which often lie closest to the bones themselves. This is particularly true of the relationship between the spinal nerves and the bones of the spine (vertebrae).

Because of this, any malpositioning of vertebrae can have a harmful influence on spinal nerves, and a chiropractor must have an intimate and detailed knowledge of the bony structure of the body in order to be able to correct any misalignments that are observed. The diagrams below show the bones of the spine in side view and those of the trunk seen from behind.

Side view of spine

Back view of spine

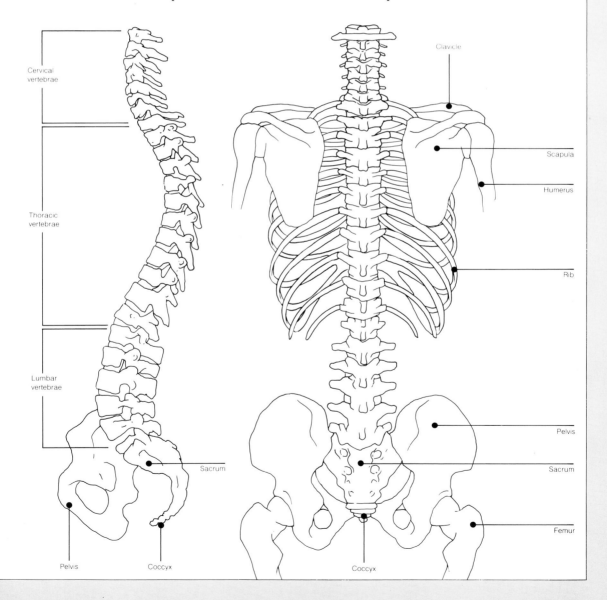

Side view labels: Cervical vertebrae, Thoracic vertebrae, Lumbar vertebrae, Sacrum, Pelvis, Coccyx

Back view labels: Clavicle, Scapula, Humerus, Rib, Pelvis, Sacrum, Femur, Coccyx

Mobilization and manipulation: ranges of movement

There are important and significant differences between the chiropractic techniques of manipulation and mobilization.

Each joint in the body has a particular range of normal movement. For instance, if you turn your head to one side it will only go so far. This distance is known as its range of active movement. Exercise generally functions within the range of active movement of a joint or joints. But if you use your hand to press gently on your head, you will be able to turn your neck a little farther. This is its range of passive movement. Mobilization techniques practised by physiotherapists usually function between the limits of active and passive movement.

A joint can, however be moved even farther, past its range of passive movement to the limit of the integrity of the joint. This is what happens when a chiropractor applies an adjustive or manipulative thrust to the joint. Chiropractic adjustment may sound painful, but a chiropractor always functions within the pain threshold of the patient, and his skills allow him to determine exactly how to achieve this adjustment in a safe manner. The force used is small, precise and extremely effective.

"Normal" function of a joint varies for each person, depending on his or her age, fitness and general physical make-up. A chiropractor is able to tell from physical examination whether or not normality has been restored, and does not need to rely solely on what the patient says.

Ranges of movement

In normal activity the range of movement of the spine (active movement) is limited by the joints between the vertebrae. By applying gentle pressure to the spine using mobilization techniques, an additional range of movement (passive movement) can be achieved. Using techniques of manipulation, the vertebral joints can be taken to the limits of their anatomical integrity, so that normal joint function can be restored.

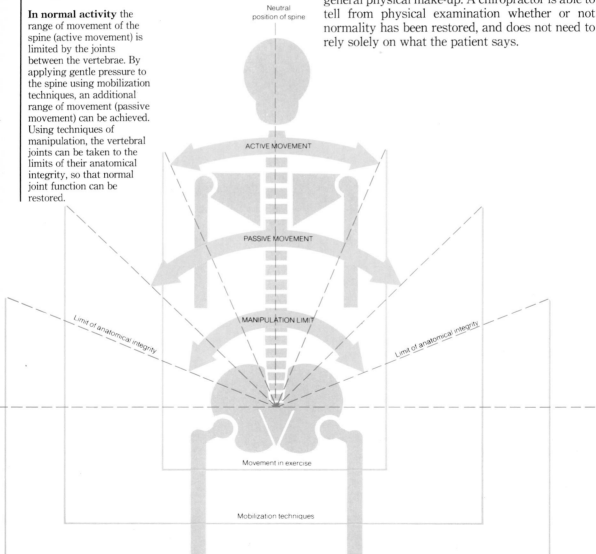

Neutral position of spine

ACTIVE MOVEMENT

PASSIVE MOVEMENT

MANIPULATION LIMIT

Limit of anatomical integrity

Limit of anatomical integrity

Movement in exercise

Mobilization techniques

Manipulation and adjustive techniques

Manipulation

Chiropractors spend a minimum of four years in full time training at a chiropractic college, where they become specialists in the use of manipulative techniques. This training also includes all the basic science and diagnostic skills learned by a medical student, apart from surgery and pharmacy. Once qualified, a chiropractor uses and refines the manipulative skills every day in the diagnosis and treatment of patients.

Chiropractic therapy aims to restore normal joint function where joint mobility has either been abnormally reduced (hypomobility) – which is usually the case – or increased (hypermobility). Any change in the normal function of a joint or joints can have far-reaching consequences on the body through the musculo-skeletal, vascular and nervous systems. These result not only in pain, for example in the low back, but can also produce a referred pain in the leg, as well as having other side effects such as alteration to the normal function of the bowels or bladder.

A chiropractor locates the joint or joints that are the cause of the patient's pain, through careful examination of the area. Once they have been located, the chiropractor uses a variety of therapeutic adjustment techniques in several consultations over a period of time to restore normal joint function to the area.

Spinal manipulation involves the application of a precise force to a specific area of the body. This force is applied with a controlled speed, depth and magnitude through a contact point on the body. For example, the chiropractor may make contact with part of the hand on the patient's spine, over a facet joint, transverse process or spinous process. (The processes are the bony projections from the vertebrae.) The chiropractor then applies a force through the hand to the part of the spine he or she is concerned with, using a precise speed and amplitude. Learning this precision requires considerable practice and skill.

Not every spinal adjustment is the same. There are at least 36 different types of chiropractic adjustment techniques, and although not every chiropractor is expert in applying all of them, training ensures that every chiropractor is aware of the wide range of techniques that can be applied in different situations, so that the most suitable ones can be chosen for each case. For example, a chiropractor would not expect to use the same type of technique on a well-built, athletic young man as on a 70-year-old woman with osteoporosis (thinning of the bones). Other specially adapted techniques are used for treating babies and children.

Conditions commonly treated by chiropractic therapy

Chiropractors specialize in treating a variety of muscle- and joint-related disorders. However, their skill is not concerned only with disorders affecting the spine and spinal nerves, but also involves muscle or joint problems anywhere in the body.

Nevertheless, about 50 per cent of patients consulting a chiropractor suffer from problems with the lower back. These can range from a simple low back pain (lumbago), through low back and leg pain (referred from the back), to severe disk problems. Some low back conditions result from biomechanical problems in the functioning of the joints of the spine, which can, in turn, cause both low back pain and referred pain in the leg.

A prolapsed lumbar disk, commonly called a slipped disk, creates severe pain not only in the low back, but also in the leg, often associated with pins and needles and numbness in the leg. The disk can move or prolapse in a number of different directions within the spinal canal, and the more simple prolapses respond well to chiropractic treatment. Even some of the more severe ones respond to careful and effective chiropractic techniques. However, in cases of neurological involvement where, for example, the function of other organs, such as the bladder, is affected, or where fragmentation of the disk has occurred, surgery is usually essential.

Neck pain, with or without referred pain to the arm, is the next most common condition for which chiropractors are consulted. Headaches and migraine can also be caused by neck problems. The causes of many of these conditions are biomechanical in nature and respond extremely well to chiropractic therapy.

Other common conditions for which patients consult a chiropractor are frozen shoulder (adhesive capsulitis), tennis and golfer's elbow, and wrist and hand problems such as arthritis, carpal tunnel syndrome and even small wrist ganglia.

Arthritic hips are frequently diagnosed in the first instance by a chiropractor and, although most eventually require surgery, the chiropractor can help to reduce the amount of pain and keep the hip more mobile while the patient waits for the operation. Other extremity joint problems treated by chiropractors include those affecting the knees, the ankles and, occasionally, the feet.

Some conditions mimic back pain, but through their training chiropractors are able to differentiate between a true back pain and one being referred from an internal organ. Typical examples include left arm pain from a heart condition and right shoulder pain from a liver complaint.

Who does a chiropractor treat?

Not only do people usually cherish the prejudice that chiropractors treat solely back problems, many also believe that the majority of back sufferers are overweight and middle-aged. Both are misconceptions. A chiropractor's patients may range in age from a one-month-old baby to a 90-year-old great grandmother. The chiropractic techniques applied to each case vary accordingly.

An increasing number of patients are children and teenagers. Many of the aches and pains complained of by children used to be put down to "growing pains", but examination of the spine can reveal the beginning of a condition which, if not corrected, may lead to chronic problems later in life. Signs of scoliosis or curvature of the spine, for example, are easy to detect, and if caught early can be straightforward to remedy. Birth itself can be extremely traumatic to a baby's spine, and chiropractors have special techniques to examine and treat babies in these cases. Preventive treatment for children is therefore important, and regular check-ups are recommended.

Expectant mothers may also benefit from chiropractic treatment, both before, during and after the pregnancy. Chiropractors are well able to adapt their techniques to treat pregnant women, who do not only suffer from low back pain. Pain between the shoulder blades can develop as the breasts enlarge and put more strain on the spine in that area. Again, a mother-to-be need not suffer in silence.

Sporting injuries are another area where people benefit from early chiropractic care. For this reason, many professional and amateur sports enthusiasts attend their chiropractor for treatment of sports injuries. In the United States, chiropractors work closely with many leading professional sportsmen, sportswomen and sports teams.

Many back problems are occupation related. The list is endless, but common among chiropractic patients are hairdressers, teachers, nurses, factory workers, shop assistants, engineers, manual labourers and musicians. Some problems are related to poor posture, while sitting or standing for long periods, whereas others are due to misuse of the body when lifting or carrying heavy objects.

Far from restricting their therapy to the treatment of the spine, chiropractors try to be as versatile as possible in their approach to biomechanical problems, or to muscle and joint disorders that may occur almost anywhere in the body. Equally, chiropractic therapy has something to offer everyone, whatever their age, sex, build or occupation.

Chiropractic and other medical systems

Although patients commonly consult a chiropractor when they have general musculo-skeletal and, especially, back problems, a chiropractor also has the responsibility of looking at and diagnosing all a patient's symptoms and referring them for additional or more appropriate treatment if necessary.

Most patients visit a chiropractor's surgery as a result of word of mouth recommendations from other patients. In more and more cases, however, orthodox medical practitioners are referring patients to chiropractors for treatment.

Chiropractors are pleased to work with the orthodox medical profession for the benefit of their patients, and they are careful to keep the patient's family doctor or specialist informed of the treatment and progress when asked. In some cases, it is also necessary for the chiropractor to refer the patient back to the doctor for further tests and investigations, for instance if chiropractic examination reveals a problem that was not evident at first. Unfortunately, not all doctors are keen to work with chiropractors in this way, and sometimes because of this, a problem that would normally be easy for a chiropractor to treat is left untreated for a long time so that in the end treatment is of only limited value to the patient.

Other patients, who have not found orthodox medical treatment satisfactory in solving their problems, may simply present themselves to a chiropractor because they are looking for "an alternative", perhaps because a friend was helped by chiropractic therapy, even though their condition is not one that is really suitable for this form of treatment. In such a case, the chiropractor will look to an alternative form of therapy, such as acupuncture, homeopathy, medical herbalism or naturopathy and then refer the patient to the one that seems most appropriate. This referral is made only after discussing the situation with the patient, to avoid the impression that the chiropractor is simply avoiding the issue.

Sometimes it may be necessary for the patient to be treated by more than one therapy at a time. Ultimately, the aim of any treatment is to relieve the patient of the problem as quickly as possible. If this requires more than one therapy at a time, and the patient complies, then the practitioners are usually happy to work together. In other instances, however, it can definitely be better to use only one therapy at a time, with another taking over once the current one has achieved its aim. In either case, the patient's progress must be monitored very carefully and liaison between practitioners must be both frequent and close.

Autonomic nervous system

Manipulation of the spine affects internal organs, primarily through influencing the sympathetic (stimulating) and parasympathetic (relaxing) nervous systems. These are known collectively as the autonomic nervous system, because they exert an involuntary control over organs and tissues. They consist of chains of nerves that run beside the spinal cord. They are connected with it through the nerve roots, and with tissues either directly or via ganglia.

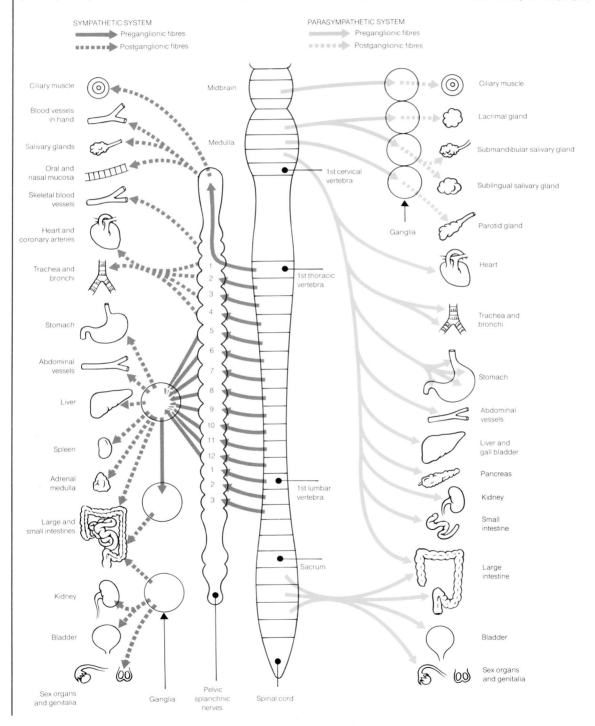

SYMPATHETIC SYSTEM
→ Preganglionic fibres
▪▪▪▪▶ Postganglionic fibres

PARASYMPATHETIC SYSTEM
→ Preganglionic fibres
▪▪▪▪▶ Postganglionic fibres

Ciliary muscle
Blood vessels in hand
Salivary glands
Oral and nasal mucosa
Skeletal blood vessels
Heart and coronary arteries
Trachea and bronchi
Stomach
Abdominal vessels
Liver
Spleen
Adrenal medulla
Large and small intestines
Kidney
Bladder
Sex organs and genitalia

Midbrain
Medulla
1st cervical vertebra
1st thoracic vertebra
1st lumbar vertebra
Sacrum

Ganglia
Pelvic splanchnic nerves
Spinal cord

Ciliary muscle
Lacrimal gland
Submandibular salivary gland
Sublingual salivary gland
Parotid gland
Ganglia
Heart
Trachea and bronchi
Stomach
Abdominal vessels
Liver and gall bladder
Pancreas
Kidney
Small intestine
Large intestine
Bladder
Sex organs and genitalia

CASE HISTORY

A chiropractor takes a case history by asking the patient a number of questions, to find out as much as possible about the problem. Typical questions include:

How did the problem start?
How long has it been going on?
Has this problem occurred before?
Where – exactly – does it hurt?
Is there pain in more than one place?
Does anything make the pain better or worse?
Is it better or worse when walking, standing, sitting or lying down?
Is there any numbness or tingling?
Has the patient suffered a fall or other accident?

Does the patient have headaches, dizziness, deafness or ringing in the ears?
Are bowel movements and urination normal?
Is the patient currently receiving treatment for any other condition?
Have there been any previous illnesses or operations?
What is the patient's general state of health?

Not all of these questions apply to every case, and if it is a recent problem with no previous history, this part of the consultation will probably take only a few minutes. A long-standing chronic problem requires a more detailed case history, which will take longer.

EXAMINATION

The patient is asked to undress down to the underwear, and a woman may be given a gown to wear for the examination.

The first part of the examination usually takes the form of orthopaedic and neurological tests of bone and nerve function. If necessary, the patient's reflexes are tested.

The next part of the examination is usually palpation, in which the chiropractor feels with his or her hands to assess the amount of movement in various joints – particularly vertebrae. The spine is taken through all its ranges of movement in flexion, extension, (forward and backward bending), sideways bending and rotation, often joint by joint along the length of the spine. Static palpation can also tell the chiropractor about the placement of bones, and the texture of soft tissues, muscles, tendons and ligaments.

If necessary, the chiropractor also takes X-rays to confirm the initial diagnosis and to rule out conditions not suitable for chiropractic treatment.

DIAGNOSIS

From the case history and the results of the examination and any X-rays, the chiropractor arrives at a diagnosis and is able to plan the appropriate treatment.

TREATMENT

Treatment of an acute condition, such as a prolapsed intervertebral disk, (commonly known as a slipped disk) may begin at the first visit, particularly if the patient is in considerable pain. But if the problem is long-standing, and if X-ray photographs have to be processed, treatment will probably be postponed until a second visit. At this visit, the chiropractor's findings are explained and a judgement expressed about whether or not the condition is amenable to chiropractic therapy. If it is, the course of treatment is explained to the patient.

Treatment may be carried out with the patient sitting or lying down, usually on a special treatment table. Before adjustment of the spine or other joints, many chiropractors first use massage or another soft-tissue technique to loosen tense muscles or strained ligaments. In exceptional cases, ultrasound may be used – high-frequency sound which stimulates circulation and reduces inflammation by stimulating the removal of toxins from the tissues.

To treat the neck, the chiropractor locates the joint affected and, while gently moving the patient's head, applies a quick, precise thrust to a joint. There may be a cracking noise (caused by the release of gas bubbles within the fluid of the joint), but this is quite normal and nothing to worry about.

Treatment of the thoracic (chest) area in the upper spine is usually done with the patient lying face down. The patient is asked to breathe deeply, and on the outward breath the chiropractor makes hand contact and again applies a quick and precise thrust to the joint or joints concerned.

The lower back is usually treated with the patient lying face down or on one side. As the patient breathes out, the chiropractor takes out any slack in the movement of the joint and applies a quick precise thrust to the joint. The adjustment may be repeated at more than one joint and on one or both sides of the spine.

In complex cases, more than one area of the spine, and indeed more than one part of the body, may be treated at the same session. After treatment, the chiropractor checks the spine to see what changes in movement have been achieved. But it may take three or four treatments before the patient can detect much difference, and these treatments will be given over a period of time. Conditions that are extremely acute or chronic may require a great many more treatments, which will obviously take substantially more time.

Chiropractic adjustment of the cervical vertebrae can restore normal mobility of the neck. The therapist stabilizes the head with one hand and applies a quick thrust to the neck with the other hand. As pressure on the joint fluid is altered a cracking sound may occur.

HOMEOPATHY

In modern medicine, the concept of the fight against disease usually means, in reality, the "fight against symptoms". Relatively seldom does the medical establishment look for the fundamental reasons why people become ill. What in their physical, mental and/or emotional make-up causes some individuals to succumb to certain diseases while others do not? And how can this unknown potential to resist illness be enhanced to either prevent or cure disease?

In contrast, homeopathy is a system of medicine that starts off by looking at the total health picture of each patient and at the individual ways in which the body's own healing powers can be harnessed.

Like cures like

The way in which homeopathy and orthodox medicine – which homeopaths call allopathy – differ is amply reflected in these two names. "Homeopathy" means "like disease", whereas "allopathy" translates as "opposite disease". In homeopathy, medicines mimic the symptoms of a disease, whereas allopathic treatments are generally designed to have the opposite effect. The philosophy underlying homeopathy is "like cures like" (*Similia similibus curantur*).

Samuel Hahnemann (1755–1843), a highly respected German doctor, developed the system of homeopathy in the nineteenth century. He did so as a result of his disillusion with the medical techniques that were current at the time – practices such as blood-letting and the administration of massive doses of crude chemicals. After abandoning his medical practice he made a living from translating. While he was working on a German edition of a major British herbal, Cullen's *Materia Medica*, he became interested by the way the bark of *Cinchona*, the "quinine" tree, worked in the relief of malaria. He also discovered that by taking the medicine he actually developed the symptoms of malaria.

After 14 years of research, Hahnemann concluded that symptoms were the outward signs that the body was fighting an illness. If the first action of a medicine was to make patients worse – to enhance the symptoms – then the second would be to make them better. He deduced that when a medicine was taken by a sick person, it created an "artificial illness", which was experienced as an aggravation of symptoms. This would be self-limiting and often barely noticeable, especially if the disease was acute at the time. The result of the aggravation, however, would be recovery from the illness.

Hahnemann and quinine

In the early nineteenth century, when Hahnemann was developing the science of homeopathy, the bark of the Cinchona tree was used to treat what was then called "the ague". This fever, with its alternating chills and sweats, we now know as malaria.

The Indians of South America first discovered that the bark of this tree, found mainly in Peru and its neighbouring countries, was effective in treating malaria. In 1640, the Countess of Cinchon brought the bark to Europe. To this day, it bears her name.

The active ingredient in Cinchona bark is quinine – which can cause severe side-effects. These include: headaches, vomiting, and fever – also characteristics

of malaria itself – deafness, noises in the ears, rashes and stomach pains.

Hahnemann wanted to find out why the medicine was effective against malaria and so took it himself to determine its effects.

For a week, he took doses of an ounce of Cinchona bark every day. When he found himelf developing the symptoms of malaria, he came to the conclusion that a drug which can cause symptoms of a disease can also cure that disease.

In addition, because of its drastic side-effects, he determined that much smaller, more dilute doses could be given to achieve the same therapeutic effect. This principle of minimum dosages became another cornerstone of homeopathy.

Quinine tree
Cinchona officinalis

A *Belladonna* headache

Worse for pressure

Throbbing, bursting pain; worse on right side

Dizziness when stooping or rising

Dilated pupils

Sensitive to bright light

Worse for noise

Dry mouth and throat

Hot skin

In homeopathic treatment the pattern of a patient's symptoms is matched with those of a remedy. The more closely the remedy pattern matches that of the patient, the more effective will be the cure.

If a person has headache symptoms like those illustrated, they would be prescribed the homeopathic remedy *Belladonna*. This plant is a well-known poison which, if taken in its natural form, would produce – among more serious symptoms – a headache with these characteristics. In its diluted homeopathic form, which is completely safe, *Belladonna* can cure such a headache.

"Proving" homeopathic remedies

Hahnemann's investigations suggested to him the idea that the way to determine the field of action of a medicine would be for a healthy person to take it, and for the "symptoms" it produced to be observed. This process is called "proving", and the people involved are called "provers". Hahnemann used himself as a guinea pig, and enlisted the help of family, friends and colleagues, in order to "prove" all the medicines that were then available.

Medicines used in provings are taken in extremely diluted or "potentized" form – the same form that is used in homeopathic remedies. The pattern of symptoms obtained in provings provides the "symptom picture" of a remedy.

Symptoms fall into three categories – those produced by all provers, those produced by a high percentage, and those produced relatively infrequently. These groups indicate the importance of the symptoms found in patients. If, for example, diarrhoea dominates in a group of abdominal symptoms for a particular remedy, this same emphasis must be found in the patient's symptoms.

A "symptom picture" not only indicates the physical symptoms such as a rash or pain, but also includes many other details such as subjective impressions and sensations that have been revealed by the provers. For this reason, people proving medicines have to give detailed accounts of the symptoms they develop after taking the remedy – especially changes in their physical health, mental state, preferences in food, sleeping patterns, personal relationships, temperament – even their attitude to the weather.

Because homeopathic remedies act over a long period, symptoms should be noted for up to 12 months. To ensure accuracy, the provers must be healthy, with regulated diet and avoidance of physical exertion and emotional stress.

The provings carried out by Hahnemann were extended by other great homeopaths of the late nineteenth century. Many *Materia Medica* of homeopathic remedies produced then are still used by homeopaths today. A prominent modern homeopath, George Vithoulkas, has modified the language used in these early *Materia Medica* and has carried out further provings. The "symptom pictures" of remedies proved last century, however, have not changed, because the nature of a remedy is still the same.

The nature of disease

As a result of his research, Hahnemann began to achieve a more satisfactory understanding of the ways the body functions and how it can be affected by disease.

By recording all the symptoms that occurred during provings, Hahnemann and his followers came to see the human body as one unit, rather than a collection of separate parts – as is the view of most allopathic practitioners. Because it is a complete, living whole, when it is disturbed or afflicted in any way, it takes coordinated action to protect or restore the harmonious balance – medically called homeostasis – that is its natural state.

The "intelligence" behind this coordinated action is known by homeopaths as the "vital force". It can be seen only by its actions – primarily, the production of symptoms as it attempts to bring the body back to a state of balance. To a homeopath, therefore, a "disease" is the totality of symptoms produced by the body in its own efforts to heal itself. The object of homeopathy is to enhance these natural reactions (symptoms) – such as vomiting in response to food poisoning – to promote healing.

Symptoms are seen as the body's way of externalizing disease. Like ripples on a pond they dissipate the energy of a disease and enable harmony to be restored. According to the principles of homeopathy, disease is prolonged if anything hampers the free flow of symptoms. This way of looking at physical illness is similar to the methods of psychotherapy. According to the latter, psychological disturbances are best resolved if strong emotions are allowed to be expressed; if they are internalized, they will continue to restrict and harm the sufferer.

Individual patterns of disease

In most diseases, there is a specific pattern of symptoms. For example, a measles rash is first seen on the face and neck, then it spreads down to the rest of the body. Although these obvious symptoms are similar in anyone who develops the illness, and although the physiology and anatomy of each individual is more or less the same, every person has his or her own unique weaknesses so far as the body's ability to heal itself is concerned.

The existence of these weaknesses means that everyone who succumbs to an illness has a slightly different experience of it. This theory resulted from the multitude of details that Hahnemann's "provers" gave him while testing the remedies. It is fundamental to the way in which homeopathic prescriptions are made, and a homeopath always looks for the individual symptoms.

In homeopathic treatment, the symptoms of a patient are matched with the pattern of symptoms produced by a remedy. The more closely the remedy matches the total pattern of the patient, the more effective the remedy will be. A good example is the homeopathic treatment of the "common" cold. An allopathic doctor would almost certainly advise taking aspirin, drinking plenty of liquids and resting. In contrast, a homeopath asks a great many questions about the exact nature of the symptoms, and prescribes one of a number of remedies depending on what these symptoms are.

For example, if you are constantly sneezing, your eyes are watering, you are hoarse, you cough a lot, you have a headache, your nose is running, creating a sense of burning on your upper lip, and (although this may seem strange) you feel better in cold rooms, you may be prescribed *Allium cepa*, a remedy that is made from red onions.

On the other hand, if you cannot sleep because you are anxious and restless, have a fever and a headache, are permanently thirsty, have burning sensations in your eyes and nose, and (again, strangely) feel better in warm rooms, a prescription for *Arsenicum album* may be given.

Acute and chronic illness

Conditions described as acute are those that develop suddenly and improve quickly, with or without the aid of a remedy. Chronic conditions are deep, long-term disorders.

Typical acute conditions are colds, fevers and vomiting. They are seen as the activity of the vital force in dealing with a disturbance. Homeopathic remedies are effective in dealing with them because they stimulate the body's own healing mechanisms, so speeding up the removal of the disturbance.

Chronic conditions appear most commonly as the result of inherited tendencies and include general weakness of body systems such as the lungs, which can result in a tendency to get coughs. These chronic states of illness are called "miasms" or "miasmic disorders" in homeopathy. From the three miasms many different constitutional patterns may be drawn. Constitutional remedies are given to remove these tendencies and improve health in general.

If an acute condition develops after a patient has taken a homeopathic remedy, this is a positive sign called an "aggravation" or "healing crisis" – it passes quickly and is no more severe than the patient's vitality can cope with. A familiar example of a "healing crisis" occurs during a fast, when headaches may develop as the body cleanses itself of toxins.

The preparation of a homeopathic remedy

1 Homeopathic remedies are usually prepared from mineral, plant, animal or other biological sources. An extraction of the substance is made by soaking it in a solution of alcohol, to form the "mother tincture".

2 This tincture is diluted with alcohol in ratios of 1 drop of tincture to 10 or 100 drops of alcohol. It is then rapidly shaken or "succussed" on this machine. This process of dilution and succussion is repeated many times so that different potencies can be achieved.

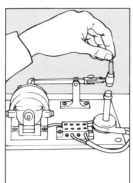

3 The resulting solution is added to tablets made of lactose and sucrose. The bottle of tablets can be stored indefinitely in a cool, dark place. If the tablets come into contact with strong perfumes or are touched, then they may lose their potency.

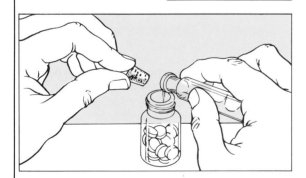

The "energy" of a substance is thought to be transferred to a solution by succussion. This solution has a potency that is increased by dilution. There are 2 scales of dilution – 1:10 (decimal scale, potency of 1X); 1:100 (centecimal scale, potentcy of 1 or 1C). A potency of 100C is also indicated as 1M.

Potency
Centecimal scale

$$1C = 1^{100} = \frac{1}{100}$$

$$2C = 2^{100} = \frac{1}{10,000}$$

$$3C = 3^{100} = \frac{1}{1,000,000}$$

$$4C = 4^{100} = \frac{1}{100,000,000}$$

$$5C = 5^{100} = \frac{1}{10,000,000,000}$$

$$6C = 6^{100} = \frac{1}{1,000,000,000,000}$$

Potentization of medicines

Hahnemann was concerned that crude chemical drugs often produced severe side-effects. At first he tried simply diluting them, so that only a little of the substance was taken, but this also reduced therapeutic effects. He then developed the process of "potentization", in which the medicine was still diluted a number of times, but was vigorously shaken or "succussed" between dilutions. This process was found to increase the therapeutic value or "potency" of the medicine and is still used today.

A medicine is diluted either 1:10 (the decimal scale) or 1:100 (the centecimal scale). For example, a potency of 30X indicates that a 1:10 dilution of the original tincture has been diluted and succussed 30 times at that ratio.

After a dilution of 24X, however, molecular chemistry suggests that there is no longer likely to be any significant amount of the original substance left in the medicine, and, not surprisingly, this has caused scepticism about the ways the remedies work. Yet homeopaths have found, from repeated experience, that many of these greater dilutions are in fact even more effective than lower dilutions. This suggests that the power of the remedy comes from the dilution process rather than from the chemical content of the remedy itself.

Some scientific study is coming closer to understanding how potentization works. It is known that a substance leaves behind "footprints" even after it has been greatly diluted. Paul Callinan, an Australian scientist experimented by freezing remedy tinctures to $-200°C$; they crystallized into "snowflake" patterns that were different for each remedy. And the more these tinctures were diluted, the clearer their patterns became. Quantum physics tells us that physical substances leave behind energy fields, and in the end, it may be this that will explain potentization fully.

The selection of potency in treatment

The lowest potencies, 6th and 30th (6C and 30C), are used if a patient has low vitality or if the symptoms are slow-moving. The 200th potency (200C) is used where the activity of the symptoms is violent – whether as a fever or as an emotional state. Higher potencies (e.g. 1M or 10M) are used to create the speediest cures with the least aggravation, and are often reserved for people with a combination of mental or emotional symptoms. An optimum potency will stimulate enough – but no more – activity to restore the patient to health in the most gentle way possible.

The hierarchy of symptoms

Before a person can be treated by a homeopath, their symptoms must be formed into a total "symptom picture". The individual symptoms are evaluated in a hierarchy that puts "Strange, Rare and Peculiar" symptoms at the top. The more unusual a symptom, the more specifically it matches the symptom picture of a remedy. Typical symptoms might be as unusual as "a sensation of blood boiling in the veins" or "something moving in the abdomen".

"Mental and Emotional" characteristics are the second level of the hierarchy. These refer to the patient's temperament. They are particularly important to homeopaths because mental and emotional states, and disturbances in them, indicate the overall state of health and balance.

The next category of symptoms is known as "General". This refers to symptoms expressed by the person as a whole, and includes appetite, sleep and menstruation. When patients say, "I am tired/cold/hot", these are referred to as "General" symptoms.

The fourth category, "Particular", refers to symptoms relating to a specific part of the body. These include all the obvious signs of an illness such as a rash, intestinal upset or fever. Although they may be the reason why a person seeks medical help, they are usually less important than other symptoms. It is the unseen, internal dysfunction in the body's healing process that is the root of the trouble.

The minimum dose

Homeopaths not only differ from allopaths in the remedies they prescribe, they also differ in the way they prescribe them. Nearly always, they give remedies first in a single dose – then watch and assess the changes in the patient's symptoms.

If a remedy is for an acute condition, such as a headache, it should work at once. When a change occurs, this indicates that the remedy has initiated the healing process, and need not be repeated.

In chronic conditions, the single dose may continue to work for months, and changes in a patient's symptoms are monitored over this time to assess how healing is occurring. When the new pattern of symptoms has been assessed the prescription may be repeated or changed.

How cure occurs – "The Law of Cure"

The first actions of the body's healing process are to protect its vital organs and its life. Similarly, in homeopathic treatment, the pattern of symptoms can be seen to move from vital organs, such as the lungs, to less vital parts, such as the skin or throat.

Levels of health

In homeopathic terms, disorders can be graded according to the effect they have on the whole person. In the diagram, levels of health are ordered from left to right according to their importance in terms of their effect on a person's ability to function.

The mind is central to human existence, and disturbances of it – depending on the degree – can utterly destroy the quality of life.

Both mental and emotional disorders can also lead to physical illness. For example, the effects of stress on health are widely recognized. The reverse is less common, however, which is why physical disorders are regarded as being less serious, in terms of this comparison. The physical level is extremely important, nevertheless, but illness can be tolerated if the emotional and mental levels remain balanced.

On the physical level, some organs or systems are obviously more important than others. Diseases of the heart are more serious than diseases of the skin.

Within each level of health there is also a degree of severity or intensity of disturbance. Group I includes the most serious disorders. Group II represents disorders that have a pronounced effect on the normal functioning of mind or body. And Group III includes relatively mild disorders that often resolve themselves without treatment and are commonly ignored.

Symptoms also move from within the body outward. Toxins may be dispelled in the form of discharges – diarrhoea, boils, catarrh – and tears may indicate the release of an emotional trauma. Sometimes symptoms move from above downward; skin problems, for example, may spread down a limb before leaving the body.

Symptoms disappear in reverse order of appearance – that is, those that appeared last go first. If a patient has had many health problems over his or her life, it is possible that some of these symptoms will come back briefly, in reverse chronological order during constitutional treatment. They will then disappear for ever – in the reverse order of appearance. For example, a woman being treated for bronchitis may briefly develop symptoms of cystitis, a previous illness, as part of the process of constitutional healing.

The Law of Cure is an important diagnostic tool for assessing the healing process and determining further treatment. Only if the change in symptoms or their movement has ceased will further treatment be required. The same remedy may be repeated if the first has exhausted its healing energy, or a different one might be needed, according to the new symptom picture.

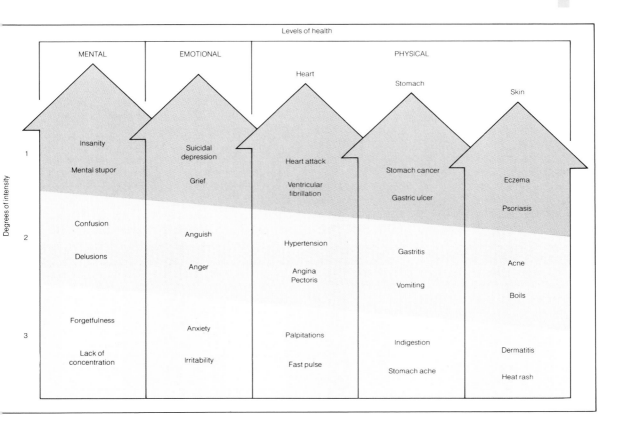

Levels of health

Homeopathy and other healing systems.

Homeopathy is seen by its adherents as an entirely different system of medicine from allopathy, because it approaches diagnosis and the prescription of medicines with a different purpose in mind. Many homeopathic practitioners would not combine homeopathy with allopathic treatment.

In Britain, however, homeopathic hospitals practice both systems of medicine alongside each other. Some family doctors include homeopathic treatment in their practices, and some patients happily consult allopathic doctors for some conditions and homeopathic ones for others. Where conventionally trained doctors also offer homeopathic treatment, however, there is a danger that their training in homeopathy lacks the depth required for using this system of medicine to its fullest extent.

Acupuncture and herbalism both treat patients holistically and try to deal with the deep constitutional factors that so often contribute to people's ill health. And like homeopathy, acupuncture also bases its treatment on using the body's own "energy".

Since these three systems have similar aims, however, there is rarely a need for them to be combined. Furthermore, homeopathy has clearly defined methods of assessing the process of healing. Thus if it is combined with other treatments, it can be hard to determine which treatment is having what effect, and this, in turn, makes further diagnosis difficult. In addition, combining treatments is not without risk. If stimulation to the natural healing process is too great, the body may move into a "healing crisis" that is both unpleasant and prolonged.

Homeopathy may be used effectively with manipulative therapies, such as chiropractic therapy and osteopathy, not only in the relief of pain or inflammation, but also in supporting the patient's constitution after manipulative treatment. Remedies must be used with caution, however, because some could reverse spinal adjustments if used too soon after manipulative treatment.

In emergencies, homeopathy can be a remarkably effective means of first aid. This is perhaps where homeopathy has gained its greatest support. It can be invaluable to have a homeopathic first aid kit in the home to deal with accidents and minor illnesses. This is especially useful for common childhood ailments. Remedies should be used discriminatingly, and if a problem does not improve quickly, professional help must be found.

CASE HISTORY

A consultation with a homeopath begins with an interview. This, in turn, starts as soon as the practitioner sees or hears the patient. The voice, words spoken, posture, dress, appearance and mannerisms all become part of the appraisal. A simple handshake takes on significance because it indicates the condition of the patient's skin – dry, sweaty, soft or calloused – as well as revealing something of the person's character.

The form of the interview depends on the practitioner and the needs of the individual patient. If the disorder is a disturbance of the status quo, then it is necessary to discover what the norm is for that patient. Homeopaths believe that it is necessary for the healer to be concerned with the patient's distress and how it is experienced on other levels beside the physical. This is easier on the physical level because there are limited patterns of human anatomy and physiology. Thus, for each symptom the homeopath will want to know about its onset, location, sensation and frequency, and will note anything unusual.

On other levels, information is gleaned by encouraging patients to discuss their problem. In this way, the practitioner has access to a great deal of subjective data. This may be both a weakness and a strength of homeopathy. Errors of judgement are reduced by the way in which homeopathic remedies are proven – because the prover's feelings and thoughts are recorded and can be compared with those of the patient. To achieve this, the usual interview technique does not make use of direct questions (except for clarification); the most important thing the homeopath does at this stage is to listen. And for this reason, such an interview takes at least an hour.

EXAMINATION

For the reasons stated above, much of a homeopath's "examination" of a patient consists of keen observation and listening. Significant factors include the patient's posture and even his or her style of dress. These can reveal much about character – artistic, traditional, neat, laid-back and casual, enthusiastic, calm or matter of fact. Also, the patient's speech may be gay, effusive, pedantic, abrupt or nervous.

A homeopath may use conventional examination techniques if necessary. A physical examination may be conducted, using conventional medical instruments, such as a sphygmomanometer, which measures the blood pressure. The patient may also be referred for various tests.

DIAGNOSIS

Once all possible data has been collected, the homeopath orders and analyses it to determine what is most important and what has given rise to the patient's problem. The theory is that something to which the patient is susceptible (such as grief or disappointment) has so disturbed the vital force – the harmony of the person – that the body has reacted to rectify the situation by displaying certain symptoms.

These symptoms may resolve themselves unaided, or form the basis of a deep trauma that creates a more obvious disturbance. For instance, grief can result in a nervous stomach and digestive disorders. Thus the analysis of the case is the most important part of homeopathic diagnosis, because it determines what is really out of order and needs treating. The pattern produced by the disturbance points to the remedy.

TREATMENT

The aim of homeopathic treatment is, having identified the cause of a disorder, to restore health by administering a remedy that is similar in its effects to the disease process. Treatment is to eliminate the cause, not merely remove its effects for the time being. For this reason, each case is reassessed during treatment to make sure that the symptoms have changed in the right direction and to check that the cause is being eliminated at a satisfactory rate. Some illnesses need to be removed quickly, whereas others, more chronic or pathological, need to move more slowly and deeply.

Each patient is unique in having different levels of energy, and this has to be taken into account. Sometimes homeopathic treatment is like rolling a boulder up a hill. If the potency of the remedy selected is not high enough, the boulder will not reach the top; the problem will not be resolved, and there will be a relapse. A partial relapse may need only another nudge of the same remedy at the same potency; a complete relapse demands a higher potency of the same medicine.

Sometimes it becomes obvious, as a remedy begins to take effect, that there was more to the problem than was at first apparent, and it is possible to identify the whole condition. This may bring with it a different set of symptoms once it is revealed, which also need treatment. If so, the case is then analysed again in its new light and an appropriate remedy selected (again with follow-up assessment). After each treatment, it is expected that the patient's level of health will improve, both physically and emotionally, as greater harmony is restored.

During treatment for chronic problems, patients may experience a short-lived aggravation (slight worsening) of current symptoms, or a recurrence of a previous disorder. Since aggravation of symptoms is part of the healing process – an indication that the vital force is functioning – these symptoms are considered to be beneficial, and no treatment is normally necessary. Patients worried about their condition should consult their homeopath for advice.

Remedies are usually prescribed in tablet form, and these are dissolved slowly under the tongue. Patients are advised to avoid coffee, mint and menthol products (including mint toothpaste) for the duration of treatment, because these may react adversely with some remedies.

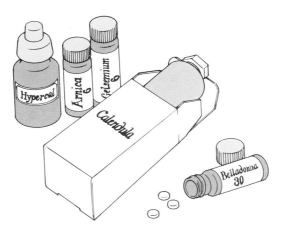

Homeopathic remedies are most commonly prescribed in the form of potentized lactose tablets. The bottles are labelled with the remedy's name and potency. Some homeopaths prefer to prescribe remedies in a powder or granular form. Lotions and ointments are used externally and are helpful in first aid situations. If remedies are kept dry and away from strong odours, they should keep indefinitely.

MEDICAL HERBALISM

The medicinal use of plants extends back over many millennia. Plants have been used for centuries by physicians and in folk remedies. While the latter provide a rich heritage of practical experience, it is with the professional practitioner that the following pages are primarily concerned. Modern medical herbalists combine clinical training and traditional knowledge with new research and diagnostic skills.

Essentially, herbal medicine is based on a holistic or whole person approach to health. At the level of the cells, improper working or dysfunction of one part of the body produces further imbalances in other parts. If the body's homeostatic (self regulating) mechanisms cannot control the situation, illness develops.

Within an individual, physical, emotional and spiritual problems all have an effect on each other – the phrase "psychosomatic illness" is just one aspect of this. On a global level, human health reflects, and is affected by, the environment as well as social and economic factors. The task of the medical herbalist is to make some assessment of the overall patterns of the health or disease of the patient in the light of these interconnecting influences.

This approach has many practical implications. It means that medical herbalism is concerned with the individual nature of the patient – there are no separately defined illnesses to be treated. By careful questioning, the herbalist builds up a complete picture of a person's health and lifestyle, and looks for clues to the causes of illness which that person experiences. Accordingly, advice and treatment can always be tailored specifically to each individual's needs.

This means that what is appropriate for one patient may be quite irrelevant for someone else, even if they have the same illness as defined by orthodox medicine. The prescription will vary, depending on what is required to encourage the body to return to health. It will also be adjusted on subsequent consultations, depending on what changes have occurred in the patient's symptoms. There are no automatically repeated prescriptions in this approach; it is based on uniquely prescribed assistance throughout the course of the healing process. Equally, advice about self help measures vary from person to person.

The aim of the medical herbalist is to assist natural healing, and to restore the patient to a state of balanced health – it is not simply to ameliorate the symptoms.

Illustration of the multiple medicinal properties of herbs

DANDELION
(Taraxacum officinale)

STEM
Sap, which is also found in the root, is applied directly to warts. Repeated application is required.

LEAF
The primary action is diuretic, increasing urine flow. The leaf is also rich in potassium.

ROOT
Acts as a gentle liver stimulant and laxative. It improves the function of the digestive system and the removal of toxins by the bowels.

Chart of some commonly used medicinal plants

FLOWER
Chamomile (*Matricaria recutita*)
Lime Blossom (*Tilia europea*)
Elder (*Sambucus nigra*)

WHOLE OF ABOVE-GROUND PARTS
Nettle (*Urtica dioica*)
Passion Flower (*Passiflora incarnata*)
Meadowsweet (*Filipendula ulmaria*)

LEAF
Dandelion (*Taraxacum officinalis*)
Comfrey (*Symphytum officinale*)
Marshmallow (*Althaea officinalis*)

BULB/CORM
Garlic (*Allium sativum*)

ROOT
Echinacea (*Echinacea angustifolia*)
Wild Yam (*Dioscorea villosa*)
Wild Indigo (*Baptista tinctoria*)

BARK
Wild Cherry (*Prunus serotina*)
Witch Hazel (*Hamamelis virginiana*)
Slippery Elm (*Ulmus fulva*)
Cramp Bark (*Viburnum opulus*)

SEED
Celery (*Apium graveolens*)
Linseed (*Linum usitatissimum*)

FRUITS/BERRIES
Cayenne (*Capsicum minimum*)
Saw Palmetto (*Serenoa serrulata*)
Hawthorn (*Crataegus oxyacanthoides*)

Diet and other factors

Apart from preparing specific herbal treatments, medical herbalists are concerned with assessing and improving a variety of different factors that affect health and disease. A vital element of herbal practice is the recognition of an individual's responsibility for health care as a major aspect of maintaining health and preventing illness.

One obvious area of daily life that has a profound effect on health is nutrition, and dietary advice is often a feature of a consultation. Typically, advice may be given on the regulation of dietary patterns and restriction of foods that can contribute to the person's ill health. Some people have allergic responses to certain foods. Others eat excessively, or aggravate their symptoms by straining their body's resources with such things as alcohol, caffeine and refined carbohydrates that are lacking in fibre. Herbalists try to help patients develop new dietary patterns which provide both greater nourishment and increased intakes of vitamins, minerals and trace elements. The aim of treatment is to replace deficiencies and generally improve vitality.

Stress is a common factor in the development of disease, and herbalists may offer advice on relaxation techniques and breathing. Or they may refer the patient for specialist support. Other aspects of lifestyle which may be addressed as part of consultation are exercise, posture, social and work environments or individual circumstances.

Whole plants for whole people

A key principle of herbal medicine concerns the importance of using extracts from the whole plant, not isolated or synthesized ingredients which perform specific functions. The rich chemical complexity of a plant or herb results in wide ranging activity within the body. This is illustrated particularly well by Garlic and Dandelion, herbs with many medicinal uses.

Not only do herbal medicines have multiple benefits for the whole body, but their overall safety is also extremely high. A serious problem in the use of some chemical drugs is that of side effects – those drug actions which are injurious to health and not directly related to the intended therapeutic results. In many instances research on medicinal plants that has aimed to isolate the "active" ingredient has produced either a highly toxic substance or an ineffectual drug. In contrast, the whole plant can provide both a safe and useful therapeutic effect.

An early study of the tropical plant *Rauwolfia serpentina* produced reserpine – a drug used to lower blood pressure. This drug is powerful, but also dangerous, and research to make it safer revealed that the original plant contained some 40 "active ingredients" which, when combined in their natural form, made the drug both safer and more effective.

The complex compounds of plant tissues commonly provide an easily assimilated medication with fewer side effects than isolated ingredients.

Meadowsweet
(Filipendula ulmaria)
Meadowsweet can be an effective and safe painkiller because it contains not only aspirin-like components, but also anti-inflammatory ingredients that counteract the irritant effects aspirin can have on the stomach.

The multi-system effects of garlic

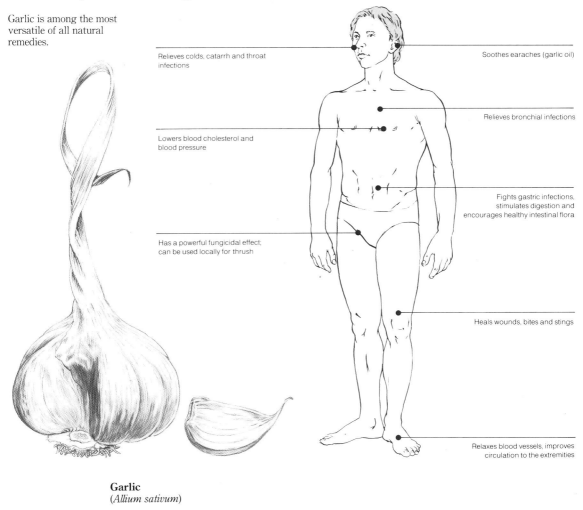

Garlic is among the most versatile of all natural remedies.

Relieves colds, catarrh and throat infections

Soothes earaches (garlic oil)

Relieves bronchial infections

Lowers blood cholesterol and blood pressure

Fights gastric infections, stimulates digestion and encourages healthy intestinal flora

Has a powerful fungicidal effect; can be used locally for thrush

Heals wounds, bites and stings

Relaxes blood vessels, improves circulation to the extremities

Garlic
(*Allium sativum*)

Furthermore, in many plant tissues there are "buffer" chemicals which counteract the unwanted effects of the primary active ingredients.

Combinations of substances found naturally in a plant may prove helpful where in isolation they may be harmful. This occurs in the plant Meadowsweet (*Filipendula ulmaria*). It contains salicylate compounds similar to those used in the common drug aspirin (itself derived from a species of Willow, *Salix alba*, which contains salicylates). Aspirin tends to irritate the stomach and may produce microscopic bleeding of the stomach lining (gastric mucosa) if used frequently. It would never be prescribed to someone suffering from a gastro-intestinal problem such as a gastric ulcer.

Meadowsweet, however, has many of the anti-inflammatory properties of the synthetic drug, but it also contains substances that soothe damaged gastric mucosa and reduce stomach acidity. It may be prescribed for people suffering not only from inflammatory conditions, such as rheumatism, but also from gastritis or heartburn.

These examples serve to highlight the approach of medical herbalists. By recognizing the widespread actions of herbal remedies they can work to balance and improve many functions of the body. Moreover, using whole extracts from the appropriate parts of plants, herbal medicine achieves a gentler, safer, and less violently disturbing therapeutic effect, assisting the natural healing process.

The "hot" and "cold" nature of ill-health

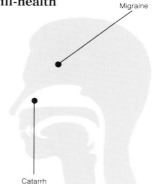

Migraine

Catarrh

CATARRH

"Hot" type
Nasal passages are inflamed and congested.
Phlegm is thick but not profuse.
Stress or nervousness is a factor.
Patient has a high metabolic rate.

"Cold" type
Pale complexion.
Puffy around nose and eyes.
Profuse watery mucus.
Patient feels chilly.
Tendency to be overweight.

MIGRAINE

"Hot" type
Congested blood vessels.
Some relief from cold application applied locally.
Pain accompanied by digestive disruption, biliousness, nausea, etc.

"Cold" type
Constricted blood vessels.
Some relief from warm application applied locally.
Hands and feet tend to feel cold.

The nature of disease

To a medical herbalist, disease is a result of the body's own attempts to restore balance and harmony or, at least, to limit the damage or disturbance caused by illness as much as possible. Any intervention and treatment is therefore aimed primarily at supporting the body's own self healing mechanisms rather than reducing or suppressing them.

In this, medical herbalism shares the view with certain other "alternative" therapies – notably homeopathy – that because the body's natural state is one of health, signs of illness are primarily manifestations of the body's struggle to defeat the disease on its own. Merely removing the symptoms of illness, therefore, may not necessarily be the same as removing the illness – the symptoms could simply have been suppressed.

In other respects, medical herbalists also try to maintain the body's normal functions in as healthy and efficient a state as possible. The body removes toxins and waste products through excretory organs, so it is important to ensure that these are functioning effectively. An assessment of the circulatory system is also important, and appropriate remedies are often used to promote circulatory flow and ensure the even distribution of blood throughout the body.

The impact of stress on the body's resources is another important factor in health and illness, and medication may involve the use of stimulants, relaxants or nervous restoratives. The latter act gently, but effectively, to nourish and restore normal nervous functioning after periods of stress, or in cases of chronic debility.

The idea of restoring balance, or homeostasis, is central to a herbalist's view of disease. A term which reflects this is "adaptogenic". In the past it was used to describe medicines – often including members of the Ginseng family – that helped to maintain bodily responses to stress, particularly in supporting the function of the adrenal glands. Nowadays, "adaptogenic" refers to herbal medicines that support the function of particular systems, such as Hawthorn for the cardiovascular system, and Oats for the nervous system.

Although some aspects of human understanding of the nature of disease have ancient origins, they also have relevance today. The concept of "hot" and "cold" characteristics in relation to disease is an example of this. A "hot" condition involves vasodilation (widening of blood vessels) and circulatory congestion. A patient with such a condition is likely to have a high metabolic rate, feel hot and, if the problem is respiratory, the mucus secretion will be thick and scanty, associated with a harsh dry, cough and inflammation.

"Cold" conditions, in contrast, involve vasoconstriction (contraction of blood vessels), and a patient experiencing them will be pale, feel cold, have pale urine, a sluggish metabolism and copious, watery nasal mucus. These concepts substantially affect the treatment of conditions such as migraines or catarrh.

Thus for herbal medicine understanding illness entails an overall assessment of personality, individual reactions to illness, and competence of all the bodily functions to accomplish the task of restoring harmony and health. In turn, these functions rely on adequate nourishment and circulation, effective detoxification and elimination of toxins, good functioning of the nervous system and hormone balance. Disease, or lack of harmony, in a person can often be an opportunity for them to take stock of their lives and correct underlying trends that may otherwise provoke further – or more serious – ill health.

Prescriptions and preparation of medicines

Herbal medicines can be prepared in various ways, and in the past many herbs were incorporated into food for their medicinal properties as much as their taste. In the home, many people still use herbal teas or infusions for their therapeutic effects. Indeed, medical herbalists may recommend certain tisanes to their patients to help them return to health. In professional practice, however, the majority of medicines are prescribed in tincture form.

Tinctures are made by macerating the roots, leaves and/or flowers of a herb and immersing them in a solution of alcohol and water for a period of time. Alcohol extracts the maximum level of compounds from the plants and also acts as a preservative. The concentration of plant material in relation to alcohol, and the strength of alcohol required, vary from plant to plant. The final medicine is then prescribed within its own particular dosage range.

Some herbal medicines have dosages very strictly controlled by law, since many members of the plant kingdom can be toxic. For this reason, self treatment should be undertaken only with great caution, and only for minor complaints. Although a qualified medical herbalist does not use poisonous plants, herbal medicines can have powerful effects nevertheless, and professional prescribing is an important safeguard.

In prescribing and dispensing a medicine, the medical herbalist assesses what is necessary for a patient at a particular time. Consequently, the same prescription is unlikely to be used for different people even if they have similar problems. It is uncommon even to repeat the same prescription for one person, since the nature of the problem and the reactions to it are constantly changing, and therefore require different treatment.

The prescription itself may vary from one herb alone to a combination of several medicines to help correct various imbalances.

Apart from tinctures prescribed for internal use, the medical herbalist may prescribe lotions, gargles, creams, ointments, and other external applications. These too will generally be prepared and dispensed by the herbalist specifically for one patient.

On occasion, herbal medicines in tablet or capsule form may be prescribed, but this is quite rare because of the practical costs and difficulties of preparation and storage. For children it may occasionally be necessary to prepare a syrup of the required herbs, although a suitably reduced dosage in tincture or infusion form can usually be tolerated by younger people.

Herbal medicine and other medical systems

Medical herbalism attempts to offer a wide range of help to restore a patient to health, either within the confines of the consultation or through referral to other health care professionals. Some of a herbalist's concepts of health date from times past, but most have been reappraised and expressed in today's language. Furthermore, modern knowledge of global ecology, combined with the traditional concept of the interdependence of individual health with the environment, provide a powerful philosophy for health care, which medical herbalists have long proclaimed. These facts are now beginning to be more generally recognized, not only as valid but of increasing importance for general health and well-being.

Practitioners of herbal medicine see and treat people with a wide range of conditions and can be regarded as providing primary medical care. Nevertheless, no one system of medicine contains all the answers to problems of ill health, and there are occasions when the medical herbalist will either work directly with other practitioners or refer patients to other specialists for different treatment.

In the case of acute conditions or medical emergencies, or if a person comes with a problem requiring urgent medical attention or surgery, a medical herbalist will immediately refer the patient to his or her family doctor or local hospital. In practice this does not occur often, however, because the majority of patients come to medical herbalists not because of acute problems but because they have been through a range of drug regimes, hospitalization, and even surgery, and are seeking an alternative opinion as a "last resort".

Occasionally patients are referred by their family doctor, but an historical rivalry and suspicion remains between herbalism and orthodox medicine, so contacts of this kind are also relatively rare.

The relationship with other practitioners of complementary medicine is often more positive, and there are many instances of acupuncturists working with herbalists in the treatment of the same patient. If a patient has postural or back problems the herbalist may refer him or her to an osteopath or a chiropractor, and in some cases combined treatment with either of these therapies may also work very well.

If stress and inability to relax is an issue for a patient, a herbalist may recommend yoga, *Tai Qi*, or remedial massage as methods of relaxation. If the problems are mental or emotional, however, a patient is more likely to be referred to a counsellor or psychotherapist.

CASE HISTORY

The first stage of a consultation is to gather information, not only about the current condition, but also about the patient's previous medical history. Identifying a condition and labelling it in conventional terms is, however, a minor part of diagnosis. A herbalist needs to know how the problem started and what conditions caused it – for example stress, infection or injury. It is also important to find out the individual symptom picture – both physical and emotional – and any factors that exacerbate symptoms.

The patient's previous medical history is then taken. This includes assessment of long term weaknesses, imbalances and inherited disorders. If, for instance, there is a history of respiratory infections this may indicate a general weakness of the respiratory system. Recurrent cystitis can indicate a degeneration of the tissues of the urinary system, which needs treating or tonifying before the condition will improve.

The effective functioning of all systems of the body is important if the patient is to fully regain health. The herbalist therefore asks questions about digestion, menstruation, circulation and other systems as a matter of course.

The nature of diet and the patient's intake of alcohol, tobacco or non-medicinal drugs has bearing on any case, so details of these are taken during the initial consultation. Other aspects of lifestyle, including stress factors, emotional or mental problems, occupational or environmental hazards, exercise habits and postural factors (especially in people with breathing difficulties), are also taken into account.

EXAMINATION

Physical examination is like that of a family doctor and in general is done for the same reasons. Medical herbalists are trained in examination procedures of conventional medicine and use the same instruments – sphygmomanometer for monitoring blood pressure, ophthalmoscope to examine the eye, otoscope for ear examination, stethoscope to listen to the heart or chest. The abdomen may be palpated (felt) to detect inflammation of organs and the tone of the bowels.

DIAGNOSIS

All the information gathered in the consultation is assessed to identify which of the many factors is (or are) causing and perpetuating the problem.

For many people there is an immediate cause, such as an infection, which has resulted in the presenting symptoms. It is, however, important to identify other factors that have contributed to ill health. Very often, an illness occurs as health is diminished through an imbalance of one or more of the body systems. For example, the development of a skin condition may be an allergic response, but the herbalist wants to know why it has occurred at this particular time.

TREATMENT

The aim of treatment is to correct the underlying causative imbalances which have led to the present condition. This may include the relief of symptoms, especially if they are serious or distressing to the patient. However, symptoms in general are seen as the body's self-healing mechanisms at work and should not be suppressed. For example, rather than attempting to dry up a cough, it is encouraged to be more productive and the phlegm loosened. The type of expectorant prescribed would thus depend on the symptoms.

The first stage of treatment is to explain to the patient the herbalist's assessment of the problem and the recommended treatment.

Encouraging awareness of self-responsibility and suggesting ways in which patients can help themselves are fundamental to the herbalist's approach to healing. Advice on the areas of the patient's own effort will be given and would include, in particular, diet and the planning of an individualized programme.

Methods of tackling stress and relaxation tech-niques would also be discussed, and often exercise is a factor in patients' self-help programmes. If emotional factors are significant in a case, the herbalist will take time to talk through problems and help the patient to find ways of dealing with them.

Medication is prescribed on an individual basis, and, generally, herbal tinctures are dispensed in the herbalist's surgery. Although dosage varies, it is common for patients to be prescribed one dose three times daily. Creams, lotions, and gargles are pre-scribed as appropriate.

Further treatment may be necessary, depending on the problem, and in most cases patients return to have their problem reassessed. Prescriptions are adjusted to suit the changes that have taken place, and further advice or counselling can be offered. Treatment may be accomplished after one session, or a patient may have to return several times for further assessment, depending on the nature of the problem. Initial consultations generally take one hour, but subsequent visits tend to be shorter.

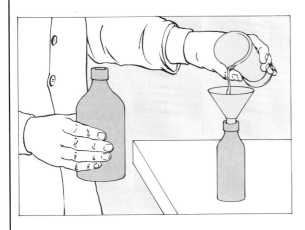

Herbal medicines are generally prescribed as tinctures. These are administered by the medical herbalist at the end of the consultation. The selected tinctures are poured into a medicine bottle and mixed together. Adjustments may be made to future prescriptions according to the needs of each patient.

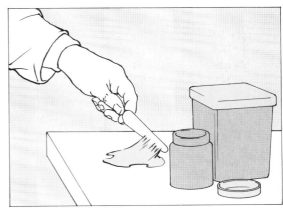

Creams and ointments, for external use, may also be prescribed by herbalists. Beeswax, aqueous cream and organic oils may be used as the base of these preparations and are blended with the herbal tincture. These are often prepared individually by the herbalist, but are also available commercially.

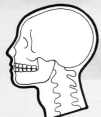

OSTEOPATHY WITH NATUROPATHY

The founder of osteopathy was an American doctor named Andrew Taylor Still, who practised during the nineteenth century. In his orthodox medical practice, Still observed that the drugs and treatments of his day were ineffectual against many of the serious diseases then prevalent. Three of Still's own children died during an epidemic of viral meningitis, and it was this devastating loss that motivated him to seek a new form of medicine. He ardently believed it necessary to return to the concept of Hippocrates (c. 460–377 BC, said to have been the father of Western medicine) that the "cure of disease lies within the body". Still claimed, furthermore, that disease could be cured by mechanical adjustment of the body.

Based on a dedicated and detailed study of human anatomy, Still formulated and began to teach the principles of a system which in 1874 he called osteopathy. Osteopathy literally means "bone disease", but Still used the word to indicate the relationship between the presence of a disorder and the misalignment of bones. Of all the bones in the human body, Still considered the most important to be the vertebrae, which make up the spinal column, because of their close relationship with the nervous system – they surround and protect the spinal cord.

Osteopathy has its roots in living anatomy and physiology. The coordinator of all bodily activity is the neuro-endocrine system – that is, the mechanism made up of the network of nerves on the one hand, and of hormones on the other. Endocrine glands secrete hormones that act as chemical messengers, and which are carried around the body in the bloodstream. The nervous system, of which the brain and spinal cord are the major organs, operates through millions of nerve cells, which penetrate all parts of the body. Nerve cells are involved in controlling voluntary or involuntary movement, in regulating the secretion of every gland, and in recording every sensation experienced – including touch, temperature, pain, balance, sight, sound, smell, taste and hunger.

Anything, therefore, that interferes with nervous activity or blood flow can affect function somewhere in the body.

If a nerve is destroyed or a blood vessel blocked, the part of the body served by it becomes paralysed, devoid of sensation or atrophic (lacking in nourishment) – or all three. The interference that occurs in an osteopathic spinal lesion is less final but can nevertheless have a functional effect (see box) and cause great discomfort.

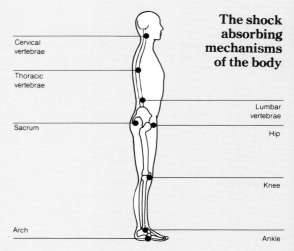

The shock absorbing mechanisms of the body

Cervical vertebrae

Thoracic vertebrae

Lumbar vertebrae

Sacrum

Hip

Knee

Arch

Ankle

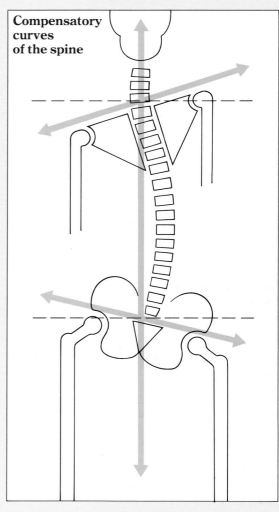

Compensatory curves of the spine

Spinal lesions

Osteopathic spinal lesion is a term that refers to any deviation from normal between two or more vertebrae, whether in position or in relative mobility.

Spinal lesion can involve intervertebral disks, articular facets, supporting ligaments or muscular attachments.

Biochemical changes can occur around the spinal joints. These changes can, in turn, affect the nerves emerging from between vertebrae, and ultimately influence a distant organ, a sense receptor or a gland.

Spinal lesions can result from injury, bad posture, occupational strain, the reflex effects of organic disturbance, or nutritional interference with the spinal tissues. There is usually more than one cause of a spinal lesion.

Likely sufferers include a car driver whose muscles tense up because of a continual draught, a passenger whose head and neck whiplash when the car stops suddenly, a careless worker who lifts something heavy without bending at the knees and letting the leg muscles take the load, an asthmatic who has a violent fit of coughing, and a golfer who does not follow through.

The list of straws that can break the human back is endless. More important are the predisposing causes, those that make it more likely for a lesion to occur: driving aggressively, wearing unsteady high-heels, stooping, using pillows that are too high or too low, typing for hours at a time with the head to one side, and carrying the world on worried shoulders. All these and more predispose the vertebral column to disturbance.

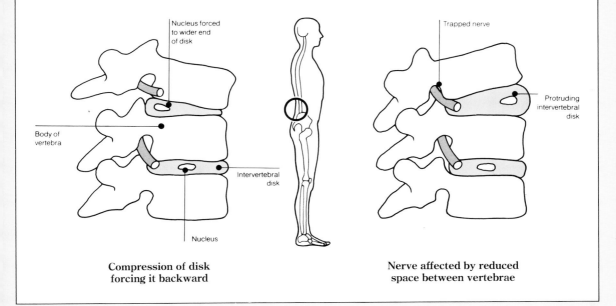

Compression of disk
forcing it backward

Nerve affected by reduced
space between vertebrae

The principles of shock absorption

The ability of the human frame to withstand the shocks of locomotion (movement from one place to another) is essential for its healthy survival. A comparison can be made with the shock-absorbing mechanisms of a car. A car ride is usually comfortable because of a combination of steel springs, hydraulic shock absorbers, and air-filled tyres. Without these means of absorbing the impact of the road against the vehicle, the car could vibrate itself – and its passengers – to near-destruction.

Humans have a similar need for protection against the normal physical impacts we encounter when moving. This need is met by the spring-like arches of the feet, the movable ankle and knee joints, the movement of the pelvis and hip joints, the elasticity of the intervertebral disks, and, finally the natural curves of the spinal column and sacrum. The combined cushioning effect makes it relatively safe to walk, run, skip, and jump.

Although the human body has extremely effective shock-absorbers, it is still possible to disturb the mechanical balance of the body. For instance, landing on the feet from a height without bending the knees has been known to transmit the force of the impact to the head and cause concussion. Fallen arches could be a cause of headaches as well as low back pain.

A distortion of the pelvic bones and of the curve of the spine above the pelvis could alter the positions of the uterus, and possibly result in menstrual difficulties or even miscarriage.

Slipped disk

A human adult has 26 vertebrae, which together make up the spinal column. Between the individual vertebrae there is an intervertebral disk, a cushion made of cartilage that separates the vertebrae. Each disk consists of a strong fibrous outer ring that binds the edges of two vertebrae together and acts as a container for a jelly-like substance. This substance is the nucleus pulposus, the material that enables an upper vertebra to balance on the one below it and gives the spinal cord stability. The nucleus pulposus is also vital in cushioning the spinal column against the shocks of everyday movement.

Problems arising from an imbalance of the vertebrae, or misalignment of one or more disks, are especially common amongst people in Western society. In general, most people take insufficient exercise, and so the ligaments and muscles that support the spinal cord become slack and ineffectual. When the spine lacks the kind of support given by healthy ligaments and muscles, the likelihood of disk problems increases, and it does not take very much strain to "slip a disk".

When a change takes place (perhaps caused slowly by continual bad posture or suddenly by trauma), the balance of the vertebrae is upset. The disk becomes wedge-shaped and the nucleus pulposus is forced toward the wide end of the wedge. The disk material can bulge outward at that end and press on a nerve root.

If the pressure is great or sustained, the disk may actually rupture (that is, split). In this case, the nuclear material oozes out and presses upon the nerve roots. This condition is known as a herniated, or slipped, disk and can cause muscle weakness, numbness and crippling pain. A slipped disk can also be a cause of sciatica. In this case, the disk presses upon the sciatic nerve, which runs from the spinal cord down the side of the leg to the foot.

Tendons and ligaments supporting the shoulder joint

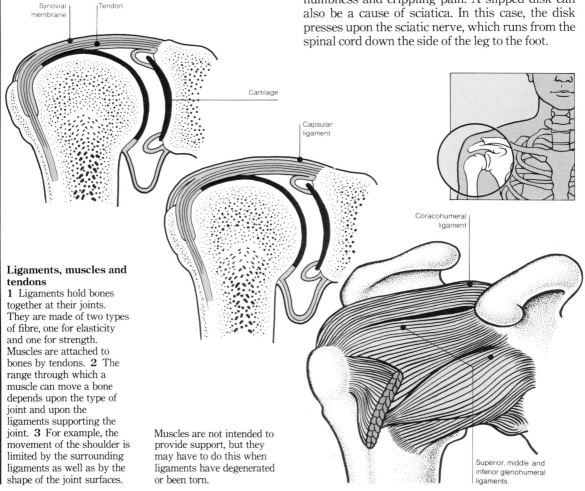

Synovial membrane

Tendon

Cartilage

Capsular ligament

Coracohumeral ligament

Superior, middle and inferior glenohumeral ligaments

Ligaments, muscles and tendons
1 Ligaments hold bones together at their joints. They are made of two types of fibre, one for elasticity and one for strength. Muscles are attached to bones by tendons. 2 The range through which a muscle can move a bone depends upon the type of joint and upon the ligaments supporting the joint. 3 For example, the movement of the shoulder is limited by the surrounding ligaments as well as by the shape of the joint surfaces.

Muscles are not intended to provide support, but they may have to do this when ligaments have degenerated or been torn.

Compensation

The term compensation refers to the ability of the body to make up for a defect or deficiency. Heart muscle sometimes enlarges to compensate for a faulty heart valve. Similarly, a single kidney can enlarge its capacity to make up for the other one if it is diseased or has been removed. All living things have the power to adapt to adverse situations, providing that the adversity is not overwhelming. The price of compensation, however, may be various degrees of discomfort.

Somebody who is hard of hearing may incline his or her head in order to hear better. After some years, compensatory changes in the muscles concerned with the posture of the neck may be evident, and it may then be difficult to restore them to normal. Having one leg that is shorter than the other often has the effect of tilting the pelvis downward on the short side. To maintain balance and straighten the body, the lower spine inclines in the opposite direction. But that could overbalance the body, so the spine bends again towards the midline higher up. These compensatory curves act to position the head in as straight a line as possible above the pelvis, but spinal integrity and comfort have almost certainly been reduced.

Some scolioses, kyphoses and lordoses (varieties of spinal curvature) are barely noticeable to the untrained eye, but they are obvious on an X-ray or under osteopathic examination.

Cranial osteopathy

The principle of osteopathy suggests that all areas of the body interact and depend on each other. Cranial osteopathy, formulated in the 1930s by William Garner Sutherland (a disciple of Andrew Still), emphasizes the part played by the primary respiratory mechanism.

Life starts with the first intake of breath, and ends with the last breath exhaled. In between, it is maintained by the differing rhythms of lung respiration, heart circulation and the flow of cerebrospinal fluid.

There are two phases to primary respiration: inhalation and exhalation. During the inhalation phase, the occiput (the bone at the back of the head) and the sphenoid (the butterfly-shaped bone inside the middle of the head) rotate toward each other so that their articulation (the place where they join) rises slightly, stimulating the pituitary gland.

To accommodate the movement, the paired bones such as the parietals (at the sides of the head) and the temporals (containing the ears) rotate outward, slightly widening the head. At the same time, because of the tension membrane connecting the cranium and the spinal cord, the spinal cord is lifted and the sacrum at the base of the spine rotates within the ilia (the broad portions of the hip bone). During exhalation, the bones and tissues return to their original positions.

Such respiratory activity is detected and analyzed by sensitive fingers held on each side of the head, on the sacrum or the limbs. An osteopath also takes account of soft-tissue changes in the body that might reduce the efficiency of the sacro-cranial relationship. Deviations from normal movement and position determine the precise and gentle treatment that is administered by a skilled cranial osteopath.

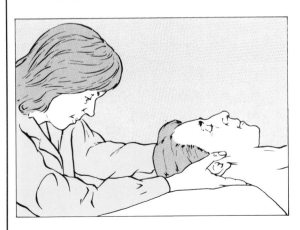

▲ **An osteopath** holds a patient's head to diagnose imbalances and correct them.

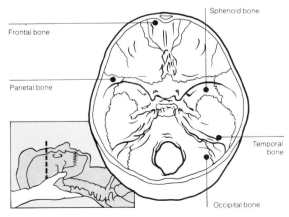

Sphenoid bone

Frontal bone

Parietal bone

Temporal bone

Occipital bone

▲ **An interior view** of the skull shows the sphenoid and adjacent bones.

Visceral osteopathy

Viscera is the term used to describe the internal organs, and visceral osteopathy is thus osteopathy as applied to them.

In the earlier part of this century, the term "bloodless surgery" referred to the non-surgical manipulation of organs and tissues in the abdomen. The approach to this form of adjustment is perhaps a little more sophisticated these days. A deeper understanding of the anatomy, physiology and possible pathology (disease) of the contents of the abdomen has increased the accuracy of the analysis of problems that are treated by manipulation.

Some healthy organs can be palpated (felt) through the abdominal wall. Some can be felt only if they are diseased, enlarged or malpositioned. Female reproductive organs can be examined via the rectum or vagina. The prostate and seminal vesicles (sac-like structures that secrete the fluid part of semen) can be felt by a finger inserted through a man's rectum.

Visceral osteopathy aims to restore an organ to its proper position, remove adhesions, massage congested tissue and encourage peristalsis (muscular movement) of the contents of hollow vessels. This is achieved by massage and manipulation of the abdomen.

In addition to direct contact, organs can also be influenced through, for example, the ganglia (nerve centres) that lie alongside the spine.

Naturopathic osteopathy

An osteopathic patient is more than just somebody with a bad back. Equally, an osteopath is more than an adjuster of bad backs. Osteopathy always tries to look into and after the whole person, as the analogy of the three-legged stool serves to illustrate.

Provided that each of the three legs of the stool are of equal strength and quality, and each is firmly embedded in the seat, the stool can be relied upon to serve its purpose for many years. Shortening a leg causes imbalance and puts a strain on the whole. Removing any leg altogether causes complete collapse.

In the human three-legged stool, one leg represents body chemistry. The efficiency of body chemistry depends a great deal upon healthy eating. The second leg represents the physical structure of the body: the organs that process the food eaten; the neuro-endocrine system; and the framework and posture of the body. The third leg represents mental, emotional, moral and spiritual attitudes – the joy of being. The seat itself reflects the influence of heredity for good or ill.

For an osteopath, health consists of the harmonious interaction of all four aspects illustrated by the three-legged stool. So, a sound physical structure requires good chemistry and a contented mind. Peace of mind comes from good nutrition and a healthy physical body (fasting and dietary assessment are often undertaken as part of treatment). Eating for nourishment should be pleasurable and easily handled by the body's organs.

A person (like the stool), however, neither floats in space nor exists alone, in a vacuum. People should be well grounded and aware of the climatic and creature environment. In addition, they need to

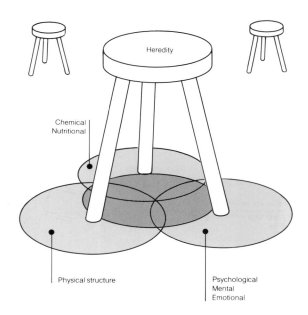

Heredity

Chemical Nutritional

Physical structure

Psychological Mental Emotional

relate constructively to their neighbours – socially, culturally, racially, religiously and politically.

Deviation from health – what we call disease – reflects disharmony of the pattern. Treating one of the stool's legs or part of a leg in isolation may alleviate symptoms and give temporary relief, but it rarely deals with the whole problem.

These are the basic principles of naturopathy. However, not all osteopaths practice naturopathy (or, indeed, visceral or cranial osteopathy).

Chart of correspondences showing possible effects of some spinal misalignments

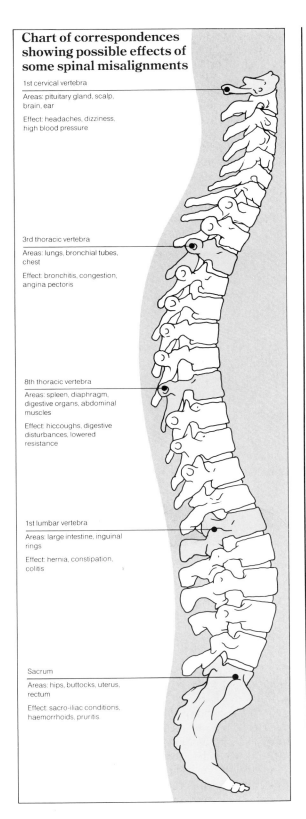

1st cervical vertebra

Areas: pituitary gland, scalp, brain, ear

Effect: headaches, dizziness, high blood pressure

3rd thoracic vertebra

Areas: lungs, bronchial tubes, chest

Effect: bronchitis, congestion, angina pectoris

8th thoracic vertebra

Areas: spleen, diaphragm, digestive organs, abdominal muscles

Effect: hiccoughs, digestive disturbances, lowered resistance

1st lumbar vertebra

Areas: large intestine, inguinal rings

Effect: hernia, constipation, colitis

Sacrum

Areas: hips, buttocks, uterus, rectum

Effect: sacro-iliac conditions, haemorrhoids, pruritis

Relationship with other systems

Medical specialisms The two branches of orthodox medicine closest to osteopathy are orthopaedics and orthopaedic surgery. Orthopaedics is the branch of medical science that treats locomotor (movement-linked) disorders, involving bones, joints, muscles and connective tissues. Orthopaedic surgery is the surgical prevention and correction of deformities. It is often the last resort for intractable spinal, hip and other joint defects.

Similar therapies There are several therapies that seek to treat mechanical problems affecting the skeleton, muscles or posture. Some of these are officially accepted as being complementary to orthodox medicine, whereas others are not.

Physiotherapy is the treatment of physical disorders using massage, heat treatment, therapy with electrical and mechanical equipment and water therapy (hydrotherapy). Many physiotherapists work in hospitals and undertake patient rehabilitation after surgery.

Some manipulative therapy is practised by masseurs who have undertaken additional training in manipulative procedures.

Chiropractic therapy is quite similar to osteopathy. It teaches that diseases are preconditioned by nerve impingement and correctable by spinal adjustments. The differences between osteopathy and chiropractic therapy are mainly of detail rather than quality. Both require in-depth medical study of the whole person on several levels.

Bone-setting is a traditional, empirical approach to skeletal defects that relies on innate skill rather than scientific training. It is probably still practised in some parts of the world.

Complementary therapies Acupuncture has a link with osteopathy in the use of associated effect points (AEPs), particular acupuncture points on the body that are said to be directly related to the viscera. AEPs are located on the line of the Bladder Channel (meridian) each side of the spine, and are effective because they influence the autonomic nerve ganglia below the surface. The same ganglia are affected by osteopathic adjustment of the spinal vertebrae.

Herbalism and homeopathy are therapies in which specific remedies may be prescribed for the pain and inflammation that often accompany musculo-skeletal problems. Where these problems arise from within – that is, from disease rather than from injury – appropriate constitutional remedies can be helpful to encourage self-healing.

CASE HISTORY

To determine the nature of a patient's problem, an osteopath takes a detailed case history by asking a series of questions. With regard to the chief complaint, the practitioner asks:

When did it start?
Where is it located?
How long have you had it?
How severe is it, and how often does it occur?
Has it occurred before?
Can it be linked to a particular time of day or time of year?
Is it associated with a particular food, or with bowel movements, menstrual cycle, stress, activity (or lack of it)?
Did it follow an accident or other injury?

The osteopath then asks about any related complaints that occurred before, together with, or after the present episode.

Has the patient had any previous physical or psychological illnesses?
What are the family influences?
Are there any inherited tendencies, or were there any childbirth problems?
What other treatments – medical or surgical – has the patient received?
Is he or she under treatment now?

The patient is finally asked for details of food intake, and whether he or she drinks alcohol, smokes tobacco or takes non-medicinal drugs. Any problems with bowel movements or urination, the menstrual cycle, sleep, the circulation, breathing, the skin or any of the senses are also noted.

EXAMINATION

After a preliminary examination of the area of chief complaint (and any areas of other complaints), the osteopath goes on to make a detailed examination of various musculo-skeletal structures. The practitioner notes the appearance of the patient standing, sitting and lying down, looking at the levels of bilateral structures (such as the ears, shoulders and hips), the spinal curves, the abdomen and chest, and the face and cranium.

Joint mobility is assessed from the range of movement of the bones of the arches, ankles, knees, hips, pelvis, spine, ribcage, arms and the bones of the skull. Finally, the practitioner analyses the nature of any fixation or malposition of bones of the spine and other joints, and assesses significant postural imbalances.

The chief body systems involved are also examined: the circulatory, endocrine, respiratory, nervous, genitourinary, gastro-intestinal, reproductive or sensory system. This, in turn, might entail investigation of the activity of the heart, lungs, abdominal and pelvic organs, eyes, ears, nose, throat and skin.

Clinical tests carried out by the osteopath include routine checks on blood pressure, heartbeat and pulse. Neurological tests may be made if indicated. The patient may be referred to hospital for X-rays or laboratory tests on blood or urine, or to check on liver function and hormone levels. Referral of the patient for a cervical smear test or biopsy (removal of a small piece of tissue for examination) may also be recommended in relevant cases.

DIAGNOSIS

The safety of the patient is paramount, and treatment is chosen according to the analysis to date. Some procedures may be used before the final diagnosis is made. For instance, omitting suspect foods from the diet may alleviate some symptoms and make further diagnosis possible; inhibiting a muscle in spasm may restore movement to a joint.

Finally a name may be given to the patient's condition. But it is not the name that determines treatment, which aims to correct specific imbalances found in the patient as a whole. Not all balances can be restored through osteopathy.

TREATMENT

Almost always, some therapeutic benefit is obtained from the first examination. Moving a joint to assess its mobility often frees it; manual examination of the abdomen sometimes moves bowel contents and gives relief. If there is an acute condition, such as excruciating low back pain, "first aid" treatment is administered on the first visit and advice given about home care, which may include hydrotherapy (hot and cold applications or baths, steam baths and the like), diet, posture and relaxation techniques.

The physical treatment programme usually begins on the second visit. The actual procedures used depend on the patient's needs as well as the nature of the problem. Neuro-muscular massage of the back, abdomen, limbs, joints or ribcage prepares muscle tissue for manual adjustment or removes congestion, improves circulation, breaks down adhesions or tones up slack tissue.

Active and passive movement of stiff joints, with or without resistance, is used to increase their range of movement and to improve lubrication of the joint surfaces. The practitioner also carries out manipulative adjustment of any spinal, rib or limb joints that have a limited range of movement, are locked at their joint facets, or involve wasted and malnourished tissue. The adjustments may involve positional release or muscle energy techniques, vibration or high-velocity thrusts.

The course of the programme may vary from one to ten or more treatments, depending on: the extent of any damage, the amount of degeneration present, the severity of the pain, how long the problem has existed, the patient's willingness to follow advice about home care between visits and, above all, the self-healing capacity of the patient concerned. An osteopath removes obstructions to healing, but it is the patient who actually does the healing itself.

Physical rehabilitation includes specific exercises, postural re-education and relaxation techniques. Depending on their relevance, certain foods, liquids or drugs may be replaced by a diet of more wholesome products. In some cases, the patient may be asked to switch to a diet of raw fruits and salads to enhance self-healing. Fasting for between 24 hours and a week may also be recommended.

It is sometimes necessary to help patients deal with problems arising through stress or fear, domestic or professional disharmony, or the long-term effects of shock or bereavement. This psychological care aims to remove factors that could have contributed to the onset of a disorder or could aggravate it.

To ensure that the same problem does not recur, the osteopath works out with the patient what the avoidable causes of the problem were and provides a programme of health care – for the home, job or sports field.

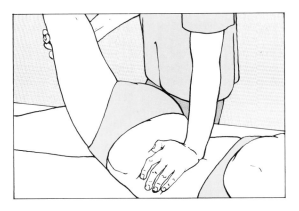

Lower thoracic vertebrae can be adjusted with the aid of leg leverage. The osteopath raises the leg while gently thrusting down on the appropriate vertebrae with the heel of the hand.

WESTERN MEDICINE

The family doctor provides primary medical care to the general public, handling the health problems and anxieties of individuals and families in a local catchment area. The general practitioner may work single handed in his or her own practice or with a number of doctors and other health professionals (such as nurses and health visitors) in group practices and health centres.

Primary health care

The family doctor is commonly the first contact a person makes when medical help is required, and is the entry point into a wide range of specialist medical services provided by hospitals, clinics and other health professionals. A doctor sees patients of all ages, and deals with a wide range of acute and chronic medical problems.

Although most doctor/patient contacts take place at the time of a patient's illness, the doctor and patient have an opportunity to form a relationship with each other over a period of time. Knowledge of the individual in terms of medical history, family, employment and social environment, all contribute to the doctor's ability to help with minor medical as well as other more complex emotional problems, life-threatening illnesses and chronic disabilities. Insight into the relationship of the patient with the family and society in general, makes the notion of "whole-person medicine" feasible in the context of orthodox medicine.

The five-minute interview.

The family doctor's role in the health of local people is limited, however, by two major constraints: the relatively large number of patients he or she looks after (up to 3,500), and as a consequence the limited amount of time available for consultation.

Consultations, which generally take place in the doctor's surgery, usually last between five and ten minutes. In order for this time to be used effectively, a competent physician must be a specialist not only in clinical knowledge, but also in the art of consultation. A patient should be able to confide in the doctor and discuss even sensitive matters in a trusting and supportive environment.

Listening for vital clues, skilled questioning and sound clinical knowledge make diagnosis in such a short time possible. A second appointment may be made for a longer interview, especially if the problem is emotional or requires specialist investigation. The constraints of time lead to frustration for both doctors and patients, and there needs to be acknowledgement of this on both sides.

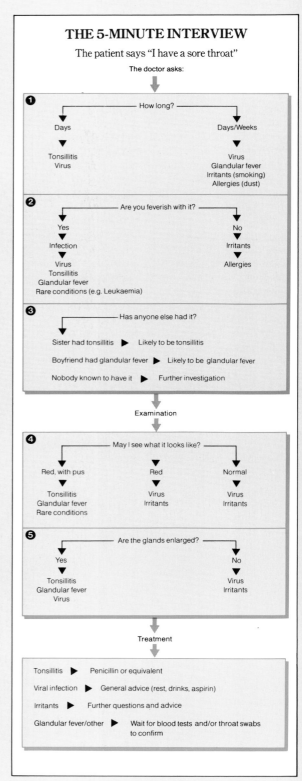

THE 5-MINUTE INTERVIEW

The patient says "I have a sore throat"

The doctor asks:

❶ How long? —

Days	Days/Weeks
Tonsillitis	Virus
Virus	Glandular fever
	Irritants (smoking)
	Allergies (dust)

❷ Are you feverish with it? —

Yes	No
Infection	Irritants
Virus	Allergies
Tonsillitis	
Glandular fever	
Rare conditions (e.g. Leukaemia)	

❸ Has anyone else had it?

Sister had tonsillitis ▶ Likely to be tonsillitis

Boyfriend had glandular fever ▶ Likely to be glandular fever

Nobody known to have it ▶ Further investigation

Examination

❹ May I see what it looks like? —

Red, with pus	Red	Normal
Tonsillitis	Virus	Virus
Glandular fever	Irritants	Irritants
Rare conditions		

❺ Are the glands enlarged? —

Yes	No
Tonsillitis	Virus
Glandular fever	Irritants
Virus	

Treatment

Tonsillitis ▶ Penicillin or equivalent

Viral infection ▶ General advice (rest, drinks, aspirin)

Irritants ▶ Further questions and advice

Glandular fever/other ▶ Wait for blood tests and/or throat swabs to confirm

Western medicine and other health services

The family doctor works in cooperation and consultation with other health care professionals. Nurses may be attached to a doctor's practice, while others work independently or in hospitals.

The family doctor is an intermediary for referrals, and maintains contact with the patient and specialist consultant while tests or treatment are being carried out. If patients seek specialist advice without referral, the specialist may lack access to medical records and there will be no consultation over treatment.

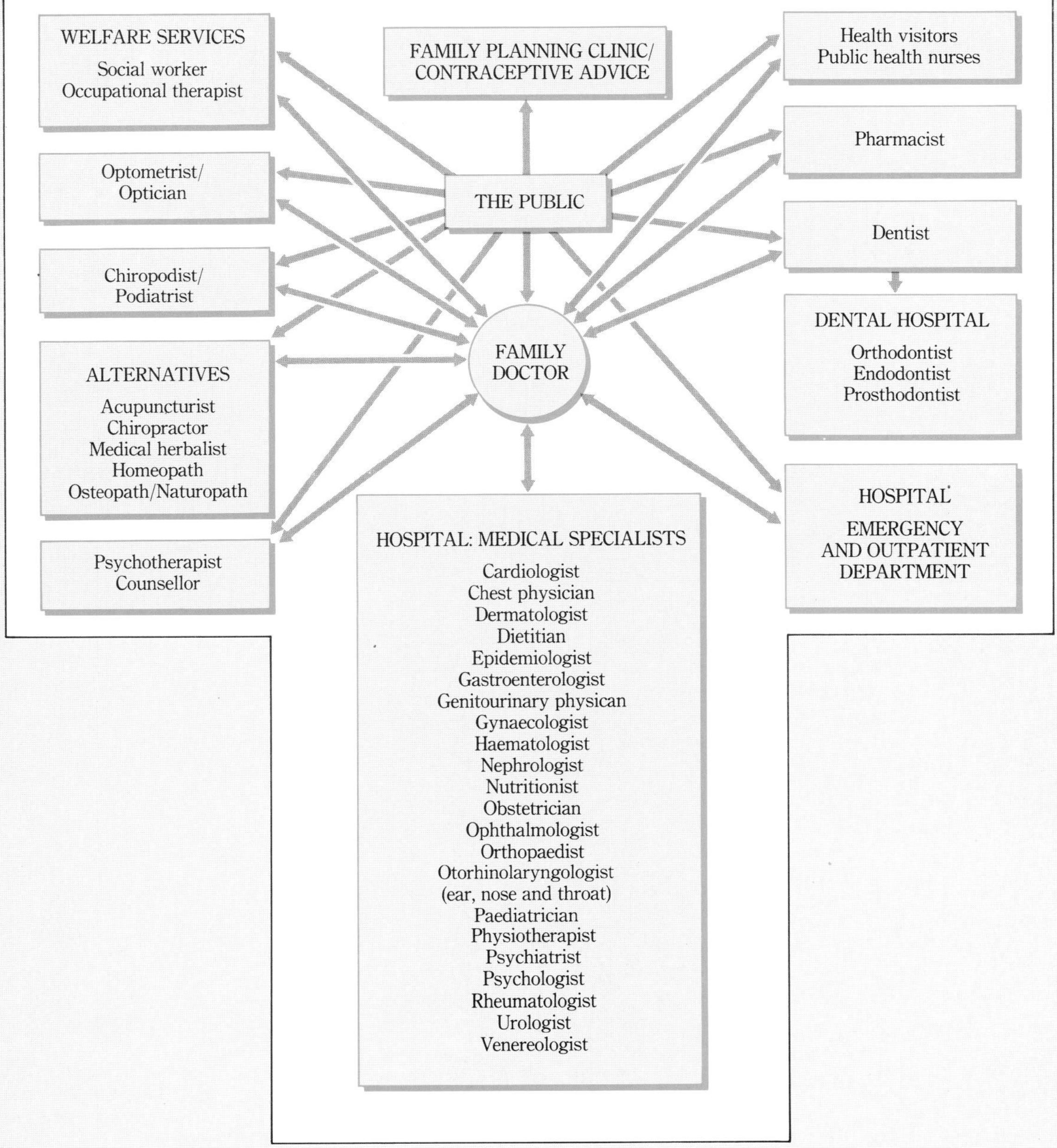

WELFARE SERVICES

Social worker
Occupational therapist

FAMILY PLANNING CLINIC/ CONTRACEPTIVE ADVICE

Health visitors
Public health nurses

Optometrist/
Optician

THE PUBLIC

Pharmacist

Chiropodist/
Podiatrist

Dentist

FAMILY DOCTOR

DENTAL HOSPITAL

Orthodontist
Endodontist
Prosthodontist

ALTERNATIVES

Acupuncturist
Chiropractor
Medical herbalist
Homeopath
Osteopath/Naturopath

Psychotherapist
Counsellor

HOSPITAL

EMERGENCY AND OUTPATIENT DEPARTMENT

HOSPITAL: MEDICAL SPECIALISTS

Cardiologist
Chest physician
Dermatologist
Dietitian
Epidemiologist
Gastroenterologist
Genitourinary physican
Gynaecologist
Haematologist
Nephrologist
Nutritionist
Obstetrician
Ophthalmologist
Orthopaedist
Otorhinolaryngologist
(ear, nose and throat)
Paediatrician
Physiotherapist
Psychiatrist
Psychologist
Rheumatologist
Urologist
Venereologist

The systems of the body

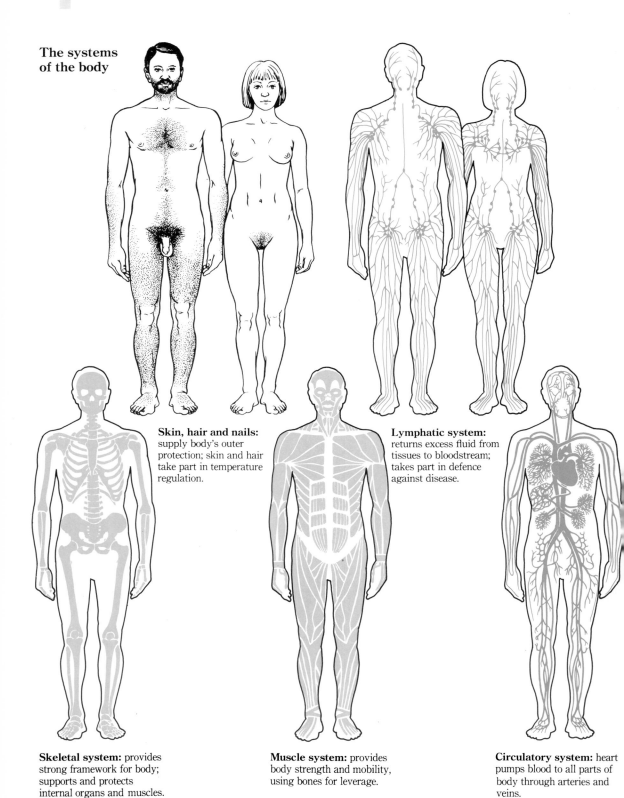

Skin, hair and nails: supply body's outer protection; skin and hair take part in temperature regulation.

Lymphatic system: returns excess fluid from tissues to bloodstream; takes part in defence against disease.

Skeletal system: provides strong framework for body; supports and protects internal organs and muscles.

Muscle system: provides body strength and mobility, using bones for leverage.

Circulatory system: heart pumps blood to all parts of body through arteries and veins.

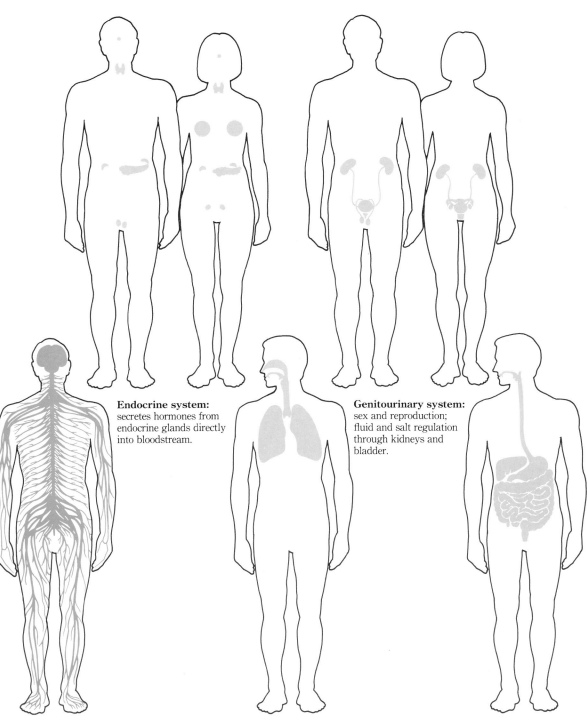

Endocrine system: secretes hormones from endocrine glands directly into bloodstream.

Genitourinary system: sex and reproduction; fluid and salt regulation through kidneys and bladder.

Nervous system: carries information from senses to brain; carries instructions from brain to rest of body.

Respiratory system: absorbs oxygen from air breathed in; expels the waste product carbon dioxide.

Digestive system: breaks down food, absorbs nutrients; removes waste matter.

The family doctor and the patient

All doctors have an initial training in anatomy, physiology, biochemistry and pharmacology (the study of drugs). At a later stage doctors concentrating on general practice pass through hospital training and study clinical therapeutics, clinical pathology (the study of disease) and medical and surgical specialisms including paediatrics, obstetrics and gynaecology.

This training enables doctors to identify which part of the body is diseased or not functioning normally, and to decide on the best form of therapy. The treatment of illnesses using drugs is generally related to a specific disorder and the body system or systems involved. Side effects of some drugs, however, may interfere with systems other than those being treated.

Doctors do not see patients only as manifesting symptoms relating to a particular system. Managing the care of an asthmatic who smokes requires consideration not only of the respiratory system but also of allergic factors, psychological and family issues. Other systems, such as the cardiovascular or digestive, may have to be considered, also. Although a family doctor has a good general medical knowledge, in some cases referral is made to a specialist with in-depth knowledge of a particular system and access to equipment. For instance, if a patient has a severe heart condition a cardiologist will be consulted.

The family doctor's understanding of community and family medicine, and cooperation with other professionals, comes from the training year after qualifying as a doctor. Trainees are attached to approved practices where they learn from recognized trainers. The techniques of consultation are also developed through role play and video tapes, thus enabling young family doctors to acquire competence in consultation. Sound clinical knowledge is essential but the ability to communicate with patients is equally important.

The organization of family medicine on a local

The family doctor and community medicine

ROUTINE MEDICATION
Chronically ill patients visit the doctor's surgery regularly for check-ups and repeat prescriptions. Common conditions include diabetes, heart and lung disorders. Patients with long-term minor psychological problems also visit the doctor frequently.

HOUSE CALLS
Visiting a patient's home is a service provided for those who are unable to come to the surgery. Seeing the social and domestic conditions can help the doctor to identify issues relating to care for the sick person and to prevention of further ill health.

ELDERLY
Many of the patients seen by doctors are elderly. Some are chronically sick, but medication keeps them out of hospital. They make frequent visits to the doctor's surgery for check-ups, medication and reassurance. House calls will be made if they cannot get to the surgery.

FAMILY PLANNING AND CHILDBIRTH
Discussing family planning and organizing facilities for childbirth, in hospital or at home, are important functions of a family doctor and other health workers. Potential problems can often be averted if pregnant women are seen regularly.

FAMILY DOCTOR

FAMILY MEDICAL HISTORY
In general, knowledge of medical history aids diagnosis and treatment. Knowing an individual's medical history, and also their family's history, can be invaluable in making early diagnoses of inherited diseases such as glaucoma, diabetes and thyroid disease.

CHILDREN
Family doctors often know children from birth and can anticipate health problems early. Some doctors have their own children's clinics – to assess growth, weight, general health and diet, and provide inoculations. Health visitors generally provide health care for babies.

KNOWLEDGE OF SOCIAL ENVIRONMENT
The family life, work and social environment of patients affect their health. Knowing the family can aid both diagnosis and treatment. The nature of work, occupational hazards or unemployment may be factors in a health problem.

DISABLED
Disablement due to accident or illness is dealt with by hospitals, but the family doctor is often involved in aftercare – providing medication and advice on self help and liaison with hospital and welfare services – wheelchair provision, allowances, occupational therapy and so on.

basis enables doctors to work closely with families over a period of time, and sometimes through several generations, despite population mobility. When a patient registers in a new area the medical records are transferred, so that previous medical matters can be referred to in consultation.

Illnesses do not exist in isolation from a person's social and family environment. Working within a local community the family doctor can become aware of trends in employment, housing issues, pollution factors, cultural and local dietary factors and so on. All of these things can help the doctor, not only in diagnosis but also in preventive medicine and care of patients. The impact of unemployment on marriages and general health, cultural isolation and age-related illnesses are all part of the broad picture of socio-medical problems.

Home visits provide a unique opportunity for doctors to offer advice on preventive and long term health matters. However, doctors generally make house calls only when patients are unable to get to the surgery.

Preventive medicine

This is one of the most important areas of the family doctor's role.

Vaccination is historically one of the most important areas of preventive health care, and major diseases have been eradicated by world health policies. Nurses or health visitors provide immunization for babies and young children, and a tetanus vaccination is given if a patient has a puncture wound. Travellers to tropical countries can obtain vaccinations from special clinics or their doctor.

Preventive care for women usually relates to reproductive functions and many women consult their doctors or visit specialist clinics regularly for check-ups. These include cervical screening, breast examination to detect abnormalities, weight and blood pressure checks, and family planning advice.

It is less common for men to have regular check-ups unless their employer demands it or they need references for insurance purposes.

Anyone visiting a doctor is given advice on general health issues such as weight, smoking and exercise, if these factors are relevant. Many diseases are caused or aggravated by obesity and poor diet, and doctors offer basic advice on weight-loss or refer for more specialist help.

House calls offer doctors the opportunity to advise on hygiene and general health care if the home environment is a factor in a patient's case. Cooperation between family doctors, social workers and health visitors is also important in the preventive health care of young children and the elderly.

Relationship with other medical systems

The long standing conservatism and mystification of doctoring has led to considerable isolation of the profession from other medical systems and support services. In Britain, the isolation of orthodox medical practice from other methods of medical care now seems to be breaking down, due mainly to an increase in information to the public and changes in post-graduate medical education.

Most forms of unorthodox paramedical or "complementary" support, (acupuncture, chiropractic therapy, homeopathy, and so on) are only available privately, although some doctors have studied these methods independently and use them in their family practices. In Britain, one of the Royal Family's physicians practices homeopathy as well as conventional medicine. However, a few doctors are also trained as homeopaths, and referrals are rarely made to homeopaths who do not also have a formal medical training.

Chiropractic therapy and osteopathy are sometimes recommended when a patient has back problems, but if the problem is acute or severe, hospital investigation or treatment is advised in the first instance. Acupuncture is not commonly used but can be helpful in the relief of pain and, occasionally, in childbirth. Doctors sometimes undertake a short training in acupuncture, which enables them to provide basic symptomatic treatment. If patients make specific requests for alternative treatment, a family doctor may be able to refer them or provide a recommended contact, but in general there is little communication between a family doctor and "alternative" therapists.

An increasingly challenging area for family doctors is to assess the complex emotional problems that face so many people today, and to review the wide range of options available. Many patients and families require help with emotional difficulties such as childhood disturbances, student breakdowns at college, difficulties within marriages and family relationships, and problems related to stress associated with work, unemployment, retirement or bereavement.

Psychiatry, family therapy, relaxation techniques, individual psychotherapy and counselling all have roles to play in helping people cope with life's difficulties. Increasingly, doctors refer patients for counselling or psychotherapy as the most effective way of dealing with stress-related or emotional problems that affect their physical well-being. This is not really a very different role from the family doctor/hospital consultant relationship, where their joint involvement in dealing with wider problems has a far-reaching impact.

CASE HISTORY

In general medicine, a patient's case history can play an important part in arriving at a diagnosis and prescribing treatment. But many people who visit their family doctor already think they know what is wrong with them: "Doctor, I've got an infected cut and I think it needs treatment." After a few questions and a brief examination, the doctor can often confirm what the patient says and prescribe treatment. The whole process takes no more than a few minutes.

Even less specific problems, such as "I feel so weak these days, I don't know what is wrong with me", may be dealt with in a short consultation by the doctor "tuning in" to what the patient says and picking up clues, rather than by asking specific questions.

The doctor may ask about the patient's diet, family life and social environment. It may be important to know if there is a history of certain disorders in the patient's family. Observing his or her general state of health and consulting existing medical records – in effect, the case history – also help to build up a picture. Often merely asking the patient what the problem could be provides valuable information; listening to what the patient has to say can be the most important diagnostic tool.

EXAMINATION

Any examination begins with observation. The doctor notes the patient's general appearance and whether there has been a significant gain or loss in weight. Skin colour, complexion, the condition of the hair and the appearance of the eyes all provide clues about the state of health. Obvious signs such as a limp or a wheezing cough also provide clues.

A physical examination may involve palpation of any painful areas, and listening to the chest with a stethoscope. The patient's blood pressure may be measured, and the doctor may take samples of blood or urine for testing. A difficult case may need further clarification by means of X-rays or special tests, usually carried out in a hospital out-patient department. Or the doctor may refer the patient to a specialist for a complete diagnosis and treatment.

DIAGNOSIS

The doctor's clinical knowledge, combined with the examination and reference to the patient's medical notes, usually enable a diagnosis to be made on the first visit to the surgery, even if the problem seems unusual or worrying to the patient. If specialist consultation or tests are involved, there may be some delay until the results of these are available. Some cases may require several visits to a hospital for specialist investigation before the results can be evaluated and diagnosis made.

TREATMENT

Medical treatment may consist of simple advice and reassurance that nothing serious is wrong. Often the doctor recommends self-help such as bedrest, a change in diet or regular doses of a mild painkiller until the condition improves. The assistance of paramedical services, such as nurses or social workers, may be required to help care for the patient.

More serious conditions may require prescribed medication, ranging from simple but potentially lifesaving antibiotics to complicated drug regimes for treating disorders such as heart failure. Some patients are reluctant to take drugs, others expect them to be prescribed routinely. Doctors recognize that all drugs should be used with discretion and not as the rule. If such treatment is necessary, the doctor chooses a drug from a knowledge of its effectiveness, possible side-effects and possible interaction with other medications (or alcohol).

Most drugs can be taken as tablets or liquids, although sometimes a course of injections is prescribed. Injection is also the most common form for vaccines, and giving these is an important part of preventive medicine in family practice – especially for children.

Some cases require surgical treatment. This can vary from simple stitching of a cut or dressing an infected wound, done in the doctor's surgery, to setting of broken bones and operations on diseased or malfunctioning vital organs performed by specialists in hospital.

For a patient suffering from an emotional disorder, the doctor may set aside extra time for the consultation – talking through a problem is part of the treatment. A patient may be referred to a counsellor or therapist for specialist help if the case is complex. In some cases of extreme anxiety, tranquilizing drugs may be prescribed to help the patient cope in the short term. But these drugs are prescribed less often than they once were, because of their addictive nature and the fact that they do not help to resolve the underlying cause of stress. In cases of severe mental disorder, the patient would be referred to a hospital for appropriate psychiatric treatment.

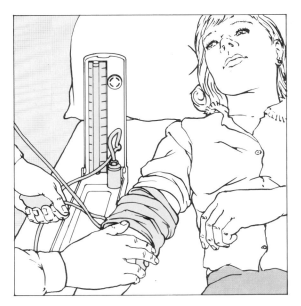

Blood pressure is measured using a sphygmomanometer. An inflatable cuff is wrapped round the upper arm and a stethoscope is applied to the artery below the cuff. As the cuff is inflated, changes in the pulse can be detected. The highest and lowest blood pressures are recorded as the air in the cuff is gradually released.

TREATMENTS FOR HEALTH PROBLEMS

The area of health care that matters most is the diagnosis and treatment of individual patients. It is with this in view that the following pages compare the six different alternative therapies.

Comparisons between the alternatives are made in the form of both individual case studies and comprehensive charts.

The diseases and disorders discussed are divided into eight sections relating to body parts and systems. At the beginning of each is an introduction to the system or systems to which the group of cases relates, and a summary of the different complementary approaches to them. Conventional Western classification has been used because of its familiarity; it is not intended to imply any bias. Each type of therapy views patients in specific and often different ways from other traditions, and these differences continue to underlie each separate approach to diagnosis and treatment.

The 30 case histories have been selected for their common occurrence, and for their relevance to an open-minded approach to health care. They are brief accounts of how individuals with particular disorders would be diagnosed and treated by the six practitioners. Each case concludes with a commentary by an independent consultant. Cross-references guide you to related disorders or to other conditions mentioned in the case studies.

The patients described are real people with real needs for treatment. Nevertheless, in practice each patient could not have been treated by all six practitioners, so instead each practitioner was asked to say only how he or she would approach treatment of the patient. The same technique is used in the "case conference" approach to co-operation between practitioners in many holistic and complementary clinics. The approaches of different therapies and therapists shed new light on each case, help a patient to understand his or her case history better, and also encourage practitioners to view their own approaches with an open mind.

The comparative charts that conclude each section indicate the suitability of each type of therapy for treating a selection of disorders, and may help you choose the method of treatment that could suit you best. Cross-references to other parts of the book are an integral part of these charts.

The patient as an individual

The greatest limitation of any general discussion about complementary therapies is that theories and concepts alone do not actually correct illness. Ill-health hurts and degrades the sufferer in a way that no other person can understand. Even other sufferers of the same sort of illness experience it in different ways.

Among the "alternative" therapies – whatever their differences – there is one essential factor that unites them and distinguishes them from conventional drug-based medicine; all emphasize the notion that every person is a unique being. The best family doctors practising conventional Western medicine also transcend the limitations of a symptom-based approach, and focus on the patient's uniqueness. In essence, the success of all treatments always depends on the individuality of the person concerned.

An open-minded comparison

As the different cases unfold, patterns in the approaches of the six practitioners emerge, and these provide insights into methods of diagnosis and treatment. They also show, with startling clarity, that there are often several approaches to most health problems – especially ones that are persistently difficult to treat.

The cases help to illustrate the strengths and weaknesses of the therapies discussed, and may even help you, as a potential patient, to choose one form of treatment rather than another.

Study of the cases will show patients the value of their own case history, and bring a realization that off-the-shelf treatments can only ever be of limited value. The case studies clearly illustrate that the best way to treat the problems of real people is to unravel the threads of each case, and deal with details individually. Only then can a therapy provide fundamental healing rather than merely relieving symptoms.

It is to be hoped that this open-minded attitude will provide interest and enlightenment for both conventional health professionals and complementary practitioners. It is still rare for those in the healing professions to share insights from other disciplines – especially if they are working in orthodox fields. A deeper understanding should also increase mutual respect between practitioners, so that patients may be referred more freely to different therapists for alternative or complementary treatment.

THE MOUTH, THROAT AND RESPIRATORY SYSTEM

As we breathe, our lungs extract oxygen from the air we inhale. On exhaling, waste products (carbon dioxide and water) extracted from the blood are removed. The respiratory system consists of passages that carry air from the nose and mouth to the lungs, and a network of blood capillaries in the lungs. Oxygen enters, and carbon dioxide is removed from, the blood through the walls of these capillaries.

The mouth is connected to the respiratory passages. It is also the entrance to the digestive system. The teeth break up food, and saliva – produced in the mouth – begins the digestive process. The throat also houses the larynx, which contains the vocal cords.

The mouth, throat and all respiratory passages are particularly susceptible to infection because they are all directly exposed to the outside environment.

WHAT CAN GO WRONG

Bacterial or viral infections frequently affect the respiratory system, resulting in coughs, sore throats, catarrh and many other disorders. Bacteria can also affect the mouth, teeth and gums, causing tooth decay and gum inflammation. Allergies can affect the respiratory system leading to such conditions as hay fever and asthma. Some disorders, such as silicosis, are caused by inhalation of foreign matter that leads to irritation and scarring of the lungs. General debilitation and deficiency states, such as scurvy, can result in damage to the delicate mucous membranes that line the mouth and lips.

Any part of the mouth, throat and lower respiratory tract may develop cancer. Smoking greatly increases this possibility, and aggravates other less serious respiratory conditions.

Complementary and alternative medical approaches sometimes view the mouth, throat and respiratory system and their disorders in different ways, as summarized in the following paragraphs.

Acupuncture

In traditional Chinese medicine, the throat, nose and voice are all part of the *Lung* system. The *Lung* protects the other *Zangfu* from external influences such as *Wind, Cold* and *Damp*, but is, at the same time, vulnerable to these influences.

There are three types of diseases of the *Lung*. First is acute invasion by external *Wind, Cold* and *Heat*, which leads, initially, to the symptoms of the common cold and (if the disease progresses) to coughs and bronchitis.

The second is retention of *Phlegm* in the *Lung*, which often occurs after a cold and can result in chronic coughs and bronchitis.

The third category is chronic deficiency of *Lung Qi* or *Yin*, which can produce tiredness, a weak voice, weak limbs or a cough. If the *Yin* is weak there will also be *Dryness* and signs of *Heat*.

The mouth is said to be under the influence of the *Spleen*. Some mouth ulcers are caused by *Spleen* dysfunction and others may be due to a *Stomach* disorder. The *Stomach* and *Large Intestine* channels pass over the cheeks and around the mouth, and can be used to relieve toothache. The condition of the teeth may be related to the *Kidney* and the *Jing*.

Chiropractic therapy

In general, chiropractic therapy would not aim to treat respiratory disorders. However, a chiropractor might be able to relieve any associated back pain, and so help the condition.

Homeopathy

The respiratory system is more vulnerable than other body systems because it is exposed to external environmental influences. Colds and coughs are the result of this, but if the body is healthy, it adapts to changes in the environment and fights off bacteria and viruses. When vitality is lowered, a person is more susceptible to illness.

Minor colds are seen as the body's struggle to adapt to adverse environmental as well as internal factors – cold weather, change in seasons, stress and over-tiredness. The vital force produces cold symptoms as a means of cleansing the system and restoring health. These symptoms are to be encouraged, to increase the discharge of toxins by loosening congestion. More serious conditions, such as bronchitis, indicate a weakness of the lungs that requires deeper, constitutional treatment to improve the overall level of health.

Allergies also indicate the inability of the body to adapt to the external environment and can be alleviated by constitutional treatment.

Medical herbalism

With all disorders, medical herbalists treat the individual rather than the condition. Respiratory infections are no exception, particularly when problems recur frequently, because the herbalist is concerned with identifying the underlying causes of the disease.

Treatment is generally aimed at boosting the vitality and the functioning of the immune system. It also helps to relieve distressing acute symptons by encouraging the body to "cleanse itself" more effectively. Factors such as diet, exercise (including breathing exercises), stress levels, posture and the functioning of other body systems are all considered in assessing treatment. This approach offers real prospects of long-term vitality and a reduction of respiratory ailments.

In allergic conditions such as asthma, the approach of overall assessment is vital, because environmental allergens are only one factor in the onset of such disorders. Diet and stress reactions are probably the most significant areas for investigation and treatment, but many such problems have complex causes and demand a holistic approach.

Osteopathy with naturopathy

The respiratory system either accepts or rejects the many influences to which it is subjected. The result depends on the health of the individual.

Bacteria and viruses require a medium within the mouth, throat, bronchi or lungs in which they can multiply and establish themselves. Lack of general fitness, and not infection, is therefore the primary cause of symptoms. The symptoms represent the body's efforts to restore harmony and should not therefore be suppressed.

Inefficiency of this system can be affected by faults in the thoracic (chest) vertebrae of the spinal cord and by interference with the breathing centre of the brain from the cranium, the bones of the skull. Some foods (especially dairy products and carbohydrates), pollution, and smoking can create catarrhal congestion in the respiratory system.

Chart of disorders

At the end of this section there is a chart listing various disorders of the respiratory system. This is a general, but not definitive, guide to the treatment of such disorders. Complementary therapies treat the patient as a whole rather than merely the disorder presented. Whether a person can be treated, and the success of treatment, depends on the nature of the condition and the general health of the patient.

ASTHMA

THE PATIENT

NG is 33, recently married and working as a counsellor. She is 1.6 metres (5 ft 4 in) tall, has a good complexion, and although slim has to control her diet to avoid putting on weight. She is very committed to her work and rarely has the time or inclination to exercise. NG's free time is generally devoted to gardening, reading and entertaining. She has a quiet and sensitive temperament, and takes her life seriously.

THE PROBLEM

NG has had asthma since she was 13 years old – two years after puberty – and it is now a chronic condition. Until recently her symptoms were erratic and she used inhalants only when necessary, but five years ago she was hospitalized with an attack and has since used inhalants and tablets daily. She is allergic to feathers and dust, and knows that stress aggravates the condition.

NG also suffers from low backache and frequently gets a stiff neck and shoulders; she perceives that this is due to poor posture.

Although she lives in the country and relaxes a lot, NG's work is stressful and she often has to deal with crises. She is self contained, but tends to worry about other people and put their needs above her own. She used to lack confidence in her own abilities, but has recently come to terms with her own strengths and weaknesses and now feels accomplished and good about herself. Due to a distaste for meat she has been a vegetarian since she was 19, and eats a healthy wholefood diet, avoiding too much dairy produce.

Apart from asthma, NG has had no other major health problems. She rarely gets colds, but has heavy and painful periods, with premenstrual tension lasting for up to a week. She also suffers from water retention before her period which causes her breasts to swell and feel painful. She had glandular fever when she was 16 years old.

TREATMENT BY AN
ACUPUNCTURIST

The immediate cause of asthma is the accumulation of fluids in the chest in the form of *Phlegm*. This involves dysfunction of either the *Lung* or *Kidney*. The *Lung* type of asthma may be the result of a common cold which has not been resolved, due to weakness of the *Lung Qi*, overwork or poor diet. The *Kidney* type arises because the *Kidney* is not strong enough to receive and hold the *Qi* and *Body Fluids* sent to them by the *Lung*.

In NG's case the primary disharmony involved both the *Lung* and the *Kidney*. The involvement of the *Kidney* was suggested by the fact that NG had difficulty breathing in, which indicated that the *Kidney* could not take hold of the *Qi*; by the fact that attacks occurred at night; and by the backache. NG's allergies are a *Lung* problem, but they could also involve the *Kidney*, as an allergy is also a constitutional problem.

There were signs of the stagnation of *Qi*, which appeared as heavy, painful periods with premenstrual tension and swollen, painful breasts. Involvement of the *Spleen* was also indicated here.

Her pulse was weak indicating weak *Qi*. The "wiry" pulse on the left indicated *Liver* stagnation and the slippery right pulse confirmed *Phlegm* accumulation in the *Lung*.

Treatment
Reducing NG's dependence on inhalants and tablets would be important, since these tend to mask the condition. However, she could only reduce her medication as her condition improved, and the process would be closely monitored.

Treatment would initially concentrate on reducing phlegm retention and wheezing, using the *Lung, Ren, Urinary Bladder*, and *Stomach* channels, and other points. The *Kidney* would be strengthened using the *Urinary Bladder, Kidney* and *Ren* channels. It would then be necessary to repair the *Lung* and *Kidney* functions, and move the stagnant *Qi* using the *Liver* and *Gall Bladder* channels.

Prognosis and conclusion
Treatment might last for up to six months. Exercise, particularly swimming, would be recommended in order to promote circulation of *Qi*. She might also think of taking up *Tai Qi* or yoga to help her to control stress.

Backache pp. 152–155 Dysmenorrhoea pp. 142–145   Introduction to acupuncture pp. 8–15

TREATMENT BY A
CHIROPRACTOR

Points of particular interest in NG's case are the pattern of development of her asthma, her low backache and stiff neck, and her premenstrual problems.

Physical examination
Initially NG's standing posture was noted. She was then asked to sit, and the whole spine was palpated (felt) to check for any stiffness or restriction in the normal movement of the vertebrae. During the examination, orthopaedic and neurological tests were carried out as necessary. X-rays of the cervical and lumbar areas of the spine and of the chest were taken to check for any abnormalities.

As well as restriction in the lower back, neck and shoulders, NG also had considerable stiffness and muscle tension throughout the thoracic area, which is common in people suffering from asthma.

Treatment
Muscle spasm in her neck, shoulders, thoracic and low back areas would be treated using general soft-tissue massage. Subsequently, those areas of the spine – especially the thoracic area – where restriction of the vertebral movement had been found would be corrected using chiropractic adjustment. Once the muscles had been loosened and the vertebrae were moving freely she would feel an improvement in her lower backache and neck and shoulder stiffness.

Loosening the thoracic area frequently helps to improve asthmatic problems, making breathing easier and decreasing the number of attacks. It is likely that treatment of the low back would help her painful periods.

The chiropractor would advise NG to consider attending yoga or relaxation classes to help her cope with stress and so avoid becoming too tense. A reduction in tension, together with an overall improvement in her well-being, would help to control and reduce her asthmatic attacks.

Prognosis and conclusion
Chiropractic treatment might be able to ease NG's asthma and would certainly improve her general health. If she required further help, the chiropractor would probably refer her either to an acupuncturist, homeopath or medical herbalist.

TREATMENT BY A
HOMEOPATH

This case is interesting because of the quality of the symptoms. As expected in asthma cases, there are many emotional symptoms, but the common symptom of anxiety is replaced by a competence in dealing with crises and a self awareness that has helped her to come to terms with her weaknesses. Such willpower is evident also in the way she tackles her weight problem. It is not surprising that she also manages to control her asthma except when she drives herself too far.

Allopathic treatment – both drugs and inhalants – have a suppressive effect on the body as they do not deal with the whole person. It is therefore not surprising that her condition is getting no better. The aim of homeopathic treatment would be to reduce her drug dependence over a period of time.

It is also likely that the patient is dissatisfied in some way with herself, because she gives little acknowledgment to her own needs and spends so much of her time counselling others.

Natrum muriaticum has many of the characteristics described above. In addition, NG's condition has tended to be worse since puberty and she suffers from premenstrual tension, which is often accompanied by water retention. She also has a stiff back, neck and shoulders. All of these symptoms fit the picture of *Natrum muriaticum*, so – after asking a few more questions related to the diet and quality of sleep – this remedy was confirmed.

Treatment and prognosis
The existing medication being used by NG would be assessed. In this case, NG would need to continue using inhalants while homeopathic treatment took its effect. As her condition improved the medication could be reduced. *Natrum muriaticum* would be given, in the 30th potency at first, to assess its effect on her condition. The potency would be increased over time to improve her constitutional health.

As the prescription progressed to the higher 1M or 10M potencies it would be possible to gain access to deep emotional levels. However, it might also be necessary to refer her for psychotherapy to enable her to cope with her underlying emotional problems. Conversely, if she does not deal with the emotional causes of her illness, there is a risk that her condition may worsen as her constitutional energy increases. Careful monitoring of her condition is therefore crucial.

Introduction to chiropractic therapy pp. 16–23

Introduction to homeopathy pp. 24–31

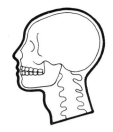

TREATMENT BY A
MEDICAL HERBALIST

Several factors contributed to NG's problem. Her sensitivity to stress was reflected by the hypersensitive reaction in her airways. The premenstrual tension and fluid retention indicated a hormonal imbalance, which was likely to aggravate the asthmatic reaction. A further problem was posture, not only giving rise to low backache, but also impeding chest movement and expansion. Glandular fever may have impaired the function of the liver and this would also need some attention.

Treatment
NG could usefully concentrate on exercises to improve posture and balance, and reduce stress. Yoga, *Tai Qi* or the Alexander technique might be useful, and breathing exercises could help. The herbal prescription would include:
- Euphorbia (*Euphorbia pilulifera*): relaxes antispasmodic muscle action of the bronchial airways and dilates the bronchial tubes; helps to loosen any accumulation of sticky phlegm.
- Ephedra (*Ephedra sinica*): powerful bronchial relaxant, also gives some cardiac stimulation (a check would be kept on blood pressure).
- Chamomile (*Matricaria recutita*): calming, anti-inflammatory action which helps to reduce reaction to stress, and increases urine flow, reducing fluid retention before periods.
- Thyme (*Thymus vulgaris*): antispasmodic expectorant, loosens thick mucus.

The prescription would be maintained and adapted as part of a programme to reduce the use of drugs and would be broadened to deal with such matters as hormone imbalance.

Prognosis and conclusion
NG should concentrate on redressing all her imbalances, particularly stress and her reaction to it. The prospects for improving her ability to cope without medication should be quite good, but while severe stress remained, her lungs would be a weak part of her constitution.

TREATMENT BY AN
OSTEOPATH AND NATUROPATH

NG showed her disease in various ways: problems associated with her periods, backache, a tendency to be overweight, and distress with her breathing.

All parts of her system were examined, including her mental and emotional condition. Giving relief during acute attacks would be desirable, but not if this ignored NG's underlying problems.

Lesions were found in most of the spine and in the sacrocranial mechanism. It seemed likely that some of NG's problems went back to when she had glandular fever – a condition often influencing the choice of treatment and the prognosis. Consideration of nutrition and stress-related factors is important. Feathers and dust are not a fundamental cause of such a condition, even though they are likely to initiate an asthmatic response.

Treatment
The osteopathic treatment would try to re-educate NG's spinal mechanism and the movements of her diaphragm and ribcage. The effects of cranial bone motion and cerebrospinal fluid flow on her pituitary gland should be improved as this controls other glands that are involved with fluid metabolism and cortisone production.

She should learn to distinguish between an inability to breathe in – the fear of some asthmatics – and the tendency to hold a lungful of air that should be released.

Reassurance and encouragement to breathe is the most important assistance someone can provide during an attack. It may also help to press deeply on the tissue on either side of the midline of the upper thoracic spine – this influences the respiratory mechanism through the sympathetic ganglia (nerve junctions linking directly to organs) and can often calm a severe attack.

NG should also give up milk products and various other foods that tend to encourage mucus production.

Prognosis and conclusion
It would probably be some time before NG saw a significant reduction in her asthma. It would also be essential for her to concentrate on improving her general health during this time.

Introduction to medical herbalism pp. 32–39

Introduction to osteopathy with naturopathy pp. 40–47

TREATMENT BY A
FAMILY DOCTOR

Asthma is a potentially very serious condition and so it should not be underestimated. While it depends on many subtle factors – such as stress, allergy, infection and irritation – there are great dangers in failing to take its treatment seriously.

Treatment

Identification and avoidance of allergic agents – such as feathers and house dust – would be essential. Desensitization injections are dangerous and should not be undertaken.

Bronchodilators would be necessary for reversing bronchial spasm and can be safely used by inhalation.

Inhaled topical corticosteroids (such as Becotide) are useful in the management of asthma in young people, although they do not give the immediate relief of a bronchodilator such as Ventolin (salbutamol). Intal (sodium chromoglycate) is also a useful inhaled drug that acts to block the antigen/antibody complex and prevents the release of histamine with the ensuing asthma symptoms. It is also used in the treatment of hay fever, although its main use is in allergic asthma.

NG had tensions and stresses that would benefit from attention, both physically and through expert supervision in her job. She should never smoke and should avoid being in a smoky atmosphere.

NG's treatment should involve regular educational supervision by her doctor. She should learn how to assess her breathing with a testing device, manage acute episodes and use maintenance medication.

Prognosis and conclusion

As an intelligent non-smoker who takes her condition seriously, NG should do well. Orthodox medicine has an important place in the treatment of asthma, and hospital admission must be considered in severe episodes. Good management of the condition is usually rewarding, however. Special attention should be paid to minimizing asthma-inducing situations such as stress, and exposure to allergic agents and irritants. Exercise and healthy breathing are also very important.

CONSULTANT'S COMMENTS

As the family doctor is correct to comment, asthma is a potentially serious disease that is still sometimes fatal. Orthodox drugs are not necessarily the only way to protect a sufferer, but they are the most readily available. During treatment by any of the complementary therapies, it is important that both the patient and practitioner consider carefully any reduction in conventional medication.

The treatments

There is no doubt that there are herbs, that can abort an asthma attack. Research in China also supports the notion that skilful acupuncture treatment can do the same. However, neither option is likely to be readily available in a Western context.

The aim of a complementary therapist is primarily to correct the underlying disturbances so that the hypersensitive reaction and other disorders that produce the bronchial spasm can be reduced. Conventional medical opinion is that this is not a valid approach, but complementary therapists will usually have clinical experience to show that it is possible to wean patients off drugs. The watchword, as always, is caution.

The homeopath makes a valuable point that, unless emotional issues are taken into account, it is possible to exacerbate an asthmatic condition by trying to improve the constitution.

The chiropractic and osteopathic emphasis on posture and spinal health is reflected in the advice of others to explore yoga, *Tai Qi* or other relaxation methods. Physical therapy can be a most effective way of untangling the psychosomatic and emotional knots that often dominate in asthmatic patients.

Summary

The complementary approaches contrast vividly with that of orthodox medicine, where the only option is to retreat from irritants under the protection of suppressive medication. It is because they provide hope of another, more positive way ahead in cases such as this, and offer optimistic strategies of support, that complementary therapies have gained much of their recent popularity.

Introduction to Western medicine pp. 48–55

BRONCHITIS

THE PATIENT

BR is a 38-year-old and is married with two children aged seven and three. She is tall and fine-boned and, although she has been slender all her life, since the weaning of her second son her weight has increased. Although she smoked regularly in her twenties, she stopped during her first pregnancy and has not resumed. She eats healthily and goes swimming when the weather is warm and she feels fit enough.

THE PROBLEM

BR has little resistance to respiratory infection. A slight sore throat can develop into bronchial congestion in two or three days. For the past seven years she has had bronchitis (an infection and inflammation of the bronchi, the tubes leading into the lungs) once or twice each winter. Several times this has resulted in bronchial pneumonia. Each incident has required stronger antibiotics and a longer period of recuperation.

The bronchitis starts in the throat and quickly descends – within four days she has pain in the lower lung on both sides, although the right side is usually the first to be affected. Often she has a fever and coughs up phlegm. There is persistent pain when she coughs, and a feeling of apathy and loss of energy.

She is emotionally, physically and mentally exhausted, but tends to use her considerable will power to override fatigue and illness.

BR is very tolerant and supportive of the weaknesses of others, but demands a great deal from herself. She left a challenging career to be a full-time mother and often feels quite isolated and intellectually unchallenged. Apart from this condition, BR's general health is good.

As in Western medicine, in traditional Chinese medicine chronic bronchitis is a disease of the *Lung*. It may be associated with several different syndromes of the *Lung*, such as *Lung Qi* weakness, *Phlegm-Heat* in the *Lung*, *Phlegm-Damp* in the *Lung*, or *Lung Yin* weakness. It may be accompanied by a general deficiency of *Qi, Blood, Yin* or *Yang* in the body.

BR appeared to be suffering from a complicated syndrome involving a weakness of the *Lung Qi* caused by repeated attacks of *Wind* and *Cold* to the *Lung*. Each attack was causing *Phlegm* to accumulate in her *Lung*, obstruct the *Qi* and lead to pain. There is a tendency for such *Phlegm* to dry and become hot, leading to retention of *Phlegm-Heat* and to pneumonia. Because her *Lung Qi* was weak, the *Qi* and *Blood* of her whole body had also become weak. This was indicated by her emotional, physical and mental exhaustion.

These attacks had occurred only since the birth of her first child, which indicated that this event, along with the birth of her second son, had probably weakened her *Qi* and *Blood*. In turn, this had weakened her *Lung* and her body's defensive *Qi*, which with repeated illness had never had a chance to recover properly.

Treatment
The *Lung Qi* should be strengthened and the body's defensive *Qi* repaired. If *Phlegm* was retained in the *Lung*, this would have to be cleared first. The *Qi* and *Blood* of the whole body should also be strengthened. Points on the *Lung, Ren, Urinary Bladder, Stomach* and *Spleen* channels would be used. BR would have to undergo a period of enforced rest while the treatment continued.

Prognosis and conclusion
A good recovery over a period of three to six months could be expected, as long as treatment was accompanied by a change in lifestyle. Breathing exercises and swimming would also be important in maintaining and in improving the condition of her *Lung* and her general health.

TREATMENT BY A
CHIROPRACTOR

BR's case was clearly not suitable for chiropractic therapy. Bronchitis is generally not treated by a chiropractor, although sometimes predisposing factors may be dealt with.

Treatment
In certain cases bronchitis may benefit from loosening of the thoracic area of the spine, in conjunction with treatment by other methods.

Prognosis and conclusion
It would be recommended that BR consult her family doctor, a medical herbalist, or some other complementary practitioner.

TREATMENT BY A
HOMEOPATH

The thread that ran through this case appeared to be BR's insecurity. This made her expend enormous amounts of energy in maintaining a "proper" home life. BR's determination probably undermined her vitality, and this was further debilitated by the antibiotics that were prescribed for her bronchitis. It may take some time before her health is restored.

Acute bronchitis is often dealt with well by *Bryonia*. This is used when colds develop in cold, wet weather, proceed rapidly to the chest (especially the right side) and may even develop into pneumonia. Those people suited to *Bryonia* may produce copious amounts of phlegm, but this is followed by dryness, which makes coughing so painful that the sufferer grasps the chest to still its movements. Apathy and exhaustion are inevitable.

There is, however, one other symptom that is relevant to this remedy which makes it unusually apt for BR. This is the concern for the home and stability, and for finding fulfilment in her role in life. It is this symptom that makes *Bryonia* effective at a constitutional level in this case.

Treatment and prognosis
If BR did not have bronchitis at the time of treatment, the remedy would be given in a 1M potency; if the condition was in an acute phase, a lower potency might be given. After a high-potency dose, it would not be abnormal for BR to develop a chest problem or a cold with phlegm or mucus production. This "aggravation" would be a sign that the body's own healing powers were attempting to push the disorder out of the system.

Because healing is working from the centre outward, BR would probably feel well, especially emotionally, despite yet another attack. Unless the symptoms became intolerable, this attack would not be treated, but would be allowed to run its course. Afterwards, other attacks should be less frequent. Each time they occurred, a dose of *Bryonia* would strengthen BR's constitution even further, so that the attacks would gradually happen less and less often.

A note of warning: BR should refrain from swimming in chlorinated swimming pools, because the chlorine might make the remedy ineffective.

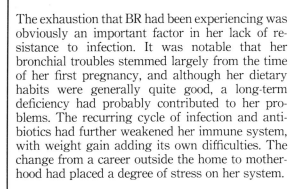

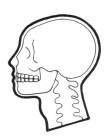

TREATMENT BY A
MEDICAL HERBALIST

The exhaustion that BR had been experiencing was obviously an important factor in her lack of resistance to infection. It was notable that her bronchial troubles stemmed largely from the time of her first pregnancy, and although her dietary habits were generally quite good, a long-term deficiency had probably contributed to her problems. The recurring cycle of infection and antibiotics had further weakened her immune system, with weight gain adding its own difficulties. The change from a career outside the home to motherhood had placed a degree of stress on her system.

Treatment
Supplementing her diet with vitamin C (preferably with iron) and Garlic would help BR to boost her immunity. Inhalations with essential oils such as Eucalyptus and Pine would help to keep her airways free from congestion. Combining rest with gentle, gradually increasing, amounts of exercise such as walking or swimming, would be of value in recuperation and maintenance of stamina.

The herbal prescription would include:
● Echinacea (*Echinacea angustifolia*): improves circulation and stimulates the immune system.
● Ginger (*Zingiber officinale*): stimulates the circulation and encourages the function of the lungs and heart.
● Sage (*Salvia officinalis*): in the short-term would improve circulatory functions and raise vitality.
● Elecampane (*Inula helenium*): warming, stimulating expectorant which eases congestion.
● Wild Thyme (*Thymus serpyllum*): loosens phlegm (increases expectoration) while relieving spasmodic attacks of coughing.

The prescription would be reviewed frequently. Increasing emphasis would be placed on building resistance, restoring the nervous system to health and healing the bronchial tissues.

Prognosis and conclusion
Dealing with acute infection and congestion, and attention to chronic respiratory and circulatory problems, would all produce improvements. BR would have to change her attitudes to her health and her lifestyle.

TREATMENT BY AN
OSTEOPATH AND NATUROPATH

There is no doubt that smokers are more susceptible to respiratory problems than non-smokers; persistent smoking damages progressively larger amounts of the breathing apparatus as each damaged part obliges another to share the load.

Although she had not smoked for seven years, smoking had weakened the whole of BR's respiratory tract from the throat to the smallest, innermost lobes of her lungs. And she was exposed to enough air pollution to irritate areas that had already been weakened, which would aggravate her tendency to bronchitis.

It is unfortunate that the suppression of symptoms by antibiotics and other drugs seldom initiates strengthening of the tissues involved – all that happens is that the body's attempts to discharge offensive toxic material are disrupted.

Treatment
When she was well enough, BR should undergo osteopathic correction of spinal and rib lesions – often caused by severe coughing – and abdominal soft-tissue treatment of the diaphragm. The respiratory system could be strengthened by gentle exercise that encourages deep breathing. She should also adjust her diet, to reduce body weight, and avoid mucus-forming foods.

When ill – especially if she had a raised temperature – BR should follow a naturopathic regime and fast (under daily supervision) for as long as is appropriate for her whole well-being rather than just for the bronchitis. She should also use steam inhalations to loosen phlegm, reduce pain, and encourage expectoration. Avoidance of antibiotics, except as a last resort, would be important for long-term recovery, especially during the fast.

She should also rest, to conserve her energy for healing purposes, and introduce selected vitamin and mineral-rich foods to her diet, with prescribed mineral and vitamin supplements if necessary.

Prognosis and conclusion
Progress would depend on BR's realizing that in order to continue helping others she should devote time to healing herself. Although this might take several years, and would depend on the degree of tissue degeneration present, with a healthier body and mind she should be able to resist infections, cease being prone to fatigue, and enjoy being alive.

Introduction to medical herbalism pp. 32–39   Introduction to osteopathy with naturopathy pp. 40–47

TREATMENT BY A
FAMILY DOCTOR

BR appeared to suffer from chronic bronchitis in a form that would be expected to affect an older smoker or someone with exposure to chronic irritants. This might have been caused by repeated serious infections, which would be the result of either a deficiency in her immune system or chronic bronchial damage caused by earlier infections.

However, BR might have been suffering from undiagnosed asthma, giving her a cough with phlegm, which was becoming worse as the primary condition remained untreated. She would therefore be investigated for asthma, which is a reversible narrowing of the bronchial tubes.

In addition she would have a chest X-ray. It would also be advisable to carry out respiratory function tests to assess the degree of her respiratory problems. If it appeared that she had an immunological problem, this could be confirmed by appropriate testing, and she would have to consult an immunologist for advice.

Treatment
BR had chronic bronchial damage resulting in recurrent infections. These would be likely to continue, and would require treatment with antibiotics from time to time. The patient could, however, do a great deal for herself.

She was marginally overweight and did not persist with exercise. It would be essential that she did some form of exercise that would ventilate her lungs thoroughly, and she should try to keep fit. She and her husband could work with a physiotherapist. BR would be taught breathing and coughing exercises, while her husband could learn how to empty secretions from her chest by postural drainage, and be instructed in giving active physiotherapy.

She should never smoke, and it would be helpful if others in the family did not smoke either.

Prognosis and conclusion
BR could help herself, and be helped by her husband. And it is likely that treatment at home would have a great impact on her health if she persisted with it. She would need to consult her family doctor from time to time, and might require periodic chest X-rays.

CONSULTANT'S COMMENTS

Chronic weakness of the chest was traditionally considered as a mark of a much wider constitutional debility. Although this patient is relatively young and active, a key feature is her emotional, physical and mental exhaustion. This is the most critical problem in her condition, and the one that needs correcting first if her liability to bronchitis is to be reduced.

The treatments
Most of the practitioners recognize that practical measures to support BR are vital. The family doctor reviews the routines of lifestyle and other measures to improve lung health, all of which would be generally approved, although the prospect of repeated antibiotic treatments would not be so welcome.

The naturopathic approach touched on by the osteopath and medical herbalist adds another dimension that would contribute to the management of the problem – one commonly practised by many European clinics and sanitoriums.

As an intrinsic part of their therapy, the homeopath, medical herbalist and acupuncturist seek to support the patient's constitution. The Chinese interpretation of this sort of bronchitic condition is sophisticated, but it also has no illusions about the difficulty of restoring strength in such cases.

The homeopath's reference to a "healing crisis" reflects the observations of many practitioners, that some congestive conditions seem to be most effectively relieved through encouraging the natural process of elimination (in this case coughing). The technique is justifiable in a case such as BR's, but would be debilitating for someone who is very infirm.

The medical herbalist, in opting for specific warming lung and immuno-stimulant remedies, has taken a sound route that could equally be applied to an elderly patient.

COMMON COLD

THE PATIENT

TH is eight years old and of average height and weight. She has two younger sisters and they are all at the same school. She dislikes sport, but eats well and has few preferences. Her mother cooks conventional Western food.

THE PROBLEM

About two years ago TH started to get frequent colds, and now these occur almost monthly and last for up to two weeks, so that it seems as though she is never well. The colds start with a sore throat, which develops into a running nose with thick yellow mucus, and is often followed by a wheezing cough.

The condition is usually accompanied by swollen glands and a high temperature in the first few days, at which time her head and neck feel hot to the touch and she sweats profusely, especially at night. She seems to be worse at night, and at about 3 am she often wakes from nightmares. The colds often start with changes in the seasons and with damp, cold weather.

Before she developed these colds TH was an openly loving and cheerful child. But now she is grumpy, weepy and whines a lot. She demands a great deal of attention and cuddling, and never seems to be happy. She has always been a restless sleeper and she dreams a lot, sometimes talking in her sleep.

TH has never been a healthy child. She was a "blue" baby and has a history of colds, nose-bleeds and deafness caused by excess ear wax. She rarely has the energy for physical activity, but used to do more before the recurrent colds began. There is a family history of chronic colds and coughs.

TREATMENT BY AN
ACUPUNCTURIST

In traditional Chinese medicine, the common cold is caused by invading *Wind-Cold* or *Wind-Heat*. The *Wind* is said to "scatter" the defensive *Qi* on the surface of the body – particularly on the head and neck – along with the *Lung Qi*. The *Lung* is the *Zangfu* organ most exposed to external attack. *Wind* "spearheads" attack by seasonal excesses of *Cold*, *Heat* or *Damp*. The determining factor in the effect of an attack is the condition of a person's *Qi*.

TH had suffered frequent colds over the previous two years, which suggested that her *Lung Qi* was compromised. The symptoms indicated that the initial attack had not been resolved, with *Phlegm* and *Heat* lodging in the *Lung*. *Heat* predominated during the height of the attack, and the symptoms worsened at night when the defensive *Yang Qi* was weakest. Each attack further weakened her normal *Qi*, and this was reflected in her moods and poor vitality.

Her history revealed that TH's *Qi*, especially her *Lung Qi*, had been weak since her early years. There was also a family predisposition to *Lung* problems. Her slippery, rapid pulse indicated the presence of *Phlegm* and *Heat*.

Treatment
Acupuncture treatment of children is common in China and can have dramatic results. In this case, points on the *Lung*, *Urinary Bladder*, *Spleen* and *Stomach* channels would be used to disperse *Phlegm* and strengthen the *Lung*, with points on the *Large Intestine* channel being added during an acute attack to reduce *Heat*. Specific massage techniques could also be used on the arms, chest and back. These can be taught to parents for use between treatments. During an acute attack, daily treatment would be preferable, although not always practical. Between attacks, weekly treatment would suffice. Dietary changes to reduce the intake of *Damp*-producing foods would be advisable.

Prognosis and conclusion
For a child of this age the prognosis would be good, although care should be taken until TH's *Qi* had repaired itself. Preventive treatment would be advisable for up to two years after her recovery.

TREATMENT BY A
CHIROPRACTOR

When a child of this age is suffering such severe symptoms it is seldom easy to find a cure. Orthodox drug treatment can often solve the problem in the short-term, but the condition usually recurs.

An alternative therapy that would treat TH as a whole, rather than just her symptoms, would probably be recommended. Acupuncture can often improve a condition such as this, and a homeopath or a medical herbalist should also be able to help.

Physical examination
A spinal check would probably be advised. It is always sensible to check a child's spine regularly in order to detect any problems early and prevent them from developing into something more serious.

In a child with a history of poor health such as TH's, it would be quite likely that, although there were no complaints of any back or neck problems, the chiropractor would be able to detect a number of mechanical problems in the spine.

Treatment
Manipulative techniques specially adapted to treat children would be used to restore normal movement in the spine where any problems had been found. This could be achieved within two or three treatments. Children usually respond quickly to spinal adjustment, and so require much less treatment than an adult would.

Prognosis and conclusion
Chiropractic therapy would not directly help such a condition, but if any problems in the spine were corrected this would improve TH's overall health, and help her to respond to any other treatment.

A check-up a month or two later would be advised, and then on a three- to six-month basis, so that any further problems could be detected and corrected early in her development.

TREATMENT BY A
HOMEOPATH

A common cold is an acute illness with a definite "exciting" cause. Usually it would be diagnosed as a single viral infection, not a recurrent one, as with this child. A patient such as this has a debilitated constitution, which the homeopath may treat as a miasm, a pattern of chronic illness that has so warped the basis on which the vital force operates that the patient's condition worsens progressively.

Diagnosis
TH had been weak since birth, but it was only in the previous two years that the colds had been present. No specific factor stood out as causing this change in the pattern.

Her symptoms corresponded to the picture of *Pulsatilla*, which is a deep remedy capable of removing the miasmic warp. The typical *Pulsatilla* patient often has chronic colds that change the personality to that of a grumpy, weepy child. The colds start in the throat with swollen glands, then produce thick yellow catarrh, a high temperature in the head area and profuse perspiration. This is often accompanied by a wheezing cough. In TH's case the picture of *Pulsatilla* was completed by the 3 am aggravation time, the nightmares, and the detrimental effect of the changing seasons or cold, damp weather.

When treating miasms the family history is important. In this case the immediate family had a history of colds. Going further back it would not be surprising to find a history of tuberculosis, because the particular miasm evident in this case is called tuberculoid.

In some cases it may be treated by a nosode, a remedy specially prepared from diseased cells, made in this instance from diseased lung tissue. Its effect is similar to vaccination, except that it is given after an illness is contracted, not before. The nosode enables the patient to fight the disease.

Treatment and prognosis
Since *Pulsatilla* fitted so well, it would not be necessary to use a nosode in this case. A single dose of *Pulsatilla* 30 given to TH should begin to build up health. She would eventually need a higher potency, and by slowly increasing the potency, health would be restored gently.

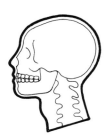

TREATMENT BY A
MEDICAL HERBALIST

The common cold is an excellent example of the importance of treating the person, not the disease. The essential thing is to build up a long-term resistance to viral infection, and not just to ease the symptoms. The history of colds in TH and her family indicated a chronic decline in vitality and resistance.

Treatment
Dairy produce and refined carbohydrates should be severely restricted in order to reduce mucus discharge and lessen the eliminative burden on TH's system. Of particular importance would be additional vitamin C, in the form of fresh fruit and vegetables. During the winter months, extra supplements of zinc and vitamin B would help to maintain the immune system and repair tissues. A careful analysis of her diet to detect any food allergies or sensitivities should be made. The herbal prescription would include:
● Chamomile (*Matricaria recutita*): calms restlessness, and helps to regulate temperature and ease inflammation.
● Elderflower (*Sambucus nigra*): encourages sweating and temperature regulation; reduces catarrhal symptoms.
● Catmint (*Nepeta cataria*): improves circulation and reduces nasal congestion; gently relaxing.
● Hyssop (*Hyssopus officinalis*): a relaxing expectorant; reduces the spasms of a wheezing cough.
● Echinacea (*Echinacea angustifolia*): powerfully anti-infective, increasing resistance to infections and cleansing the tissues.

The prescription would be regularly assessed and varied as necessary. TH would be encouraged to use herbal drinks – such as Elderflower, Lemon Balm or Rosehip. A Garlic supplement could be very valuable in helping to restore resistance.

Prognosis and conclusion
With changes in diet, and reasonable amounts of fresh air and exercise, TH could expect dramatic long-term improvements in health and vitality.

TREATMENT BY AN
OSTEOPATH AND NATUROPATH

Conventional Western food is usually excessively starchy and milky. White flour and sugar abound and so, probably, do fatty foods such as potato chips and fried bread. The body's response to such foods is invariably catarrhal in nature. If TH and her family live that way, then the family's recurrent colds and coughs are likely to persist.

Catarrh showed itself in TH as earwax, colds with thick yellow mucus, and a wheezing chest. Her swollen glands and high temperature were nature's way of dealing with toxic excesses that were not being properly handled by normal eliminative processes.

Physical examination
The physical examination showed an imbalance in TH's cranial bone structure. She had the type of head typical of someone suffering from catarrh – that is, narrow with a relatively high palate and thickened sinuses.

Treatment
TH would be put on a brief, supervised fast while her temperature returned to normal. She would then be encouraged to eat wholesome foods – those that nourish rather than provide "empty" calories.

All spinal and cranial imbalances would be adjusted in a programme gentle enough for a child of this age. Lymphatic pumping of the chest would speed waste elimination, as would hydrotherapeutic compresses and baths.

Having started life with a traumatic need for healthy blood (being born as a "blue baby"), TH would need careful building up, not least psychologically. Her nightmares could have sprung from congestion, but they were more likely to have a root in fears and insecurity. This meant that the family as a whole should be involved in TH's treatment. They should set an example in sensible eating and exercise, be reassuring without pampering or showing favour, and make health restoration an adventure for the whole family.

Prognosis and conclusion
Colds as such are not curable, indeed they *are* the cure for most people. They need to be understood and encouraged, not suppressed. TH could be helped, given time and patience.

Introduction medical herbalism pp. 32–39

Introduction to osteopathy with naturopathy pp. 40–47

TREATMENT BY A
FAMILY DOCTOR

The common cold is a short-lived illness with an incubation period of two or three days. It is caused by a virus, and may be accompanied by a low-grade fever. It is characterized by sneezing, runny nose and cough. There may be secondary bacterial infection causing catarrh. Children may develop a middle-ear infection, and some people are prone to secondary sinus infections. Asthma attacks are often triggered by colds.

Treatment
There is no specific treatment. Headache and fever may be helped by painkillers, and sometimes antihistamines or decongestants relieve distress. but the common cold does not last long and abates spontaneously. Secondary conditions such as asthma and ear infections do have to be treated.

TH seemed to have a number of problems. She had a wheezy cough and was possibly suffering from bronchospasm (asthma); and she should receive advice about this. If this was the case, the fact that her symptoms were worse at night might indicate that she was allergic to her pillows or bedding (feathers or dust), and this would make her predisposed to catarrh as well as mild asthma. Advice as to how to manage this would be given.

TH's high fever, swollen glands and cough were usual for a child suffering from colds. She would be checked to see if she was getting chronic middle-ear infections (another likely cause of her deafness), or a nasal obstruction from adenoids. She may even have had a low-grade tonsil infection.

TH seemed to have an emotional problem in her family, as shown by her attention-seeking behaviour and her nightmares. If medical attention did not lead to improvement, it should be acknowledged that the family needed some help (probably family therapy) to deal with the difficulties that had led to her emotional condition.

Prognosis and conclusion
This was a story of more than simply colds. There were various possible underlying causes for TH's condition, such as allergy or some form of asthma. Emotional problems should not be overlooked in this sort of case.

The "cure for the common cold" is a goal that has assumed almost fabulous status in the popular imagination. Most conventional medical researchers have accepted that, in their terms, it may prove elusive for a long time to come. Yet in any public gathering the air usually carries cold-causing agents and most individuals resist infection. Succumbing to a cold can be seen as the result of a temporary slip in normal defensive health.

What is of concern here is a recurrent failure of the body to defend itself. The concern is more acute because the sufferer is a child, with much original vitality but few reserves for a long fight. The therapeutic priority is, as Hippocrates put it more than 2000 years ago, "to support the healing power of life".

Treatments
Given this mandate, the homeopath starts with a major advantage. The therapy is gentle, well-tolerated by children, and often effective in increasing long-term vitality. The acupuncturist can provide one of the most sophisticated analyses and treatments of the underlying disturbance, but has to overcome a degree of reluctance among parents (rarely children) about the needles. The medical herbalist and the osteopath and naturopath share a fund of useful supportive measures and a recognition of the importance of dietary and other day-to-day factors in treating resistive vitality.

The chiropractor can be relied on to correct complicating spinal disturbances, but in the knowledge that this is a peripheral matter. Surprisingly, the family doctor is barely in a different position and is left to fend off complications such as secondary infections and allergic responses, and provide supplementary treatments such as individual or family psychotherapy.

Conclusions
Although the family doctor can deal with any serious complication of this condition, the high ground belongs to the other specialists.

CASE STUDY HAY FEVER

THE PATIENT

LJ is 30 years old and is tall and slim, with bright eyes and clear skin. Her health is generally good. She is a teacher and is energetic and enthusiastic, but her energy is easily drained by stress and excess activity. She often lacks confidence in herself and demands a lot of reassurance from those around her.

THE PROBLEM

LJ suffers from hay fever, an allergic reaction to pollens. Her hay fever symptoms are typical – an itching nose, sneezing, watering eyes and a clear discharge from the nose – and occur between May and August each year. Symptoms are worse in the morning and evening, in hot and humid weather, and when she is stressed. Her skin breaks out in a rash if she comes into contact with newly-cut grass.

In the past, LJ has taken antihistamines, which have helped to relieve her symptoms but have made her feel drowsy and rather depressed, and seem to have had no long-term effect on the condition itself. The self-help remedies that work for her include staying indoors, keeping cool and, during an attack, covering her face with a cold, damp flannel. Attacks make her sensitive to light and leave her exhausted.

LJ has suffered from hay fever since she was about 12; the first attack coincided with puberty and a large growth spurt. Apart from one of her two brothers, no other member of the family shares the problem. She has also suffered from frequent winter colds, sore throats, cystitis and occasional migraines. She had the usual childhood diseases, as well as jaundice, when she was 11, glandular fever at 14 and acute tonsillitis at the age of 18, followed by a tonsillectomy. At 26 she contracted pneumonia. A positive cervical smear test was recorded when she was 23, but the subsequent biopsy was negative.

TREATMENT BY AN ACUPUNCTURIST

In traditional Chinese medicine, hay fever is categorized as an invasion of *Wind* and *Heat*. *Wind* is indicated by sneezing and irritation of the eyes and nasal passages. The classification of *Heat* is used because it invariably appears in hot weather. The predisposing factors that allow this invasion are usually weakness of the *Lung* and *Kidney Qi*. In Chinese medicine, the important element is the energetic disharmony, rather than the specific allergy.

LJ's symptoms were typical of hay fever due to *Wind Heat* invasion. In addition, her tendency to sore throats and winter colds was evidence of weak *Lung Qi*. Her history of tonsillitis, glandular fever and pneumonia helped to confirm this. The onset of hay fever in puberty, the time when the *Kidney Qi* becomes fully active, combined with her history of cystitis, indicated a *Kidney* involvement. LJ's tongue was pale and her pulse soft and fine, both of which indicated weak *Qi*.

Treatment
Points on the *Urinary Bladder* and *Large Intestine* channels around the nose, combined with points on the *Sanjiao, Lung* and *Large Intestine* channels on the hand and wrist, would be used to alleviate sneezing and strengthen the *Lung Qi*. In addition, points on the *Kidney, Ren* and *Urinary Bladder* channels would be used to strengthen the *Kidney Qi* and support the *Lung*. Ideally, weekly treatment to strengthen the *Qi* would commence two or three months before the onset of symptoms. More frequent treatment, possibly daily, might be necessary to control symptoms once they had set in.

Prognosis and conclusion
Hay fever tends to be either very easy or very difficult to treat. Thus, five to ten treatments may be sufficient, or it may be necessary to have treatment in the period leading up to the commencement of the hay fever season for several successive years.

Bronchitis pp. 64–67 Common cold pp. 68–71 Cystitis pp. 138–141   Introduction to acupuncture pp. 8–15

TREATMENT BY A
CHIROPRACTOR

At the initial consultation, LJ's case history was reviewed in detail. Her frequent winter colds, sore throats, cystitis and occasional migraines were all noted.

Physical examination
This started with orthopaedic and neurological tests. The spine was then palpated to check for any areas where there was more or less spinal movement than normal. The examination was carried out in two stages, first with LJ sitting on a stool, then with her lying face down on the treatment table.

Particular attention was paid to the neck and upper thoracic (chest) areas in case her frequent colds, throat inflammations and migraine headaches were related to any mechanical spinal problems. Nasal stuffiness is sometimes helped by treating such problems at the base of the neck and the top of the thoracic area.

Treatment
The examination revealed some neck problems, and treatment would help LJ's recurrent colds, sore throats and migraine. Treatment would involve soft-tissue massage and specific spinal manipulation of the upper chest and neck.

LJ would also be given advice about her cystitis so that this could be helped at the same time.

Prognosis and conclusion
Although some relief might occur, hay fever is not usually treated by chiropractic therapy, and for this LJ would be better advised to consult an acupuncturist, homeopath or medical herbalist.

TREATMENT BY A
HOMEOPATH

The significant symptoms related to LJ's hay fever were her itching, red and watering eyes, and her running nose, with clear, watery mucus and spasmodic sneezing throughout the day. In addition she was irritable, especially when she was hot or in direct sunlight.

Also significant was her recurrent cystitis. This had been treated by antibiotics, and in general she had been treated with antibiotics (and also vaccinated) more than usual. Eight years of taking oral contraceptives may have disrupted her body chemistry, debilitated her vital energy and lowered her resistance to illness.

Two circumstances that had made LJ's general condition worse were the fast rate of growth during puberty, and the attack of pneumonia. Her personality – which combined excitability, lack of self-confidence, an occasional sense of frustration and helplessness, and a general need for reassurance – suggested an imbalance in her approach to life. This signified a "liver" weakness, which resulted in her tendency to collapse under strain.

Her need for foods that would give immediate energy (chocolate) and heat (spicy and hot foods) showed that she had a problem in channelling energy. Other diagnostic pointers were her improvement in sunshine and fresh air.

Treatment and prognosis
The constitutional remedy appropriate at a deep level would be *Phosphorus*, which would increase LJ's vitality and allow her body to resolve the problem naturally.

Phosphorus works by pushing things to the outside, so spots might appear after treatment. The remedy might also exaggerate her hay fever symptoms, so treatment would not be carried out during the hay fever season. A complementary remedy, *Pulsatilla*, would be used during an attack to help the body express, and thereby reduce, the hay fever symptoms. The constitutional remedy would reach deep into the body, so a flare-up of cystitis and sore throats might also be initially expected.

The mental and emotional levels usually improve first, so she could expect to feel better in herself relatively soon.

Introduction to chiropractic therapy pp. 16–23

Introduction to homeopathy pp. 24–31

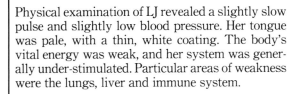

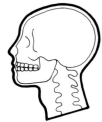

TREATMENT BY A
MEDICAL HERBALIST

Physical examination of LJ revealed a slightly slow pulse and slightly low blood pressure. Her tongue was pale, with a thin, white coating. The body's vital energy was weak, and her system was generally under-stimulated. Particular areas of weakness were the lungs, liver and immune system.

Treatment
The herbal prescription would include:
- Ma Huang (*Ephedra sinica*): increases lung function. Particularly useful for allergic conditions that affect the respiratory system.
- Eyebright (*Euphrasia officinalis*): an astringent for the mucous membranes of the upper respiratory tract. It also reduces catarrh.
- Black Sampson (*Echinacea angustifolia*): strengthens the immune system.
- Pill-bearing Spurge (*Euphorbia pilulifera*): an expectorant to relax the lungs.
- Ginger Root (*Zingiberis officinalis*): a warming stimulating remedy, which improves lung function.
- Dandelion Root (*Taraxacum officinale*): tones up the digestive system and liver.
- Mullein Leaf (*Verbascum thapsus*): soothes and relaxes the respiratory system and reduces the irritation that sets off the hay fever attack.

The prescription would be prescribed in tincture form two or three times a day for two weeks, then the condition reviewed.

A diet containing foods rich in vitamins A and C (to strengthen mucous membranes and aid resistance to infection) would be strongly recommended. Essential fatty acids, particularly those in Evening Primrose oil, would help the body form prostaglandins, hormone-like substances that help to combat inflammation and allergies.

Other dietary advice would include eating stimulatory foods, such as onions and garlic, watercress, horseradish, mustard and cabbage, and reducing caffeine intake. Cider vinegar and honey can help combat hay fever symptoms.

Prognosis and conclusion
In herbal medicine, treatment of chronic conditions often takes some time, so regular visits for several months could be anticipated.

TREATMENT BY AN
OSTEOPATH AND NATUROPATH

An interview preceding the physical examination showed that LJ combined cheerful enthusiasm with a tendency toward anxiety. In particular, personal relationships gave her both the greatest pleasure and the greatest cause for concern.

Physical examination
Manipulative examination of bones, muscles and internal organs assessed their positions, alignments and tensions.

Examination showed a slight tilt of the pelvis and some minor spinal deviations – most significantly in the neck – which needed readjustment to improve LJ's general health. There was some imbalance in the temporal bones of the cranium, which might have been interfering with the sneezing centre and aggravating the hay fever. Her slightly crooked nose – not caused by trauma – also indicated cranial imbalance. Soft-tissue congestion at the base of the cranium suggested problems with the flow of blood and lymph and with the nerve impulses to the brain.

Treatment
The main object of treatment would be to restore the integrity of the spinal, pelvic and cranial mechanisms. This would be reinforced by exercises to correct posture and encourage postural awareness. Specialized (very gentle) cranial adjustment and neuromuscular massage of parts of the head, neck, back and abdomen would be needed to decongest the sinuses. The latter would help to clear the blood, lymph and nerve channels in this region.

Naturopathic treatment would include the avoidance of mucus-producing foods, such as dairy products, especially during the summer. LJ should also avoid stressful activities during this time.

Prognosis and conclusion
Osteopathy with naturopathy could bring about changes in LJ's general health, and some improvements in her condition, at least helping to relieve symptoms during an attack.

Introduction to medical herbalism pp. 32–39

Introduction to osteopathy with naturopathy pp. 40–47

TREATMENT BY A
FAMILY DOCTOR

LJ's symptoms were typical of hay fever and suggested that it was a direct allergic reaction to grass pollens. Because people who suffer from such allergic conditions tend to be sensitive to other allergens (substances that produce allergic reactions), for which there is specific treatment available, the range of LJ's reactions was evaluated with a skin test.

This test involved injecting minute amounts of different allergens into the skin, including house dust and horse dander. LJ was found to react only to specific grass pollens.

Treatment
A course of desensitizing injections can provide a cure for allergies of this kind, but is potentially dangerous because it can produce a violent over-reaction. This option would be rejected in view of the fact that LJ's symptoms were unpleasant rather than seriously problematic.

Instead, a course of treatment to control the symptoms would be decided on. This would consist of both common sense and pharmacology. As far as possible, LJ should avoid obvious high concentrations of pollen, and should wear dark glasses to counter the effect of bright sunlight. She should consider taking a holiday abroad during the worst part of the hay fever season, because plant pollens are likely to differ, or be airborne at different times in another climate.

The use of drugs would need a careful approach, because antihistamines, the drugs most commonly used in the control of hay fever, made LJ feel uncomfortably drowsy. An alternative would therefore be tried, such as a corticosteroid administered as a nasal spray twice daily.

Prognosis and conclusion
The corticosteroids alone might not be completely effective, and could keep her awake at night. One dose of antihistamines, taken at bedtime, could be added to the prescription. A combination such as this would keep LJ's symptoms under control, reduce the swelling of the nasal lining and allow her to sleep more easily.

CONSULTANT'S COMMENTS

LJ's symptoms are characteristic of hay fever in an adult. She has experienced an unusually wide range of other illnesses, however, and this is not necessarily typical of most hay fever sufferers. On the other hand, the association of the condition with stress is more typical. Hay fever symptoms often occur first during periods of physiological or psychological stress, such as puberty, taking examinations, moving house, or coincide with certain emotional problems.

It is interesting to note in this case that all the specialists, with the exception of the family doctor, pay particular attention to previous medical conditions, whether superficially related or not, and to LJ's general emotional state. Apart from the family doctor, all anticipate the possibility of achieving a long-term change in the disorder.

In contrast, the family doctor attempts only to alleviate the symptoms and perhaps control them by pharmacological and practical means. The assumption in all the other therapies seems to be that hay fever is itself a symptom of an underlying problem. Treatment is therefore directed at improving LJ's general health as well as her specific symptoms.

Summary
Of the six different treatments, general medicine, acupuncture, homeopathy and medical herbalism can offer immediate relief. Osteopathy and chiropractic therapy may be beneficial in the long term, but seem to need the additional support of dietary or other therapies to achieve a short-term change. On the other hand, if a person with hay fever is aware of neck or upper spinal problems, consultation with an osteopath or chiropractor could well be the most appropriate way to deal with the disorder.

Introduction to Western medicine pp. 48–55

CASE STUDY SINUSITIS

THE PATIENT

VS is a Sikh, born in India but brought up in the West. He is 30 years old and is tall and slim. He is single and devotes much of his energy to his work as a teacher. He prefers to eat curries and spicy foods, but also eats European-style meals at work, and does not smoke or drink alcohol.

THE PROBLEM

VS came to the West at the age of six, and shortly afterward developed severe influenza, followed by sinusitis. At first the sinusitis developed only during head colds – which occurred three or four times a year and were treated with antibiotics – but the problem has worsened in the past three years. He is now unable to breathe through his nose, and experiences a constant ache in the sinuses. These are painful when touched and, when acutely inflamed, a bloody discharge is emitted with nasal mucus. This is usually accompanied by headache, sore throat, and occasional earache.

VS's parents are strict Sikhs who oppose his adoption of Western attitudes and his wish to remain unmarried. He regrets that he now has little to do with his family, but asserts his independent values. He maintains family traditions of perfectionism, discipline and hard work. He has had several relationships with European women, but none of these has been lasting. He is impatient with his prolonged sinus problem.

As a child, VS was often ill with colds, sore throats and headaches. These continued until his mid-teens, when he began to excel at school, both academically and at sports. He remained fit with only occasional colds until he was 25, when the frequency of colds followed by sinusitis increased. He also suffers from hay fever and is allergic to cats and horses.

Despite his enthusiasm for racket sports VS's movements are stiff. Since graduating from college he has had headaches, rising from the base of the skull up over the eyes, probably due to tension in his neck.

TREATMENT BY AN ACUPUNCTURIST

Sinusitis is primarily a disorder of the *Lung* and is usually the result of an unresolved attack by pathogenic *Wind-Cold*. The *Lung* is the *Yang* organ most easily affected by external climatic factors. *Wind* scatters the defensive *Qi* on the outside of the body, making it easier for *Cold* to penetrate. The nose is the site of attack, and this shows as the symptoms of a common cold. If the body's defences are not strong enough to drive out the *Wind* and *Cold*, discharges in the nose begin to congeal, turning into *Heat*, and becoming yellow and thick. The *Phlegm* collects in the sinuses and further blocks the *Qi*, causing pain.

VS had recently moved to a northern latitude when he had his first attack of sinusitis. This suggests that his bodily defences were not prepared for such a sudden change in climate. His increased tendency to develop colds after the age of 25 suggests that the *Lung* was progressively weakened by continual attacks and subsequent sinusitis. Blood in the discharge is a sign that the condition has turned from *Cold* to *Heat*. The *Liver* was also disordered.

Stiff movement and headaches indicated that the *Gall Bladder* channel – linked to the *Liver* channel – was being affected by excess *Yang Qi* from the *Liver*. An internal pathway of the *Liver* channel passes close to the nose and through the eye. The slippery, wiry pulse indicated *Liver* stagnation and the presence of *Phlegm*.

Treatment
This would concentrate on moving the local stagnation. Points on the *Bladder, Large Intestine* and *Stomach* channels would be used, as well as points that have a specific effect on the nasal area. Points on the *Lung* and *Large Intestine* channels would be used to readjust the *Qi* of the *Lung*, and points on the *Stomach* channel to clear phlegm. When the acute phase has passed, points on the *Lung* and *Stomach* chanels would be stimulated.

Prognosis
This case has a long history and may be stubborn to treat but, because VS is young, ten treatments would probably be sufficient. He may have a mild recurrence of symptoms if he has a bad cold. He should avoid milk products and greasy or highly spiced food.

Common cold pp. 68–71 Migraine pp. 196–199   Introduction to acupuncture pp. 8–15

TREATMENT BY A
CHIROPRACTOR

Because of the severity of the condition, it was unlikely that chiropractic treatment would be able to do very much to help VS's sinus problem. However, since VS suffers from headaches he was examined to see if there were any spinal problems that might be the cause of the headaches.

Physical examination
A number of orthopaedic and neurological tests were carried out on the neck to check bone and nerve function, which were all found to be normal. The chiropractor then palpated (felt) the spine to check for areas where it was restricted in its movement and look for areas of muscle spasm. Considerable muscle tension in the neck, upper thoracic area and shoulders was found. Normal spinal movement was restricted at the top and base of the neck. It is very common to find such neck and muscle tension in cases of chronic sinusitis.

X-rays of VS's neck and sinuses were taken to check their condition and to see how full the sinus fluid levels were.

Treatment
Chiropractic treatment would consist of soft-tissue work to ease the muscle tension, and spinal adjustment where necessary, particularly in the region of the neck. This would help with the headaches, and although it would not cure the sinus problem it would help to make breathing easier.

Following treatment, VS's sinuses may start to run, and in less severe cases the chiropractor could massage the sinuses to help clear them, but in a chronic case such as this its helpfulness is doubtful.

Prognosis
For treatment of the sinus problem, VS would most probably be referred to an acupuncturist, homeopath or medical herbalist for advice. Further antibiotic treatment would be unlikely to help and, providing there are no internal nasal defects requiring surgery, a more natural treatment would be effective. Dietary advice would be given, since a change in diet may affect VS's condition.

TREATMENT BY A
HOMEOPATH

It is significant in this case that the sinusitis followed a bout of influenza which developed after VS moved to a northern latitude. This seems to be the "exciting" cause, and there may have been emotional as well as climatic factors involved. It is also of note that, although he is estranged from his family, he still values their traditions.

His preference for spicy foods and characteristics of competitiveness and self discipline may be cultural and therefore not useful as homeopathic symptoms. It is necessary to determine which characteristics are affected by culture and race, and select the symptoms – both emotional and physical – that are specific to the individual.

Distinctive factors in this case are the bloody discharge with nasal mucus, sensitivity of the sinuses to touch, and headaches that start behind the eyes and extend to the forehead.

Lachesis covers these symptoms and, although its symptoms tend to be left-sided, they later move over to the right. It is a congestive remedy in which symptoms move upward into the head to the ears, often having started in the throat. Discharges are usually bloody and extremely offensive.

Lachesis has the specific symptoms of the snake from which it derives, being very sensitive to touch and unable to tolerate constriction or pressure. This characteristic fits VS's distance from his family. He does not reject their values, but does not want to be tightly controlled. Pride and competitiveness may disguise shyness and lack of confidence.

Treatment
Lachesis in this case would be the most appropriate remedy. A single dose of *Lachesis* in a high enough potency should reach deep into VS's constitution and tackle the disturbance that occurred when he first moved to a northern latitude. The case would need reviewing at regular intervals to assess progress, but the prognosis is good.

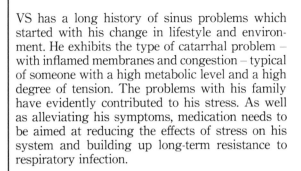

TREATMENT BY A
MEDICAL HERBALIST

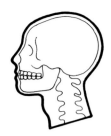

TREATMENT BY AN
OSTEOPATH AND NATUROPATH

VS has a long history of sinus problems which started with his change in lifestyle and environment. He exhibits the type of catarrhal problem – with inflamed membranes and congestion – typical of someone with a high metabolic level and a high degree of tension. The problems with his family have evidently contributed to his stress. As well as alleviating his symptoms, medication needs to be aimed at reducing the effects of stress on his system and building up long-term resistance to respiratory infection.

Treatment
VS should reduce the hotness of curries and similar foods in his diet, which will stimulate the circulation less and reduce congestion. He should avoid sugary, starchy and milky foods, and eat plenty of fruit. The practice of yoga could improve suppleness, reduce muscle tension and assist with breathing. Steam inhalations with Chamomile would help to reduce nasal congestion. The herbal prescription would include:
● Ground Ivy (*Glechoma hederacea*): reduces catarrhal congestions and astringes swollen membranes.
● Chamomile (*Matricaria recutita*): lessens irritability of nasal passages and helps to stimulate digestion.
● Golden Rod (*Solidago virgaurea*): mildly relaxing, and will have an anti-inflammatory effect on the sinuses.
● Echinacea (*Echinacea angustifolia*): stimulates the immune system to resist recurrent infections.
● Ribwort (*Plantago lanceolata*): tones the mucous membranes and reduces the build-up of catarrh.

Prognosis
Chronic catarrh, colds and sinusitis, coupled with frequent use of antibiotics, have left VS with poor resistance to upper respiratory tract problems, and it is this that requires most assistance. Herbal medicine is well suited to treating such a case, as well as providing some immediate relief of his symptoms.

VS's problem clearly reflects a history of suppressed catarrh.

Physical examination
This revealed that spinal nerves influencing his respiratory system, liver and intestines were affected by osteopathic spinal lesions. His cranium showed rigidity of certain sutures. All the bones connecting with the sinuses were involved.

Treatment
Osteopathic imbalances of the spine and articulation of the cranium would be gradually adjusted. In the meantime, VS would be given specific exercises to keep the neck supple, and relaxation techniques to try to reduce the tension that affects his problem.

A new approach is needed if VS is to change the pattern of disturbance for the better. He must avoid all suppressant drugs and find alternative procedures for getting relief from his symptoms.

Help in acute episodes would come from: cold compresses, applied both locally and around the abdomen; minerals such as potassium chloride and iron phosphate; pressure on trigger points, such as those over the eyebrows and under the occiput (back of the head); gentle lifting of the frontal bone and the parietal bones as if to separate them from the rest of the head; and, above all, fasting (no food of any kind and only water to drink if he is thirsty) for the duration of an attack.

Naturopathically, VS would be advised to undertake a balanced diet consisting mainly of fruits, salads and vegetables, with good quality protein, excluding all dairy produce. He should eat only whole grains – no refined flour and rice foods – and avoid sugar, spices, tea, coffee and fried foods. Mineral supplements will assist the transition to the new dietary plan.

VS would be encouraged to pay less attention to so-called allergens – such as cats and horses – and deal with the emotional and other strains that have contributed to his allergies, colds, sore throats, headaches, earaches and sinusitis.

Prognosis
If VS follows the advice that he is given and receives suitable osteopathic treatment, there is every hope for an improvement in his condition.

TREATMENT BY A
FAMILY DOCTOR

Sinusitis may be brought about by chronic respiratory irritation, which produces inadequate drainage of the sinuses, or by bacterial infection; it is commonly a mixture of both.

VS is a healthy, fit, non-smoker, but his problem seems to have become well established. It is unlikely that his perfectionist personality has contributed to his sinus infections, although he does have tension headaches and may have a psychological component to his catarrh. Some people suffer a type of neuralgia that feels like sinusitis; this may be triggered by irritants or stress.

Treatment

VS probably needs expert help from an ear, nose and throat specialist as well as more general, long-term help with his hay fever and allergies. It may be that he has some nasal blockage from enlarged adenoids, from polyps (distensions of the mucous membrane protruding into the nasal cavity) or even from a deviated nasal septum (a crooked wall between the nostrils, often – but not necessarily – associated with a previous injury). If this is the case, a simple surgical procedure would be effective. A specialist surgeon may also suggest cautery (with a heated wire) of swollen tissues inside the nasal passages.

If, however, VS is suffering recurrent, serious infections requiring frequent antibiotic treatment, he may require a sinus washout or some more definitive sinus draining operation.

VS's social isolation and the split from his family must be very painful for him and probably aggravates his condition. He would benefit from help from a counsellor experienced in cultural problems.

Prognosis

With some specialist attention, and if he copes with his allergies and emotional problems, VS's condition is likely to improve greatly.

CONSULTANT'S COMMENTS

Sinusitis is one condition that is usually well treated by complementary therapies, and this particular case should respond well to treatment.

The treatments

The most cautious practitioner is the chiropractor, who wisely recognizes the limitations of manipulation in relieving secondary sinus congestion. The osteopath clearly agrees, placing great reliance on classic naturopathic techniques instead – techniques that should, incidentally, form the basis of all other treatments.

The significant feature of cases like this one is the degree of secondary inflammation, congestion and infection. It is, in fact, necessary to institute radical cleansing techniques before any readjustive treatment can be expected to bring real relief. The family doctor points out that there should be a close examination of the tissues involved, to rule out any mechanical or organic obstructions. This is really a fundamental requirement, although a well trained therapist should be able to make a reasonable assessment.

Otherwise, the herbalist, acupuncturist and homeopath all have valid strategies to offer in theory. It would need an experienced hand to judge the intervention correctly and it is on this that the success of treatment would hinge.

After basic treatment is underway it is clear that attention should be paid to the cultural and social dimensions of this case. This may involve drawing attention to the possible aggravating effect of spicy foods, emphasizing climatic factors, or looking at the role of emotional strains in sensitizing the sinus tissues.

Summary

Any component of a regime that affects this patient's social life or self-image may come adrift and crash on the rocks of his carefully constructed survival strategy.

It is most likely that this patient would value direct treatment rather than special diets or exercises. The practitioners may well be judged by their ability to assume that role.

CONDITION	ACUPUNCTURE	CHIROPRACTIC	HOMEOPATHY
ADENOID ENLARGEMENT Caused by repeated respiratory infections in childhood	Treatment effective in both acute and chronic cases.	Would not treat, but would refer to a family doctor or other practitioner.	Treatment effective in both acute and chronic cases.
BREATHLESSNESS Caused by lung disorders, heart disorders or anaemia	Treatment effective in both acute and chronic cases, but depends on the cause.	Treatment may sometimes be effective, depending on cause. Would otherwise refer to another practitioner.	Treatment and its effectiveness depend on the cause.
CATARRH Inflammation of nose or throat mucous membranes	Treatment effective.	Would not treat; would refer to another practitioner.	Treatment effective in both acute and chronic cases, but sometimes works slowly because it corrects metabolic disorders.
COLDSORE Small blister or ulcer caused by virus	Treatment effective.	Would not treat; would refer to another practitioner.	Treatment effective when the condition is part of a constitutional problem.
COUGH Forceful action of chest and throat; clears airways of mucus	Treatment effective in both acute and chronic cases.	Would not treat; would refer to another practitioner.	Treatment effective when dealing with the whole health picture.
CROUP Acute inflammation of membrane of bronchial tubes, trachea and larynx	Treatment effective.	Would not treat; would refer to another practitioner.	Treatment effective in acute cases.
EMPHYSEMA Chronic lung disease causing abnormal accumulation of air in tissues	Treatment can be effective.	Treatment can sometimes help with the breathing difficulties.	Treatment can help, but its effectiveness is limited by the level of physical deterioration.
GINGIVITIS Inflammation of gums	Treatment can be effective.	Would not treat; would refer to another practitioner or a family doctor.	Treatment effective when related to the constitutional condition.
GLOSSITIS Inflammation of tongue	Treatment can be effective.	Would not treat; would refer to a family doctor or other practitioner.	Treatment effective when related to the constitutional condition.
GUMBOIL Abscess on gum	Would not treat.	Would not treat; would refer to a family doctor or other practitioner.	Treatment effective at first aid level.
HALITOSIS Bad breath	Treatment can be effective.	Would not treat; would refer to another practitioner.	Treatment must be related to the underlying cause.
INFLUENZA Acute viral infection	Treatment effective; best administered daily.	Would not treat; would refer to a family doctor or other practitioner.	Treatment effective in cutting down recovery time; leaves no after-effects.
LARYNGITIS Inflammation of vocal cords	Treatment effective in both acute and chronic cases.	Would not treat; would refer to a family doctor or other practitioner.	Treatment reduces pain and speeds recovery time.
MOUTH ULCER Open sore on membrane of mouth	Treatment effective.	Would not treat; would refer to a family doctor or other practitioner.	Treatment effective. This condition is a sign of lowered vitality and is best treated constitutionally.
MUMPS Viral infection of salivary glands; may affect pancreas, testicles or ovaries in adults	Treatment is effective in relieving symptoms.	Would not treat; would refer to a family doctor.	Treatment speeds recovery, and reduces complications or any lingering aftermath.

MED. HERBALISM	OSTEOPATHY	GEN. MEDICINE	COMMENTS
Treatment effective; definitely to be considered before surgery.	Treatment can help, especially with the aid of naturopathy.	Treatment with decongestants helps acute cases. Chronic nasal obstruction requires surgery.	See also **Tonsillitis**, pp. 82–83
Treatment can be helpful, depending on the cause.	Treatment depends on cause, and is difficult in cases of heart or lung disease.	Treatment varies with underlying cause, which may include anaemia, asthma, cardiac failure, lung disease or obesity.	See also **Asthma**, pp. 60–61 **Hypertension**, pp. 94–97
Treatment effective.	Naturopathic treatment very effective.	Treatment is for sinus infection or allergies. Avoid tobacco. Refer to specialist for treatment of nasal blockage.	See also **Common cold**, pp. 68–71; **Sinusitis**, pp. 76–79
Treatment effective in correcting background weaknesses and clearing up the problem.	Naturopathic treatment can help.	Often no treatment required; otherwise an antiviral agent may help.	See also **Mouth ulcer**, pp. 80–81
Treatment effective.	Would treat the cause, not the symptoms.	Usually no treatment for common viral condition, but suppressants may help at night.	See also **Bronchitis**, pp. 64–65; **Common cold**, pp. 68–71
Treatment effective in most cases. Might refer to family doctor.	Would treat any structural cause; would otherwise recommend naturopathy.	Acute condition needs medical supervision and may require urgent hospitalization. Chronic condition occurs in some children.	See also **FIRST AID**, pp. 226–229
Treatment helpful in relieving symptoms of the chronic condition and strengthening respiratory tissues.	Would give rehabilitation treatment only.	This chronic condition is not really treatable except for support. A few sufferers may need oxygen.	See also **Bronchitis**, pp. 64–67
Treatment effective.	Naturopathic treatment can help.	Treatment with antibiotics may be needed. Can be caused by poor dental condition or by serious underlying disease such as leukaemia.	See also **Gumboil**, pp. 80–81; **Tooth decay**, pp. 82–83
Treatment likely to help, depending on causes and severity.	Naturopathic treatment can help.	Often benign viral condition associated with a cold, but may need treatment for chronic deficiency state.	See also **Common cold**, pp. 68–71
Treatment effective both locally and systemically.	Treatment can help, especially with the aid of naturopathy.	Treatment with antibiotics may be needed. Refer for diagnosis by dental X-ray and appropriate treatment.	See also **Gingivitis** pp. 80–81
Treatment effective for most people, depending on the cause.	Treatment can help, especially with the aid of naturopathy.	Give advice on dental hygiene. May indicate underlying illness such as lung disease.	See also **Constipation**, pp. 108–111
Treatment effective in helping patients through the illness and lessening its severity.	Naturopathic treatment can help.	Treatment is supportive, with plenty of fluids and medication to reduce fever. Secondary infections may need antibiotics.	See also **Sinusitis**, pp. 76–79
Treatment usually effective.	Treatment can help, especially with the aid of naturopathy.	In acute cases rest the voice, keep the atmosphere humid, avoid irritants such as tobacco. Would refer chronic condition to specialist.	See also **Common cold**, pp. 68–71, **Cough**, pp. 80–81
Treatment completely effective locally; also effective internally to prevent further attacks.	Naturopathic treatment is indicated here. Condition is often stress-related.	Acute cases may resolve spontaneously; treatment by topical steroids may help. Chronic ulcers may indicate stress or badly-fitting dentures.	See also **Coldsore**, pp. 80–81
Treatment can be helpful; care must be taken with adults especially, to prevent complications.	Treatment can help, especially with the aid of naturopathy.	Condition resolves spontaneously; treatment supportive to prevent complications.	

CONDITION	ACUPUNCTURE	CHIROPRACTIC	HOMEOPATHY
PHARYNGITIS Inflammation of pharynx	Treatment effective	Would not treat; would refer to a family doctor or other practitioner.	Treatment speeds recovery and improves general health, so preventing a relapse.
PLEURISY Inflammation of membranes around lungs	Treatment effective, especially if condition is in its early stages.	Would not treat; would refer to a family doctor or other practitioner.	Treatment often effective.
PNEUMOCONIOSIS Disorder of lungs caused by inhalation of dust particles	Treatment can improve lung function, but all depends on stage of disease.	Would not treat; would refer to a specialist.	Treatment improves general health and copes with secondary symptoms.
PNEUMONIA Severe infection of lungs	Treatment can be effective.	Would not treat; would refer to a family doctor.	Treatment effective, but good nursing care is needed so it may be necessary to refer to hospital.
PULMONARY EMBOLISM Blockage of blood supply in lung	Would not treat; would refer to a specialist.	Would not treat; would refer to a specialist for immediate treatment.	Would refer to hospital as an emergency, but treatment may be effective.
QUINSY Infection of tissue around tonsils	Would refer to a family doctor.	Would not treat; would refer to a family doctor or other practitioner.	Treatment effective for the acute stage, but the poor lymphatic drainage needs further treatment.
SILICOSIS Disorder of lungs caused by inhalation of silica dust	Treatment would improve lung function, but would depend on stage of disease.	Would not treat; would refer to a specialist.	Treatment may help to relieve symptoms and raise general level of health.
SNORING Noisy breathing during sleep	Treatment would depend on cause.	Would not treat; would refer to another practitioner.	Treatment effective if the cause, such as catarrh, is identified.
THRUSH Fungal infection of mouth	Treatment can be effective.	Would not treat; would refer to another practitioner.	Treatment effective because it improves general health and vitality.
TONSILLITIS Inflammation of tonsils	Treatment effective in both acute and chronic cases.	Would not treat; would refer to another practitioner.	Treatment effective, but difficulties arise when antibiotics are used extensively.
TOOTHACHE Pain in or around a tooth	Treatment effective in both acute and chronic cases. Referral to dentist might be necessary.	Would not treat; would refer to a dentist.	Treatment effective, but would always refer to a dentist.
TOOTH DECAY Disintegration of tooth	Treatment would depend on cause. Referral to dentist is likely.	Would not treat; would refer to a dentist.	Treatment effective if the condition is part of a pattern of constitutional deterioration.
TRACHEITIS Inflammation of windpipe	Treatment effective in both acute and chronic cases.	Would not treat; would refer to a family doctor or other practitioner.	Treatment effective in the acute stage, but must be linked to the total condition.
TUBERCULOSIS Bacterial infection; usually affects lungs at first, but may spread	Would not treat.	Would not treat; would refer to a specialist.	Would not treat because this is a notifiable disease.
WHOOPING COUGH Childhood disease of respiratory tract	Treatment effective.	Would not treat; would refer to a specialist.	Treatment effective, lessening the severity and length of the attack and preventing after-effects.

MED. HERBALISM	OSTEOPATHY	GEN. MEDICINE	COMMENTS
Treatment reasonably effective.	Treatment can help, especially with the aid of naturopathy.	Acute cases associated with colds recover spontaneously; antibiotics will treat bacterial infections. Allergies and smoking may cause chronic condition.	See also **Common cold**, pp. 68–71
Would treat, but would refer to a family doctor if severe, or if tuberculosis were involved.	Would not treat.	Treatment with antibiotics for bacterial infections; may also be caused by virus.	See also **Bronchitis**, pp. 64–67
Treatment can be helpful in relieving irritation and sensitivity, reducing symptoms and supporting lung function.	Would not treat.	Treatment supportive for this chronic industrial disease, comparable with emphysema.	
Treatment can be helpful and would probably follow orthodox treatment. In a bacterial case would refer to a family doctor.	Would not treat.	Treatment with antibiotics usually successful. X-ray diagnosis is helpful.	See also **Bronchitis**, pp. 64–67
Unlikely to treat.	Would not treat.	Treatment may be by conservative management, anticoagulants, or exceptionally, surgery.	See also **Hypertension**, pp. 94–97
Would treat with caution; might need to refer to a family doctor.	Treatment would be both structural and naturopathic.	Sometimes resolved by massive antibiotic therapy; otherwise refer to specialist for surgery.	See also **Tonsillitis**, pp. 82–83
Treatment would be limited to helping lung competence as far as possible.	Would not treat.	Would provide supportive treatment.	
Treatment can be helpful depending on the cause.	Treatment can help.	Would treat with decongestants or for allergy or infection. Might refer for surgery for polyps or adenoids.	See also **Catarrh**, pp. 80–81; **Sinusitis**, pp. 76–79
Treatment very effective.	Naturopathic treatment is long-term if the condition is antibiotic-induced.	Would treat by antifungal drugs. Condition may be related to obesity, diabetes or immunodeficiency.	See also **Allergy**, pp. 86–89; **Diabetes**, pp. 112–115; **Obesity**, pp. 128–131
Treatment effective locally and systemically for chronic condition.	Treatment can help, especially with the aid of naturopathy.	Would treat acute cases with antibiotics, unless viral. Would refer chronic cases for surgery.	See also **Adenoid enlargement**, pp. 80–81
Treatment of limited help before referral to a dentist.	First aid treatment can be effective.	Would treat acute cases with analgesics; would refer chronic cases to a dentist.	See also **Tooth decay**, pp. 82–83
Treatment can help, but would also refer to a dentist.	Would not treat except to help prevent further problems.	Would refer to a dentist.	
Treatment can be reasonably helpful.	Treatment can help this condition.	Acute cases recover spontaneously; treat by keeping warm and avoiding dust and smoke; possibly use antibiotics. Allergies and smoking may cause chronic condition.	See also **Common cold**, pp. 68–71; **Laryngitis**, pp. 80–81
Would not treat, but would treat people with lung problems following earlier tuberculosis.	Would not treat.	Would treat by antitubercular chemotherapy in conjunction with a specialist; prognosis is good.	
Treatment can often be effective even after orthodox treatment. May be necessary to refer to a family doctor.	Treatment can help this condition.	Recovery is usually spontaneous, but small infants may require antibiotics; would refer serious cases to hospital for supportive treatment.	

THE HEART, BLOOD, AND WHOLE BODY SYSTEMS

The cardiovascular system is made up of the heart, blood and blood vessels. The heart is a muscular sac that pumps blood into the blood vessels and around the body. Blood consists of a fluid (plasma) and three types of blood cells (red, white and platelets). There are three types of blood vessels. Arteries transport oxygenated blood from the heart to the tissues of the body. Veins return blood, containing waste products from the body tissues, to the heart. Capillaries link arteries and veins; they have thin walls that allow nutrients and waste materials in the blood to pass through them.

Many systemic disorders, those that affect the whole body, are carried through the blood.

WHAT CAN GO WRONG

There are many disorders of the blood itself, the most common being anaemia, in which there is a lack of the red blood cells that carry oxygen. The blood may also be infected by bacteria, causing septicaemia or bacterial endocarditis (infection of the membrane lining the heart), or it may carry viruses around the body in conditions such as glandular fever and measles. In the tropics, there are many parasitic blood-borne infections, such as malaria. The cells in the blood may be affected by cancerous changes, resulting in leukaemia. Some blood disorders are genetic; they include haemophilia, in which a clotting factor is absent.

Blood vessels may be damaged by degenerative diseases such as arteriosclerosis, in which fatty deposits block small vessels. This is a primary factor in causing high blood pressure and conditions such as strokes, heart attacks and peripheral arterial disease.

Complementary and alternative medical approaches sometimes view the heat, blood and whole body systems and their disorders in different ways, which can be summarized as follows.

Acupuncture

In traditional Chinese medicine, the *Heart* controls the circulation of *Blood* in conjunction with the *Lung*, which controls the circulation of *Qi*. The functions of the *Heart* and *Lung* are closely linked in this respect. Together their action is known as the *Qi* of the chest, or *Zong Qi*.

On its own, the *Heart* may become deficient in *Qi*, resulting in palpitations, breathlessness or pallor. This is because the *Heart Qi* is not regulating the *Heart* function properly. If the heart is deficient in *Blood*, insomnia, poor memory and lack of concentration can result. This disturbance of mental function is associated with the other important role of the *Heart* in Chinese medicine, as the residence of *Shen* or "spirit". The *Shen* is the equivalent of consciousness in the widest sense of the word. Its disturbance can produce symptoms ranging from those mentioned above to mental illness, loss of consciousness and coma.

The *Blood* may become deficient in the body as a whole, although this cannot be equated with anaemia – which is only one symptom of deficient *Blood*. In addition, either internal or external *Heat* may invade the *Blood*, causing it to "move recklessly". This can result in spontaneous bleeding, such as nose or uterine bleeding. Other disorders involving bleeding may result from weak *Qi*, especially of the *Spleen*, which helps to maintain the integrity of the blood vessels.

Chiropractic therapy

In general, conditions affecting the circulatory system are not amenable to treatment by chiropractic therapy. Occasionally, circulatory problems such as high blood pressure are identified during examination. If the problem appears to be caused by stress or diet, advice will be given, but frequently patients are referred for more appropriate help. Neck and lower back problems can often affect the general circulation.

Homeopathy

The circulatory system is involved in many illnesses because inflammation, a condition in which blood flows to an injured or infected site, is a healthy body's first response to imbalance, either on a local level (with sore throats or wounds), or on a general level (such as fever).

The process of purifying the blood can affect almost any illness and is a basic factor in increasing vitality. Often a simple headache is caused by toxins in the blood. A basic action of homeopathic remedies is to stimulate the organs of secretion – the kidneys, liver and skin – and enable the blood to be cleansed of toxins. In more acute illnesses, homeopathic remedies may stimulate sweating and so reduce a fever.

In general, disorders of the heart and circulation are not treated separately from the whole person's physical, emotional and mental health, because all these factors are involved in any illness. Remedies are generally prescribed according to the entire symptom picture.

Medical herbalism

Adequate and efficient circulation is imperative for all the activities in the body, so urgent attention to any disorders of this system is vital. The circulatory system must be able to absorb nutrients from food, and the respiratory system must efficiently provide it with oxygen and remove waste gases from it. Normal nervous activity is also essential to coordinate heart muscle action and, through general muscle tone, to effect proper return of venous blood to the heart. Treatment is therefore not only aimed at the circulatory system.

As well as assessing the functioning of other body systems, the herbalist may recommend adjustments to the diet, especially if the patient smokes or drinks alcohol excessively. Advice on exercise and assistance in reducing stress levels are also fundamental components in dealing with circulatory disorders.

The circulatory conditions of many of a medical herbalist's patients will have been treated with orthodox drugs and this is taken into account when planning a treatment programme. Even when a patient is dependent on drugs, herbal treatment can lead to improvement in circulation and lowering of blood pressure, as well as contributing to renewed vitality and general health.

Osteopathy with naturopathy

The circulatory system cannot be considered in isolation, because it interacts with every other system of the body. Disorders are approached by looking for causes within the whole person, especially those relating to emotions. If a blush can be emotionally induced, so can a hot flush or a heart attack.

Degenerative conditions, such as hardening of the arteries, have their basis in abuse – either inherited or self-induced. Environmental factors, such as viruses and climate, play their part, but are usually not a primary cause.

If good health is to be maintained, blood must be of a good quality and consistency, and unrestricted in its flow through blood vessels. Good nourishment, both from food and oxygen, is essential for making healthy blood. The muscular control of the blood vessels depends on healthy spinal nerves. Diet, spinal lesions, abdominal pressures and breathing efficiency are all considered during osteopathic investigation and treatment of cardiovascular disorders.

Chart of disorders

At the end of this section there is a chart listing various disorders of the heart, blood and circulation, and of systemic disorders. This is a general, but not definitive, guide to the treatment of such disorders. Complementary therapies treat the patient as a whole rather than merely the disorder presented. Whether a person can be treated, and the success of treatment, depends on the nature of the condition and the general health of the patient.

ALLERGY

ACUPUNCTURIST

THE PATIENT

PB is 20 years old, 1.7 metres (5 ft 8 in) tall and of slim build. He is a student at business school. Most of his spare time is spent in bars and discos and he drinks heavily. His mother is health-conscious and brought her family up on a wholefood diet, but PB eats less nutritious food during the day, with a preference for fried foods. He enjoys hiking and cycling, but otherwise dislikes strenuous exercise.

THE PROBLEM

Since childhood PB has had a severe allergy – an abnormal reaction of tissues – to animals, especially cats and horses. The symptoms were first noticed when he was three years old. He becomes short of breath with wheezing, severe sneezing and watering eyes. Cause for concern occurred a few months ago when he borrowed a friend's jacket which had been used when horse riding; he reacted violently and had to seek medical help to control the wheezing and relieve the skin irritation.

PB is a friendly, fun-loving young man with a lot of energy, both physically and intellectually. He is quick-witted and humorous, and does not take life too seriously. He writes poetry and listens to lyrical music when alone, but prefers to keep the company of others.

Throughout his life PB has been healthy, having only occasional colds. He does, however, suffer from sinus trouble, and finds it difficult to breathe through his nose most of the time. The nasal mucus is thin and clear except if he gets a cold, when the condition sometimes worsens into a running nose and catarrh. When under stress he can develop shortness of breath and wheezing, and since his allergy attack he carries a proprietary inhaler with him. The allergy and wheezing attacks improve with rest and warm compresses.

Of the common childhood illnesses he had caught only German measles in a mild form, and was vaccinated against measles, whooping cough, diphtheria and poliomyelitis as a baby.

The determining factor in allergies, in terms of traditional Chinese medicine, is the condition of the person's "normal" *Qi*. If this is damaged, the ability to cope with changes in the external environment is reduced and, instead of adapting, the *Qi* reacts violently; this is seen as a conflict between the normal (defensive) *Qi* and the external, pathogenic *Qi*. These conflicts tend to occur on the exterior of the body: in the nose – the opening to the *Lung* – or on the skin. The *Lung* and the skin have a close relationship.

PB's initial childhood symptoms showed that the *Lung Qi* had been weakened at an early age, and this was confirmed by his chronic sinus trouble and difficulty in breathing through his nose. This may have resulted from an early, unresolved cold. Stress worsened the condition and rest helped to alleviate it, thus indicating that the underlying condition was one of deficiency. The recent worsening of the condition, with the appearance of skin rashes, suggested a connection with his heavy drinking and preference for fried foods, both of which would be producing *Heat* in his *Liver* and *Stomach*. This *Heat* could easily transfer to the *Blood*, and thus the skin, predisposing him to rashes.

Treatment
The treatment during the acute phase would alleviate the symptoms of running nose and skin rash using the *Large Intestine, Lung, Stomach* and *Spleen* channels. The main treatment, during periods when there was no acute attack, would be for the underlying *Lung* weakness, using the *Lung, Ren* and *Urinary Bladder* channels. The *Liver* channel might also be used. PB would have to reduce his drinking and cut down on fried food; he should try to eliminate dairy products from his diet because they inhibit the function of the *Spleen* and *Lung* in transforming fluids, thus leading to *Dampness*.

Prognosis and conclusion
Allergies are either very easy or very difficult to treat. Improvement may be either dramatic or only gradual. Mild symptoms may persist, but these must be treated as important warning signs about the patient's state of health.

Asthma pp. 60–63 Sinusitis pp. 76–79

Introduction to acupuncture pp. 8–15

TREATMENT BY A
CHIROPRACTOR

Allergic conditions of this nature are not problems amenable to treatment by chiropractic therapy. Usually, a family doctor can refer patients with severe allergies for desensitization treatment. Otherwise, the chiropractor would suggest that PB consults either a homeopath or medical herbalist for treatment or advice.

TREATMENT BY A
HOMEOPATH

Allergies develop as the sensitivity of a person increases. They may be confined to one or two irritant factors, but if these factors are removed the problem of hypersensitivity does not go. It simply transfers to other irritants. The homeopath therefore sees the problems of allergies as constitutional – that is, affecting the whole body.

Irritability of the skin and of the lining of the respiratory system were PB's main physical symptoms. Itching, inflamed red skin on contact with the jacket, watering eyes, violent sneezing and sudden wheezing attacks pointed to *Sulphuricum*. When this remedy is indicated, excessive bodily activity usually results in heat and itching of the skin. In the mucous membrane (lining) of the respiratory tract this gives rise to violent sneezing and runny eyes, and the production of thin mucus, which in turn causes wheezing.

There is violence and suddenness in the *Sulphuricum* symptom picture, and this was represented in PB. *Sulphuricum* patients are basically healthy individuals, lively, intelligent, quick-witted and fun-loving. A great deal of energy revolves around the self and pleasure. PB was egocentric, and his self-indulgence came out in his poetry writing. The other side of *Sulphuricum* patients came out in PB's dislike of exercise and the fact that he did not take life too seriously.

The fast metabolism of typical *Sulphuricum* subjects means that they may eat without putting on weight, and prefer fatty foods as PB did. Usually respiratory problems can be eased by breathing warm moist air.

Treatment
The treatment in this instance would be constitutional, so a high potency single dose of *Sulphuricum* would be given. Because PB had had a bad attack of wheezing, he would be left with his inhaler, to use when necessary although as little as possible. In breathing problems the patient's anxiety can be more of a problem than the symptoms, and to take away PB's inhaler might create breathing difficulties because of anxiety.

The remedy might not need repeating, but because it acted on the whole body might produce a skin rash during the process of cure.

Introduction to chiropractic therapy pp. 16–23

Introduction to homeopathy pp. 24–31

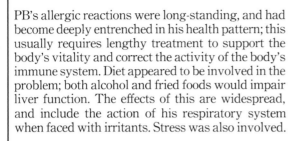

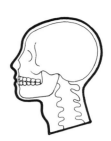

TREATMENT BY A
MEDICAL HERBALIST

PB's allergic reactions were long-standing, and had become deeply entrenched in his health pattern; this usually requires lengthy treatment to support the body's vitality and correct the activity of the body's immune system. Diet appeared to be involved in the problem; both alcohol and fried foods would impair liver function. The effects of this are widespread, and include the action of his respiratory system when faced with irritants. Stress was also involved.

Treatment

An improved diet, the use of essential oils in inhalations or compresses, and deep breathing exercises could all have a part to play in lessening the severity of PB's symptoms and building up a greater resistance to irritants.

The herbal prescription would include:
- Eyebright (*Euphrasia officinalis*): to tone up the mucous membranes and reduce the inflammation and watery catarrh.
- Lobelia (*Lobelia inflata*): relaxes irritable, hypersensitive airways.
- Euphorbia (*Euphorbia pilulifera*): bronchial dilator; relaxes the spasmodic tightening which gives rise to wheezing and breathlessness.
- Meadowsweet (*Filipendula ulmaria*): reduces any irritation to the digestive tract from underlying food sensitivities, and appears to generally lessen allergic responses.
- Golden Seal (*Hydrastis canadensis*): promotes improved digestion and liver function, especially in connection with food sensitivities; it is a useful adjunct to those remedies aimed more specifically at the lungs.

The prescription would be varied according to changes in health. The state of the respiratory system would be particularly significant in this.

Prognosis and conclusion

Herbal treatment would aim to look for any underlying sensitivities. If PB could make some changes in his lifestyle (although he is at a difficult age to do so) there would be good scope for positive results in the long term, as well as relief from immediate symptoms.

TREATMENT BY AN
OSTEOPATH AND NATUROPATH

It might be sensible for PB to avoid contact with animals, but the key to his problem did not lie in the animals but in his inherited tendencies, physical or psychological damage, the structural condition of his body, and nutrition. The possibility was considered that childhood vaccinations had sown the seeds for allergic reactions, especially those inoculations that were animal-based. Many intolerances and allergies begin when very young children drink cow's milk or, possibly, eat eggs. Whatever started PB's allergy, his problem was not being helped by his eating and drinking habits. If he changed these habits the fact that he had been brought up by a health-conscious mother would probably help his recovery.

Physical examination

Osteopathic investigation looked for factors that might have increased his sensitivity or interfered with his ability to inhibit, or suppress naturally, "bad" responses. The spine, cranium (skull) and connective tissues were examined in order to assess the function of the cranial nerves that emerge from the base of the brain.

Treatment

Therapy would include spinal and cranial adjustments, and the use of specific minerals and other nutritional supplements. Homeopathic remedies could help as part of a regime of self-cleansing.

Osteopathic treatment would aim to balance the involuntary nervous system (the part responsible for automatic, involuntary actions) nutritionally, structurally, mentally and emotionally.

PB should adopt a lifestyle that encouraged self-healing. This would include eating nourishing foods instead of those that are fat-fried or mucus-forming. It would mean more exercise, moderate drinking, and no smoking. He should look into any stressful and distressing circumstances that might initiate his allergy attacks, and attempt to find ways of controlling or cutting short an attack without suppressing it with drugs.

Prognosis and conclusion

PB was young enough for good long-term effects as long as he cooperated with the specialist.

TREATMENT BY A
FAMILY DOCTOR

Allergies are reactions to foreign substances (allergens). They are extremely common, take many forms and may affect different body systems. For instance, foods or drugs may cause sickness and skin rashes; airborne substances (pollens and dusts) produce asthma- or hay fever-type symptoms; certain chemicals, such as biological detergents or zinc oxide in sticking plasters, may cause skin eruptions. Many allergens are easily identified and are therefore avoidable, but widespread allergens such as house dust or pollens pose different problems for sensitive people.

It is common for allergic people to have identified, from experience, the allergens which affect them. Sometimes, however, confirmation is useful by means of tests in which the skin is exposed to contact with the substances under investigation, or the substances can be inhaled as a dust.

Treatment
The best treatment for PB would be prevention – he should avoid animal dusts. If he knew when he would be in contact with allergens he could use a prophylactic inhalant such as a sodium chromoglycate preparation to alleviate eye and nose allergies. Oral antihistamines (there are modern ones which do not cause drowsiness) are helpful, and steroid sprays for asthma and inflammation of the respiratory passages are a major advance.

PB was absolutely right to use a broncho-dilator inhalant, but if he experienced prolonged exposure to harmful dusts he should use a steroid. Steroid creams are also valuable. PB had a degree of stress-induced asthma and would need to learn to identify stresses and how to cope with them – or avoid them altogether. He had already developed soothing self-help therapeutic manoeuvres such as rest, compresses and bathing.

Prognosis and conclusion
There is considerable interest in allergies at the moment; some are certainly very troublesome and a few can be dangerous. Confirmation can be extremely difficult and based on tenuous circumstantial evidence. The most significant allergies are like PB's and tend to cause respiratory problems. If he takes suitable action to avoid allergens, and takes the right medication, PB could get considerable relief from his condition.

Introduction to Western medicine pp. 48–55

CONSULTANT'S COMMENTS

Allergies are in effect a hypersensitivity of one aspect of the body's defences. Most relevant in this case is that they can involve deep-seated alteration to the body's natural means of regulating its own internal environment.

Each therapy has its own merits. The conventional view is strong on simple practicality, but avoidance of irritation and the use of suppressive medication can be counterproductive – and there is also the problem of side-effects.

The acupuncturist has perhaps the most impressive image of the disturbance in constitutional terms, but confirms the difficulty that acupuncture can have in dealing with deep-seated allergies. (Its record in dealing with simpler cases is more impressive.)

The homeopath also explores the background constitution of PB, and possibly has the best chance of making an impact here. Using potentized homeopathic preparations of an allergen (a substance which produces an allergic reaction) has been shown in clinical trials to be effective.

The osteopath and naturopath provides a useful reminder of the possibility of parallel food sensitivities, but also recognizes that treatment might involve choosing from a wide range of regimes. Unlike the chiropractor, he sees a role for manipulation, although this would be only a small part of the treatment.

The medical herbalist, by contrast, opts for cautious measures, but ones which can provide a measure of long-term relief.

Summary
The choice facing the patient is between the practical, yet rather negative, prognosis of the family doctor and a bewildering variety of other approaches. One might safely suggest homeopathy as the most gentle natural alternative.

ANAEMIA

THE PATIENT

SD is a 45-year-old businesswoman who is successful and hard working. She is divorced with two children, the eldest of whom has just left home. Her work is the centre of her life, but she also plays golf from time to time with business associates. She is slightly overweight and flabby, because of lack of exercise and her sedentary lifestyle. Diets generally fail because she eats to alleviate stress, and her life is demanding and stressful most of the time. She has a dull, greyish complexion that lacks vitality.

THE PROBLEM

SD has been feeling unusually tired during the past three months. Her periods have always been heavy, but have been exceptionally so over the last year, and she has frequently had to take time off work to rest. Blood tests have shown her to be anaemic (anaemia is a deficiency of haemoglobin in the blood) and a hysterectomy has been recommended by a specialist. She also feels very tearful and is unable to cope with routine problems.

SD is an ambitious woman but often undervalues herself. Although she has good relationships at work she has no regular personal relationship and few close friends. Her mother died two years ago and her brother moved from the area six months ago.

Apart from her period problems, SD has been generally healthy. Her pregnancies were normal, with easy deliveries. She tends to be constipated and uses laxatives. She has considerable back trouble, especially if she has been to a lot of meetings. The affected areas are the neck, the upper and the lower back. She had a whiplash injury four years ago. Her shoulders are tense and raised, and her chest is slightly caved in.

TREATMENT BY AN
ACUPUNCTURIST

Anaemia is a symptom of deficiency of *Blood* in traditional Chinese medicine. Deficiency of *Blood* may originate in disharmonies of the *Heart, Spleen, Liver* or *Kidney*. It may also be caused by excessive loss of blood, especially loss of menstrual blood in women.

SD's symptoms of anaemia, dull complexion, dry skin, loss of vitality, constipation, tearfulness, inability to cope, pale tongue and choppy pulse, all confirmed a diagnosis of deficiency of *Blood*. Her heavy periods were a contributory factor, suggesting stagnation of *Blood* in the uterus resulting from stagnation of *Liver Qi* due to stress. Combined with overwork, which consumes *Qi* and *Blood*, this had produced poor circulation of *Qi* and *Blood* leading to back pain.

Her age suggested that SD was entering her menopause, when the *Kidney Jing* declines, producing weakening of *Qi* circulation to the uterus leading, in turn, to stagnation. Low back pain may be an indication of *Kidney* involvement. The emotional stress of losing her mother and of her brother moving may also have been contributory factors, exacerbating her lack of emotional nourishment.

Treatment
Strengthening the *Blood* alone would not deal with SD's problem. The stagnation of *Blood* in the uterus should be addressed first, using *Spleen, Stomach, Ren* and *Liver* channels. Treatment to move stagnant *Blood* would be interspersed with treatment to strengthen the *Qi* and *Blood* using different points on the same channels. The *Kidney* and *Urinary Bladder* channels might also be used to strengthen *Kidney Qi*.

Treatment to regulate menstruation and reduce blood loss would help her as she entered the menopause. SD would be advised to rest more, eat foods that nourish the *Blood*, and take regular exercise in addition to golf.

Prognosis and conclusion
Successful acupuncture treatment should make hysterectomy unnecessary. Weekly treatment could extend for three to six months. Consultation with an osteopath would be recommended in order to deal with SD's back problem once her general health had improved.

Constipation pp. 108–111   Backache pp. 152–155

Introduction to acupuncture pp. 8–15

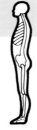

TREATMENT BY A
CHIROPRACTOR

Apart from her anaemia, which was contributing to her tiredness and tearfulness, SD had a number of other problems which needed to be dealt with, especially her heavy and painful periods, and her spinal problems.

Physical examination
The whole of SD's spine was examined, beginning with the routine orthopaedic and neurological tests, which in this case all showed her to be normal. Palpation of the neck, thoracic (chest) and lumbar areas revealed restriction of spinal mobility at the levels of cervical 5 to 6, thoracic 4 to 5 and the lumbo-sacral area, with associated muscle spasm. Her muscles were found to be particularly tense across the shoulders, this being associated with her rounded shoulders and poor posture.

X-rays were taken and these revealed generalized spondylosis (wear on the disks and joints) in the cervical area (especially the 6th), which had probably been accelerated as a result of her whiplash injury.

Treatment
SD's treatment would consist of generalized soft tissue work to the whole of the spine, followed by general mobilization to help loosen up the tension. This would be followed by specific spinal adjustment to cervical 5 and 6, thoracic 4 and 5 and the lumbo-sacral junction on both sides. Although she might feel immediate release of the muscle tension, it would take three or four treatments before she felt any great relief from back pain.

Her other problems would also be discussed. She would be prescribed iron and an iron-rich diet for her anaemia. It is likely that she would need to consult a gynaecologist concerning her severe period problems; these would also be aggravating her low back condition.

She might consider seeing an acupuncturist, homeopath or medical herbalist, as she obviously needed some overall, constitutional help. She would be encouraged to take more regular exercise.

Prognosis and conclusion
There would be potential for great improvements in SD's health and her sense of well-being.

TREATMENT BY A
HOMEOPATH

As the menopause approaches, the monthly cycle often changes to one of excessive bleeding, which can give rise to anaemia. This was one such case.

There were three aspects to the case: the protracted, heavy periods; the resulting anaemia; and the general constitution that underlay the whole tendency.

The anaemic symptoms of tiredness and a greyish complexion arose from a demanding lifestyle and excessive blood loss. To heal the patient it would be necessary to enable her to pass through the menopause without a crisis. *China* 30C would help the body to replace the loss of vital fluids quickly. It is often used on a first-aid basis in this context, together with *Ferrum protoxalate*. Underlying the menstrual picture was an image of an ambitious woman whose life revolved around work, but who was lonely and unsure of herself. Her posture confirmed this. Her work was successful, but underneath she was very worn down. *China* would still cover this picture, but other remedies needed to be considered.

SD was suppressing a lot of the grief for her mother, she had little emotional support and the cause and effects of her marriage break-up would have to be taken into account before a constitutional prescription could be given. Remedies such as *Arsenicum, Lachesis, Sepia, Pulsatilla, Lycopodium* and *Natrum muriaticum* would be considered.

Lachesis might enable SD to express her dammed-up emotions. *Sepia* would also cope with the back pain, her flabbiness and the constipation. One of these might be selected at a later stage of treatment.

Treatment
The first phase of treatment would be with *China* 30C to restore energy and repair the state of the blood. It should also balance the menstrual cycle.

Because *China* would act quickly, SD would be advised to avoid squandering her extra energy on her work. *China* would cope mainly with the physical problems, but without paying attention to emotional issues these problems would recur. *Ferrum protoxalate* 3X, night and morning for up to a week, would speed up the recovery from anaemia because it would replace lost iron. Blood tests would be recommended to assess her progress.

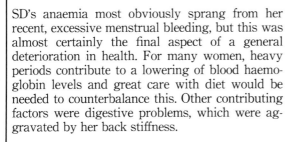
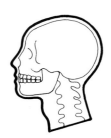

TREATMENT BY A
MEDICAL HERBALIST

SD's anaemia most obviously sprang from her recent, excessive menstrual bleeding, but this was almost certainly the final aspect of a general deterioration in health. For many women, heavy periods contribute to a lowering of blood haemoglobin levels and great care with diet would be needed to counterbalance this. Other contributing factors were digestive problems, which were aggravated by her back stiffness.

Treatment
The first area to concentrate on would be diet. Dietary supplements of iron, vitamin B complex and folic acid would be important. Introducing more green, leafy vegetables into her diet would be helpful. She should increase her intake of fibre-rich foods to help to relieve constipation, and the latter would also be helped by exercise. Regular testing of her haemoglobin levels would be necessary to assess the effects of the treatment and supplements, and monitoring of blood pressure would be useful.

The herbal prescription would include:
- Yellow Dock (*Rumex crispus*): an iron-rich remedy which acts to increase bowel movements and stimulate liver function.
- White Deadnettle (*Lamium album*): improves uterine blood flow and lessens pelvic congestion.
- Yarrow (*Achillea millefolium*): stimulates the digestion and encourages the healing of damaged blood vessels that produce heavy bleeding.
- St John's Wort (*Hypericum perforatum*): calms and tonifies the nervous system.
- Lime Blossom (*Tilia europaea*): increases peripheral circulation and appears to improve the condition of fragile capillaries.

The prescription would be varied as necessary, particularly with regard to menstrual problems and the likelihood of menopausal problems developing.

Prognosis and conclusion
SD would need to re-evaluate her lifestyle in order to change the pattern of decreasing vitality. With attention to her diet and herbal treatment the prospect for improvement in her condition would be good, both for her anaemia, and for correcting the underlying trends producing this problem.

TREATMENT BY AN
OSTEOPATH AND NATUROPATH

SD was anaemic because she was generally unhealthy: a result of heavy periods, constipation, back problems, careless diet and probably of hereditary influences. Heavy bleeding can cause anaemia and can be the result of the energy that is needed to control body functions – including menstruation – being in a depressed state. Equally, she was feeling drawn, tired, colourless and generally unhealthy because of her anaemia.

A gynaecological examination ensured that there was no disease responsible for the undue bleeding. SD's back was examined for spinal lesions and incorrect postural attitudes. The effects of her whiplash injury were confirmed. She also showed poor respiratory function, which can contribute to a variety of circulatory problems.

Heart function and blood pressure readings and blood tests would be taken to monitor progress once it was confirmed that the anaemia was of a "simple" kind, rather than a more complex type.

Treatment
Osteopathic lesions would be adjusted. SD would be made aware of her posture, and encouraged to carry herself better to improve her breathing. Brisk walking and other exercise that requires deep breathing would be essential for her recovery.

A programme of mineral and vitamin supplements, with appropriate homeopathic and herbal remedies, would aim to regulate her periods. SD would be encouraged to eat for health, rather than as an antidote to stress; dark green leafy vegetables, walnuts, raisins, brewer's yeast and wheatgerm are examples of iron-rich foods that contribute more than just iron supplements to the diet.

Prognosis and conclusion
There would be considerable hope for an improvement in her anaemia with an upgrading of her general state of health. If, however, heavy periods were the prime cause of SD's anaemia and if health measures made no difference to her condition, there might be a need to surgically remove the uterus (hysterectomy) to prevent SD's health from deteriorating further.

TREATMENT BY A
FAMILY DOCTOR

There are many causes of anaemia, which is essentially a lack of the oxygen-binding protein haemoglobin, in red blood cells. This may result from haemoglobin deficiency, caused, for example, by insufficient iron, faults in haemoglobin production, or loss of red blood cells (for example, through bleeding).

SD was suffering from heavy periods, and her anaemia was an iron-deficiency anaemia caused by chronic blood loss. Her blood tests demonstrated a typical picture of pale, small cells, and the level of iron in her blood serum was low.

Treatment
It would be important to deal with the cause of the problem, that is, her bleeding. SD might be able to reach her menopause without having a hysterectomy with the help of certain hormones, but heavy bleeding such as this in later menstrual life is sometimes quite resistant to treatment, and a hysterectomy might be the best answer in the long term. The advantage of the operation would be that she would not need to take medication – either iron or hormones – and that she would not have to endure regular episodes of heavy bleeding and pain. In the short term, iron supplements would be prescribed, and an improvement in her energy level should be apparent in a month or two.

Prognosis and conclusion
SD should look and feel much better once she was no longer anaemic. If she had the hysterectomy, she would feel much more like taking exercise and would have eradicated the source of her continual mild malaise. She would still have to face her oncoming menopause and come to terms with being a single person again. Once her health had improved she should feel positive about herself, and this might help her make new, close relationships.

Low-grade anaemia is a very common, and often undiagnosed, cause of prolonged malaise. Women may have the double burden of chronic iron-deficiency anaemia and heavy and painful periods. This can be helped quite significantly with medicines containing iron, painkillers and hormones, but a number of women need to have surgical help, and can need counselling and support to come to terms with their problem.

CONSULTANT'S COMMENTS

Common anaemia can be a deceptive condition and steps must always be taken to establish its exact nature. Blood disorders, cancer and pernicious anaemia (caused by vitamin B_{12} deficiency) are serious causes and must be checked for. In this case, the diagnosis of iron deficiency is supported by the heavy menstrual bleeding.

Treatments
No treatment can ignore the need to increase iron intake in this type of anaemia. The conventional iron supplement can sometimes cause constipation and could be inappropriate in SD's case. Better results are likely with iron-rich foods, as recommended by the naturopath and medical herbalist, although blood tests would be needed to monitor this.

The problem facing most of the specialists, however, is what to do about the excessive blood loss and whether a hysterectomy may be necessary. It is possible that SD's womb could be saved, but her chances of doing so would be much reduced without measures to improve the health of her pelvic region. In this context, the measures proposed by the chiropractor and osteopath to correct her spinal problems might be surprisingly effective. Improving the blood supply of the womb, as in the prescription of the medical herbalist, is similarly well directed.

Summary
Concentration on improving the health of the pelvic region, as proposed by the three practitioners above, is likely to be especially effective in this case. In contrast the homeopath and acupuncturist, by attending to the constitutional nature of the problem, would be likely to help if the patient's general health was poor. A hysterectomy would still be available if all other measures failed.

HYPERTENSION

THE PATIENT

SL is a 55-year-old man. He is 1·8 m (5 ft 10 in) tall and weighs 89 kg (14 stone). He has a loud, cheerful voice and a red complexion. He formerly worked abroad in a government office, but took early retirement 12 months ago after a check-up revealed high blood pressure (hypertension).

Although he is an active gardener, SL is overweight, a problem caused largely by good eating, excessive drinking and entertaining while he was abroad. He finds maintaining a strict diet difficult because he enjoys food and continues to entertain regularly. He is married with one daughter aged 25. He does not smoke.

THE PROBLEM

The typical symptoms of high blood pressure occur when SL over-exerts himself. He cannot walk fast or climb stairs without becoming short of breath, and his exercise is therefore limited. He was aware of increasing shortness of breath for four years before he started to suffer from chest pains. Drugs have been effective in stabilizing the condition, but he does not like using them.

SL is bright and outgoing, with a fine sense of humour. He enjoys the company of others and rarely spends time on his own, except when gardening. His work for the government did not stimulate him, but he found his social life as an expatriate satisfying. He returned to his home town last year and is rekindling old friendships and becoming involved in rural activities. His ease in communicating with people has enabled him to settle down well in his new environment.

SL grew up in the countryside and had a robust constitution. He suffered from scarlet fever when he was four years old but otherwise had no serious illnesses. He smoked during his late teens and twenties but stopped after developing bronchitis when he was 28 years old. He suffers from occasional indigestion and constipation.

TREATMENT BY AN
ACUPUNCTURIST

Hypertension is often related to an imbalance between the *Liver* and the *Kidney*, where the *Yang* of the *Liver* is excessive and the *Yin* of the *Kidney* is deficient.

SL showed signs of an excess of *Liver Yang*, such as aching in the crown of the head, dizziness and a red face. This was accompanied by buzzing in the ears (tinnitus), which indicated a deficiency of *Kidney Yin*. He also suffered from shortness of breath, when he exerted himself, and chest pains, which suggested either a *Qi* or a *Yang* deficiency affecting the *Heart* and leading to poor circulation of *Blood* and to pain.

It is possible for different organs in the body to manifest contradictory *Yin* and *Yang* signs, and the *Kidney* may be both *Yin* and *Yang* deficient. The *Liver Yang* had been overstimulated by SL's excessive alcohol consumption, and this had burnt up the *Liver Yin*, which in turn depleted the *Kidney Yin*. Because *Yin* nourishes *Yang*, the *Kidney Yang*, which is the basis of *Yang* in the whole body, had become weak. Thus, SL's *Heart Yang* was undermined. The *Heart* was also affected by excess weight and lack of exercise.

Treatment
The treatment would involve reducing the *Liver Yang* and strengthening the *Kidney* to support the *Liver Yin*. Points on the *Liver, Gall Bladder, Ren, Du, Kidney* and *Urinary Bladder* channels would be used, along with points which have been empirically shown to lower blood pressure. Blood pressure would be monitored throughout treatment.

Yang should also be strengthened to support the *Heart* and control the breathlessness and chest pain. Points on the *Ren, Pericardium, Kidney, Du* and *Urinary Bladder* channels would be used.

A major part of the treatment would need to be undertaken by SL himself. He must avoid alcohol, eat less rich food – particularly sweet and fatty foods – and lose weight. He should take gentle exercise, taking care not to over-exert himself.

Prognosis and conclusion
SL would need treatment for at least six months, weekly at first. Treatment would not aim to replace the drug regime, but it would help to ease his breathlessness and chest pain and generally prevent a worsening of his condition.

Constipation pp. 108–111

Introduction to acupuncture pp. 8–15

TREATMENT BY A
CHIROPRACTOR

Hypertension is a serious condition that is usually progressive and can be life-threatening. It is not generally suitable for chiropractic treatment. The chiropractor would refer cases of severe hypertension to a family doctor for advice and attention. Sufferers from hypertension might also benefit from the advice of an acupuncturist, medical herbalist or homeopath.

TREATMENT BY A
HOMEOPATH

SL fits well into the stereotype of the jolly, fat, red-faced extrovert. But his condition is serious and his constitution weakened through years of abuse.

The overall pattern of overeating, indigestion, constipation, chest pains and shortness of breath are typical symptoms of the remedy *Calcarea*. This is a potentized preparation of oyster shell and contains calcium carbonate. The remedy is often indicated when the calcium metabolism is imbalanced, affecting blood pressure and metabolic rate.

A person for whom this remedy is appropriate would have been lively and robust with a ruddy complexion when they were healthy. However if their health is disturbed, they become acutely ill, usually with a high fever.

Calcarea is one of the major remedies used by a homeopath. It is known as a "polycrest" because it covers a broad range of disorders. The most common type of *Calcarea* patient is a robust person with a slow metabolic rate, who may develop kidney stones.

Belladonna, with its symptoms of high fever and pounding full pulse, may be appropriate in this case but only in an acute phase of the condition. *Calcarea* would be needed to improve his chronic ill health.

Treatment
Belladonna would be prescribed initially to help lower the blood pressure, which would be monitored closely throughout treatment. Once the condition improved, *Calcarea* would be prescribed in high potency to correct the underlying constitution and the calcium metabolism.

This remedy might be repeated after several months, depending on SL's response. As his health improved, the role of "conventional" or allopathic drugs could be assessed, and it might be possible to reduce them gradually and under continual assessment of his progress.

Prognosis
In many cases homeopathic medicine can help patients with hypertension, especially if the condition is mild, and treatment is combined with advice on diet, exercise and relaxation. It would be more difficult in SL's case, since he had been using allopathic drugs for some time. In such severe cases, great care would be taken, and treatment and prognosis would depend on the drugs being used.

Introduction to chiropractic therapy pp. 16–23   Introduction to homeopathy pp. 24–31

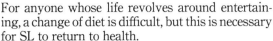

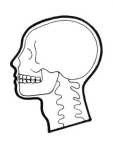

TREATMENT BY A
MEDICAL HERBALIST

For anyone whose life revolves around entertaining, a change of diet is difficult, but this is necessary for SL to return to health.

Initial steps that would be of great value include eliminating salt from the diet to help kidney function and reduce fluid retention, and reducing intake of fatty meats, rich sauces and the like. A positive approach – variety in food and exploration of healthier versions of favourite dishes – would be more helpful than a mere list of things to avoid.

Alcohol is definitely a problem, and consumption should be reduced. Encouragement from his wife and friends would be of vital importance. The use of garlic – either in food or as a supplement – helps to lower blood cholesterol levels and has at least a short-term effect on reducing blood pressure.

In addition to gardening, swimming would be a very helpful form of exercise, to maintain heart and lung muscles.

Treatment
The herbal prescription would include:
- Hawthorn (*Crataegus oxyacanthoides*): improves the blood supply to the heart and stabilizes the heartbeat.
- Lime Blossom (*Tilia europea*): dilates peripheral blood vessels and has a mildly relaxing effect, thus helping to reduce blood pressure.
- Dandelion Root (*Taraxacum officinale*): tonic to the digestive system and a mild liver stimulant.
- Dandelion Leaf (*Taraxacum officinalis*): similar to Dandelion Root, but more active as a diuretic; also provides considerable amounts of potassium to replace that lost in drinking wine.

Blood pressure should be regularly monitored and the prescription amended as necessary.

Prognosis
Weight reduction would be the first – though difficult – aim, but this should accompany a general change in dietary habits which would make slimming easier and carry substantial health benefits. A gradual but substantial reduction in blood pressure would certainly be possible for SL.

TREATMENT BY AN
OSTEOPATH AND NATUROPATH

The direct cause of a problem such as SL's is increased resistance to the flow of blood through the arteries and veins. The examination assessed the state of his heart, blood pressure, blood vessels and kidneys, and considered the causes of this increased resistance, which could be nutritional, structural or psychological.

In some cases of hypertension the body can be encouraged to rejuvenate its blood vessels. In all cases, the quality of blood flow through the vessels can be improved. Also, careful dieting will help purify the blood.

Physical examination
The structural examination was concerned with the integrity of the spine, pelvis, ribcage and abdomen. It looked for congestion in the soft tissue of the neck and in the back of the head, affecting the nourishment and drainage of the head. The cranium was analysed for cerebro-spinal and cranial nerve influences. The effects on the heart of excess weight being carried, and the efficiency of the kidneys, were both checked.

Treatment
The osteopathic treatment would involve a programme of structural adjustment to improve nerve supply to organs and blood vessels. This would aid the elimination of toxins as the efficiency of liver, lungs, kidneys and skin improves. Cranial manipulation and massage of the abdomen could induce relaxation and a drop in blood pressure.

Naturopathic treatment would recommend a controlled fast to take some of the load off the system. Animal products should be replaced by plant foods, and stimulants such as coffee, tea and alcohol should be avoided.

SL should try to avoid physical, mental and emotional stress, and adjust his attitudes to life and to his social activities accordingly.

His blood pressure should fall as a result of these measures, and he could then gradually reduce his dependence on drugs.

Prognosis and conclusion
Osteopathic help would improve SL's health in general and help his system to restore itself. However he would need to make important changes to his lifestyle if improvement were to be long-term.

Introduction to medical herbalism pp. 32–39

Introduction to osteopathy with naturopathy pp. 40–47

TREATMENT BY A
FAMILY DOCTOR

High blood pressure is common in middle age and later, and usually shows no outward symptoms unless it is dangerously raised. It is most often diagnosed by a routine medical check or a medical examination for insurance purposes.

Overweight men who smoke and take little exercise are a high-risk group, and medical surveillance in middle age is good preventive medicine, because raised blood pressure is associated with an increased risk of vascular disease (strokes and heart attacks).

Treatment
Blood pressure should be taken several times over a period of weeks or months to ensure accurate and reliable measurements before treatment is started. Gentle exercise, combined with a loss of weight, may reduce it to normal levels. Failing this, however, there are many drugs – including diuretics, beta blockers and the more modern calcium antagonists – which are effective and do not cause undue side-effects. SL should take regular medication, and his doctor would help him with his angina (chest pain on exertion).

SL was overweight and unfit, and would be at risk of a vascular catastrophy if he remained so. It would be wise to assess cardiac damage with an electrocardiograph (a trace of the heartbeat). He would then need advice about exercise – which is very important – and dietary education. SL should take in fewer calories, lose weight and try to remain on a diet low in animal fats. A low-salt diet might also be recommended. It is not likely that drugs could stabilize his weight, and appetite suppressant drugs are dangerous.

Prognosis and conclusion
Regular medical supervision and appropriate treatment, in combination with exercise, weight-loss and a sensible diet, should allow SL a normal life. He could drink a little alcohol quite safely. Smoking would be particularly dangerous. SL would be unlikely to need surgical help – such as coronary by-pass surgery – unless he became afflicted by increasing angina.

People can – and do – die young from the consequences of high blood pressure. Treatment would be essential and require regular supervision.

Introduction to Western medicine pp. 48–55

CONSULTANT'S COMMENTS

This is a classic case of a man's past and continuing lifestyle being on a collision course with his health. Without a radical change of lifestyle or the help of powerful drugs, this man is moving toward an early death.

The treatments
SL's condition is serious, and it is unlikely that conservative natural therapy will make much inroad into this problem unless it is associated with a major change in his approach to exercise, diet and lifestyle. This change would have to include a conversion of conviction; otherwise the resultant misery might be even more life-threatening.

It is also unlikely that any natural treatment would compete with conventional drug treatment for critically high levels of blood pressure. It is difficult in this case to judge whether it would be possible to wean the patient off medication.

If the patient were willing to change his lifestyle sufficiently, treatment by complementary therapies might be effective in improving the circulatory, lung, kidney and liver functions enough for the blood pressure to fall. Once this had been achieved the patient's drug regime might be gradually reduced, if not stopped completely – hopefully in cooperation with his family doctor. However, some drugs for high blood pressure are difficult to withdraw from, especially if they have been used over a long period, and this would present the practitioners with a problem.

Summary
In less severe cases it is likely that herbal, homeopathic, acupuncture and naturopathic treatments could reduce blood pressure significantly. There is growing agreement in the medical profession that methods other than drug treatments are more appropriate in dealing with mild cases of high blood pressure.

VARICOSE VEINS

ACUPUNCTURIST

THE PATIENT

SV is 58 years old and worked as a teacher until she took early retirement four years ago and became a part-time store assistant. Her husband died two years before she retired, and this prompted her change in occupation. Her two children live in other parts of the country, and she rarely sees them, but finds that the social contact of her new job alleviates her loneliness. She is slim and elegant and looks younger than her age, with bright eyes and a clear healthy complexion. She swims and does yoga regularly.

THE PROBLEM

Twenty years ago SV developed varicose veins (enlarged, twisted veins) and these have worsened dramatically since she started working in a shop. She wears support stockings but still finds her legs feel heavy and aching after several hours of standing. Putting her feet up and bathing them in hot water reduces the discomfort. The veins are unsightly, being raised and knobbly on both sides of her calves and inner thighs. They first developed in the left leg.

SV is cheerful and outgoing. Although deeply affected by the loss of her husband six years ago, she has been determined to make a new life for herself. She travels a lot and keeps busy knitting, going to evening classes and playing bridge. Her energy is sometimes overwhelming, and she has a tendency to talk quickly.

Her family has always been healthy, and her mother is still living at 90 years old. SV has suffered from insomnia since her husband's death. She generally has no trouble getting to sleep at 11 pm or midnight but wakes around 1 am and finds it difficult to sleep again until 3 or 4 am. She has a chronic stiff neck with fibrous nodules occurring on each side of the cervical (neck) vertebrae – particularly in the winter – and has some difficulty turning her head from side to side.

Varicose veins involve poor circulation of blood in the legs and the breakdown of the walls of the veins; they are therefore thought to be due to stagnation of *Blood*. The condition is classified as a dysfunction of *Qi*, in its roles as the driving force in the circulation of *Blood*, and in maintaining the integrity of the *Blood* vessels. The *Lung* and the *Spleen* are the main organs responsible for the circulation and production of *Qi* respectively; they have a close relationship with the *Heart*, which is responsible for the circulation of *Blood*.

Insomnia is caused by insufficient *Blood* of the *Heart*. The *Heart Blood* is said to "house" the *Shen*, or spirit, which includes the "mind" and its functions, such as clarity of thought, consciousness, memory and sleep. When the *Shen* is not "housed" properly, it is said to "float", disturbing the mind and the sleep.

Both of SV's occupations involved much standing, which weakened the venous circulation in her legs. Her varicose veins had worsened since the death of her husband. This suggested that sadness had weakened her *Lung Qi*, aggravating an already existing condition of *Qi* weakness, and further undermining her *Blood* circulation. This had affected her *Heart Shen* leading to insomnia: she was waking at 1 am, the time when the *Heart* is at its lowest ebb. The insomnia had further weakened her *Qi*. Her pale, flabby tongue and weak pulse confirmed this. Her stiff neck, especially in winter, was consistent with poor circulation of *Qi*.

Treatment
The treatment would involve promoting *Qi* and *Blood* circulation in the legs using points on the *Heart, Pericardium, Spleen, Stomach* and *Urinary Bladder* channels. With the addition of points on the *Ren* channel it would also serve to promote *Qi* and *Blood* production, calm the *Shen* and stop the insomnia. Points on and near the neck would be used to enhance local *Qi* and *Blood* circulation.

Prognosis and conclusion
Acupuncture treatment could not repair the long-standing damage to the veins in SV's legs. It can, however, enhance the circulation and thus stop the discomfort associated with the condition.

TREATMENT BY A
CHIROPRACTOR

Varicose veins are not a condition normally treated by chiropractic therapy.

SV's neck was examined. All orthopaedic and neurological tests were normal. Palpation revealed general stiffness and muscle tension in the neck. X-rays revealed generalized spondylosis (wear and tear), as would be expected in a woman of her age.

Treatment
The treatment would consist of soft-tissue work to release the muscle tension, followed by specific spinal manipulation to the neck. Within three or four weeks of treatment her neck would feel more mobile, and the fibrous nodules would have disappeared.

She would need to avoid being on her feet all day, which was certainly aggravating her condition, even though she was wearing support stockings. Unfortunately her job necessitated long periods of standing. It would be important that she rest, with her feet up, in the evening and even sleep with the end of her bed raised 15 cm (6 in) or so, because this frequently helps in the long term.

The possibility of having the veins "stripped" would be discussed. This is a procedure frequently carried out on varicose veins. It is a minor operation, and her family doctor could refer her to a specialist who would perform the operation.

Prognosis and conclusion
Operations for vein problems are frequently successful, although a job which demands continual standing would be not recommended. SV would be advised to consult the chiropractor again should the stiffness return at any time.

TREATMENT BY A
HOMEOPATH

Varicose veins indicate a sluggish constitution with easily-relaxed smooth muscle tissue (which is present in veins). While exercise improves the condition, congestion of the veins makes it worse, hence the aggravation when standing.

SV's case illustrated this well. It was only after her work necessitated standing so much that her varicose veins became troublesome. The veins affected were in the calves and inner thighs, and the trouble started on the left side. Various remedies fit this picture. *Carbo vegetabilis, Hamamelis* and *Pulsatilla* are usually for the right side, while *Sepia, Lachesis* and *Graphites* are for varicose veins on the left side.

SV was slim, so there was not the pressure of weight to worsen the load on the veins. Swimming and yoga keep the muscles of the legs supple, and these activities usually help to prevent the formation of varicose veins.

She had determination, and recognized the need to keep herself motivated to cope with loneliness following the death of her husband. However, the disruption of her sleep pattern showed the disintegrating effect of this event. Her exuberance and tendency to talk quickly were over-compensations for bereavement.

Lachesis would also have a positive effect on her stiff neck. A good indicator of the accuracy of selecting a remedy is always that, as well as fitting the main hierarchy of symptoms, it also fits all the other symptoms.

Treatment and prognosis
Lachesis in a high potency would greatly improve SV's general health and change her sluggish constitution. It would also help her to deal with her grief and its resulting symptom of insomnia. It would eventually help her varicose veins, too. She might then only need occasional repeat doses, perhaps years apart, to maintain a high level of health.

Another way of prescribing would be to give the *Lachesis* in a low potency at first to start healing the veins, and then to build up the potency slowly to create deeper changes in health. In view of the grief and insomnia, however, the first alternative would probably be better.

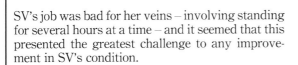

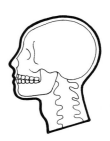

TREATMENT BY A
MEDICAL HERBALIST

SV's job was bad for her veins – involving standing for several hours at a time – and it seemed that this presented the greatest challenge to any improvement in SV's condition.

Treatment

The first area of attention would be to improve the tone of her calf muscles with specific exercises, especially encouraging her to elevate the legs whenever possible to assist drainage. She should raise the foot end of her mattress slightly so the congestion could be drained overnight. Cold water applications on her legs would also help to tone her tissues. This treatment could be reinforced by applying lotions or ointments containing Marigold (*Calendula officinalis*) or Horse Chestnut (*Aesculus hippocastanum*).

The herbal prescription would include:
- Lime Blossom (*Tilia europaea*): helps to improve circulation through the extremities and restore greater elasticity to the blood vessel walls, with a gentle, overall relaxing effect to help reduce tension and aid natural sleep patterns.
- Horse Chestnut (*Aesculus hippocastanum*): astringes and tones swollen vein walls and reduces inflammation.
- Golden Seal (*Hydrastis canadensis*): an astringent; also improves digestion.
- Scullcap (*Scutellaria laterifolia*): relaxes the central nervous system.
- Hawthorn (*Crataegus oxyacanthoides*): improves circulation and tones the blood vessel walls.
- Yarrow (*Achillea millefolium*): increases peripheral circulation, and acts as a mild diuretic to help reduce fluid retention in the legs.

The prescription would be reviewed, taking account of the patient's digestive system, circulation and the like.

Prognosis and conclusion

SV had unfortunately chosen a job which was aggravating her condition, already made worse from years of teaching, and she might need to reconsider this. Exercises for the legs, especially with legs raised, would be essential and, combined with herbal treatment, offer the best hope for improvement in her condition.

TREATMENT BY AN
OSTEOPATH AND NATUROPATH

Veins carry blood that is returning to the heart. Arterial blood is pumped by the heart; venous blood needs muscle action to propel it back from the tissues to the heart. There are valves within the leg veins that prevent blood from flowing back down the legs. SV's valves were inefficient and the vein walls had poor tone, hence her enlarged, twisted blood vessels close to the surface.

The pressure of SV's pregnancies was partly responsible, and hereditary tendencies had to be considered. The state of the circulation through the liver would also be considered because blood leaving the liver is joined by blood from the veins of the legs and can have an effect on leg circulation.

Physical examination

In examination, account was taken of SV's general health. Abdomen, spine, general circulation and breathing efficiency were assessed, as was her bowel activity (left leg varicose veins are often associated with constipation).

Treatment

Spinal lesions would be adjusted, especially those that influence nerve control of muscles within the blood vessel walls. Breathing would be improved by work on the thoracic (chest) vertebrae and the rib cage. Cranial balancing would improve breath control and circulation. Massage of the abdomen would improve circulation through the liver.

SV should raise the foot of her bed about 10 cm (4 in) so that blood would be encouraged to flow towards her heart while she was asleep; she should avoid sitting for long periods, especially on a seat that presses on the backs of her thighs; if she has to stand at work she should shift her weight from leg to leg. Elastic stockings are helpful. SV should spray her legs with cold water, using a scent spray – the legs should be left to dry in the air.

She should improve the quality of her blood so that it flows less sluggishly. This would involve attention to what she ate, and deep breathing with a brisk walk would mobilize abdominal organs each time the diaphragm moved up and down.

Prognosis and conclusion

While it is impossible to restore elasticity to a vein once it has been lost, it should be possible to make SV's varicose veins less uncomfortable.

Introduction to medical herbalism pp. 32–39

Introduction to osteopathy with naturopathy pp. 40–47

TREATMENT BY A
FAMILY DOCTOR

Varicose veins are swollen superficial veins which develop in the legs because faulty valves allow pressure to build up in the blood in the veins. They tend to run in families, and although they are more common in older people and the obese, they can occur in healthy active young people. They sometimes worsen during and after pregnancy. Varicose veins can ache and are often most unsightly. In the elderly, who have thin fragile skin, small injuries can cause severe bleeding and the legs can develop an intractable, irritant rash. Because the skin's supply of healthy oxygenated blood is diminished, varicose veins in the elderly can lead to leg ulcers which are very difficult to treat.

Treatment
Weight loss (not necessary in SV's case) and exercise are essential, but some veins demand surgical treatment. Various procedures can be carried out which include "stripping" the whole or part of the vein or injecting the "roots" or bunches of veins with a chemical that makes them shrivel up.

SV could probably be helped by vein stripping. Her doctor could refer her to a specialist, who would advise her on the most appropriate procedure. Her job was not helping her condition, so she should wear special stockings at work and learn to move on her feet to improve the circulation in her calves.

Prognosis and conclusion
SV's veins could be greatly helped by surgery, and her recovery would be assisted by being relatively fit. Furthermore, she did not have a long history of the problem. After surgery there would still be a tendency for varicose veins to recur, and it would be important to maintain lightness and fitness, and to avoid prolonged standing with little movement.

Her personality seemed very strong and this could only help her to do very well.

Varicose veins are a common condition, although in early life they are seldom a serious medical problem. Complications can occur, however, and advice concerning the merits of surgery should be sought before irreversible skin changes have a chance to develop.

CONSULTANT'S COMMENTS

Unlike the arterial system, the venous system has no direct pumping action at all. Instead it has a series of passive one-way valves, and relies for its "pump" on the squeezing action of the leg muscles surrounding the veins, and on the internal effects of the movements of the diaphragm during breathing.

When the leg muscles are kept active, the diaphragm exercised, and the strength of the vein walls maintained, the system works very well. If the veins are weakened by heredity, hormones (as in pregnancy) or dietary deficiency, and if inactivity of the leg muscles is compounded by frequent standing or sitting, then the veins may stretch and bulge.

Non-surgical treatment of varicose veins is therefore directed at improving venous circulation or the strength of the vein walls. The question is whether it can succeed.

The treatments
The osteopath and naturopath, and the medical herbalist, suggest the most practical measures for improving the tone and circulation of the leg, and tone of the veins, directly. Their suggestions should form the basis of measures to reduce deterioration, but whether these would actually improve matters is much less sure; improvements have been noted, but only in a few cases.

The roles of homeopathy and acupuncture would be in improving general background influences, while manipulative treatments would help reduce some of the postural strains on the condition.

Conclusions
Non-surgical methods must be the recommended course in the short term, and for the longer term in order to avoid deterioration and complications. The family doctor's option of vein stripping might turn out to be the most realistic for cosmetic purposes, but it would not deal with any underlying problems.

Introduction to Western medicine pp. 48–55

GUIDE TO TREATMENT OF HEART, BLOOD AND SYSTEMIC DISORDERS 1

CONDITION	ACUPUNCTURE	CHIROPRACTIC	HOMEOPATHY
ANEURISM Localized abnormal dilation of a blood vessel	Treatment is in prevention and post-operative care; in acute case would refer to a general practitioner.	Would not treat; would refer to a specialist.	Treatment is long term and will help restore the basic level of health. Healing time depends on present state of health. Would refer to family doctor.
ANGINA Severe pain radiating from heart	Treatment can be very effective, especially when combined with changes in diet and lifestyle.	Would not treat; would refer to a specialist or other practitioner.	Treatment will prevent the disease getting worse, but is unlikely to effect a complete cure. Would refer to family doctor.
ARTERIOSCLEROSIS Thickening and hardening of the arteries	Treatment most effective in the early stages of the illness.	Would not treat; would refer to a specialist.	Treatment can help improve the basic level of health and arrest progress of disease. Improvement likely to be limited.
BRUISING Dark mark beneath the skin caused by a blow	Treatment of spontaneous bruising due to internal *Spleen* disharmony is effective; treat bruises due to injury with *Moxa*.	Would not treat; would refer to another practitioner.	Treatment works well as a first aid measure; it also helps in cases where bruising is a constitutional problem.
CANCER Disorder in which body cells multiply and destroy healthy tissue	Treatment possible for very early signs of breast and cervical cancer; in serious cases can treat associated symptoms.	Would not treat, would refer to a specialist.	Treatment may halt the disease and even cure it, depending on how far it has progressed. Would refer to general practitioner. Surgery may be unavoidable.
CHICKENPOX Infectious disease with skin eruptions and fever	Treatment is effective if carried out early and frequently (once a day).	Would not treat; would refer to a family doctor.	Treatment speeds recovery and helps with complications and any aftermath.
ENDOCARDITIS Inflammation of membrane lining the heart	Treatment reasonably effective if condition is associated with rheumatic fever, but results are poor if associated with congenital deformity.	Would not treat; would refer to a specialist.	Treatment is effective, especially where the condition is a complication of an acute illness.
FEVER Abnormally high body temperature	Treatment very effective in both acute and chronic cases.	Would not treat; would refer to a family doctor.	Treatment is effective and helps recovery without complications or aftermath. Naturopathic treatment may also be used.
FOOD ALLERGY Reaction to specific foods	Treatment effective when dealing with underlying disharmony leading to allergic reaction.	Would not treat; would refer to another practitioner.	Treatment is effective, but involves raising the general level of health rather than dealing with specific symptoms.
GLANDULAR FEVER High fever and enlargement of lymph glands in acute phase	Treatment effective in most cases.	Would not treat; would refer to another practitioner.	Treatment effective in acute cases, but results may be slow in chronic illnesses.
HAEMOPHILIA Hereditary lack of factor needed for blood to clot	Use of needles would be dangerous. Treatment with Chinese herbs may improve the condition but in general it is not possible to treat directly.	Would not treat.	Constitutional treatment can be effective in improving general level of health. First aid blood-clotting remedies such as *Lachesis* are useful.
HAEMORRHAGE Abnormal external or internal bleeding	Treatment of chronic condition (not internal) most effective when combined with Chinese herbal treatment; would refer most acute cases to hospital.	Would not treat; would refer to a specialist.	Treatment effective in acute cases, but the condition may require stitching or more careful investigation.
HEART BLOCK Failure of heart tissue to conduct normal impulses	Would refer to a family doctor.	Would not treat; would refer to a specialist.	Would refer immediately to hospital because specialized resources may be needed. Constitutional treatment may follow.
HEART FAILURE Heartbeat too weak to maintain normal circulation	Treatment in chronic cases is effective in strengthening heart function by strengthening *Qi* and *Yang* of whole body.	Would not treat; would refer to hospital or a specialist. Urgent medical treatment usually required.	Would refer immediately to hospital because specialized resources may be needed. Constitutional treatment may follow.
HYPERTHERMIA (HEAT STROKE) Raised body temperature	Treatment can be effective.	Would not treat; would refer to a specialist.	Treatment is effective, but may need more detailed investigation.

MED. HERBALISM	OSTEOPATHY	GEN. MEDICINE	COMMENTS
Unlikely to see; would refer to a family doctor in case immediate hospitalization is needed.	Would not treat.	Would not treat. Depending on location, major drastic surgery may be required, but the condition may be inoperable.	See also **Haemorrhage**, pp. 102–103
Treatment effective in the long term. Condition may need nitroglycerin for acute pain.	In acute case would give first aid and send for ambulance; in chronic case would recommend naturopathy to avoid recurrence.	Treatment by drugs is effective, plus stopping smoking, taking exercise and adjusting diet. Bypass surgery may be needed in severe cases.	See also **Hypertension**, pp. 94–97
Treatment effective over a period of time. Would treat the causative factor.	Would treat to avoid worsening; naturopathy would cleanse bloodstream.	Cannot be treated; bypass surgery for essential arteries is possible. A low fat diet and stopping smoking help.	See also **Hypertension**, pp. 94–97
Treatment is effective. If a fracture is suspected may need to refer to hospital.	Treatment by osteopathy can be effective; recommend hydrotherapy; homeopathic treatment with *Arnica* is effective.	Rest or physiotherapy are the best treatments for post-traumatic bruises; spontaneous bruising may mean a bleeding disorder.	See also **FIRST AID**, pp. 226–231
Treatment helps resistance; patient is likely to be receiving other treatment as well.	Naturopathy would help a patient cope with symptoms and encourage healing.	Refer to specialist.	See also **CANCER**, p. 225
Treatment relieves severity of the illness.	Recommend naturopathic treatment; condition should be allowed to take its course.	Would provide supportive treatment such as calamine lotion or anti-itching medicine pending spontaneous recovery.	
Would treat, but might need to refer to a family doctor, especially if condition is bacterial in origin.	Would not treat except for first aid.	Would not usually treat unless chronic viral condition. Refer urgently to specialist for diagnosis.	See also **Hypertension**, pp. 94–97
Treatment is effective, but may need to refer to a family doctor, depending on cause.	Management treatment only, for comfort; fever should rarely be suppressed.	If severe, would treat with antipyretic drugs following diagnosis. Small children may suffer convulsions.	See also **FIRST AID**, pp. 226–231
Would treat for the sensitivity, and give dietary advice.	Would treat the whole patient, not the allergy, using naturopathy.	Treatment with antihistamines, and occasionally steroids, is helpful in acute cases. Refer to dietician or allergist.	See also **Allergy**, pp. 86–89
Treatment helpful both in the febrile stage and to speed convalescence.	Treatment can help; also recommend naturopathy.	Recovery generally spontaneous. Would provide supportive treatment in case of complications such as hepatitis.	
Would not treat the condition directly, but could apply first aid in emergencies.	Would not treat.	Injections of absent clotting factor can be given for minor injuries; condition is hereditary and incurable.	See also **FIRST AID**, pp. 226–231
Would treat mild cases; severe condition requires orthodox treatment and/or hospitalization.	Treatment can help localized and surface condition; would not treat traumatic visceral condition, but can treat underlying physiology.	Would treat to stop acute bleeding; severe cases may require transfusion and surgery.	See also **Anaemia**, pp. 90–93; **FIRST AID**, pp. 226–231
Would treat mild form; severe condition might require hospitalization.	Would not treat as such, but patient can be helped as a whole if cause is nutritional.	Requires diagnosis by electrocardiogram, and specialist help may be needed. Some cases do not require treatment.	See also **Heart failure**, pp. 102–103
Would treat chronic case; would refer to a family doctor if orthodox treatment were necessary.	Would not treat.	Treatment generally effective. May require specialist diagnosis or help.	See also **Anaemia**, pp. 90–93
Treatment effective unless temperature is very high, when orthodox drugs may be needed.	Would treat in emergency, using conventional first aid.	Would not treat; this severe reaction to some medication and disease requires urgent specialist intensive care.	See also **FIRST AID**, pp. 226–231

CONDITION	ACUPUNCTURE	CHIROPRACTIC	HOMEOPATHY
HYPOTENSION Low blood pressure	Treatment is effective by strengthening *Qi* and *Blood* of whole body.	Would not treat; would refer to another practitioner.	Treatment is effective both in first aid (for example fainting) and in chronic cases.
HYPOTHERMIA Below normal body temperature	Treatment is very effective; older patients may need herbs also.	Would not treat; would refer to a family doctor.	Treatment may support general nursing care and attempts to raise temperature; treating shock may prevent pneumonia.
ISCHAEMIA Obstruction of circulation to a part of the body	Treatment is effective in promoting *Qi* and blood circulation in local area and generally.	Would not treat; would refer to a specialist.	Treatment depends on cause. Remedies such as *Arnica* dissolve clots quickly, and *Aconite* can cause rapid dilation of blood vessels. More investigation may be needed.
LEUKAEMIA Excess production of white blood cells	Might treat associated symptoms, depending on history and severity of the disease.	Would not treat; would refer to a specialist.	Treatment has been known to arrest the disease, depending on its stage, and deal with secondary symptoms. Would refer to a family doctor.
MALARIA Fever caused by mosquito parasites infecting the blood	Treatment for acute and chronic cases commonly used in China.	Would not treat; would refer to a family doctor.	Treatment is effective. Remedies have also been used in preventive treatment.
MEASLES Infectious disease with skin rash and fever	Treatment very effective if carried out early and frequently (once a day).	Would not treat; would refer to a family doctor.	Treatment speeds recovery and helps with complications and any aftermath.
NOSEBLEED Bleeding from the nostrils	Treatment very effective in chronic cases; would refer to a family doctor if the cause is not obvious.	Would give first aid treatment only.	Treatment is effective.
PALPITATIONS Heart flutter	Treatment is effective in regulating *Qi* of the heart; would refer to a general practitioner if cause is not obvious.	Would not treat; would refer to a family doctor.	Treatment is effective in acute cases resulting from shock or fear. In chronic cases results depend on cause.
PHLEBITIS Inflammation of a vein	Treatment can be effective; care is needed because of the risk of complications.	Would not treat; would refer to a family doctor.	Treatment is effective, but other forms of treatment such as exercise are indicated.
RHEUMATIC FEVER Infection causing serious fever and joint pain	Treatment daily or twice daily has a good effect in reducing the fever.	Would not treat; would refer to a family doctor.	Treatment is effective in acute stage and in repairing damage later.
ROSEOLA INFANTUM Non-infectious rash of infants, following a high fever	Treatment is effective in reducing symptoms.	Would not treat; would refer to a family doctor.	Treatment for relief of discomfort can be successful.
RUBELLA German measles	Treatment effective in shortening course of disease and reducing its severity.	Would not treat; would refer to a family doctor.	Treatment speeds recovery and helps with complications and any aftermath.
SCARLET FEVER Acute contagious disease with fever, rash and sore throat	Would not treat; would refer to a family doctor.	Would not treat; would refer to a family doctor.	Treatment speeds recovery and helps with complications and any aftermath.
SEPTICAEMIA Blood poisoning from septic wound	Treatment can be helpful.	Would not treat; would refer to a family doctor.	Condition may respond excellently to treatment. If response is slow would refer to a family doctor.
THROMBOSIS Blood clot	Treatment can be helpful.	Would not treat; would refer to a family doctor.	Treatment with remedies such as *Arnica* is excellent in acute cases. Would refer to family doctor in chronic cases.

MED. HERBALISM	OSTEOPATHY	GEN. MEDICINE	COMMENTS
Would treat, but would refer to family doctor if condition were severe and unresponsive to treatment.	Naturopathic treatment is effective, unless problem is due to organ failure.	Would treat chronic cases, which are usually the result of overtreatment by antihypertensive agents. Acute cases may be referred to hospital.	See also **Fainting**, pp. 204–205
Would treat, but severe acute cases require urgent medical attention.	Would treat in emergency.	Some elderly patients can be treated at home; others may need hospital care. Best treatment is prevention.	See also **FIRST AID**, pp. 226–231
Would treat, but severe cases would need referral for intervention such as surgery.	Treatment effective if interference to blood flow can be removed.	Treatment with drugs that inhibit intravascular clotting may be helpful. Total condition, as in heart attack or arterial thrombosis, needs hospital care.	See also **Anaemia**, pp. 90–93
Treatment effective in boosting immune system, but would refer to a family doctor for conventional medication.	Would not treat.	Refer to specialist; otherwise supportive treatment for chronic conditions.	See also **CANCER**, p. 225
Would treat, but unlikely to see acute cases.	Would not treat, but naturopathic measures can improve general health.	Treatment usually means hospital referral. Preventive medication indicated for countries where disease is rife.	See also **Homeopathy**, p. 24
Treatment is helpful to improve vitality and reduce severity of illness.	Naturopathic measures enable body to handle this condition without complications.	Recovery spontaneous, but secondary ear and chest infections may develop in young children. Vaccination of children is recommended.	See also **Earache**, pp. 204–205
Would give first aid initially. Treatment effective for a recurrent condition.	Treatment very effective.	Treatment is effective in acute cases. Chronic cases may need simple specialist treatment.	See also **FIRST AID**, pp. 226–231
Treatment can be effective, depending on cause.	Treatment would be as effective as the uncovering and disposing of reasons for the condition.	Treatment is sometimes needed, but the condition is common and usually harmless.	See also **Hypertension**, pp. 94–97
Would treat, depending on the cause, but would refer to a family doctor if necessary.	Treatment can help; would recommend naturopathy.	Physiotherapy, strapping and general advice are usually sufficient. Treatment by analgesics and anti-inflammatory medication can be helpful.	See also **Varicose veins**, pp. 98–101
Treatment could be helpful; would be unlikely to treat in acute phase.	Presentation unlikely; would recommend naturopathy and fasting.	Refer to hospital. Condition is rare but may have serious complications.	See also **Rheumatoid arthritis**, pp. 160–163
Would not treat until cause had been established.	Treatment can help; would recommend naturopathy.	No treatment required.	See also **Fever**, pp. 102–103
Would treat to ease passage of illness.	Treatment can help; would recommend naturopathy.	No treatment required but may cause problems in early pregnancy. All girls should be immunized.	
Would treat in the mild form or if a recurrent problem.	Treatment can help; would recommend naturopathy.	Treatment is by antistreptococcal antibiotics. Occasionally leads to complications.	See also **Fever**, pp. 102–103
Would treat, but would refer to a family doctor if condition were severe.	Treatment would depend on cause; naturopathy can help.	Usually refer to hospital; blood cultures required for accurate diagnosis and treatment.	
Would treat chronic problems associated with condition; unlikely to see acute cases.	Would treat a venous condition, not an arterial one; naturopathy is very helpful.	Usually refer to hospital for coronary condition, and may refer for cerebral condition (stroke) or deep-vein thrombosis.	See also **Heart failure**, pp. 102–103; **Stroke**, pp. 206–207

THE DIGESTIVE AND ENDOCRINE SYSTEMS

The digestive system breaks down food and modifies it so that nutrients can be absorbed by the blood. Waste products are excreted as faeces. The system consists of the alimentary canal, which begins at the mouth and continues through the oesophagus, stomach, small and large intestines and rectum to the anus. Secretions that help digest food are produced by the salivary glands, pancreas, liver, gall bladder and stomach.

The pancreas is also an endocrine gland. The endocrine system consists of the pancreas and the pituitary, thyroid, adrenal and reproductive glands (ovaries and testes). These produce chemicals called hormones, which are secreted directly into the bloodstream. In conjunction with the nervous system, hormones control the internal environment of the body.

WHAT CAN GO WRONG

The most common digestive disorders are related to diet, stress and lifestyle, and include constipation, piles, irritable bowel syndrome and ulcers. The liver is affected by viruses such as hepatitis and can be damaged by cirrhosis, a fibrous degenerative change often caused by excess alcohol consumption. High levels of bile salts in the gall bladder can cause gallstones.

Irritation of the digestive system by substances such as alcohol, aspirin and spicy foods can cause gastritis. Diarrhoea and vomiting may result from viral infections or from toxins produced by food poisoning organisms. Certain parasites can cause dysentery, particularly in the tropics. Cancers of the oesophagus, stomach and large intestine are common.

The body can be affected by over- or under-production of hormones. This can result in damage to glands or disorders such as hyper- and hypothyroidism. Diabetes is caused by the under-production of insulin by the pancreas.

Complementary and alternative medical approaches sometimes view the digestive and endocrine systems and their disorders in different ways. A summary of these views follow.

Acupuncture

In Chinese medicine, the digestive system and metabolism is almost exclusively under the influence of the *Spleen* and *Stomach*. The sources of *Qi* and *Blood* are the *Lung* and the *Spleen*. These derive their "essence" from air, food and drink.

The *Stomach* is responsible for breaking down food so that the *Spleen* can extract and refine the "essence". This can then be transformed into *Qi*. The *Qi* derived from food is combined with the *Qi* refined from air, and together these sustain and maintain all bodily functions. The intestines have a role in further extracting "essence" and fluids and thus making faeces. In terms of treatment, however, their functioning is mainly related to the *Spleen* and *Stomach* channels.

The endocrine system is not recognized by Chinese medicine. Some sources claim that channels known as the "eight extraordinary channels" have a strong influence on the endocrine system. However it is not safe to create parallels between the two systems of medicine unless it is done on the basis of sound clinical observation.

Chiropractic therapy

In general, chiropractic therapy would not aim to treat disorders of the digestive and endocrine systems. However, a chiropractor might be able to relieve any associated back pain, and so help improve the condition.

Homeopathy

The body's metabolism is controlled by the autonomic nervous system and hormones. These create a natural rhythm of digestion and assimilation of nutrients and excretion of waste materials. The primary action of homeopathic remedies is to balance the natural rhythm of the metabolism. Some imbalances are apparent in constipation or diarrhoea, but chronic imbalances may result in such disorders as Crohn's disease or gallstones.

Emotions, such as fear or anger, release hormones that can interfere with the metabolic rhythm. Anger may irritate the liver or gall bladder and produce excessive bile, causing biliousness or colic. Fear can stimulate muscular movement (peristalsis) in the intestines and cause diarrhoea. Prolonged emotional reactions such as anxiety or repressed anger can lead to pathological changes in the metabolism and resultant illness.

Medical herbalism

Ensuring efficient digestive functioning is a central task for medical herbalists. They assess digestive competence in all disorders, and conversely look at the effects of other factors on digestion. Stress, exercise and musculo-skeletal factors often affect the digestive tract.

The main focus of attention in dealing with digestive disorders is a careful review of dietary intake – including foods, liquids, drugs and vitamin supplements. Food allergies and long-term drug intake – particularly of antibiotics – are increasingly common influences on digestive function. Antibiotics are known to kill benevolent intestinal bacteria, and can cause digestive problems.

The complex interaction of the digestive, nervous and endocrine systems provides considerable risks of imbalances developing, which can lead to illness. The elimination of waste matter through regular bowel movements is another aspect that is vital to health. The health hazards resulting from reabsorbed toxins through the bowels make this a priority for herbalists. Also of great concern, and central to much ill-health these days, is the ability of the liver to cope with the increased stresses that are frequently placed on it – rich and processed foods, alcohol, drugs and emotional or environmental pressures. As part of the treatment of a wide variety of disorders, herbalists aim to assist liver function, encouraging its detoxifying and regulating effects.

Osteopathy with naturopathy

The efficient functioning of the digestive system is central to good health. Without the effective absorption of nutrients and the elimination of waste matter from the intestines, many disorders can develop.

If the system is well balanced it can adapt to changes and external influences. For example, a high intake of sugar could disturb the pancreas and lead to diabetes, but this is unlikely if metabolism is healthy. The metabolism initiates a homeostatic process that removes excess sugar from the body through the urine.

Persistent abuse overrides the body's ability to defend itself, and chronic disease can result. Once this stage has been reached, orthodox medical measures may be the only recourse to preserve life.

The naturopathic approach to disorders of the digestive system is to consider the factors that are the cause of problems, and to assess the body's response to bacterial, viral, nutritional, traumatic or emotional influences. The aim is to prevent serious, chronic conditions developing, by improving nutrition, adjusting physical structure and addressing emotional issues.

Chart of disorders

At the end of this section there is a chart listing various disorders of the metabolism and digestive and endocrine systems. This is a general, but not definitive, guide to the treatment of such disorders. Complementary therapies treat the patient as a whole rather than merely the disorder presented. Whether a person can be treated, and the success of treatment, depends on the nature of the condition and the general health of the patient.

CASE STUDY CONSTIPATION

THE PATIENT

JM is tall at 1.9 metres (6 ft 3 in), slim and aged 31 years. He works for an international trading company and often goes abroad for short periods of time. He has been happily married for four years. His eating habits vary according to his circumstances, but he generally eats a light breakfast, snack lunch and large evening meal. He smokes occasionally and drinks socially, but not excessively. He takes less exercise than he would like because of his erratic lifestyle.

THE PROBLEM

The amount of travel involved in JM's work is aggravating chronic constipation (difficulty in defaecation). He finds that his bowel movements can be normal until he travels, and then he is unable to achieve a movement for several days. Constipation has been a problem since his teens, and is often related to stress. He has occasionally used laxatives. His father and sister also suffer from constipation.

The symptoms usually include a bloated abdomen which is painful and hard to the touch in the pelvic area, and sharp pain in the stomach. The pain comes in waves and is better for bending and clutching, or lying down. His tongue is coated with yellow fur and his breath is foul smelling when the condition is severe.

JM is a warm, gentle man who delights in novel experiences and is enthusiastic about all that he does, but is easily discouraged if things go wrong.

JM has been in excellent health all his life, having little more than the occasional cold. He had German measles (rubella) as a child and chickenpox when he was 21 years old. He has a strong stomach, being able to eat almost anything and, apart from amoebic dysentery five years ago, has never been troubled with diarrhoea. He has a very long back and often complains of stiffness, especially of the neck and lower back, and sometimes he experiences pain in the lumbar area.

TREATMENT BY AN ACUPUNCTURIST

Classification of constipation in Chinese medicine can be reduced to two broad categories: constipation caused by retardation or weakness of *Qi* or *Yang*, in which the faeces move too slowly or not at all; and constipation caused by *Dryness* (weak *Yin* or *Blood*) or excess of *Heat*.

In JM's case, constipation appeared to be related to stress and anxiety, with travel as a major contributory factor. This stress had depressed the outward, smooth flow of *Liver Qi*, which in turn had inhibited the downward flow of *Qi* in his *Stomach* and intestines. The faeces had failed to move and he had become constipated. The stagnation had become severe, producing the symptom picture described; if it persisted, then it would turn to *Heat*, producing a yellow coating on the tongue and foul breath. His normally erratic bowel movements, his tendency to be easily discouraged, and his stiffness, all suggested retardation of *Liver Qi* as an underlying disharmony. There was clearly an inherited factor in his predisposition to this problem.

Treatment
In the acute phase the principle would be to move the *Qi*, reduce *Heat* and moisten the intestines. A selection of points from the *Stomach, Spleen, Large Intestine, Kidney, Sanjiao* and *Gall Bladder* channels could be used. Since the acute phases are self-limiting, treatment would hasten a return to normality, while reducing the severity of symptoms. The underlying disharmony of *Liver Qi* would need to be dealt with to reduce JM's susceptibility when under stress. He should be careful to avoid hot, spicy and fried foods, all of which create *Heat* in the *Stomach* and intestines. Regular exercise, along with relaxation exercises and meditation, would help to prevent his *Qi* becoming knotted up during stressful times.

Prognosis and conclusion
Acupuncture could help to limit the degree to which JM was susceptible to constipation, but might not completely eliminate it. This is because there was an inherited factor, and because it would depend on his willingness to undertake remedial measures on his own behalf. Chinese or Western herbal medicine work well with acupuncture in preventing or controlling constipation.

Backache pp. 152–155

Introduction to acupuncture pp. 8–15

TREATMENT BY A
CHIROPRACTOR

Constipation is not a condition normally treated by chiropractic therapy. However, some sufferers with low back problems do become constipated as part of their overall back condition. In JM's case, however, his main problem seemed to be linked with his history of bowel disorders, as indicated by the condition of his tongue and breath. In all likelihood acupuncture, homeopathy or medical herbalism could offer help with his constipation. JM required dietary advice as well as any other treatment he might obtain.

His back was examined to see if any treatment would be advised. All the orthopaedic and neurological tests were normal, but palpation revealed generalized soft-tissue tension throughout the cervical, thoracic and lumbar areas. The examination also revealed joint fixations in the 1st and 2nd lumbar vertebrae on both sides, in the mid-thoracic and lower cervical areas.

Treatment
The treatment would consist of general techniques to loosen up the muscle tension, followed by specific spinal adjustment of lumbar, mid-thoracic and lower cervical vertebrae, as necessary.

Prognosis and conclusion
Within about four treatments his general stiffness would be considerably eased. JM would probably find that he needed to consult the chiropractor regularly every three to six months for a check-up to keep his spine in good condition. Anyone with a long back has a tendency to back trouble, and it is always more important to prevent any severe problems occurring, rather than just to treat the condition as it arises.

TREATMENT BY A
HOMEOPATH

Constipation is a particular problem of our age because of our sedentary lifestyle and the highly processed food we eat. It is most common in people with a sluggish metabolism. There may be other causes too; as in JM's case.

While JM's eating habits did not help his bowels to function, the specific symptoms may be covered by several remedies. The symptoms to be isolated here were bloating of the abdomen in constipation, with hardness to the touch, abdominal pain which was better when bending or lying down and worse when eating, the yellow, furred tongue and foul breath. A relevant symptom was that the constipation was worse when he was away from home.

Usually this might single out *Lycopodium* as a remedy. However, the remedy selected was *Bryonia*, which is usually indicated for constipation caused by dryness. Dryness is the result of an under-functioning or slowness of the metabolism. On the mental level it can be found as "holding back", usually when a person feels insecure.

Bryonia is a remedy used for insecure people whose life revolves around the stable situations of home and work. When well-supported, for example when happily married, they indulge their sensuous nature in other ways (such as experimenting with foods), but are never outrageously adventurous. Their insecurity can be seen in the fact that they are easily discouraged, or when away from home constipation strikes as they "hold back".

The difference between *Lycopodium* and *Bryonia* is a very subtle one and relates to attitude. The *Lycopodium* patient is continually driven and eaten away by insecurity. The *Bryonia* patient is content once a regime is established in which he can live, as in JM's case.

Treatment and prognosis
When JM was safely at home a high potency of *Bryonia* could be administered. This would not be given during the constipation stage because it might aggravate the problem. The aim would be to give JM confidence, so that he could travel freely without a hint of insecurity. If this could be achieved he would stop "holding back" and constipation would cease to be a problem. The *Bryonia* might need repetition, but at infrequent intervals, which might be years apart.

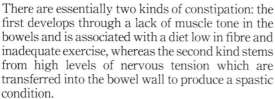

TREATMENT BY A
MEDICAL HERBALIST

There are essentially two kinds of constipation: the first develops through a lack of muscle tone in the bowels and is associated with a diet low in fibre and inadequate exercise, whereas the second kind stems from high levels of nervous tension which are transferred into the bowel wall to produce a spastic condition.

JM's picture was generally of an over-toned bowel. The development of constipation since puberty and a strong link to stress was typical of this problem. Travelling can itself be stressful, and prolonged sitting impairs bowel movements and "locks in" abnormal bowel tone.

Treatment
A key factor for JM would be exercise and posture. His height made it likely that there would be inadequate relief of tension stored in back or abdominal muscles, and stretching and relaxing exercises combined with breathing to exercise the diaphragm could be very valuable in reducing bouts of colicky pains and restoring normal tone.

The herbal prescription would include:
- Chamomile (*Matricaria recutita*): relaxant to the bowels and a mild liver stimulant.
- Fennel (*Foeniculum vulgare*): reduces flatulence and colic symptoms.
- Hops (*Humulus lupulus*): reduces excess bowel spasm and also improves digestion.

Under certain circumstances there might be a useful role for a bulk laxative such as Linseed or Psyllium Seed, which gently provoke bowel movements without increasing muscle tone.

Prognosis and conclusion
Changes in JM's lifestyle, including exercise, relaxation, postural and breathing techniques would be vital for the long-term improvement in his condition, which would be important for his general health. With herbal medication there would be good prospects for such improvement, and not simply short-term relief, which might aggravate the underlying problem.

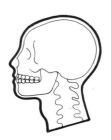

TREATMENT BY AN
OSTEOPATH AND NATUROPATH

While it is not unusual for travelling to upset bowel rhythms, not all travellers suffer from constipation, so there must have been other factors involved in JM's problem. A major clue lay in his tendency to eat almost anything; hardly a virtue where health is concerned. Without discrimination about what is eaten, even the toughest constitution will eventually show a lack of ease, and his diet generally was not geared toward good health. The state of his tongue and breath, the bloated abdomen, and the stomach pain were indicative of either nutritional indiscretion or diseased organs. JM's response to stress was an added burden, as was his lack of exercise and the periodic low back pain.

Physical examination
Examination showed no obvious disease of the organs. JM's spine and pelvis were examined and showed interference with nerve supply, and therefore with the control of some digestive organs. Normal bowel activity depends on effective functioning of the entire digestive system. For example, the main secretion of the liver is bile, and bile is the body's natural laxative.

If the treatment programme was not successful within a few weeks, it might be necessary for JM to have a barium X-ray investigation to eliminate the possibility of intestinal obstruction.

Treatment
The aim of treatment would be to ensure that all related organs functioned effectively. This would involve helping JM to free his mind of anxieties, guiding him in sensible eating and drinking, and adjusting all osteopathic lesions. He would be given specific exercises to encourage peristalsis (movement of bowel contents) and to strengthen his abdominal and back muscles. He should chew his food carefully, because starchy food that is not chewed sufficiently is not easily broken down by the digestive system, and what reaches the large intestine undigested becomes a burden to the elimination process.

Prognosis and conclusion
Constipation that has not been caused by a specific disease does not usually persist after osteopathic and naturopathic treatment.

Introduction to medical herbalism pp. 32–39

Introduction to osteopathy with naturopathy pp. 40–47

TREATMENT BY A
FAMILY DOCTOR

Constipation may be a symptom of various bowel disorders, some of them serious, but it commonly has a functional cause – such as depression, pregnancy, anal discomfort, lack of physical activity or dietary indiscretions.

It would be difficult to prove that JM's degree of constipation was producing the pain and bloating, although many people believe that malaise and headaches are caused by constipation. It was possible that he had an irritable bowel that was responding to the stress of travelling.

Treatment

Assuming that JM's constipation was not caused by a tumour, and was related directly to the functioning of the bowels (medical investigations, if appropriate, could exclude other causes) he could treat himself without much help from a doctor. He should pay attention to what he felt his bowel required and respond to this; for example, he should only attempt movements when he feels that they are necessary, and should not rush off to work on an empty stomach.

Diet would be important and should contain plenty of roughage – extra fruit, vegetables and bran could be added. Purgatives should be avoided because, at worst, they can lead to bowel obsession and laxative addiction. A reasonable fluid intake prevents too much water being removed from the stool by the bowel. Stool softeners can be prescribed which can be very effective. Regular exercise is generally stimulating, and lack of it can be a cause of constipation. JM should develop regular dietary habits. It seemed that once he had broken his normal routine by travelling he was failing to re-establish it on his return.

Prognosis and conclusion

A high fibre diet and faecal softeners might well overcome JM's difficulty in re-establishing normal patterns of defaecation.

Although constipation is blamed for lots of symptoms in otherwise normal, healthy people, whether it is the cause or the effect is debatable. Psychological factors should not be overlooked.

CONSULTANT'S COMMENTS

In a case of constipation starting in early life, provoked by stress and found in a slim, tense individual, a diagnosis of bowel tension is the most likely. The syndrome of "irritable bowel" in which diarrhoea and constipation alternate, is merely a rather more troublesome form of the same condition.

In such cases, stimulating laxatives are counter-productive, even if they work in the short term. Even bran, the form of fibre popularly thought to help cure this problem, should be used with caution since it acts to irritate the bowel. The priority instead must be the relaxation of visceral tone, combined with the use of gentle sources of fibre or bulk laxatives.

The treatments

The medical herbalist, acupuncturist, homeopath, and osteopath and naturopath each recognize in their own way the characteristics of this form of constipation. Their treatments are designed accordingly. As something of a specialist in eliminative matters, the medical herbalist possibly has the immediate advantage in the direct improvement of bowel function, but the others would make progress on background constitutional factors.

Chiropractic and osteopathic manipulation of the spine can often unlock aspects of pelvic tension, and are likely to help JM – with his vulnerable body shape – in particular.

The family doctor, although providing useful suggestions, reflects the conventional medical viewpoint that infrequent bowel movements are not a serious issue. This differs from almost all other medical traditions, and indeed some modern research, that see the potential for toxic problems in sluggish faecal contents.

Conclusions

There should be no difficulty in correcting this problem if it is approached constructively.

Introduction to Western medicine pp. 48–55

DIABETES

THE PATIENT

TG is 23 years old, 1.6 metres (5 ft 5 in) tall, but well built and with a tendency toward overweight. He has spent the past six months in Israel working in a kibbutz. He is outgoing, sociable and very active, playing football and tennis regularly. He completed a business studies course a year ago. He does not smoke, but on average drinks beer heavily three or four nights a week.

THE PROBLEM

While on the kibbutz, TG began to feel tired and listless, lost weight (despite eating a great deal), and developed an abnormally persistent thirst. These symptoms worsened dramatically, and he went to a hospital where he was diagnosed as diabetic.

Diabetes mellitus is a complex condition. It often runs in families, although by no means always so. The condition is caused because the pancreas produces too little of the hormone insulin to break down sugars in the body. As a result, sugars are excreted in the urine. This causes great thirst and loss of weight and can, after some time, result in cataracts in the eyes, or the development of chemicals called ketones in the blood. These, if allowed to accumulate, may lead to physical collapse and even coma. Diabetes is generally treated through diet and insulin injections.

TG was given insulin injections and a controlled diet, which successfully regulated his condition. He finds the regime of insulin injections very restricting, however.

He gets acute sinusitis most winters and tends to develop colds in wet periods of the year. He has been slightly overweight since his late teens because of a fast food diet and high beer consumption while he was studying. His uncle is also diabetic.

TREATMENT BY AN
ACUPUNCTURIST

Diabetes is called "wasting and thirsting" syndrome in Chinese medicine. It is usually classified as upper, lower or middle wasting syndrome. Upper wasting syndrome is characterized by thirst, lower wasting syndrome by profuse urination (polyuria), and middle wasting syndrome by great hunger. They are seen as arising from dysfunction of the *Lung*, the *Kidney*, and the *Stomach* and *Spleen* respectively. Very often all three syndromes are involved.

In this case the disease appeared to be having most effect on the *Lung, Stomach* and *Spleen*. The main symptoms were great thirst, hunger, loss of weight, tiredness and listlessness. TG's susceptibility to colds and sinusitis was evidence of long-standing *Lung* dysfunction. His consumption of beer and fast food (fried, fatty, greasy and sweet) had created *Heat* in the *Stomach* (he had been overweight) and had impaired the *Spleen* function.

Treatment
Diabetes always requires long-term treatment, particularly in cases where it has a hereditary component. Treatment would concentrate on reducing *Heat* and restoring normal function to the *Lung, Stomach* and *Spleen*. The effects of treatment on TG's blood and urine sugar levels would be closely monitored.

In traditional Chinese medicine, as much as in orthodox Western medicine, diet plays an important part in the management of this disease. TG should be particularly careful to avoid sweet, fatty, fried and greasy foods, and also alcohol. Eating regular meals and not overeating are also important. Moderate exercise only would be recommended, because strenuous exercise might deplete the *Qi* and hinder recovery.

Prognosis and conclusion
Patients whose diabetes is being controlled by diet often respond well to acupuncture treatment. In some cases, dependency in insulin may be reduced, but only after prolonged treatment. In cases of early onset diabetes, such as this one, improvement of general health could be achieved with acupuncture treatment, but it would be unlikely to result in diminishing the insulin dependency.

TREATMENT BY A
CHIROPRACTOR

Diabetes is not a condition amenable to chiropractic treatment. TG would be referred to a family doctor. Other alternative methods of treating this condition and its symptoms help with general health.

TREATMENT BY A
HOMEOPATH

As with many chronic illnesses, the symptoms of diabetes must be assessed on an individual basis. Because of this, it is necessary to go behind the diagnosis of diabetes to look at the disease process that led to it in the first instance.

TG's family history was important because it showed an inherited weakness. He was a popular, outgoing young man with a lot of energy, and an enthusiasm for new experiences which took him to a kibbutz. His consumption of beer, which is rich in sugar, was probably responsible for overbalancing his diabetic tendency; this preference for beer rather than sweets was a significant symptom.

Treatment and prognosis
Phosphorus has all these symptoms. People suited to this remedy tend to have erratic energy levels, usually with a lot of vitality and exuberance, but alternating with a sudden lack of energy, resulting in listlessness and apathy. TG's tendency to suffer sinusitis and colds in wet weather, and to feel worse when hot, further substantiated *Phosphorus* as an appropriate remedy.

If TG's diabetes had been controlled by diet alone, it would have been appropriate to use a single dose of *Phosphorus* (1M). This might have further disturbed the sugar imbalance temporarily and would have required careful monitoring until sugar levels settled down to new values.

Because TG was using insulin regularly, treatment would be complicated. This would be especially true if the patient has been insulin-dependent for some time. In a case such as TG's it would be unlikely that he could reduce his dependence on insulin – the goal of treatment would be to improve the general level of health alongside the use of insulin. The blood and urine sugar levels would be monitored closely throughout.

Because *Phosphorus* works constitutionally, other aspects of health would also improve. His energy level should stabilize and there should also be an improvement in his sinusitis. Further repetition of the remedy would be given if there was deterioration of general health. This might help prevent TG's condition remaining untreated until problems occurred at the diabetic level.

Introduction to chiropractic therapy pp. 16–23

Introduction to homeopathy pp. 24–31

TREATMENT BY A
MEDICAL HERBALIST

People who suddenly develop diabetes at quite an early age are likely to have to take insulin for a very long time, if not for the rest of their lives. The effects of any herbal medicine would have to be carefully monitored by testing blood sugar and urine sugar levels.

Apart from diabetes, TG displayed a weakness of his respiratory system – exacerbated by cold, damp conditions – which would need balancing to ensure, in him, a harmonious functioning of all his body systems.

Treatment
TG had already been given dietary advice, but some addition to this would be necessary. It would emphasize the value of wholefoods (grains, pulses, vegetables and fruit) which slow down the rise in levels of the sugar glucose in the bloodstream, and help prevent strain on insulin production. Of vital importance would be his beer consumption, which needs to be very greatly reduced. It would also be important for TG to control caffeine intake, and to eat at regular intervals – especially for a very active person – in order to avoid sugar levels dropping below safe limits.

The herbal prescription would include:
- Goat's Rue (*Galega officinalis*): acts to reduce sugar levels, working directly on the pancreas.
- Burdock (*Arctium lappa*): mild diuretic (increases kidney function and urine output) and general tissue cleanser; it also helps to lower glucose levels.
- Gentian (*Gentiana lutea*): bitter stimulant for both liver and pancreatic activity, improves digestion and regulates insulin production.
- Elderflower (*Sambucus nigra*): diuretic and mild circulatory stimulant, which also helps to relieve sinus congestion and catarrh.

TG would benefit from intake of raw Garlic because this stimulates the immune system by increasing the production of white blood cells. Garlic also helps to remove glucose from the blood, thus reducing blood sugar levels.

Prognosis and conclusion
Improvement and control would take a long time and involve discipline and hard work. With careful monitoring of sugar levels TG's general health and the diabetic condition could improve, but he might never make a complete recovery.

Introduction to medical herbalism pp. 32–39

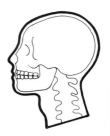

TREATMENT BY AN
OSTEOPATH AND NATUROPATH

Many people have a hereditary hormonal imbalance of some kind. It need not be significant unless the way of life of the individual stresses the body beyond its hormonal ability to maintain homeostasis (equilibrium of the internal environment). Such imbalances can then be the forerunners of various diseases, such as problems of the ovaries and thyroid gland, asthma, and diabetes.

In this case, the pancreas has probably degenerated to a state where it can no longer provide the insulin needed for sugar metabolism. There is therefore no option but to introduce insulin into the body. It is important in most cases of diabetes, however, to consider other aspects of the problem.

There are glands other than the pancreas that may be involved – sometimes the pancreas is the victim rather than the cause of the problem. There are always nutritional factors, and these were evident in TG's case.

There is often a mental and emotional component which in this case was not immediately apparent, but is likely to be present in some form. There is always a structural imbalance to be found, either in the cranium or in the spinal column.

Treatment
Osteopathic investigation is concerned with more than the overt symptoms, distressing though these are. The treatment of TG would try to remedy any imbalances found. It would require a change in his attitude toward his health and a study of his physical and mental constitution.

Prognosis and conclusion
If TG has to rely on injected insulin, attention to his general health would make it easier for him to cope with the disease, and lessen any side-effects of such long-term medication.

Introduction to osteopathy with naturopathy pp. 40–47

TREATMENT BY A
FAMILY DOCTOR

When diabetes starts at an early age, insulin injections will be required for the rest of the patient's life. If the disease arises in later life, it may be managed by diet and tablets alone. The complications of diabetes – such as eye damage and disease of the blood vessels – can be lessened significantly by sensible management.

Treatment
It would be important for TG to understand his condition and to come to terms with it. Diabetics who inject insulin are likely to experience alarming hypoglycaemic attacks, which are caused by too much insulin and therefore too little sugar. They have to learn how to avoid these, and deal with them swiftly when they occur. TG would need to learn to cope with his condition with the help of a diabetologist and a dietitian. He would need regular medical examinations – including ophthalmic examination – and would have to undertake regular tests on his blood and urine to test their sugar levels.

TG would probably use modern "pen" injections with which he could learn to make subtle adjustments to his daily insulin requirements; these would allow him a full and normal life. He would be reassured that he could get fully fit, as demonstrated by several international athletes who are diabetic. Diabetics have managed, with injected insulin, to lead normal lives for more than 50 years.

It would be important that his family doctor knew about his condition and that his records were marked. He should also keep dextrose injections at home and carry dextrose tablets with him in case of low-sugar attacks.

Prognosis and conclusion
Young people quickly learn to adapt to this condition but need skilled advice and counselling. Long-term medical follow-up is necessary and a good relationship with the clinic is very important.

There is often a family history of diabetes, but it would not be necessary for a healthy diabetic to avoid having children.

CONSULTANT'S COMMENTS

This case is clearly an early-onset type of diabetes. That the young man required injected insulin so quickly, suggests that his diabetes arose out of an aggressive disruption of his pancreas. Until insulin was discovered, this form of diabetes was usually fatal.

The treatments
No natural treatment could expect to lead to the restoration of insulin production by the pancreas after such severe damage. Artificial insulin suppresses pancreas activity, and it is difficult to conduct a safe weaning off such a drug. This would become the hardest problem in treatment.

There are, however, other considerations, as some of the practitioners have pointed out. The benefit of diets that slow down the absorption of sugar is now beyond doubt, and it is often possible to fend off reliance on artificial insulin with a strict diet. Evidence of this is supported by the success of dietary treatment of late-onset diabetes, in which there is progressive exhaustion of the pancreas. This often occurs after a lifetime coping with refined carbohydrates such as sugar and white flour.

Naturopathy, herbal medicine, acupuncture, and homeopathy can also be relied on to help with general health. To the extent that such regimes can protect the pancreas from strain, and can support the wider constitution, they would have some application to TG's case. But it is always wise to keep blood sugar levels under observation, in case improvement in health requires an adjustment of the dose of insulin that is injected.

Through constitutional treatment, it might be possible to reduce some of the long-term effects of insulin-dependent diabetes, such as deterioration of sight or the circulation, and disorders of the urinary tract or skin.

Introduction to Western medicine pp. 48–55

GASTRIC ULCER

THE PATIENT

PB is 65 years old. He is a retired painter and decorator with abundant greying hair and a ruddy complexion. He is 1.7 metres (5 ft 8 in) tall, and is well-built. Since retirement, three years ago, he has put on weight due to lack of exercise. He occupies his time with gardening and do-it-yourself projects around the home, and looks after his nervous wife, who rarely leaves the house. He eats regularly, but frequently consumes tinned and frozen foods: he also enjoys fried food.

THE PROBLEM

About six weeks ago, PB began to get pain in his upper abdomen a few hours after eating. He found that he needed to eat frequently, and would wake up in the night feeling hungry and suffering from stomach pains. His wife recently persuaded him to seek advice and his condition was diagnosed as a gastric ulcer.

PB is a quiet, easy-going man. He is pleased to be retired, but distressed by his wife's ill health and anxiety. He frequently visits his two children and his grandchildren who live nearby.

PB was healthy until his early thirties when he developed bronchitis. This condition recurs regularly – especially after head colds – although he stopped smoking ten years ago.

His bronchitis leaves him wheezing and short of breath, and this has contributed to his lack of physical fitness by restricting his activities.

TREATMENT BY AN
ACUPUNCTURIST

In traditional Chinese medicine, gastric ulcer is classified as epigastric pain. It may be the result of a number of different *Ying, Yang* and *Qi* disorders, and is usually related to disorders of the *Stomach, Spleen* and *Liver*.

The *Stomach* receives food and liquids and transforms them into an essence, which is processed and distributed by the *Spleen*, the residue being passed to the intestines for further refinement. The proper function of the *Stomach* is therefore dependent on downward movement, which, if it fails, produces either stagnation of *Qi* leading to pain, or rebellious *Qi* (upward movement) leading to belching, nausea or vomiting. The *Stomach* and *Spleen* are closely related, and the proper functioning of the *Stomach* is partly dependent on the support of the *Spleen*.

In PB's case, the main symptoms all pointed to weakness of the *Stomach* and *Spleen Qi*. The weakness was indicated by the fact that the pain came when the *Stomach* was empty. He appeared to have a long-term condition of weak *Lung Qi*, shown by his shortness of breath and susceptibility to colds and bronchitis. Diseases of the *Lung Qi* often weaken the *Spleen*. The weak pulse and the pale, flabby tongue confirmed generally weak *Qi*, but especially of the *Stomach*.

Treatment
The treatment would concentrate on strengthening the *Stomach* and *Spleen* functions in order to stop the pain and allow a return to normal digestion. The *Lung Qi* would need to be strengthened in order to support the *Spleen*. The *Spleen, Stomach, Lung, Urinary Bladder* and *Ren* channels would be used.

PB would be advised to take regular, gentle, exercise such as walking. He should avoid fried, fatty and spicy foods, as well as raw foods and cold drinks, all of which would put a strain on his digestion and weaken his *Spleen*.

Prognosis and conclusion
Since the ulcer problem began only six weeks ago, positive results would probably be achieved after about ten treatments. The *Lung* disorder, however, might take up to six months to treat. Strengthening the *Qi* would help PB cope better with the anxiety and stress in his emotionally demanding life.

TREATMENT BY A
CHIROPRACTOR

From the case history it was evident that PB was not a suitable case for chiropractic treatment.

Treatment
PB obviously needed dietary advice and help with his anxiety problems. He also needed to take more regular exercise.

Prognosis
The chiropractor would generally refer cases such as this to an acupuncturist, homeopath, medical herbalist, or to the patient's family doctor for treatment and advice.

TREATMENT BY A
HOMEOPATH

PB is seriously ill, with more problems than simply an ulcer. Homeopathic treatment would aim to improve his general level of health in addition to treating the specific condition.

Ulcers often result from poor dietary habits, prolonged periods of stress, or negative emotions such as anger or anxiety. An appropriate remedy would not only improve the physical condition but would also help a patient to cope better with stress.

PB's diet of canned or frozen foods lacks nourishment and contains a lot of fat. To use dietary factors as symptoms it is necessary to ask how much the diet reflects the culture of the community to which he belongs. PB's diet is partly due to his culture, but also to ignorance and a lack of interest in preparing food. His personal preference for fatty food is a significant symptom in selecting the best remedy.

Pain experienced several hours after eating and during the night, combined with the frequent need to eat, are common symptoms of gastric ulcers. Several remedies produce this symptom picture and to select the appropriate one, more specific characteristics must be identified.

PB is fastidious in keeping his garden immaculate and continually improving his home, and has a strong sense of duty in looking after and supporting his wife. He also has a ruddy complexion. *Arsenicum* and *Nux vomica* both have these symptoms. However, *Nux vomica* is often indicated in cases where ulceration is related to the abuse of the digestive system through poor diet.

Treatment
Since this is a serious condition, *Nux vomica* would be prescribed in low potency to improve the physical symptoms. Over time, depending on how PB responded to treatment, the prescription would be repeated in higher potencies.

The pain and discomfort should disappear first, then the remedy would be administered in 30th potency to deal with the deeper emotional factors and aspects such as appetite and desire for fatty foods. His bronchitis and wheezing may respond to the same remedy, but another may be required to alleviate these problems.

A homeopath would also help PB to identify means of reducing the stresses in his life, since they contribute to his ill health.

MEDICAL HERBALIST

PB displayed a pattern of health often found in people with gastric ulcers: a history of smoking, an inadequate diet, and a degree of stress – in this case concern for his wife's health.

Treatment
The legacy of chronic bronchitis left by smoking should be tackled at the same time as the digestive problem. Dietary guidance would be of great importance. He would be advised to avoid fried food and sugar-rich foods such as biscuits, chocolate and canned foods; alcohol should also be severely restricted. Small but regular meals would probably place less of a burden on his digestive system. Further advice would be necessary as he adjusted to these initial changes.

It seems that PB's worries about his wife would be best relieved by treating her problems directly, but PB's stress due to this situation would also be addressed in consultations. The herbal prescription would include:
● Licorice (*Glycyrrhiza glabra*): highly soothing to inflamed gastric membranes, reduces excess acidity and would have a pronounced healing effect on the ulcerated surfaces.
● Marshmallow Root (*Althaea officinalis*): rich in mucilage, gives a soothing effect to the gut wall.
● Golden Seal (*Hydrastis canadensis*): astringent and digestive stimulant. Improves liver function and helps the effects of other remedies.
● Comfrey (*Symphytum officinalis*): strong local healing agent that would stimulate cell proliferation at the site of the ulcer.
● Elecampane (*Inula helenium*): stimulating expectorant that would increase the removal of mucus from the bronchial airways.

The prescription would be reviewed in the light of changes in repiratory and digestive function, and blood pressure would be monitored regularly.

Prognosis and conclusion
PB's pattern of exercise should be improved along with his diet, in order for his weight to reduce and to ensure effective functioning of the heart, lungs and digestion. With effort and advice, considerable benefits to overall health could ensue, along with local healing of the stomach.

OSTEOPATH AND NATUROPATH

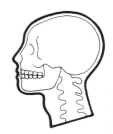

A number of factors could be seen to have contributed to the deterioration that resulted in PB's gastric ulcer. Nutritional abuse is a common predisposing factor. Damage to the lungs from years of smoking reduced the effective movement of the diaphragm with a loss of natural massage of the digestive organs. Emotional stress or shock may have precipitated the disharmony that led to PB's ulceration.

Physical examination
Although PB did not suffer directly from back pain, the spinal nerve supply was certainly involved for one of three reasons: an osteopathic lesion of the spine may have affected the function of the stomach; the stomach may have been the primary problem and affected the spine; or the bronchial problem may have affected a spinal segment which had in turn influenced the digestive system.

Treatment
Osteopathic treatment would reduce spinal lesions and restore suppleness to the spine and rib cage. Visceral osteopathy could influence peristalsis (muscular movement of the contents of digestive tract) and help to ease the pain of the ulcer.

An important aspect of treatment in this case would be naturopathic. PB would be advised to undertake a balanced regime of vegetable nutrition. If pain would allow it, a short (closely supervised) fast would allow the stomach wall lining to start healing without being disturbed. Concentrated proteins which produce acid secretions in the stomach should be avoided for a while and he should forgo fried foods. He should also avoid mucus-forming foods – such as milk, cheese, biscuits and chocolate – in order to ease his wheezing chest.

A programme of gentle exercise would encourage circulation and breathing. Relaxation and, if necessary, psychotherapy might enable PB to cope with his wife's distress more positively.

Prognosis and conclusion
PB would need a total approach to his problems; conditions should be created in which the ulcer in the wall lining could heal, leaving the tissues healthy enough to accept all sensible foods without breaking down again.

TREATMENT BY A
FAMILY DOCTOR

Gastric and duodenal ulcers are both known as peptic ulcers. They seem to be brought about partly by high stress, and they are provoked by irritants such as aspirin and alcohol.

Peptic ulcers can be diagnosed by direct vision using a flexible quartz-fibre light (endoscopy). This simple procedure, carried out by a specialist, is quick and much more reliable than barium meal X-rays. It is important to exclude the possibility of a malignant ulcer (stomach cancer) and a biopsy may be done at the time of an endoscopy.

Treatment
Surgical treatment has been largely superseded by modern drugs – such as Cimetidine – which inhibit the formation of hydrochloric acid in the stomach. They may be taken as a limited course or on a long term basis, and can act as an effective treatment rather than just palliatively. Use of antacids and avoiding provocative agents – such as aspirin, alcohol, coffee, strong tea and tobacco – would certainly give some relief of the symptoms.

PB would not need a specialized diet and should be encouraged to eat normally. He was, however, overweight and suffered from chronic bronchitis. Plumpness and a ruddy complexion were warning signs of a serious deterioration of health.

Prognosis
Accurate diagnosis is extremely important in the case of an ulcer, as is adequate treatment, because the condition carries the risk of life-threatening bleeding developing, and of perforation of the stomach if the condition worsens.

Medical treatment should make PB much better and his ulcer would probably heal. However, it could also happen that his anxiety about his wife and the frustration of looking after her would worsen his ulcer. If possible he should get help from his family or a good neighbour scheme in caring for her. His doctor might know of a local carers' group with whom he could discuss his difficulties.

CONSULTANT'S COMMENTS

Inflammation and ulceration of the stomach or duodenal wall is a complex process, most often involving dietary and stress factors, but by no means limited to them.

The treatments
This individual, as the family doctor and others have pointed out, has warning signs that point to a wider breakdown in health. It is therefore important that, in seeking to relieve the stomach trouble, such broader signs are not masked or neglected. Particular care with prescriptions is noted by both the medical herbalist and the family doctor, and both have, in this case, avoided the dangers of misapplication. Even "holistic" assessment of the problem might miss other signs of deterioration if too much attention was paid to the stomach.

Because the circumstances point ominously to an imminent breakdown in health, all treatment should be prepared for that. Acupuncture, in experienced hands, is probably the therapy that is most sensitive to such developments, and must be recommended for that reason.

As far as symptomatic relief is concerned, dietary advice is difficult to counter. Experience of gastric inflammation suggests that improvements often follow adjustments to the diet that are specific to the individual – although smoking, coffee, tea, spices, aspirin and alcohol are notorious offenders, and avoidance of them is likely to benefit anyone. Such improvements are more likely in gastric than duodenal ulcers, however. Dietary change may have wider benefits as well.

For additional local relief, herbal remedies can have dramatic effects, and can often relieve some of the associated problems at the same time.

Summary
It seems likely that domestic and emotional pressures dominate this patient's life at present, so this could be an appropriate case for treating both husband and wife, as the herbalist suggests. Without relief of these stresses, it may be that all therapies do no more than scratch the surface of the problem.

THE PATIENT

ST is a 50-year-old. He is married with two teenage children and has a successful business with two partners. He is about 1·8 m (6 ft) tall, heavily built and slightly overweight. He eats a rich diet, dislikes exercise, smokes at least 10 cigarettes a day and drinks aperitifs before and wine with meals.

THE PROBLEM

ST suffers from aching and inflamed ankles and big toe joints. The symptoms are relieved by aspirin. In the four months since the condition first developed it has become worse and now causes him discomfort when walking. He dislikes being ill and has put off seeking medical advice.

ST's condition has been diagnosed as gout – an accumulation in the blood of the chemical uric acid, which has not been excreted by the kidneys as it should. A high concentration of uric acid causes inflammation of the joints, such as the ankles and big toes. If neglected, the disorder may cause damage to the kidneys.

ST lives a busy, stressful life, but would not consider any of his activities unusual for a man in his situation. He enjoys entertaining and dining with friends and business associates. He has felt relaxed and satisfied for the last four years since his business stabilized, but the previous ten years saw him coping with the strains of his mother's ill health, bringing up his children and difficulties at work.

ST has had few illnesses – even winter colds – during his life, but he does have a rattling smoker's cough. He suffered from slight high blood pressure when he was 45 years old. This was brought under control in several months by weight reduction and drug treatment.

Although he has few overt symptoms ST does not look healthy. He has broken veins on his cheeks, pale skin and dark rings under his eyes. He moves stiffly and complains of an aching back and neck in the mornings.

TREATMENT BY AN
ACUPUNCTURIST

Gout is not a common condition in China, but in traditional Chinese medicine this type of condition is generally seen as an accumulation of *Damp* and *Heat* in the body. The accumulation of *Damp* is often related to the *Spleen* failing to process and distribute *Fluids* properly. The *Heat* is often related to dietary factors. If untreated at this stage, the *Damp* and *Heat* could build up in the lower *Jiao* (the urinary system as defined by Western medicine).

ST's liking of rich food and alcohol contributed to the accumulation of *Damp* and *Heat* in his system. Smoking cigarettes added further to this. His cough suggested that there was retention of *Phlegm* and *Heat* in his *Lung*, thus impairing the *Lung's* function of circulating *Qi* energy.

ST's build indicated that he was a *Yang* type. His dislike of exercise and his stiffness, along with emotional stress and frustration (which possibly contributed to the *Liver Qi* being depressed), were further inhibiting smooth movement of *Qi*. He was therefore less able to cope with his rich diet, the *Damp* and *Heat* accumulating more easily because the *Qi* could not disperse them.

Treatment
Dispersal of the local stagnation of *Damp* and *Heat* to reduce swelling and pain would be necessary, but the main aim of the treatment would be their dispersal throughout the body. Points on the *Spleen* channel would be used to deal with *Dampness*, while points on the *Large Intestine* and *Liver* channels would be used to reduce *Heat* and improve circulation of the *Qi*.

This treatment would help to prevent a further deterioration in ST's health which, if not checked, could lead to a stroke (*Wind-Stroke* in Chinese medicine) and damage to the *Kidneys*.

Prognosis and conclusion
Treatment in the acute stage of gout would be effective in reducing the pain and inflammation. Progress in dealing with ST's general health would depend on his willingness to make changes to his diet, and to reduce his consumption of alcohol and cigarettes. He should also consider regular exercise as a contribution to his future well-being.

Hypertension pp. 94–97   Obesity pp. 128–131   Backache pp. 152–155   Introduction to acupuncture pp. 8–15

TREATMENT BY A
CHIROPRACTOR

At the initial consultation, particular attention was paid to the origins of the aching and to the inflamed ankle and toe joints. ST had an aching back and neck – usually felt in the mornings – and an examination of the spine assessed any restriction of normal mobility.

Physical examination
ST was asked to stand while the chiropractor moved his back in forward and side flexion, and backward extension. It was evident that his spine was not as flexible as would be expected in a man of his age. The ankle and toe joints were examined, and any heat, inflammation and restriction in the flexibility of these joints was noted.

From the case history and examination it was clear that this was not a simple muscle or joint problem.

Treatment
If the patient wanted to alleviate his stiffness and neck problems, chiropractic treatment would be given. However chiropractic treatment could not be applied specifically to treat the condition of gout.

ST would be advised to take some gentle exercise, improve his diet and alter his eating habits to avoid aggravating the condition and further contributing to his generally poor state of health.

Prognosis
Chiropractic therapy would be unlikely to help ST with the problem of gout, but might be able to improve his general health and stiffness. The chiropractor would refer ST to his general practitioner so that further tests could be carried out and specific treatment for gout given.

TREATMENT BY A
HOMEOPATH

ST is very much an example of modern day life. His basically healthy constitution has been destroyed by the continual harm to his body caused by stress, sedentary lifestyle and rich diet. At first a strong, healthy body will bear up well, but eventually, under continued bombardment, the weakest systems of the body can be disturbed.

A homeopath must identify the factors that perpetuate the condition. Health often improves automatically, even without further treatment, if perpetuating factors are removed. In this case diet and lifestyle are major factors that need to be considered if ST's health is to improve significantly.

There are two other aspects to which a homeopath must pay attention – the acute attack of gout and the predisposing constitutional weakness. Aching and inflamed ankle and big toe joints that are worse from walking are common symptoms of gout and therefore not suitable for the selection of a reliable remedy.

However, the following symptoms provide vital clues for this purpose: the patient's dislike of exercise; his desire for the stimulation of alcohol and tobacco; his dislike of being ill; his love of the good life and entertaining friends; his tenacity and energy to persevere with his business; and his history of high blood pressure.

Treatment
A remedy that has many of these characteristics is *Nux vomica*, and this would be prescribed to strengthen ST's underlying weak constitution. The aim of this treatment would be to improve his general level of health, which would, in turn, deal with the gout and blood pressure problems. In an acute phase of the condition, *Ledum* 30 could be used, because it also fits the patient's symptom picture. If *Ledum* were given without the constitutional remedy, it would probably not have a long-term effect.

A major part of treatment would be to discuss ST's lifestyle and damaging habits. It would also aim to find ways of lessening stressful factors or of enabling the patient to cope better with stress. The long-term management of the case would depend on how effectively this was done.

Introduction to chiropractic therapy pp. 16–23

Introduction to homeopathy pp. 24–31

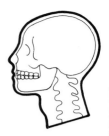

TREATMENT BY A
MEDICAL HERBALIST

ST showed many signs of a chronic neglect of his health. The pattern of long-term stress, imbalanced diet, lack of exercise, and tobacco and alcohol consumption produced the warning signs of an impending breakdown in his system. His appearance, the cough, his lack of mobility and the hypertension were all signs of a sequence of deterioration in health in which gout was just the latest phase (rheumatoid arthritis seems to be likely in the future).

Treatment
The first objective would be to change ST's diet and to severely restrict the foods likely to add to the uric acid burden – such as fatty meat and fish, rich sauces, refined sugars and carbohydrates, and alcohol.

Exercise is obviously a difficult subject, but the benefits and desirability of some form of activity could not be overemphasized. Any exercise should be enjoyable; swimming would be ideal, perhaps going as a family or with friends as an incentive to gradually building up stamina.

The herbal prescription would include:
● Celery Seed (*Apium graveolens*): increases the excretion of uric acid via the kidneys by having an alkalizing effect.
● Willow Bark (*Salix alba*): anti-inflammatory, and acts as a bitter tonic to the digestion.
● Silver Birch (*Betula alba*): diuretic, so increases the kidneys' ability to eliminate toxins; also reduces inflammation.
● Burdock (*Arctium lappa*): general cleanser working through the kidneys and bowels to improve elimination of waste matter from the tissues.

Dosage would need to be gradually built up to prevent over-reaction. The prescription would be reviewed and adjusted as necessary after two weeks. The action of the liver would be likely to need stimulation.

Prognosis and conclusion
ST was clearly in a dangerous downward spiral toward chronic ill-health. Herbal treatment would help him, but any recovery would also depend heavily on his own efforts to reverse this trend.

TREATMENT BY AN
OSTEOPATH AND NATUROPATH

Gout is commonly associated with so-called "rich living", but so are many other conditions, such as high blood pressure and bronchitis. Living bodies protest in a variety of ways when they are abused, and the first approach to ST's case should be to get him to appreciate how his illness arose. Osteopathy/naturopathy is concerned with education as well as with musculo-skeletal adjustment.

Uric acid is a derivative of purines, chemicals which are the end-products of the digestion of proteins. Foods that contain the highest concentrations of purines include offal, fish roe, herrings and sardines. There are moderate amounts in other meat and fish, and in cereals, spinach and asparagus. The presence of fats in the system interferes with the excretion of uric acid.

Treatment
Because gout is associated with the functioning of the kidneys, investigation and osteopathic treatment would be made of the nerve supply from the spine to the kidneys and bladder, and of other organs that work in harmony with the kidneys.

Treatment in this case, however, would be primarily naturopathic. ST would be advised to eat nothing but fresh fruit and salads during an attack, and to make these foods the basis of his diet once he recovers. At the same time, the health of the kidney system should be improved so that it could handle a reasonable amount of uric acid when necessary.

During an acute phase, ST should rest and try to avoid analgesic and other drugs, which only add to the toxic load. In addition, cold compresses would draw out the heat of inflammation. Doses of potassium chloride, iron phosphate and magnesium phosphate (preferably in colloid form) would also help. Sodium phosphate, and silica and calcium fluoride would complete a useful formula of minerals to help ST's metabolism in general.

He would be advised on relaxation techniques, and should avoid pressure on the painful areas. Inflammation is the body's way of dealing with the problem and should be encouraged not suppressed.

Prognosis and conclusion
Naturopathy could help to improve ST's overall health. If he follows advice there should be a great improvement in his condition.

Introduction to medical herbalism pp. 32–39

Introduction to osteopathy with naturopathy pp. 40–47

TREATMENT BY A
FAMILY DOCTOR

Gout is often found in successful middle-aged men and requires a serious medical approach and a reappraisal of lifestyle. Untreated, gout is likely to be progressive. The attacks increase in frequency and severity, and further complications ultimately lead to kidney failure.

Certain factors, such as alcohol excess, over-consumption of protein, stress, fatigue and fluid depletion may provoke attacks in certain individuals.

Gout tends to run in families. Accurate diagnosis is essential to differentiate gout from other arthritic conditions such as rheumatoid arthritis. The clinical picture may be confirmed by blood tests, which will show persistently raised uric acid levels.

Treatment
ST would require medical treatment for acute attacks with standard anti-inflammatory drugs. It is likely that to prevent further arthritis – and ultimately kidney damage – he would require continuous and lifelong treatment with a medication that encourages the kidneys to excrete more uric acid.

ST could make a big difference to his future by greatly reducing his alcohol intake as well as by taking dietary advice from his doctor (although the effect that dietary change has on uric acid levels is small by comparison with drug therapy).

He would be well advised to stop smoking completely, to lose weight and to become physically fit. A suitable exercise would be swimming.

Prognosis and conclusion
Anyone with gout who is also suffering from raised blood pressure is likely to develop kidney and heart disease. Although ST's blood pressure is now under control, this could be a danger. There is also a risk of osteoarthritis.

ST would need a great deal of support from his family doctor and possibly a dietician. His medical management would be complicated, and his doctor might decide to use agents other than diuretics if his blood pressure again increased.

CONSULTANT'S COMMENTS

Gout is an extremely painful condition and is likely to severely disrupt a patient's life and sense of well-being.

The treatments
In this case, as the family doctor and most of the therapists point out, the gout is just part of a dangerous deterioration in health that requires radical corrective measures. This factor and the threat to the kidneys make easy optimism about his prospects a little doubtful.

The concern of the homeopath and acupuncturist to strengthen the predisposing constitution is a sound one, and this approach would be recommended in all therapies. Some firm direction as to diet and alcohol intake is also essential. One untoward effect of gout is that the crippling pain provides a major incentive, for even the most devoted hedonist, to change his or her ways.

The osteopath/naturopath and herbalist correctly point to the high protein, purine-rich foods that encourage more uric acid production in the body. Avoidance of these has been shown to be essential in gout treatment, and the emphasis on a cleansing dietary regime is also likely to be well-founded. Both herbal and naturopathic techniques have a strong reputation in Europe for effective gout treatment and can provide a substantial alternative to the "lifelong treatment with medication" held out by the family doctor – providing that the patient is willing to follow advice and change his lifestyle.

Summary
Whether, in this case, complementary therapies will be able to overcome the damage already done to the patient's constitution is the critical question.

It is important that therapists distinguish between this and other arthritic and rheumatic conditions. Gout requires its own approach, especially since failure to treat it effectively can result in damage to the kidneys.

Introduction to Western medicine pp. 48–55

CASE STUDY HAEMORRHOIDS

THE PATIENT

PL is a 31-year-old single parent, with a six-year-old son. She is thin and has a fair complexion. Her full-time job at a community project involves meeting a lot of people, which she enjoys, but also finds stressful because she is essentially very shy. She takes little exercise, eats erratically, and loses interest in food from time to time, especially when she is depressed.

THE PROBLEM

Since giving birth to her son, PL has suffered from painful haemorrhoids, commonly known as piles – swollen veins on the wall of the anus. These are now a constant problem needing daily treatment with ointments. They bleed frequently and are often sore, and she has been advised by a general medical practitioner that surgery is the only solution.

The condition improves slightly if PL eats a high-fibre diet, but it has never completely disappeared. Her pregnancy was punctuated with morning sickness, cystitis and depression, which resulted from the stresses in her personal life. The labour was prolonged, and the baby needed a forceps delivery.

PL's moods are variable, especially since the birth, and she tends to feel depressed. She is very involved in and enjoys bringing up her child.

Apart from glandular fever when she was 23 years old, PL has had no major illnesses. She often gets colds in winter, but they are rarely severe or prolonged. Her health has deteriorated since her pregnancy with the development of the haemorrhoids, mild asthma and recurring cystitis. Her standing posture is slightly distorted so that she appears to lean backward with her pelvis pushed forward.

TREATMENT BY AN ACUPUNCTURIST

In traditional Chinese medicine haemorrhoids are classified as stagnation of *Blood* due to an accumulation of "turbid" *Qi* around the anus. This accumulation of *Qi* can occur for a variety of reasons: because of the straining involved in constipation or labour; because weak *Qi* sinks, and in extreme cases may cause prolapse of the anus; or because the *Qi* of the *Liver*, and through it the *Qi* of the whole body, is stagnant and not circulating properly.

PL's problems seem to have begun after excessive straining during labour. This caused local stagnation of *Qi*. In addition, she was leading a stressful life, eating irregularly, had a tendency to lose her appetite with attendant weight loss, often suffered from colds in the winter, and had variable moods. All these indicated a weakness of both *Qi* and *Blood*. That her asthma and cystitis also dated from the pregnancy suggested that these, too, were rooted in a weakness of *Kidney Qi*.

Treatment
The local stagnation of *Blood* and *Qi* would be dispersed by using points on the *Du* and *Urinary Bladder* channels. The *Qi* and the *Blood* of the whole body would need to be strengthened, as well as the *Qi* of the *Kidney*. For this, points on the *Lung*, *Stomach*, *Spleen*, *Ren*, *Kidney* and *Urinary Bladder* channels would be used. Treatment would initially be administered once or twice a week, but could be more frequent if the symptoms were severe.

Prognosis and conclusion
Treatment would help the anus to heal, and prevent further inflammation, pain and bleeding. In serious cases, however, acupuncture may only be a palliative, and surgical or other means may be needed to ameliorate the condition. PL clearly needed to think about eating and exercising regularly, both of which would help to prevent any further development of haemorrhoids.

Common cold pp. 68–71 Asthma pp. 60–63 Cystitis pp. 138–141

Introduction to acupuncture pp. 8–15

TREATMENT BY A
CHIROPRACTOR

Although PL had a distorted standing posture her other complaints were such that she would be better served by seeing a practitioner other than a chiropractor.

Once her haemorrhoids had improved, chiropractic treatment might be useful to prevent any progressive postural (and therefore structural) problems later in life.

TREATMENT BY A
HOMEOPATH

In PL's case, there was a clearly identifiable point of change – her pregnancy – after which the deterioration of her health accelerated. This can be thought of as an "exciting cause" that brought on her haemorrhoids, asthma, cystitis, moodiness and depression. The prolonged labour suggested one particular remedy, but there was not enough information on which to base a prescription. Her fair complexion and shyness, combined with such a love of company that she put herself through a great deal of stress, indicated the remedy *Pulsatilla*.

Pulsatilla tends to suit placid people although, unlike PL, they are usually overweight. PL fended for herself well, although she suffered for it. Each of us is subject to individual life experiences that ultimately determine how our character is expressed. So although PL was primarily introverted, she found a role that satisfied her need for the company of others but also created anxiety when she had to communicate with them.

In doing this, PL was going against her natural instincts and, lacking the support she needed, fell into depression and moodiness. She also found relief in her own company, which is rather unusual in the symptom picture for *Pulsatilla*. The emotional problems that she experienced during pregnancy undoubtedly exacerbated the symptoms that *Pulsatilla* mimics.

Treatment and prognosis
Here it was not the haemorrhoids that were significant, but the "exciting cause". *Pulsatilla* is one of the remedies most commonly indicated for haemorrhoids during pregnancy or after childbirth. The aim of treatment would be to remove all the symptoms caused by the pregnancy.

A high potency (1M) would be selected and given in a single dose. The case would be reviewed after a month, and the remedy repeated if necessary. One treatment usually works well, and a lasting improvement in symptoms could be expected.

Introduction to chiropractic therapy pp. 16–23

Introduction to homeopathy pp. 24–31

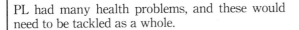

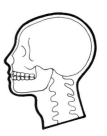

TREATMENT BY A
MEDICAL HERBALIST

PL had many health problems, and these would need to be tackled as a whole.

Treatment
PL should establish a more regular pattern of eating, using nourishing wholefoods which would provide dietary fibre to assist bowel movements. Live, natural yoghurt would restore the digestive bacteria to the gut, which were destroyed by the repeated use of antibiotics in the treatment of cystitis. It would also help to lubricate stool movement.

PL should take some form of exercise, such as swimming. She should also pay attention to posture, the pelvic-spinal relationship being important in her ailments; yoga might be useful.

The herbal prescription would include:
- Dandelion Root (*Taraxacum officinale*): a gentle liver stimulant that improves liver function depressed by stress, glandular fever, dietary imbalance and so on. It is also a digestive tonic and a mild laxative.
- Buchu (*Barosma betulina*): anti-infective for the urinary system, building resistance to recurrent cystitis and healing damaged membranes of the bladder.
- Lobelia (*Lobelia inflata*): relaxes irritable airways that produce asthma attacks and calms such spasms.
- Gentian (*Gentiana lutea*): bitter digestive stimulant which improves liver function.
- Golden Seal (*Hydrastis canadensis*): mild laxative and digestive stimulant which enhances the action of other remedies for the digestive and urinary systems.
- Horse Chestnut (*Aesculus hippocastanum*): tones the swollen vein walls of the haemorrhoids and reduces inflammation.

The herbal prescription would be reviewed fortnightly to begin with. Applications of Horse Chestnut and Witch Hazel (*Hamamelis virginiana*) to the haemorrhoids would also be recommended.

Prognosis and conclusion
PL's whole system would need overhauling and alterations to her lifestyle would be important. Wider health considerations should be tackled alongside measures to ease the haemorrhoids.

Introduction to medical herbalism pp. 32–39

TREATMENT BY AN
OSTEOPATH AND NATUROPATH

Haemorrhoids are a painful condition, but because recovery from a surgical excision can be protracted and uncomfortable they should be treated conservatively at first.

Haemorrhoids react badly to excessive heat, which makes them swell more. If they itch and are scratched, the surrounding tissue can become fibrous and harder to treat.

Haemorrhoids are frequently aggravated by stress, and this should be taken into account.

Physical examination
The cranial and spinal nerve supply to the liver and intestines were investigated, as was blood and lymph circulation related to the bowel.

PL was examined rectally and vaginally to check whether birth trauma had disturbed the positions of the pelvic organs; the uterus and any scar tissues could be putting pressure on the bladder as a factor in cystitis, or be pressing on the lower bowel and hampering venous flow.

Treatment
Any spinal lesions would be osteopathically adjusted, and soft-tissue treatment of the abdomen and lower back would be carried out.

Exercises to lessen the effects of gravity on the area would help – such as raising and lowering the pelvis when in bed to encourage its contents to shift away from the rectum.

She should avoid straining when passing stools, and after each visit to the lavatory she should splash the anus with cold water, which acts as an astringent and makes the veins contract. After dabbing dry she should apply Pilewort ointment.

PL would be advised to undertake a strict diet, preferably vegetarian. She should avoid milk, sugar, denatured grains, fried foods and hot, spicy foods. She would benefit from relaxation techniques and talking about her problems. Counselling might help her gain inner confidence.

Prognosis and conclusion
There would be a good chance of PL's avoiding surgery, and of seeing an improvement in her condition as well as in her general health.

Introduction to osteopathy with naturopathy pp. 40–47

TREATMENT BY A
FAMILY DOCTOR

It is not uncommon for haemorrhoids to affect women after childbirth. There is often a family history of this condition which is, in essence, a dilation of the veins of the lowest part of the rectum.

She had other problems which, although they were not directly related to the haemorrhoids, made them more difficult to cope with.

Treatment
Surgical treatment might be helpful, but major surgical excision is not often necessary. Minor procedures, such as injecting the haemorrhoids or obliterating them with small, tight rubber bands (banding), are much less unpleasant and time consuming, and can be very effective. She would be referred to a specialist if this was required.

Regular meals and exercise would be helpful. PL was aware of this, but for various reasons was not taking advantage of these forms of self help. Haemorrhoids are worse in overweight and sedentary people, but this was not a problem for PL.

Although operative procedures might be of assistance, PL could expect further trouble from a combination of her tension, tendency to depression and erratic diet.

She had experienced a difficult pregnancy, and had suffered since then from problems near the genital area, which probably had an emotional component. She had deep seated psychological difficulties; communication caused her anxiety, she was unhappy and she had eating problems. However, PL was intelligent and enjoyed working with people. She would therefore be likely to benefit from psychotherapy, either individually or in a group.

Prognosis and conclusion
Haemorrhoids can be greatly helped by attention to diet, fitness and lifestyle. They may require operative intervention, but significant surgery is seldom required. PL had a mixed problem, and probably the haemorrhoids themselves were only a minor aspect of this.

CONSULTANT'S COMMENTS

Similar in many ways to varicose veins of the legs, haemorrhoids can often act as an important signpost to wider disturbances affecting the circulation and tone of the organs within the pelvis. Persistent difficulty in emptying the bowels, pelvic fluid retention, recurrent urinary infections, poor low spinal posture, a sedentary lifestyle with insufficient exercise, and smoking are all potentially associated with weakened and expanded veins in the anus.

Pelvic congestion in women, often connected with pregnancy and the premenstrual syndrome, can be particularly damaging because of the weakening effect some hormones have on veins. And both sexes can inherit a tendency to have weak veins.

The treatments
The family doctor, medical herbalist and osteopath each attend to mechanical and other contributory causes. They recognize that exercise and diet are important in controlling the condition, and each looks at the other contributory factors in the pelvic area. Both herbalist and osteopath propose topical measures or specific exercises to tackle the problem superficially.

The homeopath and acupuncturist choose to treat the problem constitutionally. Their approaches are more likely to influence constitutional factors as a result – the weakening of vein walls, hormonal and fluid impact on the tissues concerned, congestive factors, and so on.

Summary
Each approach has merit in treating this condition. The final choice will depend on those features judged most significant in each individual sufferer. Choosing natural therapy in an attempt to avoid surgery is well worth while.

CASE STUDY OBESITY

THE PATIENT

TR is 38 years old, 1.8 metres (6 ft) tall, heavily built and overweight at 115 kg (18 stone). He is a social worker and, since his mother died three years ago, he has lived alone. He takes little exercise, but goes sailing most weekends in the summer. He generally eats "fast foods", and prefers rich meat dishes and hot spicy foods. He eats three meals a day and snacks between meals. He drinks a glass or two of beer most evenings, but more when in company.

THE PROBLEM

Since childhood TR has had a tendency to be overweight, and both his mother and father had weight problems. He rapidly gained weight at puberty and stayed an average 100 kg (16 stone) during his twenties and early thirties. He put on weight again when his mother became ill five years ago. He has tried dieting, but gets disheartened easily. His dislike of exercise is a contributing problem. Having developed high blood pressure recently, and feeling depressed about his personal appearance, he is now more determined than ever to lose weight.

TR is relaxed and easygoing, which combined with his sense of humour makes him popular with colleagues and clients. However, he feels that he is poor at making long-term relationships, especially with women, and therefore feels lonely at times.

As well as obesity, TR suffers from eczema and has allergic reactions to bites, stings and some detergents. He gets frequent colds at the change of seasons, and his sinuses are often affected, being painful, tender and worse for cold air and blowing his nose.

His nose seems to be permanently stuffy, causing him to breathe through his mouth most of the time. The mucus is thin and watery, and more copious in the mornings and early evenings. He has developed back pain in the past four years, located in the lumbar and cervical (neck) areas. His neck is very stiff, especially in the mornings.

TREATMENT BY AN
ACUPUNCTURIST

Obesity is seen as being caused by excessive consumption of sweet, greasy, fried and fatty foods. These foods hinder the function of the *Spleen* in digestion and distribution of *Qi* and *Body Fluids*. As a result, both *Phlegm* and *Dampness* accumulate in the body.

TR was trying to compensate for poor emotional nourishment of his *Heart Shen* by excessive physical nourishment of his *Spleen*. The food was undermining the ability of his *Spleen* to assimilate properly, leading to hunger. Poor emotional expression had depressed his *Liver Qi*.

TR's eczema suggested that his diet, along with the depressed *Liver Qi*, were producing *Heat* in the *Blood*; his allergies were probably an extension of this. His nasal problems suggested that his *Lung* was disordered, resulting from poor nourishment by the *Spleen*. His back pain suggested poor *Qi* circulation due to poor *Liver* function and insufficient exercise; it may also have indicated weak *Kidney Qi*, again because of poor *Spleen* function. High blood pressure indicated that his health was deteriorating.

Treatment
First, ear points would be used to control eating and help calm the *Shen*. Second, the accumulated *Phlegm* and *Damp* (fat and fluid) would be dispersed and eliminated using *Spleen, Stomach, Ren, Urinary Bladder* and *Sanjiao* channels; the *Heart* channel would be used to calm anxiety. Third, the *Spleen, Stomach* and *Lung* channels would be used to strengthen the function of their related organs, while strengthening the *Qi* to reinforce TR's sense of responsibility, confidence and self-esteem; the *Liver Qi* would be balanced to improve the outward flow of *Qi*, encouraging emotional expression. If necessary, the eczema would be treated separately.

Prognosis and conclusion
Acupuncture would help to provide a way of breaking the vicious circle of obsessive eating and low self-esteem. Much would depend on TR's attitude and determination to tackle the problem seriously. His high blood pressure would improve as his *Qi* began to circulate, but this would need to be monitored regularly.

Hypertension pp. 94–97 Eczema pp. 182–185 Backache pp. 152–155.

Introduction to acupuncture pp. 8–15

TREATMENT BY A
CHIROPRACTOR

Obesity itself is not a condition that would normally be treated by a chiropractor. However, as in this case, many obese people do suffer with neck and low back problems brought on by their overweight. Often, the back problem is no more than a muscular or facet strain which, although it is usually very painful at the time, can be easily treated. But until the weight problem is sorted out, recurrences are commonplace.

Examination of TR showed no abnormal findings and his X-rays showed normal wear and tear. Palpation revealed general stiffness of movement in the low back and neck areas, with associated muscular tension locally. The most likely causes of these were his overweight and general lack of exercise.

Treatment
The treatment would consist of soft tissue work to the low back and cervical areas with appropriate specific adjustment as necessary. The aim would be to restore normal movement, as much as was possible, to the low back and neck areas to relieve the general pain and stiffness.

TR would be encouraged to lose weight by working out an acceptable dietary regime, and to establish a regular exercise routine. Walking and swimming would be appropriate forms of exercise to start with.

For treatment of his eczema and sinus problems the chiropractor would refer TR to a homeopath or medical herbalist.

Prognosis and conclusion
Although chiropractic therapy could not directly help TR with his obesity, it would alleviate any consequent spinal problems, and this might encourage him to take more exercise.

TREATMENT BY A
HOMEOPATH

Some obesity is caused by overeating, although other types result from poor functioning of the metabolism. With two obese parents and a problem of overweight since he was young, it seemed likely that TR's problem was metabolic. However, it could equally have been cultural. The weight increase at puberty could support either argument: his weight might have increased then because of hormonal change, or because he was already self-conscious and consoled himself by eating.

The metabolic argument was supported by constitutional features of TR's health. He was easygoing to the point of laziness, and the slowness of his metabolism could be seen in the eczema, with its dry, flaky nature which homeopaths label the "psoric" miasm.

The main remedy indicated was *Calcarea*, also called *Calcium carbonicum*. The symptom picture of this remedy is typically the rosy-cheeked, easygoing, popular fat person, who may also be shy. This remedy would also relate to TR's eczema, his sinus problem at the change of seasons, his high blood pressure and the stiffness in the cervical region which was worse in the morning.

Treatment and prognosis
When a patient has climbed on to the merry-go-round of eating, it is often impossible to come off it. So although TR needed a diet and exercise programme, it might be asking too much of him to follow one. Here the homeopathic remedy would be invaluable in giving him confidence. A single dose of *Calcarea* 1M might alter his metabolism and enable him to stick to a diet.

At first TR would be seen regularly to monitor his blood pressure, but this problem, and his back pains, might be expected to disappear once the weight loss started. Regular consultations would also support TR as he started to lose weight. Although *Calcarea* is a slow-acting remedy, weight loss and changes in confidence should be expected after one or two weeks. As the remedy improved TR's basic general health, his sinus problems would probably disappear, although at first the catarrhal discharge might increase. The eczema might also get worse at first, but after two to four weeks it would improve.

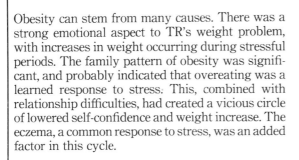

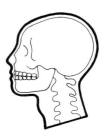

TREATMENT BY A
MEDICAL HERBALIST

Obesity can stem from many causes. There was a strong emotional aspect to TR's weight problem, with increases in weight occurring during stressful periods. The family pattern of obesity was significant, and probably indicated that overeating was a learned response to stress. This, combined with relationship difficulties, had created a vicious circle of lowered self-confidence and weight increase. The eczema, a common response to stress, was an added factor in this cycle.

Treatment
Careful dietary advice would be required, encouraging TR to take a positive interest in food rather than using it as a comforter. In terms of exercise, TR's interest in sailing could be a good starting point, and swimming might be acceptable, although the condition of his skin might discourage him from this. Canoeing and other water sports would be other possibilities. Also, more relaxing and stretching exercises, as in yoga, could be very valuable.

The herbal prescription would include:
- Burdock (*Arctium lappa*): a strong cleanser for the body tissues, which helps to remove toxic waste products.
- Yarrow (*Achillea millefolium*): improves digestion and breakdown of foods, relieves sinus congestion and relaxes blood vessels, which helps to lower blood pressure.
- Fennel (*Foeniculum vulgare*): gently improves liver function and acts as a mild diuretic.
- Dandelion Root (*Taraxacum officinale*): a mild laxative which encourages liver and digestive function and eliminates toxins.

The prescription would be regularly reassessed and altered to suit changes in his health pattern.

Prognosis and conclusion
TR's obesity was deeply entrenched in his personality and lifestyle, and the negative effects on his health were becoming serious. With dietary advice and herbal medicine his overall health could improve greatly, and this would also encourage weight loss.

TREATMENT BY AN
OSTEOPATH
AND NATUROPATH

Encouraging weight loss as a first step in this case could have some advantages, but in the long run it would be better to work toward an improvement in TR's general health, with weight loss as a consequence.

TR should eat sensibly rather than go on diets. Balanced eating would provide adequate but not superfluous nourishment. It would avoid the formation of mucus in his sinuses, and reduce the toxic overload on his system.

Physical examination
This revealed an imbalance of TR's spinal mechanics and, in particular, strain on the abdominal and back muscles caused by the weight he was carrying, and by poor breathing. There was also cranial imbalance, especially of the bones that house his sinuses.

There were no sign of disease in any of the organs that would account for his symptoms, although his circulation, liver and kidneys showed the effects of nutritional abuse.

Increased blood pressure, and the state of his skin, were also reflections of TR's attitudes to his life. Expression of irritation through his skin, heightened blood pressure because of stress, and poor eating habits arising from insecurity, would all need to be taken into account.

Treatment
Although difficult for TR, a short supervised fast would be recommended and would precede all other considerations. During the fast and the subsequent dietary regime of raw fruits, vegetables and salads, the cleansing of his tissues would be aided by neuromuscular massage, lymphatic drainage, breathing and stretching exercises, and relaxation therapy. Finally, attention would be given to spinal and pelvic adjustments, to rib mobilization, and to cranial balancing.

TR would be asked to give his skin a daily friction rub – to nourish its surface layers – and to take a good brisk walk at least once a day, filling his lungs with fresh air.

Prognosis and conclusion
The prospects for improvement are fairly good because TR had decided it was time to do something about his health.

Introduction to medical herbalism pp. 32–39

Introduction to osteopathy with naturopathy pp. 40–47

TREATMENT BY A
FAMILY DOCTOR

Obesity is associated with decreased life expectancy and an increased incidence of many other health problems, in particular diabetes and cardiovascular diseases. It often runs in families and it is difficult to determine the relative importance of heredity and family feeding habits. There are also a number of endocrine conditions that may be associated with increased weight. Food intake and bodily activity are the two factors that normally regulate body weight.

Obesity produces tiredness, shortness of breath, aches and pains leading to osteoarthritis, skin infections, varicose veins and piles (haemorrhoids). TR was developing back problems and was hypersensitive to certain irritants.

Treatment
Dietary control and increasing physical activity would be the primary treatments. There would be little place for appetite-suppressant drugs, and they are often ineffective anyway. Fluid-reducing tablets (diuretics) are inadvisable and dangerous. Obesity is caused by fat not fluid.

Some obese patients are treated by various surgical means, such as bypassing part of the gut. These manoeuvres have not been fully evaluated and do not aim at the underlying cause of the problem.

Dieticians are the main specialists in this field and can help to avert dangerous situations in which patients starve themselves to produce sudden weight loss. There are various organizations and counselling groups that can be supportive for people who are trying to lose weight. It is important to understand that losing weight should be a slow and steady process; weight lost suddenly is often regained. A number of patients may achieve substantial weight loss only after prolonged dieting in hospital.

Psychological help is often valuable and might be considered in TR's case, in spite of his apparent cheerfulness.

Prognosis and conclusion
TR urgently needed to make great changes. Probably a combination of psychological help and dietary advice would be required. Regular exercise would also be essential. If he could make the necessary changes, the outlook would be good.

CONSULTANT'S COMMENTS

The practical difficulties of dealing with long-term overweight are reflected in the cautious comments of most therapists.

There is growing evidence that obesity is as much a problem of metabolic rate as of the amount of food eaten. The rate at which food is "burnt off" determines whether or not someone can eat a lot of food and stay slim. Metabolic rate is the result of a complex interplay of regulatory functions in the body, most notably hormonal. These are determined in part by heredity, in part by feeding patterns in the first years of life, and in part by eating habits and exercise patterns later in life.

TR's best chances of breaking the mould would come with regular exercise, which progressively inceases metabolic rate, not with crash dieting. It is now established that severe dieting lowers the metabolic rate, and tends to increase weight problems in the long term.

Treatments
The practitioners, faced with the difficulty of the case, concentrate on aiming to change these wider influences on the problem. The family doctor would refer to a dietician and psychotherapist. The chiropractor would try to relieve skeletal strain. The medical herbalist would prescribe remedies that might influence aspects of the metabolic processes.

The homeopath and naturopath attempt the broadest regimes of treatment. The latter, as well as the acupuncturist and medical herbalist, sees fluid retention in the tissues as important in TR's case, because it provides a reservoir of toxic materials.

Summary
In spite of the odds stacked against him, TR could lose weight safely. It is possible that he might be helped by one or other of the approaches described here. However, all would finally turn on his willpower to change his body's relationship to food.

TREATMENT OF DIGESTIVE, METABOLIC AND ENDOCRINE DISORDERS 1

CONDITION	ACUPUNCTURE	CHIROPRACTIC	HOMEOPATHY
ACIDOSIS Accumulation of acids in body	Treatment can be helpful.	Would not treat, but would refer to a dietitian for advice.	Treatment may depend on identifying the underlying cause. This is usually a secondary symptom.
APPENDICITIS Inflammation of appendix	Treatment very effective in acute and chronic cases; but there is danger if the appendix is very inflamed. Referral to hospital may be necessary.	Would not treat; urgent medical attention usually required.	Treatment may be effective, but would refer to hospital in case surgery is needed.
BILIARY COLIC Pain caused by an obstructing gallstone	Treatment can be helpful	Would not treat; urgent medical attention usually required.	Treatment effective in acute cases, and as a constitutional measure in chronic cases.
CHOLECYSTITIS Inflammation of gall bladder	Treatment effective in both acute and chronic cases in reducing inflammation and restoring the flow of *Bile*.	Would not treat; urgent medical attention usually required.	Treatment effective in acute cases, and as a constitutional measure in chronic cases.
CIRRHOSIS Degenerative disease of liver	Treatment effective to improve liver function and prevent further deterioration, but depends on the cause.	Would not treat, but would refer to a specialist.	Treatment can raise the overall level of health. Would refer to a family doctor, since hospital treatment may be needed.
COELIAC DISEASE Allergic reaction of small intestine to the protein gluten	Treatment would be constitutional, but reform of diet would be essential until allergic reaction improved.	Would not treat but would refer to dietitian or naturopath.	Treatment for whole constitution to deal with allergic response. Short term dietary changes essential.
COLIC Acute abdominal pain	Treatment can be helpful.	Infantile colic can occasionally be treated.	Treatment is effective.
COLITIS Inflammation of colon	Treatment very effective in both acute and chronic cases, especially in the early stages.	Would treat some cases, but dietary advice is usually required.	Treatment effective, and helps to stabilize chronic conditions.
DIARRHOEA Frequent passage of watery stools	Treatment very effective in both acute and chronic cases.	Would not treat, but would refer to a dietitian for advice.	Treatment is effective.
DIVERTICULITIS Inflammation of part of colon	Treatment has a good effect in restoring and maintaining normal bowel function, depending on history and severity.	Would treat some cases, but dietary advice is usually required.	Treatment effective in acute cases; in chronic cases diet and exercise are also important.
DYSENTERY Bacterial or viral infection of intestines	Treatment effective if condition is bacterial in origin.	Would not treat, but would refer to a family doctor or other practitioner.	Treatment effective in acute cases.
FLATULENCE Excessive gas in stomach and intestines	Treatment can be helpful.	Would not treat, but would refer to a family doctor or other practitioner.	Effectiveness of treatment may depend on cause. Diet and way of life may also need attention.
GALLSTONES Stones in gall bladder	Treatment frequently used in China to expel stones up to 1 cm ($\frac{3}{8}$ in) across.	Would not treat, but would refer to a specialist.	Treatment is effective in correcting the metabolic imbalance, and may also reduce the size of the stones.
GASTRITIS Inflammation of stomach and intestines	Treatment effective in both acute and chronic cases.	Would not treat, but would refer to a family doctor or other practitioner.	Treatment effective in both acute and chronic cases.
GASTROENTERITIS Viral or bacterial infection of intestines	Treatment effective in both acute and chronic cases.	Would not treat, but would refer to a family doctor or other practitioner.	Treatment is effective.

MED. HERBALISM	OSTEOPATHY	GEN. MEDICINE	COMMENTS
Treatment can be effective, depending on nature and degree of condition.	Would not treat if due to renal or diabetic diseases.	Treatment depends on cause.	
Treatment effective for chronic low-grade inflammation. Would refer acute case for medical or surgical help.	Would treat a chronic condition; acute state needs hospitalization in case surgery is necessary.	Would not treat; condition requires surgery.	See also **Peritonitis**, pp. 134–135
Would treat, but acute condition may require hospitalization.	Would give first aid treatment.	Treatment would be analgesic to reduce pain. May require referral to hospital for diagnosis and possible surgery to remove stones.	See also **Gallstones**, pp. 132–133
Treatment is effective, especially in chronic conditions.	Would not treat acute condition except for first aid. Chronic conditions are treatable with naturopathy if not due to large stones.	Treatment may be analgesics and antibiotics. May require hospital referral for accurate diagnosis.	See also **Gallstones**, pp. 132–133
Would treat chronic case, but depending on cause, such as alcoholism, might refer to other agencies as well.	Would not treat.	Treatment is to stop drinking; non-alcoholic causes require diagnosis. The condition is essentially non-reversible.	See also **Alcoholism**, pp. 210–213
Herbal treatment to strengthen constitution would be combined with dietary advice.	Naturopathic treatment can be effective – dietary changes essential.	Dietary advice and referral to nutritionist.	See also **Allergy**, pp. 86–89
Treatment is effective.	Success of treatment depends on the organ or vessel involved and the reason for spasm.	Treatment may be analgesics for renal and biliary conditions; intestinal condition is usually benign.	See also **Constipation**, pp. 108–111
Treatment effective, often where other treatments have failed.	Treatment, including naturopathy, effective if there are no organic changes.	Condition is often benign and associated with stress. May refer to specialist for accurate diagnosis. (Ulcerative condition may need surgery.)	See also **Constipation**, pp. 108–111
Treatment is effective, but extreme cases may need orthodox treatment.	Treatment, including naturopathy, usually effective to deal with the causes, not the symptoms.	Treatment is usually increased intake of liquids; drugs may help. Babies may become dehydrated.	See also **Gastroenteritis**, pp. 132–133
Treatment can be very helpful. Counselling may also be highly desirable, as for many digestive disturbances.	Would treat the chronic condition; would recommend improving the nutritional state.	Treatment is usually dietary advice, perhaps with antibiotics.	See also **Constipation**, pp. 108–111; **CANCER**, p. 225
Might treat, but may need to refer to a family doctor or hospital for rehydration and medication.	Would not treat amoebic dysentery; would treat other types.	Treatment is replacement of fluid loss, if necessary intravenously, plus antibiotics if appropriate.	See also **Diarrhoea**, pp. 132–133
Treatment is very effective.	Treatment can help, especially with the aid of naturopathy.	Treatment is general advice on diet and avoidance of stress. May be associated with other gastro-intestinal upsets.	See also **Constipation**, pp. 108–111
Would treat, but acute condition may require hospitalization.	Would not treat.	Often associated with cholecystitis or infections. Frequently harmless. Surgery may be necessary.	See also **Biliary colic**, pp. 132–133
Treatment effective, but depends on the cause.	Treatment can help, especially with the aid of naturopathy.	Treatment includes dietary advice, reduction of smoking, alcohol and stress, taking antacids such as milk and soda water, plus medication.	See also **Gastric ulcer**, pp. 116–119
Would treat, but severe acute symptoms might need orthodox treatment.	Treatment can help, especially with the aid of naturopathy.	Treatment is similar to that for diarrhoea and dysentery, particularly replacing fluid loss.	See also **Diarrhoea**, pp. 132–133

CONDITION	ACUPUNCTURE	CHIROPRACTIC	HOMEOPATHY
GOITRE Enlargement of thyroid gland	Treatment can be helpful, depending on the nature and history of the condition.	Would not treat, but would refer to a family doctor or other practitioner.	Treatment effective, but length may depend on previous treatment.
HEARTBURN Acid rising from stomach causing burning sensation	Treatment effective in both acute and chronic cases.	Would not treat, but would refer to a family doctor or other practitioner.	Treatment effective, but diet, way of life and any constitutional weakness also require attention.
HEPATITIS Inflammation of liver	Treatment effective in reducing inflammation and restoring normal function in both acute and chronic cases.	Would not treat, but would refer to a family doctor or other practitioner.	Treatment can be effective, but because of problems of infection would refer to a family doctor.
HYPERTHYROIDISM Excess secretion from thyroid gland	Treatment can be effective.	Would not treat, but would refer to a family doctor or other practitioner.	Effective treatment depends on the cause, and this will need specialist diagnosis.
HYPOTHYROIDISM (MYXOEDEMA) Deficiency of thyroid secretions	Treatment can be effective.	Would not treat, but would refer to a family doctor or other practitioner.	Effective treatment depends on the cause, and this will need specialist diagnosis.
INDIGESTION Incomplete digestion causing belching and abdominal pain	Treatment effective in acute and chronic conditions.	Dietary advice may help condition. If there is a structural problem, manipulation may help.	Treatment very effective in acute and chronic conditions.
IRRITABLE BOWEL SYNDROME Intermittent or continuous painless diarrhoea.	Treatment effective.	Dietary advice is required; would refer to a family doctor or other practitioner.	Treatment is frequently effective.
JAUNDICE Yellowness of skin and eyes due to excess bile in blood	Treatment can be effective.	Would not treat, but would refer to a family doctor or other practitioner.	Effective treatment depends on the cause. This is often a secondary symptom.
NAUSEA Desire to vomit	Treatment effective in both acute and chronic cases.	Would not treat, but would refer to a family doctor or other practitioner.	Treatment is effective, but this condition is a secondary symptom and must be treated holistically.
PANCREATITIS Inflammation of pancreas	Treatment can be effective, depending on the severity of the condition.	Would not treat, but would refer to a family doctor or other practitioner.	Treatment effective in the acute stage, but underlying condition also needs treatment.
PERITONITIS Inflammation of membrane of abdominal cavity	Treatment not recommended, but can be effective in expert hands.	Would not treat, but would refer to hospital.	Treatment effective in the acute stage, but would automatically refer to hospital in case surgery is needed.
STOMACH ACHE Pain in stomach	Treatment effective in both acute and chronic cases.	Would not treat, but would refer to another practitioner.	Treatment effective in both acute and chronic cases.
THYROIDITIS Inflammation of thyroid gland	Treatment can be effective.	Would not treat, but would refer to a family doctor or other practitioner.	Treatment effective in acute stages.
VOMITING Forceful emission of all or part of stomach contents	Treatment is effective in both acute and chronic cases.	Would give first aid treatment only; would refer to another practitioner.	Treatment effective in both acute and chronic cases, and in dealing with underlying causes.
WORMS Parasitic infestation of intestines	Would not treat; would refer to a family doctor.	Would not treat, but would refer to a family doctor.	Treatment effective in the long term because it corrects the environment of the intestines.

MED. HERBALISM	OSTEOPATHY	GEN. MEDICINE	COMMENTS
Would treat, but patient is likely to be undergoing orthodox medication and surgery.	Would not treat.	Treatment is often possible. Would refer to specialist for diagnosis.	See also **Hyperthyroidism**, pp. 134–135
Treatment is effective.	Treatment can help, especially with the aid of naturopathy.	Treatment as for gastritis. Diagnosis is important to avoid confusion with angina.	See also **Constipation**, pp. 108–111; **Gastritis**, pp. 132–133
Would treat, but would refer to family doctor for tests to determine type of problem.	Treatment can help, especially with the aid of naturopathy.	Treatment is supportive, avoiding alcohol. Severe cases require hospital care.	See also **Gastric ulcer**, pp. 116–117
Treatment can be very helpful.	Condition needs symptomatic care, nutrition and nursing.	Treatment is by suppressive medication. Some cases require surgery. Long term follow-up with blood tests will be needed.	See also **Alcoholism**, pp. 210–213
Treatment can be very helpful.	Condition needs symptomatic care, nutrition and nursing.	Easily treated with thyroxine (replacement hormone), plus regular monitoring with blood tests.	See also **Goitre**, pp. 134–135
Treatment usually effective.	Naturopathic treatment usually effective. If spinal lesions are apparent, adjustments will be made.	Treatment with antacids is generally effective.	
Treatment as effective as any other, but cannot help everyone.	Treatment is very effective when combined with naturopathy.	Treatment is by diet plus advice to reduce stress. Antispasmodics may be helpful.	See also **Gastric ulcer**, pp. 116–117
Would treat the cause, not the jaundice itself.	Treatment depends on causes; bile duct obstruction may need surgery.	Treatment as for hepatitis. Accurate diagnosis is essential.	See also **Constipation**, pp. 108–111; **Hepatitis**, pp. 134–135
Treatment can be helpful.	Effective treatment depends on finding causes.	Treatment by drugs can be helpful depending on cause.	See also **Hepatitis**, pp. 134–135
Would probably treat chronic condition.	Treatment would be subject to investigation; would recommend naturopathy and fasting.	Would refer acute cases to hospital. Chronic cases may receive supportive treatment at home.	See also **FIRST AID**, pp. 226–231
Unlikely to see or treat.	Would not treat; patient must be hospitalized.	Would refer urgently to hospital.	See also **Diabetes**, pp. 112–115
Treatment often highly effective, but depends on the cause.	Would treat, especially if the cause is dietetic.	Would treat following diagnosis.	See also **Constipation**, pp. 108–111
Would treat the whole person.	Would recommend naturopathic treatment if dietetic.	Treatment is with beta-blockers in acute cases. Would refer for diagnostic blood tests.	See also **Goitre**, pp. 134–135
Treatment can be helpful, but severe acute condition may require orthodox treatment.	Treatment depends on cause.	Treatment is for fluid loss and electrolyte imbalance.	See also **FIRST AID**, pp. 226–231
Treatment effective, but needs care.	Some can be expelled by fasting. Would refer to family doctor.	Treatment effective with drugs once the worms have been identified.	See also **Diarrhoea**, pp. 132–133

THE REPRODUCTIVE AND URINARY SYSTEMS

Reproduction is a complex process controlled by a delicate balance of hormones. The female reproductive system consists of two ovaries, which produce female hormones and ova (eggs), and their Fallopian tubes which lead into the uterus (womb). The cervix is the entrance to the uterus and is situated at the inner end of the vagina. The female hormones control the menstrual cycle, which has a rhythm of approximately 28 days.

The male reproductive organs, the penis and testes, are external. The testes are the male equivalents of the ovaries, secreting male hormones and producing sperm.

The urinary system is connected to the reproductive system by its close proximity in the lower abdomen. In men the urinary passage (urethra) passes through the penis. In women the urethra runs alongside the vagina and emerges above the vaginal entrance. Infections of one system can easily spread to the other, particularly in women.

The urinary system is one of the excretory systems of the body. It is made up of the kidneys, which produce urine, the ureters which transport urine to the bladder, the bladder where urine collects, and the urethra through which urine is discharged from the body.

WHAT CAN GO WRONG

The urinary system can be infected by bacteria causing pyelitis (inflammation of the kidney) or cystitis (inflammation of the bladder). Urinary infections are more common in women. Stones of minerals present in the urine can become deposited in the urinary system, causing intense pain and sometimes kidney damage. The kidney is a delicate organ and may be damaged by vascular changes associated with hypertension or caused by the formation of crystals that occurs in gout.

Women may suffer from functional disorders of the reproductive system, such as period pains and heavy menstrual bleeding. Problems may also occur as a result of pregnancy. Both men and women may be subfertile or infertile for various reasons. The ovaries, womb and cervix in women, and the testes and prostate gland in men, are susceptible to cancer.

Complementary and alternative medical approaches sometimes view the reproductive and urinary systems and other disorders in different ways. A summary of these views follows.

Acupuncture

In traditional Chinese medicine the reproductive and urinary systems are under the influence of the *Kidney*. The *Kidney* is said to store *Jing*. *Jing* controls growth and development, including the development of the reproductive system and the healthy production of sperm and eggs. Reproductive dysfunction may be the result of weak *Kidney Qi*, but can equally be caused by poor *Qi* circulation to the genital area, and involve channels that pass through it. The uterus is an important organ with its own pathology. It is closely linked with the function of the *Heart*, *Liver* and *Spleen*, and with the condition of the *Blood*.

Urinary diseases are caused by improper functioning of the *Urinary Bladder* and the *Kidney*. Deficient *Yang* of the *Kidney*, for example, may produce either excessive or deficient urination.

Chiropractic therapy

Back problems are often associated with pregnancy, since the weight of the growing foetus puts additional strain on the spine. Women suffering from back problems should, if possible, seek treatment before getting pregnant, but therapy during pregnancy can also be helpful. Very often, further treatment is necessary after the baby has been born.

Gynaecological, bladder, kidney and prostate problems are often accompanied by back pain. The conditions generally require specialist help, and the back problem often clears up as the disorder improves. However, muscle spasm in the lower back may result from such disorders, and would benefit from chiropractic therapy.

Heavy periods and period pains often improve if lower back problems are treated.

Homeopathy

Disorders of the kidneys reflect the disease process of the whole body, their rhythm and discharge changing according to the health of the individual. The reproductive system is regulated by hormones, and many female disorders relate to the cycles or rhythms governed by hormonal changes. Homeopathic treatment can be helpful in restoring rhythmic balance.

Medical herbalism

Recurrent urinary infections are seen as both causes and consequences of lowered vitality, since this reduces immunity to infection. Disorders of the reproductive system can also affect the health in many ways, and the hormone imbalance may be caused in part by factors such as poor diet, stress and impaired circulation.

Herbal medicines are very effective in supporting hormone production and can act locally on the affected tissues or organs. At every stage of the female reproductive cycle, from puberty to menopause, and in pregnancy, much can be done to encourage normal activity. Infections of the genito-urinary tract may, in acute circumstances, require orthodox medication. Herbal medicine, however, has much to offer in both the short- and long-term approaches to such problems. Male disorders such as prostate conditions are also effectively helped by herbal treatment.

Osteopathy with naturopathy

The reproductive and urinary systems can develop disorders as a result of hormonal imbalance, structural lesions, inadequate nourishment or emotional trauma. Osteopathic lesions of the pelvis and low back invariably lead to disorders of this region, because the nerves controlling the activity of the pelvic organs emerge from the lower lumbar and sacral areas.

Restoring spinal harmony is of value in pregnancy if there is discomfort or backache. Deliveries are also easier if low back problems are dealt with in advance.

Hormonal influences on the reproductive system start in the head – the location of the hypothalamus and pituitary glands. Cranial osteopathy aims to maintain the integrity of the bones of the skull and the membranes that line it, so that pituitary function is unrestricted.

Chart of disorders

At the end of this section there is a chart listing various disorders of the reproductive and urinary systems. This is a general, but not definitive, guide to the treatment of such disorders. Complementary and alternative therapies treat the patient as a whole rather than merely the disorder presented. Whether a person can be treated, and the success of treatment, depends on the nature of the condition and the general health of the patient.

CYSTITIS

THE PATIENT

FL is 24 years old, tall and slim. She works as a secretary in a lawyer's office and is planning to get married in 6 months' time. Most evenings and weekends are devoted to a busy social life. She plays tennis and squash regularly and swims during the summer. She does not smoke, and drinks wine and spirits in moderation. She is weight-conscious, and avoids sweet and fatty foods; her preference is for spicy dishes.

THE PROBLEM

For the past two years FL has had recurrent cystitis – inflammation of the urethra, the passage leading from the bladder to the outside of the body. The problem arises approximately every 2 or 3 months, and is usually treated with antibiotics. It sometimes develops after sexual intercourse, but in many cases there is no obvious causal factor.

The symptoms include painful and frequent urination and an inability to pass sufficient urine, resulting in a sensation of urine retention. If the symptoms are not treated within 2 or 3 days, blood appears in the urine and her kidneys begin to ache. She has used potassium citrate and large quantities of fluid to flush out the infection, but these measures have not been completely successful.

FL is vivacious and easy-going, and enjoys her active life and work. She is both excited and nervous about her marriage, but feels emotionally satisfied and looks forward to the stability of a long-term relationship.

FL was a healthy child despite having all the usual childhood illnesses. At the age of 14 she developed recurrent tonsillitis and had her tonsils removed. She has an oily skin with a tendency to spots. Her periods are regular but heavy; bleeding lasts for 5 days and she has mild period pains in the early stages. Apart from sore throats and colds during the winter she is fit.

TREATMENT BY AN
ACUPUNCTURIST

In traditional Chinese medicine cystitis is primarily a disease of the *Urinary Bladder*. The function of the *Urinary Bladder* is to store and excrete urine, so dysfunction leads to either excessive urination or retention of urine.

The most usual direct cause of cystitis is *Damp* and *Heat* accumulating and obstructing the *Qi* of the *Urinary Bladder*, thus leading to pain and dysfunction. Weak *Qi* may also cause dysfunction. Since the *Kidney* is a paired organ of the *Bladder*, it is often also involved in cystitis.

FL's symptoms were typical of *Damp* and *Heat* affecting the *Bladder*. If such a condition remains untreated, the *Heat* becomes excessive and damages the *Blood* vessels, causing blood to appear in the urine. The *Kidney Qi*, which assists the *Bladder* in its function, also becomes obstructed, causing pain in the *Kidney* area.

FL's oily skin and tendency to spots possibly indicated a systemic condition of *Damp* and *Heat* in the *Blood*, which was contributing to her condition. In addition, she expressed a liking for spicy foods, and these produce *Heat* in the body. It was possible that the heavy bleeding during menstruation was due to *Heat* in the *Blood*.

Treatment
Initially the treatment would be aimed at eliminating *Damp* and *Heat*, stopping the pain and re-establishing normal *Bladder* function by promoting the circulation of *Qi*. Points on the *Ren*, *Stomach*, *Spleen*, *Liver* and *Urinary Bladder* channels would be used. If there was *Damp* or *Heat* affecting the *Blood*, this would be dealt with by using points on the *Large Intestine*, *Spleen* and *Urinary Bladder* channels.

Prognosis and conclusion
Acupuncture can be very effective in treating cystitis, and speedy relief can be achieved during an attack. An initial course of five to ten treatments should improve the condition significantly, although treatment for the constitutional aspects of the problem might need to be more prolonged. FL would need to adjust her diet if this was found to be contributing to the problem.

Common cold pp. 68–71 Dysmenorrhoea pp. 142–145   Introduction to acupuncture pp. 8–15

TREATMENT BY A
CHIROPRACTOR

It was evident from the case history that FL was not a suitable case for chiropractic treatment.

Prognosis and conclusion
Since there was no evidence of a kidney or bladder problem – for example, stones blocking the ureter – FL could be effectively treated by an acupuncturist, homeopath or medical herbalist. If the problem had been more serious than simple recurrent cystitis, she would be referred to her family doctor for further investigation.

Recurrent use of antibiotics would be unlikely to help the problem in the long term. FL would benefit from advice on the likely causes for her cystitis, on how to prevent her attacks and on how to reduce the effects of the attacks if they occurred.

TREATMENT BY A
HOMEOPATH

Cystitis is essentially an acute problem. In FL's case there are few distinguishing symptoms. In cystitis, it is common for a woman to feel a frequent urge to urinate as well as pain on urination, followed by a sensation of not having emptied the bladder; there may also be blood in the urine. Cystitis also frequently occurs or becomes worse after sexual intercourse.

There was, therefore, nothing in FL's physical symptoms that allowed for an individualized remedy to be selected. However, her preference for spicy dishes and for highly seasoned foods was a help in diagnosis. Dietary preference ranks as a "General" in the homeopathic hierarchy of symptoms. *Phosphorus, Nux vomica, Sepia* and *Sulphur* were possible choices of remedy because they cover both the cystitis symptoms and the preference for spicy food.

Treatment and prognosis
Cure would be established most quickly by selecting a remedy of an optimum strength that would create enough of a reaction in the body's healing process, but no more. *Nux vomica* would be suitable as a treatment for this busy woman who enjoys her work and socializing and is out-going and dynamic.

The remedy would be given in a 6th or 30th potency when an attack occurred, the potency depending on the latter's intensity. The faster the symptoms developed, the more likely that the 30th potency would be chosen. The symptoms should disappear quickly if the correct potency is given.

If too high a potency were selected, the symptoms might get worse before a cure sets in. One that is too low might not give enough stimulation to the body's healing mechanism, in which case the dose would have to be repeated.

Once FL's cystitis had cleared up, other treatment might be necessary to deal with the constitutional problems – producing a tendency toward colds, sore throats and heavy periods. As a result, she would become generally healthier and less susceptible to illness.

Introduction to chiropractic therapy pp. 16–23

Introduction to homeopathy pp. 24–31

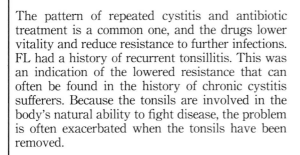

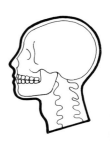

TREATMENT BY A
MEDICAL HERBALIST

The pattern of repeated cystitis and antibiotic treatment is a common one, and the drugs lower vitality and reduce resistance to further infections. FL had a history of recurrent tonsillitis. This was an indication of the lowered resistance that can often be found in the history of chronic cystitis sufferers. Because the tonsils are involved in the body's natural ability to fight disease, the problem is often exacerbated when the tonsils have been removed.

Treatment
FL had already adopted first aid measures – such as increasing fluid intake. These could be extended to include taking salt water after intercourse and the use of local warmth, such as a hot water bottle, to ease the discomfort of acute cystitis. Dietary measures would include increasing the consumption of fruit, drinking herb teas – such as chamomile – to ease inflammation in the bladder, and avoiding alcohol and highly spiced foods.

The herbal prescription would include:
- Couch Grass (*Agropyron repens*): strongly diuretic (acts to increase water output from the kidneys), with an anti-inflammatory, healing effect on the lining of the bladder.
- Buchu (*Barosma betulina*): diuretic and urinary antiseptic; would be taken after the acute phase had passed to restore damaged mucosa.
- Kara-Kara (*Piper methysticum*): anti-inflammatory agent; also stimulates the circulation and acts as a diuretic.
- Echinacea (*Echinacea angustifolia*): improves resistance to infections and stimulates circulation; aids recovery from inflammation and infection.

The prescription would be reviewed regularly to assess progress. Treatment would also be aimed at any more widely spread inflammation and low-grade infection. The possibility of pelvic inflammation should be considered and treated if necessary – Echinacea would probably be of great value here.

Prognosis and conclusion
After some time, if she follows advice and avoids causative factors, FL's ability to resist urinary infections could be markedly improved. There would also be short-term easing of the acute phases.

TREATMENT BY AN
OSTEOPATH AND NATUROPATH

Inflammation of the bladder can be caused by exposure to chill winds, mechanical pressure, external or internal infection, and irritating foods. It can also involve the health of the kidneys. The indiscriminate use of antibiotics can be counter-productive, often leading to a recurrence of cystitis-like symptoms. FL's tonsillitis and spotty skin could have been due to a toxic overload which was possibly still the root of her problems. Circumstances preceding FL's first bout of cystitis should be investigated, so that the cause, rather than merely the symptoms, could be dealt with.

Physical examination
The spine was examined, especially at the emergence of the nerves feeding the kidneys and bladder. It was necessary to check the inside of the pelvis, by way of the vagina, to find out whether anything was pressing on the bladder. Many cases of recurrent cystitis are resolved when pressure is taken off the bladder.

Treatment
FL's spine would be osteopathically mobilized. Deeper breathing would be encouraged and appropriate hot or cold abdominal compresses chosen. The aim would be to improve total body health, not just the acute symptoms.

A detailed analysis of FL's diet would be carried out. An alkali-forming diet, consisting only of fresh, ripe fruits and salads, would be essential during an attack. For some days after the symptoms eased it would be advisable for FL to avoid consuming concentrated proteins (meat, cheese and eggs) and starches, unripe fruit, curries, alcohol and coffee.

It would be helpful for FL to empty her bladder before and after sexual intercourse, and to avoid chills; if cold she should have a warm bath. Drinking large amounts of water would not necessarily help, because many processes take place before that water reaches the bladder.

Prognosis and conclusion
With help from her osteopath, and the many possible self-help opportunities, FL should see a great improvement in both her symptoms and her general health. She should avoid using drugs.

Introduction to medical herbalism pp. 32–39

Introduction to osteopathy with naturopathy pp. 40–47

TREATMENT BY A
FAMILY DOCTOR

Cystitis is much more common in women than in men because of the shortness of the urethra, the tube linking the bladder and the outside of the body, and is usually caused by a urinary infection. This type of cystitis can be diagnosed by a test on a urine specimen, but inflammation of the urethra, through damage during sexual activity or by infection, can produce symptoms very similar to cystitis. Thrush (a fungal infection) and allergy to spermicidal jelly, soaps or detergents may also produce a confusingly similar irritation.

Treatment
Prolonged, untreated cystitis can be serious, and may lead to kidney infection. A true urinary infection should be treated with antibiotics, and a follow-up test is a good idea.

FL could get advice either from her doctor or from self-help books on cystitis. She was right to drink plenty of water, which keeps the urine dilute and thus makes urination less painful; potassium citrate can also be helpful.

It would be especially useful for FL to drink and to empty her bladder after sexual intercourse. Her doctor might suggest taking a single dose of an antibiotic at these times. If her sex life were being affected, a lubricant could be used to limit any damage to the urethra.

If she were using a contraceptive cap or a spermicide this might cause some irritation, so it might be a good idea for her to use an oral contraceptive; this would also help her with her heavy periods. Sometimes cystitis arises from, or is caused by, sexual difficulties, and in this case it might help for a patient to go to a family planning doctor who has experience of counselling.

Prognosis and conclusion
FL should be able to reduce her attacks. Cystitis may sometimes have simple causes, but there can be serious reasons for the condition, and proven infections should be treated with antibiotics.

If normal measures and self help did not reduce the incidence of attacks, further investigation of her condition would be necessary. This would eliminate the possibility of any urinary tract abnormality that might be causing her infections.

CONSULTANT'S COMMENTS

Provided that this is in fact a "simple" urinary infection, then it would be quite accessible to treatment by natural therapies. There are herbs, for example, that have a dramatic and often long-term effect on acute or recurrent cystitis attacks, and the Chinese have always considered such conditions to be relatively easy to treat with acupuncture.

Possible complications arise in other areas. It is necessary to find out whether the infection is confined to the urinary system and what sort of infection it is, and to exclude kidney or vaginal infections and even venereal diseases, such as NSU (non-specific urethritis) or gonorrhoea.

Any of these complications could affect the course of treatment – some antiseptic herbs such as Juniper should not be used in kidney infections. If other types of infections of the vagina are involved, such as chlamydia or candida (thrush), much broader issues of depressed immunity must be taken into account. It is illegal for anyone other than a registered medical practitioner to treat venereal diseases.

The treatments
The family doctor pointed out the need for precautionary measures, and also the general overlap that exists between problems of the urinary system and vagina. However, he might be surprised at the benefits reported by patients with similar problems who have been treated by complementary therapies. He would also be in a minority in his recommendation of the contraceptive pill.

The other approaches all have potential benefits. The naturopathic approach is fundamental, and herbal medicines can produce swift relief. Both acupuncture and homeopathy treat the acute condition and also embrace the broader issues in this patient's story.

DYSMENORRHOEA

THE PATIENT

LF is 34 years old, of medium height and build, with an olive complexion and dark auburn hair. Her weight tends to fluctuate because she overeats when she is depressed, with a particular desire for sweet foods. As a vegetarian she eats a wholefood diet, with a preference for spicy foods. She is a social worker but copes well with the stresses involved, and takes regular exercise, especially swimming and cycling.

THE PROBLEM

In her late 20s LF developed dysmenorrhoea (period pains) which have since worsened. They were particularly severe when she was 31, which was a stressful time. At present a dull ache occurs around 12 hours after bleeding begins, affecting her lower abdomen and back. The pain is relieved by warmth and movement, but is accompanied by extreme weakness, shaking and sweating. Painkillers are not effective. The bleeding is heavy and lasts for 5–7 days; the blood is dark with many clots. Her periods are accompanied by diarrhoea and profuse urination in the first 6–12 hours.

LF is a cheerful, easy-going woman, but tends to get depressed. This is often because of her difficulties in sustaining relationships with men. Her life is much more settled now than it has been for some time, but the period pains are not significantly better.

In general, LF's health is good and she is fit. However, at the same time as her periods began to get painful she developed severe and sharp abdominal pains which lasted for 10–15 minutes and were accompanied by nausea and shaking; they often occurred during exercise. Medical examination revealed no abnormalities, and the pains rarely occur now. She had a motor accident at 24 years old and injured her left knee. She has had trouble with the sacroiliac joints at the base of her spine in the past year.

TREATMENT BY AN
ACUPUNCTURIST

Traditional Chinese medicine stresses that women have a different physiology and pathology to men. This centres on a woman's reproductive function. The *Uterus* is thus almost as important an organ in women as each of the other *Zangfu*. It has an especially close relationship with the *Liver*, the organ that ensures smooth movement of *Qi* and thus *Blood*; with the *Spleen*, which ensures a sufficiency of *Blood*; and with the *Heart*, which circulates the *Blood*. The condition of the *Blood* is very important in relation to menstruation.

LF's menstrual symptoms suggested that her *Qi* and *Blood* were both weak and stagnant, this being confirmed by her wiry and slightly thready pulse, and by the pale, purplish colour of her tongue. Her tendency to depression, associated with emotional dissatisfaction in her relationships with men, suggested retardation of *Liver Qi*.

The abdominal pains which occurred as her periods began to become painful might have been a symptom of this; however, the fact that they often accompanied exercise suggested that a weakness of *Qi* was at the root of all these problems. If the *Qi* is weak it slows down, leading to stagnation and coldness. This was further confirmed by the pain being improved by warmth, and by the diarrhoea and profuse urination. This last symptom, combined with the fact that the period pain affected her lower back, suggests a *Kidney* involvement.

Treatment
The treatment principle would be to move stagnant *Blood* in the *Uterus* to stop pain, while at the same time strengthening the *Qi* and *Yang*, especially of the *Kidney*. Points on the *Ren*, *Stomach*, *Spleen* and *Liver* channels would be used, in combination with points on the *Urinary Bladder* channel. Needling and moxa would be used to strengthen the *Qi* and *Yang* after menstruation. In the week before menstruation, acupuncture points to move stagnant *Blood* would be used.

Prognosis and conclusion
Weekly treatment for three months would be necessary initially, after which, given improvement, twice-monthly treatment would continue for another three months. Menstrual problems usually respond well to acupuncture.

TREATMENT BY A
CHIROPRACTOR

Although chiropractors do not usually treat period pains as an isolated symptom, many patients do report an improvement following the treatment of a low back problem. Reduction in normal spinal mobility in the low back area can affect the nervous system to give referred pain in a number of areas, for example in the legs or in an internal organ such as the uterus or intestines. Restoring normal function to the lumbar spine, and thus restoring normal nerve function, can help to reduce any effect on an internal organ. That is not to say, however, that all women suffering with low back pain also have painful periods.

Physical examination
LF was suffering with pain around the sacroiliac joints, and her spine was examined to see if any treatment might be appropriate. There was considerable strain and restriction of movement around the lumbo-sacral and sacroiliac areas. Neither orthopaedic and neurological tests nor X-rays revealed any abnormalities. In particular the X-rays did not reveal any fibroids (benign growths in the uterus), which can be a contributing factor to period pains.

Treatment
Chiropractic treatment would restore normal mobility to the joints in the pelvic area, and reduce soft-tissue strain. It would consist of spinal adjustment to the lumbo-sacral and sacroiliac areas.

While she was undergoing the chiropractic treatment, LF would be advised to go for a gynaecological check-up, either through her family doctor or a local clinic.

Prognosis and conclusion
Over a number of treatments, mobility would be restored and the strain reduced in LF's lower back. This, apart from being of benefit to her overall health, would probably help her period problems.

TREATMENT BY A
HOMEOPATH

The incidence of period pains has greatly increased in the present generation. This fact probably needs more investigation because it appears to be linked to stress and diet. Pollution, in food or elsewhere, tends to increase dysmenorrhoea because it overloads the liver.

LF's dysmenorrhoea was typical, occurring after a particularly stressful time and accompanied by heavy, prolonged periods. The facts that she took regular exercise, and that her diet was quite good, probably prevented the condition from being more serious. However, her vegetarian wholefood diet was not necessarily the best for her; sweets and overstimulating spices reduced its value considerably, especially when combined with overeating.

In such cases, the pain often occurs before the menstrual flow starts. It was noteworthy that LF's pain started 12 hours after the flow. Several other symptoms were also unique to this patient; pain was accompanied by trembling, sweating, diarrhoea and profuse urination. The abdominal symptoms and the extreme weakness after exertion also fitted to give a picture of *Natrum carbonicum*.

Patients indicated for *Natrum* (sodium) remedies are sensitive and serious about life, but the *Natrum carbonicum* patient is inclined to be cheerful and easy-going. Specific difficulties lie in feeling good enough to accept love. Relationships can give rise to depression, which increases as anger at the situation is suppressed. Thus it was not surprising to find that LF escaped into overeating.

Treatment and prognosis
LF's energy might be judged as good and therefore deserving of a high-potency single dose of *Natrum carbonicum* 1M or 10M. There were enough unusual symptoms to represent a strong individualistic action in LF's vital force, and thus show an imbalance of rhythm. With this type of imbalance great improvement would be possible in a short time. A high potency could create a rapid shift in symptoms and thus resolve the situation more speedily and thoroughly. Changes should be obvious by the next menstrual period, and progress should continue after each successive period.

Introduction to chiropractic therapy pp. 16–23

Introduction to homeopathy pp. 24–31

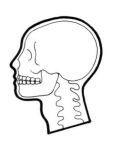

TREATMENT BY A
MEDICAL HERBALIST

In general, LF's problem revolved around muscle spasm, but there was certainly a degree of congestion which needed attention. The recent sacroiliac pains suggested the value of incorporating manipulative treatment into the approach to her health problems. Counselling could well be useful in the longer term to help with relationship difficulties and the accompanying depression.

Treatment

In other areas LF could derive benefit from exercises such as yoga in preference to cycling, which might not be so helpful to her abdominal and pelvic muscles because of the crouched position on the bicycle. Her dietary tendency to "binge" obviously reflected emotional pressures.

The herbal prescription would include:
- White Deadnettle (*Lamium album*): improves uterine blood flow and relieves pelvic congestion.
- Blue Cohosh (*Caulophyllum thalictroides*): tonic to the uterus, with a marked anti-spasmodic effect.
- Cramp Bark (*Viburnum opulus*): muscle relaxant, helpful for colicky spasms as well as the period pains.
- Chamomile (*Matricaria recutita*): general calming relaxant, which lessens muscle tensions, and a mild diuretic which increases fluid elimination.

The prescription would be reviewed according to changes in period symptoms and overall health, keeping an eye especially on circulation through the lower abdominal area and on competence of the urinary and digestive systems. It would also be important to monitor the patient for any signs of pelvic inflammation or infection.

Prognosis and conclusion

LF had settled into a pattern of painfully difficult periods, and it would probably take some time to correct the underlying imbalances and establish better menstrual flow. Herbal treatment can be extremely effective in these circumstances, and there were good prospects for the future.

TREATMENT BY AN
OSTEOPATH AND NATUROPATH

There were a number of possible reasons for LF's problem. The motor accident could have had both a physical and emotional effect on LF's reproductive cycle. If she had hurt her back, especially the lumbar and sacral vertebrae, there could be disturbance of the nerve and blood supplies to the ovaries and uterus. The accident, or a traumatic emotional incident, could have resulted in a shock that disturbed her hypothalamus and pituitary gland, and changed her menstrual routine.

Because LF's pain was evident once the period had started, it was possible that the uterus was the principal source of distress. The sharp abdominal pains and nausea she suffered when the problem started could have been caused by an infection acquired at the time that resulted in a persistent low-grade inflammation.

Physical examination

A gynaecological examination was essential to assess the state of LF's pelvic organs and tissues, and this revealed that her uterus was tilted back far enough to occupy intestinal space. This could account for the menstrual diarrhoea. The heavy bleeding was probably hormonal, there being no fibroids or other tumours present in the uterus.

Osteopathic spinal and sacroiliac lesions were also found, and these needed to be corrected, regardless of whether or not they were a primary cause of the dysmenorrhoea.

Treatment

LF's pelvic imbalance would be corrected to realign the pelvic floor (internal muscles and ligaments supporting the reproductive organs). Soft-tissue massage could reduce inflammatory adhesions (places where tissue sticks together) and help strengthen the pelvic floor. Alternating hot and cold baths, and special exercises would aid pelvic circulation. Her eating habits and the way in which she coped with her emotions could be aggravating factors, and if properly handled could make her menstrual problem less severe.

Prognosis and conclusion

LF could expect reasonably rapid improvement in her symptoms with treatment, but she would also have to take measures herself to improve her physical and mental health.

Introduction to medical herbalism pp. 32–39   Introduction to osteopathy with naturopathy pp. 40–47

TREATMENT BY A
FAMILY DOCTOR

Period pains range from the normal to the abnormal. Many people consider that some degree of pain is normal and inevitable, but it seems that expectations of such pain can have a considerable influence on whether it is felt or not. There are a number of medical conditions associated with menstrual pain, and these should be considered.

Doctors usually speak of primary or secondary dysmenorrhoea. Primary dysmenorrhoea is much more common and usually starts soon after puberty. It is said to lessen after childbearing. Numerous theories have been put forward to explain the pain; many suggest it is caused by muscular contraction. Psychological factors accentuate the symptoms.

Secondary dysmenorrhoea results from acquired conditions such as fibroids, endometriosis (uterine-type tissue growing elsewhere in the pelvis) and pelvic inflammation from infections.

In LF's case, in which the menstrual pain was of late onset, secondary dysmenorrhoea could not be ruled out. She also had bowel and bladder symptoms suggesting pelvic congestion. Her doctor would need to refer her to a specialist, having examined her in the surgery and organized swabs and smears. The gynaecological specialist would be likely to do a scan and might look at the uterus, ovaries and Fallopian tubes directly with a quartz-fibre light (laparoscopy); this simple surgical investigation would give a precise diagnosis.

Treatment
If LF had secondary dysmenorrhoea caused by fibroids, endometriosis or infection, she might be treated with surgery, hormones or antibiotics. If, however, no cause was found, it would be likely that her doctor would recommend a hormone preparation (such as the contraceptive pill); at her age, as a healthy non-smoker, this would be perfectly reasonable. Certain analgesic agents (anti-prostaglandins) could also be tried.

Prognosis and conclusion
It would be difficult to predict LF's future without specialist diagnosis. She should consult her family doctor and a specialist as a start.

CONSULTANT'S COMMENTS

Disturbances in the functions of the female reproductive system provide a particular challenge to any system of healing. Gynaecological therapy through the ages has evolved largely as an empathic female preserve. The male-dominated practice of modern gynaecology and obstetrics is an unusual phenomenon.

A therapy might well be judged by its connection with traditional practices, and by the extent that it can adapt its tenets to an approach in which subjective assessments are as valued as objective measurements, and functional disorders are as meaningful as pathological ones.

Treatments
It is necessary to take precautions in diagnosis, and the family doctor is commendably concerned to check for possible evidence of disease. However, if disease is excluded, modern medicine has very little to offer, except for pain relief or the use of the contraceptive pill or other hormones.

By contrast, other therapies can all contribute to helping the body to adjust its own reproductive functions. Chiropractic and osteopathic manipulation, and the ancillary measures suggested, arise from the earliest practices and can often markedly improve general pelvic health. Homeopathy is well-geared to treat the disorders of rhythm so central to menstrual disturbances.

Chinese medicine provides probably the most sophisticated analysis of such disorders, and can make a considerable difference to such conditions. Herbalism, as the therapy of the traditional "wise woman", has access to a rich fund of gynaecological remedies, and has a good reputation for treating menstrual disorders.

Conclusions
Unless there were confirmed causes of disease, LF would have good reason to expect her problems to improve with one or more of the natural treatments suggested here.

CONDITION	ACUPUNCTURE	CHIROPRACTIC	HOMEOPATHY
ADULT NOCTURIA Need to pass urine at night (not involuntarily)	Treatment can be effective, depending on cause of condition.	Would not treat; would refer to a family doctor or other practitioner.	Treatment may be effective if linked to the constitution. Would refer to family doctor if prostate were involved.
AMENORRHOEA Abnormal lack of menstrual periods	Treatment can be effective, depending on cause of condition.	Would not treat; would refer to a specialist.	Treatment effective in both acute and chronic cases.
BACKACHE IN PREGNANCY	Treatment would depend on cause of condition.	Treatment usually effective.	Treatment effective in both acute and chronic cases.
BED WETTING Involuntary urination during the night	Treatment is effective.	Treatment can help in certain cases, especially with children.	Condition responds well to constitutional treatment, but may require child guidance advice.
BLOCKED FALLOPIAN TUBE Condition causing infertility	Treatment can be effective, depending on cause of condition.	Would not treat; would refer to a specialist.	Treatment may be effective, depending on the cause. Acute cases may need to be referred to a hospital.
BREAST CANCER	Would not treat; would refer to a specialist.	Would not treat; would refer to a specialist.	Treatment can sometimes be effective in early stages, but vitality of the patient is important. Would refer to a family doctor or a specialist.
CERVICAL CANCER Cancer of neck of womb	Would not treat; would refer to a specialist.	Would not treat; would refer to a specialist.	Treatment sometimes effective in early stages, but vitality of patient is important. Would refer to a family doctor or specialist.
FIBROIDS Growth in muscular wall of womb	Treatment can be effective, depending on severity of condition.	Would not treat; would refer to a specialist.	Treatment may halt growth of condition and improve health, in rare cases may cure. Would refer to gynaecologist.
FLOODING Excess menstrual bleeding	Treatment can be effective, depending on cause of condition.	Would not treat; would refer to a specialist.	Treatment effective in both acute and chronic cases.
HORMONAL INFERTILITY Infertility caused by an endocrine disorder	Treatment can be effective, depending on cause of condition.	Would not treat; would refer to a specialist.	Treatment sometimes effective.
HOT FLUSHES Warmth and reddening of face and neck; common symptom of menopause	Treatment can be very effective.	Would not treat; would refer to another practitioner.	Treatment effective at the menopause.
IMPOTENCE Inability of a man to produce or sustain a penile erection	Treatment can be effective, depending on cause and severity of condition.	Would not treat; would refer to a specialist.	Treatment may work well in short-term cases, and has also been known to work in long-term ones.
INCONTINENCE Inability to control bladder or bowels	Treatment can be effective, depending on cause and severity of condition.	Would not treat; would refer to a specialist.	Treatment may be effective, depending on cause.
KIDNEY STONE Mass of substances that form in kidney	Treatment is effective, but depends on size of stones.	Would not treat; would refer to a specialist or another practitioner.	Treatment effective when condition is dealt with constitutionally.
LABOUR PAINS Pain during childbirth (not strictly a disorder)	Treatment is effective in about half the cases; it also regulates and eases the contractions, relaxes the uterus and can be used to induce labour.	Would not treat except under additional medical supervision.	Treatment is effective.

MED. HERBALISM	OSTEOPATHY	GEN. MEDICINE	COMMENTS
Treatment is reasonably helpful.	Treatment can help, especially with the aid of naturopathy.	Would not treat; action depends on diagnosis of cause by a specialist.	See also Cystitis, pp. 138–141; Insomnia, pp. 218–221
Treatment often helpful, depending on the cause; may refer for a pregnancy test.	Would treat the underlying causes if amenable.	Treatment depends on diagnosis of cause.	See also Anorexia, p. 222–223; Dysmenorrhoea, pp. 142–145
Treatment may have limited effect because it will be gentle owing to the pregnancy. Postural techniques and massage are also valuable.	Treatment usually effective, but depends on the cause.	Would refer to midwife or antenatal class for advice, counselling or physiotherapy.	See also Backache, pp. 152–155
Treatment often effective. Counselling may be needed.	Treatment can help this condition.	Would treat an infection; family therapy helps if condition in children is emotional.	See also Sleep walking, pp. 222–223
Treatment unlikely, but may be valuable.	Would not treat.	Would refer to gynaecologist.	See also Salpingitis, pp. 148–149
Would refer for orthodox treatment. However, would treat the whole person, and possibly help with side-effects of other treatment.	Would not treat as such, but all health improvement measures could be encouraged.	Would refer to a surgeon for diagnosis and possible surgery, radiotherapy or chemotherapy.	See also CANCER, p. 225
Would refer for orthodox treatment. However, would treat the whole person, and possibly help with side-effects of other treatment.	Would not treat.	Would refer to a surgeon for possible operation, radiotherapy or chemotherapy.	See also CANCER, p. 225
Treatment can help associated problems or aggravation of the condition, but surgery may well be needed.	Treatment can help, especially with the aid of naturopathy.	Would leave alone or refer to a surgeon for possible removal.	See also Dysmenorrhoea, pp. 142–145
Treatment often helpful, depending on the cause.	Treatment can be effective if condition does not require surgery.	Treatment with oral hormones is often very successful; might refer for diagnosis.	See also Dysmenorrhoea, pp. 142–145
Treatment can help, sometimes dramatically well.	Treatment effective in some cases.	Would refer to an endocrinologist following blood tests.	See also Amenorrhoea, pp. 146–147
Treatment very helpful in assisting menopausal changes, rather than in delaying them as in some treatments.	Treatment can help, especially with the aid of naturopathy.	Treatment by reassurance and often hormonal medication is effective.	See also Premenstrual syndrome, pp. 148–149
Treatment often helpful.	Treatment can help, especially with the aid of naturopathy.	Treatment is by counselling, specialist sexual therapy, mechanical aids or injections.	See also Alcoholism, pp. 210–213, Depression, pp. 214–217
Treatment can be of great help.	Treatment can help, especially with the aid of naturopathy.	Treatment depends on diagnosis of cause.	See also Bed wetting, pp. 146–147
Treatment can help considerably, given caution and care.	Would not treat.	Would treat acute pain and refer to a specialist for diagnosis and treatment.	See also Nephritis, pp. 148–149
Treatment can be very helpful.	Treatment can help.	Treatment is supportive by midwife and obstetrician.	

CONDITION	ACUPUNCTURE	CHIROPRACTIC	HOMEOPATHY
MALE INFERTILITY Inability of a man to produce fertile sperm	Treatment can be effective, depending on cause of condition.	Would not treat; would refer to a specialist or another practitioner.	Treatment less effective than in female infertility.
MASTITIS Inflammation of breast (common during breast-feeding)	Treatment is effective.	Would not treat; would refer to another practitioner.	Treatment brings speedy relief and improves the quality of the milk.
MENOPAUSAL PROBLEMS Disorders occuring when menstruation ceases	Treatment often effective.	Would not treat; would refer to another practitioner or a specialist.	Treatment helps women to adjust quickly to changes at this time.
MISCARRIAGE Spontaneous, premature termination of pregnancy	Treatment can be very effective.	Would not treat, but would refer to a family doctor.	Treatment may prevent this or remove any tendency to it, unless the cause is mechanical.
MONILIASIS (CANDIDIASIS) Fungal infection of vagina	Treatment can be very effective.	Would not treat; would refer to another practitioner.	Treatment effective because it improves general health and vitality.
MORNING SICKNESS Nausea during early pregnancy	Treatment can be very effective.	Would not treat; would refer to another practitioner.	Treatment effective in both acute and chronic cases.
NEPHRITIS Inflammation of kidney	Treatment can be effective.	Would not treat; would refer to a specialist or another practitioner.	Treatment effective if the condition is dealt with constitutionally, but may need careful investigation.
PREMENSTRUAL SYNDROME Varied symptoms appearing before each menstrual period	Treatment can be very effective.	Would not treat; would refer to another practitioner.	Treatment often effective.
PROLAPSE Displacement of uterus into vagina	Treatment can be effective, but depends on severity of condition.	Would not treat; would refer to a specialist.	Treatment strengthens the muscles in the long term. Mechanical aid may be needed in the short term, plus attention to habits and posture.
PROSTATITIS Enlargement of prostate gland due to infection or tumour	Treatment can be effective in both acute and chronic cases for pain; in promoting normal urinary function and reducing inflammation.	Would not treat; would refer to another practitioner.	Treatment effective in both acute and chronic cases.
SALPINGITIS Inflammation of Fallopian tubes, usually caused by infection	Treatment can be effective in both acute and chronic cases.	Would not treat; would refer to a specialist or another practitioner.	Treatment effective in both acute and chronic cases.
VAGINISMUS Spasm of lower vaginal muscles	Treatment can be effective.	Would not treat; would refer to a specialist.	Treatment is effective.
VAGINITIS Inflammation of vagina	Treatment can be effective.	Would not treat; would refer to another practitioner	Treatment is often effective.
VENEREAL DISEASE Group of infections contracted through sexual contact	Would not treat; would refer to a specialist.	Would not treat; would refer to a specialist.	Not permitted to treat by law but, historically, treatment has been effective. Would refer to family doctor.
VULVITIS Inflammation of vulva	Treatment can be very effective.	Would not treat; would refer to a specialist or another practitioner.	Treatment is effective.

MED. HERBALISM	OSTEOPATHY	GEN. MEDICINE	COMMENTS
Treatment often helpful.	Treatment can help, especially with the aid of naturopathy.	Would refer to an endocrinologist following blood tests.	See also **Hormonal infertility**, pp. 146–147
Local treatment is especially helpful.	Treatment can help, especially with the aid of naturopathy.	Would treat acute cases with antibiotics; would refer chronic cases to a breast clinic.	See also **Cyst**, pp. 190–191
Treatment often very effective.	Naturopathic treatment can help at this time of life.	Hormonal therapy sometimes helpful.	See also **Hot flushes**, pp. 146–147
Treatment can be helpful. Would probably refer to a family doctor.	Would carry out preventive treatment only.	Would generally refer to hospital.	
Treatment often very effective. Would refer to a family doctor for local treatment if necessary.	Treatment can help, especially with the aid of naturopathy.	Would treat with antifungal drugs. Condition may be related to obesity, diabetes or immunodeficiency.	See also **Cystitis**, pp. 138–141
Treatment can be very effective, especially combined with dietary advice.	Treatment can help.	Treatment may be simply dietary advice, occasionally anti-emetics; severe cases may require hospitalization.	See also **Backache in pregnancy**, pp. 146–147
Would refer to a family doctor in an acute stage. Treatment may be quite helpful in chronic condition.	Would not treat except nutritionally.	Would refer to a specialist.	See also **Cystitis**, pp. 138–141
Treatment can be very effective.	Would treat, especially if there are structural and nutritional causes.	Treatment may include painkillers or cyclical hormones.	See also **Dysmenorrhoea**, pp. 142–145
Treatment may be reasonably effective with exercises. May refer for mechanical treatment.	Treatment depends on degree of condition; in mild cases it is very effective.	Treatment may be effective, but surgery may be needed.	
Treatment often effective.	Treatment can help, unless the condition is degenerate.	Treatment can be effective, but may need to refer to a specialist.	See also **CANCER**, p. 225
Treatment reasonably effective over a period of time. May refer if condition is an acute infection.	Mild cases can be treated.	Treatment antibacterial; may need to refer to hospital.	See also **Dysmenorrhoea**, pp. 142–145
Treatment usually helpful. Patient may need counselling.	Would treat if psychosomatic, or if physical causes can be unravelled.	Treatment is by counselling or referral to a psychosexual therapist.	See also **Anxiety**, pp. 222–223
Local treatment can be helpful.	Naturopathic treatment can be effective if cause is not venereal.	Treatment is usually effective.	See also **Cystitis**, pp. 138–141
Would not treat.	Would not treat.	Would refer to a specialist clinic.	See also **AIDS**, p. 224
Treatment could be of value, especially locally.	Would not treat if venereal in origin; otherwise treatment is effective.	Treatment can be effective, but needs care.	See also **Vaginitis**, pp. 148–149

THE SKELETON AND MUSCLES

The skeleton is the supporting framework of the body. Individual bones are linked by joints, most of which allow movement. Connections are made by means of fibrous ligaments. Muscles are attached to the skeleton and contract around the joints to achieve mobility. Muscle contraction is stimulated by impulses from the nervous system.

The skeleton is composed of two parts. The axial skeleton consists of the skull, vertebral column, breastbone and ribs. The appendicular skeleton is made up of the bones of the upper limbs, the shoulder-blades and collar bones, the lower limbs and pelvic bones.

Muscle is the flesh that lies between the skeleton and the skin. It is made up of bundles of fibres which contract and relax to enable movement. Tendons are tough, non-elastic bands of tissue that attach muscles to bones.

WHAT CAN GO WRONG

Bones, joints, tendons, ligaments and muscles may be damaged through injury or repeated misuse caused by bad posture or inappropriate exercise. Bones become weakened in later life, especially among menopausal women, through loss of calcium (osteoporosis), which results in greater susceptibility to fractures. In childhood, bone development may be disturbed by hormonal or vitamin deficiency.

Degeneration of joints occurs as a result of wear and tear, and is part of the normal ageing process. Athletes, who use their joints excessively, can also suffer from joint degeneration. This process is called osteoarthritis. It should not be confused with rheumatoid arthritis, which can effect any joint at any age.

Tendons can be damaged by overuse, and result in conditions such as tennis elbow and Achilles tendonitis. Muscle diseases (such as muscular dystrophy) are rare, although elderly people frequently suffer from an inflammatory condition of the muscles (polymyalgia rheumatica).

Complementary and alternative medical approaches sometimes view the skeleton and muscles and their disorders in different ways. A summary of these views follows.

Acupuncture

In traditional Chinese medicine, the musculoskeletal system is dependent on *Qi* and *Blood* for growth, nourishment, strength and vitality. *Qi* and *Blood* reach the peripheries via the *Jingluo* (channels). Trauma and injury to the bones and muscles, including sprains and bruises, interrupt the flow of *Qi* and *Blood*, resulting in stagnation and causing pain and restriction of movement. The aim of acupuncture treatment is to re-establish the circulation of *Qi* and *Blood*, relieve pain, and allow the damaged area to return to its normal function.

If the circulation of *Qi* and *Blood* in the *Jingluo* is weakened because of poor *Zangfu* (organ) function, the muscles may be "invaded" by *Heat, Cold* or *Damp*. These influences cause problems such as rheumatism and arthritis.

The muscles are also under the influence of the *Spleen*, and diseases affecting the muscles are often treated by strengthening the *Spleen*. Similarly, the sinews and tendons are under the influence of the *Liver* and *Gall Bladder*, and disorders can be treated using these channels. The bones are under the influence of the *Kidney*, and poor development, brittleness or softening of the bones can all be signs of *Kidney* weakness.

Chiropractic therapy

All joints in the body should function normally within their given range of movements. Any alteration to this function – either by restricted or increased movement – leads to abnormalities in the biomechanics of the joint. This can, in turn, cause stress and strain on the muscles, tendons and ligaments in the area. The result is the immediate, or gradual, development of pain in the area, or referred pain. Chiropractic treatment aims to restore the normal function of joints and their associated soft-tissues.

Homeopathy

Homeopathic treatment can speed up the healing of broken bones and reduce the accompanying pain and inflammation. At a deeper level, homeopathic remedies can remove toxins that have built up in joints or muscles and have given rise to congestive disorders such as rheumatism.

In treating any part of the body, it is necessary to look at it in the context of the body as a whole. The circumstances surrounding the onset of any disorder must be considered. These might include such factors as stress, strong emotions (such as anger or resentment), weather, food, posture or the menopause. As always in homeopathy, the characteristics of the individual patient, aside from the symptoms directly related to the disorder, must be taken into account.

Medical herbalism

Musculo-skeletal disorders are viewed in the context of the overall health patterns of the individual patient. The focus initially is on the posture, levels of exercise, nutrition and elimination of waste matter from the body. The last of these is particularly important in rheumatic conditions.

The effects of stress are also felt throughout the body, and can contribute to these disorders in many ways – such as by provoking excess muscle tension and increasing vitamin/mineral deficiency. As a consequence, herbal treatment may involve counselling and practical advice on suitable exercises, nutritional planning and medication. These aim to support general vitality as well as relieve the condition in question.

Osteopathy with naturopathy

The health of the musculo-skeletal system is established in the mother's womb. It depends on how well she nourishes herself during pregnancy and afterwards during the first few months of feeding. Breast milk is the product of the mother's eating, drinking, smoking and drug-taking habits, and can make or mar the future skeletal structure of the growing child.

Osteopaths can be consulted to assess and improve children's health. For adults, treatment and advice can be given to help repair damage that has been done over time or has occurred as a result of injury. Often there are indications that other body systems are involved. For example, pain in the right shoulder could relate to gall bladder disorders, and headaches may be the result of muscle tension at the base or sides of the head.

Chart of disorders

At the end of this section there is a chart listing various disorders of the musculo-skeletal system. This is a general, but not definitive, guide to the treatment of such disorders. Complementary and alternative therapies treat the patient as a whole rather than merely the disorder presented. Whether or not a person can be treated, and the success of treatment, depends on the nature of the condition and the general health of the patient.

BACKACHE

THE PATIENT

AG is 33 years old and works as a carpenter and a sculptor. He is 1.7 metres (5 ft 8 in) tall and of slender build, with dark hair and a fair complexion. He is strong and fit, playing squash and jogging regularly. His work is physically demanding. He does not smoke and drinks alcohol in moderation. He is quiet, soft-spoken and enjoys his own company, although he socializes with other artists whenever he has the time. He was divorced two years ago.

THE PROBLEM

AG has a dull pain between his shoulder blades and at the base of his spine. This has been caused by the lifting and chiselling involved in his work but it has become worse in the last three years since he started working on large wooden and stone sculptures.

He has had to develop strong arm and shoulder muscles to use the chisels, and he has strained his back on several occasions. The pain is more acute in the early mornings and is eased by gentle movement. He sometimes strains his back and is in acute pain for several days, which requires total rest and painkillers.

AG has studied the Oriental exercise *Tai Qi* to improve his posture, but this has not helped his backache significantly. He has a nervous temperament and is currently under a lot of pressure preparing for exhibitions while keeping his carpentry business going.

AG has suffered occasionally from asthma attacks since his mid-teens. He frequently gets head colds which result in sinusitis. Often he is unable to breathe through his nose because it is permanently blocked up. He feels fit, but finds it hard to relax and sometimes has problems sleeping. He gets headaches located at the back of the skull when he is under pressure and finds that his neck gets very stiff at these times.

TREATMENT BY AN
ACUPUNCTURIST

Backache has various causes in traditional Chinese medicine, depending on its location. Pain in the upper back associated with work and posture would generally be attributed to poor circulation and, therefore, to stagnation of *Qi* in the channels running over areas of muscle strain.

Pain in the lower back is often the result of overstrain caused by lifting or bending, or to weakness of the *Qi* of the *Kidney*, which is said to control the circulation of *Qi* in the lower back. Stagnation of *Qi* may also lead to stagnation of *Blood*, in which case the pain would be more severe.

AG's backache appeared to be caused mainly by the physical strain of his work combined with the stress involved in working both as a carpenter and a sculptor. Overwork had weakened his *Qi* in general, this being exacerbated by a weakness of his *Lung Qi* (and possibly his *Kidney Qi*). This has produced symptoms of asthma, and frequent colds leading to a blocked nose and sinusitis.

The circulation of *Qi* and *Blood* to his neck was also weak, which resulted in stiffness and headaches. The *Qi* circulation in his back was slow at night when he was lying down, producing stiffness and pain in the mornings. Repeated straining of his lower back had also harmed the *Qi* of the *Kidney*.

Treatment
The treatment would be directed both at improving the circulation of *Qi* and *Blood* to the affected areas, and at strengthening AG's overall body *Qi*, specifically the *Qi* of his *Lung* and *Kidney*. Local points and points on the *Lung, Large Intestine, Urinary Bladder, Du, Ren, Stomach* and *Kidney* channels would be used. AG would also benefit from chiropractic or osteopathic treatment to improve the general condition of the spine. This should be done in consultation with the acupuncturist.

Prognosis and conclusion
Much would depend on AG being able to allow himself more time to rest and recover from his work regime, especially during the course of treatment. If he was able to do this, a concentrated course of 10–15 treatments would probably suffice. Relaxing exercise – such as swimming – would help to improve the circulation in his back.

Asthma pp. 60–63 Sinusitis pp. 76–79

Introduction to acupuncture pp. 8–15

TREATMENT BY A
CHIROPRACTOR

Special note was taken of the dull pain between the shoulder blades and in the low back, as well as the stiff necks and headaches which came when AG was working under pressure. AG's working posture and his heavy lifting had, over the years, caused more wear and tear on the spine than would normally be expected at his age.

His general posture was observed, and then the spine was palpated to check for areas of muscle tension and restricted spinal movement, which were noted at the following vertebrae: thoracic 5–7, lumbar 2–4 and cervical 1–3. Muscle tension in the cervical (neck) area – especially at the base of the skull – combined with the thoracic problem, was probably the cause of his headaches.

Various orthopaedic and neurological tests were carried out, but no further abnormalities were detected. The spine was X-rayed and damage was found in the upper part of the neck, at thoracic vertebrae 5–7 and lumbar vertebrae 2–4.

Treatment
AG's treatment would consist of soft-tissue massage to the whole spine, followed by specific chiropractic adjustments where problems had been found. Not all of the spine would be adjusted during the same treatment because this might cause too much of a reaction. The chiropractor would try to relax the muscles and restore normal mobility.

Ways in which AG could help himself reduce the amount of stress and strain on his back would be discussed. This would include, in particular, the specific postures AG would have to develop in his work.

AG should continue with his *Tai Qi* and consider taking up yoga and relaxation classes. Squash and jogging can aggravate a bad back, so he should approach these with caution. AG should have a firm bed, good seating, and follow a healthy diet.

Prognosis and conclusion
AG should quickly see considerable improvement in his backache. Once the back problems had diminished he would be advised to attend the chiropractor on a regular basis – about every three to six months. This is important when the major cause of back pain is occupational, so that the problem remains under control.

TREATMENT BY A
HOMEOPATH

There are some cases that a homeopath would rather not tackle, and this is one of them. AG's backache seemed to be caused by overstress and physical strain related to work. Deep constitutional treatment to improve his muscle tone and general health, combined with osteopathy, chiropractic therapy or Alexander technique to help correct spinal and postural imbalances, would be necessary.

Treatment and prognosis
Either *Rhus tox* 6 or *Arnica* 6 could be given to relieve AG's immediate symptoms of soreness between the shoulder blades and in the lower back. These remedies are commonly used in first aid, and AG's symptoms – worse in the morning and improving after gentle movement – fit their symptom pictures. However, to take these remedies continually, without correcting the structure of the back, would simply mask symptoms and might lead to more serious spinal damage.

Once AG's spinal imbalances had been corrected, *Rhus tox* 6 could be taken to prevent further serious damage, particularly after a strenuous bout of sculpting. If the backache was acute, the remedy could be taken every hour for a maximum of three hours.

If this strategy did not relieve the condition, either the remedy would be wrong, or the condition would be too serious to respond. Homeopathic remedies should not be taken like aspirins. At any sign of change – for better or worse – treatment should cease and the remedy be repeated again only if the situation worsens. If the treatment is effective, there should be a widening gap between each relapse or the symptoms should be less intense. If, however, the symptoms worsen after the remedy is taken, this is usually the homeopathic "aggravation" and a deep level of recovery will follow. First-aid treatment of this type is often very effective.

Constitutionally, AG needs treatment to deal with root causes other than the physical strain. Such treatment would also aim to deal with his general health, including the nasal congestion and asthma. *Silica* would be an appropriate constitutional remedy for AG; weak backs are common in its symptom picture. One dose of 30 C would be given and repeated, according to the changes that occurred after several months.

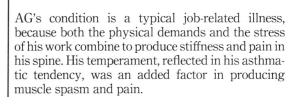

TREATMENT BY A
MEDICAL HERBALIST

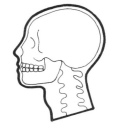

TREATMENT BY AN
OSTEOPATH AND NATUROPATH

AG's condition is a typical job-related illness, because both the physical demands and the stress of his work combine to produce stiffness and pain in his spine. His temperament, reflected in his asthmatic tendency, was an added factor in producing muscle spasm and pain.

Treatment
AG would be referred to a chiropractor or an osteopath for manipulative treatment, but this could be combined with a herbal prescription and advice.

The herbal prescription would include:
● Lime Blossom (*Tilia europea*): general relaxant which improves circulation. It helps to reduce tension and insomnia without acting as a sedative.
● Cramp Bark (*Viburnum opulus*): strong muscle relaxant, acting both to reduce asthmatic spasms and tensions in the skeleton.
● Lobelia (*Lobelia inflata*): reduces irritability and inflammation of the airways, helping both sinusitis and asthmatic attacks.
● Devil's Claw (*Harpagophytum procumbens*): analgesic and anti-inflammatory, reducing pain as an aid to long-term balancing of causes.
● Valerian (*Valeriana officinalis*): a warming antispasmodic, which reduces the muscle tension and calms the nervous system, improving headaches and other symptoms of stress. It relaxes blood vessel walls and improves circulation.

The prescription would be reviewed regularly and adjusted according to progress.

The practice of *Tai Qi*, while not giving significant relief to his backache, would provide AG with the benefits of relaxation, improved posture and breathing. If possible, taking short but fairly frequent breaks from sculpting would help prevent over-straining his muscles. Massage using a dilution of essential oil of Lavender – especially of the back, neck and shoulders – would have great benefit, both in reducing muscle tension and improving circulation.

Prognosis and conclusion
Initially, work pressure would be likely to prevent a marked improvement, but treatment and advice could contribute to a general change in the cycle of over-strain and backache, with overall benefits to health and vitality.

Posture can be affected by physical or emotional stress, both of which were likely in view of AG's strenuous job and nervous temperament. Injury (trauma) and overuse play their part in damaging groups of muscles, ligaments or intervertebral discs. Some muscles may go into contraction and spasm, while others may be overstretched. Being a sculptor seemed to have created just such a situation. Furthermore, the value of playing squash and jogging were questionable; both were likely to have aggravated the problem.

Backs can be predisposed to strain by poor nourishment of the supporting tissues – a possibility, as AG's history of head colds and sinusitis indicated constitutional weakness.

Physical examination
After investigation to make sure that there was no organic disorder responsible for AG's backache (such as lungs damaged by the dust inevitable in his work, or by inability to breathe through his nose), AG's entire musculo-skeletal system was analysed, including the shoulders, arms, hips and legs, spinal column, pelvis, ribcage, cranium, and neck. X-rays were taken.

Treatment
Spinal imbalances would be treated manipulatively and with deep soft-tissue massage to restore the integrity of the spine.

There is a limit to the number of times vertebrae can be restored to harmony with each other if the cause of their disharmony is continually repeated. At some stage disk damage would become irreversible and nerve irritation unbearable. Caution would be recommended and AG's activities would need to be discussed. He might have to agree to change the way he worked and played, especially if the X-rays showed degeneration of disks or other injury-induced abnormalities.

Prognosis and conclusion
With osteopathic help, and as long as he is careful, AG should see a significant improvement in his condition. Work on his general health would probably aid recovery.

Introduction to medical herbalism pp. 32–39

Introduction to osteopathy with naturopathy pp. 40–47

TREATMENT BY A
FAMILY DOCTOR

Backache is common in adults of all ages and may be related to structural damage – as in disk and body lesions – or to muscular strain and tension. AG was a fit young man who used his muscles in his trade and his problem seemed to be one of a mixture of stress and postural pain.

Treatment
It is unlikely that AG would need any anti-inflammatory medication, although if he did tear a muscle lifting heavy sculpture materials this might be temporarily helpful. He did not need to be physically fitter, but could gain a lot of help from a good osteopath, physiotherapist or chiropractor.

AG was aware that he needed help with his posture, but *Tai Qi* had not benefited his back. He might find that a mixed treatment of relaxation techniques and physiotherapeutic principles – such as the Alexander technique – would be very helpful. Relief of the psychological pressures on him would probably be beneficial, too.

Squash and jogging would not be the best exercises, but swimming could strengthen AG's back without causing strain or percussive damage. He would be well-advised to invest in a good orthopaedic bed.

Prognosis
Although older people tend to suffer much severe mechanical back pain, it is very common in all age ranges when associated with physical and emotional tensions. Although muscle relaxants, pain-killers and anti-inflammatory drugs may all be intelligently used, management should really treat the whole person.

CONSULTANT'S COMMENTS

Occupational back and muscle aches pose a number of tricky questions for both sufferer and therapist. It is obvious that AG's body is telling him that it is ill-suited to the life it is being asked to live. The questions follow from any attempt to correct the mismatch.

Is the work genuinely too harsh to cope with? This is unlikely in AG's case. There is ample evidence from around the world that the human frame can, when well-tuned, cope with amazing burdens without damage. The question to ask is: if the work is tolerable, in what ways is AG's body inadequate to do it without damage?

It is in attempting to answer this last question that the different therapies design their own individual approaches.

Treatments
Homeopathy, acupuncture and medical herbalism each look to constitutional angles of the patient's difficulties. They are aware that his approach to his work will affect the degree of relaxation or tension and the mechanical efficiency in his musculo-skeletal system.

Each of these treatments is unlikely to be complete without osteopathic or chiropractic manipulation as well. The family doctor also recognizes the functional nature of this condition.

The osteopath and chiropractor share a common general approach to this condition – that specific manipulation of the spine should be associated with a wide regime of exercises and other disciplines so that AG can learn to use his body in a different way. Both therapists are aware of the dangers of manipulating the spine too frequently.

Conclusion
If AG is able to improve his posture and avoid physical and emotional strain at work, there is every chance that the condition will improve.

Introduction to Western medicine pp. 48–55

OSTEOARTHRITIS

ACUPUNCTURIST

THE PATIENT

RR is 64 years old, 1.7 metres (5 ft 8 in) tall, slim and balding. He is fit and healthy, and his dark "outdoor" complexion makes him look younger than he is. His grown-up children have left home and he keeps himself busy with his profession as a vet, and with the breeding of horses. His lifestyle is active and demanding, but he does not feel the need to relax because he enjoys his work intensely. He does not smoke or drink alcohol, and eats regularly. His wife is health-conscious and prepares wholefoods.

THE PROBLEM

In the last five years RR has noticed increasing discomfort in his right hip. The dull but severe ache affects him particularly at night and after sitting for a long time. There is no swelling and the pain is eased by gentle movement. The condition has been diagnosed as osteoarthritis, a degenerative disease of the joints, which affects the cartilage involved in articulation.

RR developed a limp, favouring his right side, after a serious riding accident seven years ago in which his right hip and shoulder were injured. His right shoulder is noticeably higher and less broad than the left, and his right leg is shorter than the left. He has no back trouble, but sometimes wakes with a stiff neck. (He suffered concussion as a result of his accident and on one previous occasion.)

RR is an ambitious man with great drive and resilience. He prefers to be busy and is also active in the local community as a councillor – in fact he seems to thrive on stress. He enjoys his own company and rarely entertains, but gets on well with people in general. He enjoys his successes and is distressed by defeats, but always tries again. His hip is a cause for concern because it is beginning to restrict his mobility.

RR has never been ill except for a serious attack of glandular fever while he was a student. He rarely gets colds or influenza, and after having marginal high blood pressure, he cut down on his cholesterol intake and brought the condition back to normal.

In traditional Chinese medicine both rheumatoid arthritis and osteoarthritis are known as *Bi* (or "blockage") syndrome. *Qi* energy becomes blocked at the joints by one, or a combination of *Cold*, *Damp*, *Heat* or *Wind*. In most cases, the patient's internal pattern of disharmony dictates the external influence to which they are most susceptible, but weakened *Qi* of the whole body can be the predisposing factor.

RR's condition stemmed from his riding accident, which had resulted in poor *Qi* circulation to the affected hip. As he grew older, the natural decline of his *Qi* and *Blood* meant that his hip had become particularly susceptible to invasion by external *Cold* and *Damp*. The inactivity of sleeping or sitting was allowing the already impeded *Qi* to stagnate, leading to stiffness and pain. However, movement alleviated the discomfort by promoting *Qi* circulation. RR's active lifestyle suggested that he had allowed little time for a full recovery from his injury. He was continuing to drain his *Qi* through excessive stress, but was also maintaining a strong degree of vitality, overcoming his high blood pressure by dietary changes.

Treatment
To promote *Qi* circulation, local, adjacent and distal points on the channels passing over and near the affected hip would be chosen, particularly the *Gall Bladder* and *Urinary Bladder* channels. Associated channels, such as the *Sanjiao*, would also be used. In addition, points on the *Large Intestine, Stomach, Spleen* and *Ren* channels would be used to enhance his *Qi* circulation generally, and to combat invasion by *Cold* and *Damp*. RR would be encouraged to adjust to a less demanding lifestyle. Therapeutic exercise and dietary changes to eliminate *Damp* would be suggested.

Prognosis and conclusion
The degenerative changes of osteoarthritis can be reversed with the help of acupuncture, and a decline in the condition to a point where hip replacement might be inevitable can be avoided. A rough yardstick often used is one month of treatment for every year the condition has existed. RR had good vitality and, if this could be diverted to making the changes necessary to allow healing, the prognosis would be good.

Hypertension pp. 94–97   Rheumatoid arthritis pp. 160–163   Introduction to acupuncture pp. 8–15

TREATMENT BY A
CHIROPRACTOR

Arthritic hips can occur at all ages, but are more common in older people. The usual symptoms are mild to severe pain in the hip joint, which may be accompanied by pain in the groin and the front of the thigh, and sometimes there is low back and buttock pain as well. Some arthritic hips occur following an accident or injury earlier in life, and others occur as part of the aging process.

Physical examination
RR was examined, and a marked reduction in the degree of movement in the right hip was found, accompanied by some pain and discomfort. Examination of the neck revealed mild stiffness and restriction of movement.

X-rays were taken of RR's pelvis and hip joints. In view of his stiff neck and his history of concussion, X-rays were also taken of RR's cervical spine to check for any problems there. The X-rays showed severe arthritic changes in the right hip to the extent that a hip replacement operation was probably going to be necessary. In spite of the accidents, his neck X-rays revealed only normal wear and tear, and this would account for his occasional stiff neck in the morning.

Treatment
Even though a hip operation seemed likely (RR should consult his family doctor for referral to an orthopaedic surgeon for consideration of this option) he would be offered chiropractic treatment to make life more comfortable. This would consist of soft tissue work to the muscles of the buttocks and hips, which would be extremely tender and very tight, especially around the right hip. This treatment would be followed by general mobilization techniques to the hip in order to keep it moving as freely as possible. Such treatment would need to be carried out at least once a week.

Prognosis and conclusion
Although in very severe cases chiropractic can do little to cure the condition, considerable relief from discomfort can be given. Hip replacement operations are usually extremely successful.

TREATMENT BY A
HOMEOPATH

Osteoarthritis is a degenerative disease which takes many years to develop. Frequently there is a history of injury to the joint in which it arises. Homeopathic treatment can be expected to arrest further development of the disease and alleviate symptoms such as pain. Improved mobility after treatment is common, but full resolution in older people depends on many factors such as diet, exercise and the cause of the disease.

In RR's case the history of injury was significant as a causative factor. It had put extra stress on his right hip and shoulder, as shown by the posture of the shoulder and the shortness of the leg. Serious consideration might therefore be given to a manipulative therapy such as osteopathy or chiropractic therapy. The diagnosis of osteoarthritis would need to be established with the help of RR's family doctor and X-rays.

The condition might need potentized *Calcarea* at some point in the treatment, particularly to affect the use of calcium by the body. For immediate treatment *Rhus toxicodendron* would be indicated on the evidence of the dull pain that was worse at night and when sitting, suggesting that the condition was worse for rest, coupled with the history of injury and RR's restlessness. RR had drive and determination, but created tension in his body, as shown by the high blood pressure and the retreat into his own company.

Treatment and prognosis
Because of the physical nature of the problem, a low potency of *Rhus toxicodendron* would be used at the start of the treatment, even though a higher potency would be constitutionally appropriate. *Rhus toxicodendron* 6 would be repeated twice daily for 7–10 days, followed by a gap of days or even weeks while the body's response was monitored. Sometimes such continued doses aggravate the symptoms, and relief is obtained only when the medicine is stopped. A patient is usually instructed to stop taking the pills should any change occur.

As RR's treatment progressed, a higher potency might be given as a single dose when appropriate, repeated only when there was a relapse, although once a response began any relapse should not be as intense as the previous state, and there should be gradual and steady improvement.

Introduction to chiropractic therapy pp. 16–23

Introduction to homeopathy pp. 24–31

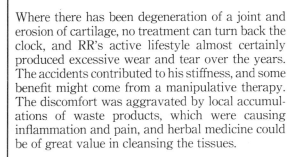

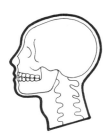

TREATMENT BY A
MEDICAL HERBALIST

Where there has been degeneration of a joint and erosion of cartilage, no treatment can turn back the clock, and RR's active lifestyle almost certainly produced excessive wear and tear over the years. The accidents contributed to his stiffness, and some benefit might come from a manipulative therapy. The discomfort was aggravated by local accumulations of waste products, which were causing inflammation and pain, and herbal medicine could be of great value in cleansing the tissues.

Treatment
RR had a reasonably healthy diet. He was slim and quite fit, but swimming would be of value in maintaining mobility while easing the binding in his joints. His work tended to aggravate the condition because it involved a lot of standing. His self-inflicted stress was also probably contributing to the condition, but this was part of his nature.

The herbal prescription would include:
- Celery Seed (*Apium graveolens*): increases elimination of uric acid and other wastes via the kidneys.
- Lignum Vitae (*Guaiacum officinale*): improves peripheral circulation and reduces inflammation.
- Willow Bark (*Salix nigra*): anti-inflammatory and analgesic; also acts to stimulate digestion.
- Hawthorn: (*Crataegus oxyacanthoides*): helps to restore blood flow to normal and regulate blood pressure.
- Ginger (*Zingiber officinale*): circulatory stimulant that encourages tissue cleansing and ensures adequate supply of nutrients.
- Devil's Claw (*Harpagophytum procumbens*): reduces inflammatory response and relieves discomfort.

The prescription would be amended according to changing needs, such as increased elimination.

Prognosis and conclusion
A great deal could be done to prevent further deterioration of RR's condition by cleansing his system of irritant metabolites, improving circulation and relieving the discomfort. A degree of change in his habits would be necessary for maximum benefit, although this might be more difficult to achieve.

TREATMENT BY AN
OSTEOPATH AND NATUROPATH

The hips are positioned to carry the weight of the upper part of the body, to provide postural stability, to permit movement during crawling, walking and running, and to allow for sitting and bending.

Physical examination
RR's hips were tested through a range of motions. If there was no restriction to expected movement in any direction there was unlikely to be any significant arthritic change in the joint. It seemed evident that his present hip problem was related to the riding accident, not just because of the hip, but because of problems with the spine, pelvis and legs as a whole.

There was a detailed examination of the areas that were injured in the accident, looking for neuro-muscular blockages, which are painful to the touch and often result in problems elsewhere in the body; for example the shoulder injury had a bearing on RR's neck discomfort.

An X-ray showing hips, pelvis, spine and lower lumbar vertebrae would be essential for confirmation of the clinical findings.

Treatment
If the problem was purely anatomical, a heel lift would be used for a few days, after which pelvic balance and pain relief would be reviewed. If the problem was not anatomical, the standard osteopathic procedure of reintegrating the whole musculo-skeletal structure would be used.

The fact that movement eased RR's hip suggested that he should avoid static positions that would affect the lubrication of his hip joint.

Inflammation is a healing process, but if the inflammation continues, the cartilage crucial to articulation within the joint is destroyed and bone changes take place. Such degenerate arthritic changes are irreversible, and, as seemed likely in this case, surgery can become inevitable.

Prognosis and conclusion
In RR's case there were a number of linked aspects that needed attention. The prospects for improvement could be assessed more accurately after three or four treatments. The entire treatment programme might extend over a much longer period.

Introduction to medical herbalism pp. 32–39

Introduction to osteopathy with naturopathy pp. 40–47

TREATMENT BY A
FAMILY DOCTOR

Osteoarthritis is a process of wear and tear that damages the cartilage faces of joints. We may all expect to develop the condition to some degree as we become older. RR's problem was typical. Badly affected joints tend to be ones that have suffered previous damage; osteoarthritis in the lower limbs is a common problem among athletes. Obesity also causes damage to weight-bearing joints.

Sometimes there can be difficulty in distinguishing osteoarthritis from other joint diseases, such as rheumatoid arthritis. The age of the patient and the clinical picture usually gives an accurate diagnosis, but special blood tests can often identify similar conditions. X-rays often confirm the disease as well as indicating the degree and distribution of bone damage.

Treatment

For most cases of osteoarthritis there is little specific treatment, but RR was fortunate in that there is the surgical option of a total hip replacement (THR). This has become an important treatment in severe cases, although there can be complications and artificial hips seem to have a limited life. The operation is less likely to succeed on repetition, so surgery is generally recommended only for older patients with considerable disability. Operations to alter the patterns of weight-bearing in the joint can also be successful, but have been largely superseded by THR. Non-surgical options would include analgesics, appliances such as walking sticks, and physiotherapy and heat treatment. It would be vital for RR to remain light in weight and to keep the muscles that support the joint in good condition.

Anti-inflammatory drugs (there are many) may be used and could help RR's night pain, but in general, osteoarthritis is not an inflammatory disease and the pain is most often related to physical use of the affected joint.

Prognosis and conclusion

RR would probably have a THR at some time, but someone as determined as he was should do well as long as he remained fit and strong. Physiotherapy could help him, and he should take suitable exercise at home.

CONSULTANT'S COMMENTS

Deterioration of the joint tissues through injury or wear and tear is often seen as one of the most discouraging of medical prospects, a view reflected by the family doctor. On the other hand, osteoarthritis sufferers usually report that their condition is not a fixed entity, at least in its early stages before severe joint breakdown has occurred. Any natural variation in symptoms opens out the possibility of encouraging the body to improve on its performance, and of halting further deterioration. Even repair is conceivable, and accounts of long-term improvement are not unusual.

Treatments

Attitudes to the potential for progress in any type of case vary with individual practitioners. Strategies such as the stimulation of circulation to counter the effects of cold and damp are common to medical herbalism, naturopathy and homeopathy, and the first two of these would also concentrate on the elimination of metabolic waste products.

Arthritic deterioration seen as an outcome of toxicity is an almost universal perception in older medical traditions, but is a concept that modern medicine does not consider. Acupuncture and homeopathy would address the widest aspects of each individual condition.

The role of manipulation is interesting. The possible need for surgical replacement of the damaged hip is clearly not ruled out by the experts in this field, yet there is also a strong case for supportive manipulation.

Conclusions

Over-confidence is not appropriate to this condition, but it is often worth delaying the decision about surgical joint replacement until more conservative strategies have been tried for several months.

RHEUMATOID ARTHRITIS

THE PATIENT

PL is 50 years old with two teenage daughters, and is experiencing menopause. She is married to a farmer and works hard as a housewife and as a caterer for a small electrical company. Her life has always been physically active, and she is strong and healthy. She has dark hair and a fair complexion, and is tall and well built, but not overweight. She is outgoing and friendly, and enjoys a drink at the local pub at weekends.

THE PROBLEM

During menopause PL developed swollen and aching joints in the thumb, forefinger and wrist of her right hand. She believed it was due to the wear and tear of having her hands in water, but several months later, despite using rubber gloves, the same symptoms developed in her left hand and wrist. Her family doctor diagnosed the condition as being mild rheumatoid arthritis.

PL has always worked with her hands and is distressed about the discomfort she is suffering. She takes her responsibilities as a farmer's wife and catering manageress seriously, and is concerned that she now finds some of her routine work – such as kneading bread and so on – painful.

PL has had no serious illnesses during her life, and no stresses other than those normally associated with bringing up a family in a small community. She used to have heavy and painful periods for which she sought medical advice and found relief with proprietary drugs. The menopause has not troubled her so far, and her pregnancies and deliveries were normal.

TREATMENT BY AN
ACUPUNCTURIST

In traditional Chinese medicine, rheumatoid arthritis is known as *Bi* (or blockage) syndrome. The *Qi* is blocked at the joints, usually by one or more of the external factors *Cold*, *Damp*, *Heat* or *Wind*. Each brings about specific symptoms. A patient is usually vulnerable to the particular external factors involved due to an underlying internal disharmony. Menopause is the time at which *Jing* (constitutional energy) begins to decline.

Overuse of a particular part of the body is often a factor in the location of the disease. Although she seemed strong and healthy, PL's life had been physically demanding.

The location of the pain indicated stagnation of *Qi* and *Blood* in the *Lung* and *Large Intestine* channels of the hand. Invasion of *Cold* and *Damp* was confirmed by the fact that her symptoms were worse in cold, wet weather. Her age, her two occupations and the fact that she had raised two children had all contributed to a deficiency of *Qi* and *Blood*, and to her inability to resist the incursions of *Cold* and *Damp*.

Treatment
The treatment would be aimed at activating the body's defences against *Cold* and *Damp*. Points at or adjacent to the painful area would be used, particularly on the *Lung* and *Large Intestine* channels. Points on the *Spleen* channel would be used to activate the *Spleen* organ to eliminate *Damp*, while points on the *Large Intestine*, *Stomach* and *Ren* channels would be used to activate the *Qi* and *Yang* to combat the *Cold*. Moxibustion could be used.

PL should avoid cold, raw foods, cold drinks, and any foods causing *Damp* in the body – such as milk products and anything sweet, fried, fatty or oily. Tea, coffee and alcohol should also be avoided. Bathing the hands in a solution of hot water and the essence from fresh boiled Root Ginger would be effective in relieving symptoms.

Prognosis and conclusion
Treatment of arthritis by acupuncture is usually very effective; an average course consisting of ten treatments. The pain may not disappear completely, and PL would probably experience discomfort when overworked or run down and exposed to cold, damp weather.

Dysmenorrhoea pp. 142–145

Introduction to acupuncture pp. 8–15

TREATMENT BY A
CHIROPRACTOR

At the initial consultation the chiropractor took a case history and then examined PL's wrists and fingers to check the amount of swelling and restriction in the joints.

Treatment
Gentle massage and mobilization of the joints can frequently help the condition, so long as it is not in the reactive phase, when the joints are particularly hot and swollen.

Prognosis and conclusion
If the chiropractor thought that massage could help PL then he or she would probably refer her to a qualified masseuse. Referral to a medical herbalist, osteopath/naturopath, acupuncturist or homeopath would be considered to alleviate the symptoms and generally improve her health.

TREATMENT BY A
HOMEOPATH

When a homeopath examines someone with a chronic illness such as rheumatoid arthritis, the procedure is quite different from that of a conventional or allopathic doctor. This is because the homeopath labels the illness not as the disease to be treated but as the end-product of the disease. In other words, reducing the inflammation may not remove the cause of the illness, which would continue to harm the person's health.

To understand the disease process in PL, it was necessary to find out the way in which her constitution functioned, and how she herself had changed. Important indications were what she reacted to and how she reacted – i.e. the individual aspects of the disease process.

Several factors stood out: the rheumatoid arthritis had started during the menopause; first the right hand and then the left were affected. Being a responsible person, she was concerned that she could no longer fulfil her everyday commitments; she was outgoing and sociable; and she had had heavy, painful periods.

Treatment and prognosis
Both *Sepia* and *Pulsatilla* would be suitable remedies. Although *Sepia* is more notable as a left-sided remedy, those who respond to it are "busy bees" who wear themselves out in their concern for others. *Pulsatilla* is also indicated here, because *Pulsatilla* types thrive on a well-structured environment, and PL's lifestyle is typical of this.

After further questioning, *Sepia* could be seen as the main remedy that would be able to go deep enough to affect the constitutional weaknesses. *Pulsatilla* could be given in a 6th or 30th potency to alleviate the acute inflammation and pain. A much higher potency of *Sepia* would be necessary to ensure more lasting changes.

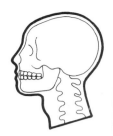

TREATMENT BY A
MEDICAL HERBALIST

Rheumatoid arthritis is an example of an anti-immune disorder in which the body attacks its own tissues. It usually develops in people with a history of low-grade infections – particularly of the respiratory and urinary systems – and PL seemed to be a typical sufferer from the condition. The onset had occurred at menopause, and her history of painful, heavy periods, indicated a hormonal factor in PL's problem. There was also some exacerbation due to her active lifestyle.

Treatment
Movements involving strain on the affected joints – such as carrying heavy loads – should be reduced as far as possible. She should adjust her diet in order to reduce any toxin build-up, by avoiding sugary foods and animal fats. Herbal medicine would initially aim at removing toxic irritants and reducing the need for an inflammatory response.

The herbal prescription would include:
- Celery Seed (*Apium graveolens*): stimulates the function of the kidneys, encourages digestive excretion, lowers levels of acidic waste products.
- Wild Yam (*Dioscorea villosa*): has a potent anti-inflammatory action (probably based on the action of steroids in the remedy) and greatly improves circulation to the extremities.
- Dandelion Root (*Taraxacum officinale)*: mild laxative and liver stimulant, increasing excretion by the bowels.
- Lignum Vitae (*Guaiacum officinale*): improves the blood supply to the extremities by widening the blood vessels, and thereby encourages cleansing of tissues in affected areas.

The prescription would need regular review, for example to further encourage kidney function, to stimulate circulation or to increase the easing of inflammation and discomfort.

Prognosis and conclusion
PL's life on a farm and her catering job may have contributed to the problem over the years by encouraging a rich diet with especially high levels of animal fats (cheese, milk, bacon and the like). Changing this could thus prove difficult for her. With careful monitoring of elimination, circulation, hormonal balance and so on, a considerable improvement will be seen.

TREATMENT BY AN
OSTEOPATH AND NATUROPATH

Rheumatoid arthritis has the image of an incurable disease with no apparent cause, although drugs can alleviate it for a time. Viruses may well be involved, but this does not explain why some people are affected by offending viruses and others are not. Experience in complementary medicine has shown that there are factors of lifestyle that coincide with either the onset or the persistence of arthritic symptoms.

Physical examination
In PL's case it was reasonable to assume that she had used her wrists beyond their capacity to cope with the strains placed upon them. It was also apparent that there was an unusual background to her problem, because its outset coincided with her menopause. Rheumatoid arthritis involves more than the joints – the body as a whole seems to proclaim the condition. This fact should govern how a sufferer from this condition is treated.

Treatment
The vertebrae involved in the nerve supply to the affected joints would be investigated and treated. Soft-tissue treatment of muscles, tendons and lymphatic channels connected with the distressed areas would be given. Visceral osteopathy would ensure that all the organs were playing their proper part in the body economy.

Respect for the joints involved in heavy work is important – somebody else (or machines) would have to do these jobs or the problem would never be resolved.

A programme of nutrition, including fasting during acute episodes, herbal and mineral supplementation, and cranial osteopathy would be suggested. The aim would be to avoid suppressive drugs and restore harmony to the menopausal hormone picture.

Prognosis and conclusion
Osteopathy, in combination with PL's own efforts, would help to relieve her arthritis. Hydrotherapeutic procedures and herbal or homeopathic remedies should also be considered.

Introduction to medical herbalism pp. 32–37

Introduction to osteopathy with naturopathy pp. 38–47

TREATMENT BY A
FAMILY DOCTOR

Rheumatoid arthritis is a disease that varies considerably, but can be devastatingly deforming and may be only part of a major, complex rheumatoid disease with organs as well as joints being affected. PL presented a typical early picture of a symmetrical and possibly progressive condition. The diagnosis was suggested by her family history and the clinical picture, but could be confirmed by specific tests and X-rays.

Treatment
There is no known cause of rheumatoid arthritis and no specific preventive measures. PL should keep up her general fitness and strength, but avoid over-exercising painful joints. Although rest would be invaluable for relieving symptoms, excessive rest and the splinting of joints can result in muscle wastage and joint deformity. It must be undertaken only in collaboration with a skilled physiotherapist.

Painkillers are often important in treatment and may be used in conjunction with a variety of specific anti-inflammatory agents (aspirin, gold, chloroquine and even steroids). If she suffered much pain and sleeplessness she might be treated with stronger analgesics and possibly hypnotics.

Should the condition worsen, PL would be put under the care of a rheumatologist and his or her physiotherapy team. She would also need skilled care and counselling from her family doctor, who could also organize help from the local social services occupational therapy department. The Rheumatoid Arthritis Association could offer helpful advice.

PL might, however, need little treatment, and her condition could remain mild – as it often does among older women. About half the patients who present symptoms similar to those of PL have a full remission with little or no evidence of residual damage or deficit.

Prognosis and conclusion
PL would have good reason to be optimistic. Acute symptoms could be controlled, and working out the right amount of exercise and rest with a physiotherapist would enable her to continue with her work – unless she were in the unhappy minority with a progressive form of the disease.

CONSULTANT'S COMMENTS

This is a puzzling and complex condition that might not worsen, might improve spontaneously, or might progress into an increasingly crippling disorder. It is wise to be cautious about accepting any claims that a treatment can correct rheumatoid arthritis. There is evidence, however, that complementary therapies have been effective in alleviating it – although, of course, this sometimes may coincide with spontaneous remission.

The treatments
The homeopath stresses the dangers of concentrating too much on the symptoms of the disease. The complexity of the immunological and inflammatory processes involved in rheumatoid arthritis mean that profound changes are taking place in the whole body. Even the narrowest medical explanation must accept this.

While anti-inflammatory drugs have brought much comfort to millions of sufferers around the world, concern about their side-effects is now intense. It can fairly be said that the medical strategy is to relieve symptoms and hope for spontaneous remission.

The acupuncturist, medical herbalist, and osteopath/naturopath all opt for measures that seek to remove irritant "toxins" or impurities – or, in the case of the acupuncturist, *"Damp"* – from the body, or at least to reduce their production. This approach, developed through centuries of clinical experience around the world, has much to commend it. Toxicity can be reduced, and painful symptoms of this condition relieved, through the dietary changes outlined by several of the practitioners.

Summary
It is difficult, with complex disorders such as this, to make a firm recommendation. There is real hope, however, for sufferers pursuing a broad-based therapeutic approach outside conventional drug treatment.

SLIPPED DISK

THE PATIENT

KL is 55 years old and has three grown up children. She lives in the country and runs a local store with her husband. Her only active recreation is walking the dog, but she has had to stop this recently because of her back trouble. Her skin is fine with a healthy glow and she looks young, but her muscle tone is poor and she has a flabby abdomen and thighs. She eats a regular wholefood diet.

THE PROBLEM

As a teenager KL pulled a muscle in her lower back and felt the vertebrae "lock" when she reached down to pick strawberries. This condition improved, but continued to trouble her after strenuous exercise or lifting heavy objects, and was especially bad in cold weather.

This autumn, KL moved house and did a lot of lifting. One morning she tried to stand from a sitting position and her back "locked" again. This time she could not move without help. The condition was diagnosed using X-rays as a slipped disk (prolapsed intervertebral disk) and she was advised to rest. The pain was acute, affecting all of her lower body and making it difficult to urinate. It was improved by complete stillness, lying on her back with pillows under her knees, and hot compresses.

KL is an active, cheerful person and is kept busy running the shop. She has been healthy throughout her life. Her first and third pregnancies were normal, but she experienced a lot of bleeding through the second and had to rest a great deal.

When KL has colds they often develop into sinusitis. This usually clears up without treatment, but occasionally requires antibiotics. She developed varicose veins (on the front of her calves) after the third child was born, and these are unsightly, but not uncomfortable. She gets fibrositis during cold windy weather and the nodules appear between her shoulder blades and up to her neck. These can be very painful, but warmth alleviates the problem. She has heavy periods and has been anaemic at times.

In traditional Chinese medicine a slipped disk is classified as acute back sprain, and because it involves traumatic injury, stagnation of *Qi* is accompanied by stagnation of *Blood*; this means that pain is severe and that there is usually restriction of movement.

KL had a history of injury to her back. This resulted in stagnation of *Qi*, which was therefore failing to warm and maintain strength in the lower back, and *Cold* had been allowed to penetrate – thus the pain was worse in cold weather. This further blocked the circulation of *Qi* and *Blood*, weakening her back still further. After moving house, KL began to suffer from classic signs of acute injury, with stagnation of *Qi* and *Blood* causing acute pain and immobility, and obstructing the flow of *Qi* to her bladder. There were also signs – such as poor muscle tone and fibrositis – that KL's *Qi* was in decline after a demanding life, and that this was leading to generally poor *Qi* circulation.

Treatment
Points on the *Du* or *Urinary Bladder* channels, or empirical points, would be used. Acupuncture would work to activate the stagnation of *Qi* and *Blood* in the area of injury, relaxing spasm, alleviating pain and restoring movement. However, caution would be needed because there would be extreme weakness in the injured area, even after the pain had been relieved and some movement restored. Further treatment to strengthen the local flow of *Qi* and *Blood* would enhance healing and help to prevent recurrence. General treatment to strengthen the *Qi* and *Blood* of the whole body would also be advised.

Prognosis and conclusion
Acupuncture can have dramatic effects in treating acute back sprain. Daily treatment while the injury was acute would be ideal. Once the acute phase had passed, ten twice weekly or weekly treatments would probably be sufficient. If treatment was applied within a week the prognosis would be better than if treatment was delayed, because the stagnation of *Qi* and *Blood* would become fixed. Referral to an osteopath would be considered in order to deal with any structural problems once strength had returned to the back.

TREATMENT BY A
CHIROPRACTOR

Slipped disks, otherwise known as prolapsed inter-vertebral disks, are conditions frequently treated by chiropractors. They usually respond well to precise manipulative treatment. Disks between the vertebrae can prolapse (or bulge) in a number of different directions, and the symptoms experienced can be many and varied. As well as prolapsing, disks can also fragment – that is, pieces can come away from the disk itself. In cases like this, and in certain disk prolapses, surgery may be essential.

Physical examination
Many of the orthopaedic and neurological tests showed the presence of abnormalities. Acute muscle spasm was found in the low back. KL's problems with urination caused considerable con-cern because this often indicates a severe problem. In this case, however, the condition was not so severe that it would necessarily require surgery.

Treatment
The use of ice packs on the low back would be advised to help reduce inflammation to the point where KL would be able to move more easily. Once this had been achieved, a more thorough examin-ation could be carried out, and gentle treatment begun to reduce the disk prolapse and pressure on the nerves, thus relieving the pain in the back of the legs. Work would also be done on the muscle spasm in the low back; treatment of this would consist of soft-tissue work, with perhaps some ultrasound or other therapeutic treatment. KL would also be asked to carry on with the ice regime.

Prognosis and conclusion
Even if KL did need to have a spinal operation, which can be the case with slipped disks, the chances are that she would make a good recovery. However, she would be advised, once recovered, to try a regular exercise routine – such as swimming – to tone up her low back and stomach muscles. She would have to take life a little more easily, with less lifting and carrying. She would be advised to sit down occasionally, rather than stand all day.

At some stage in the future it might be a good idea for her to seek chiropractic therapy to improve her fibrositis problem.

TREATMENT BY A
HOMEOPATH

For primary treatment of a slipped disk, a homeopath would refer the patient to an osteopath or a chiropractor. The role of the homeopath would be to support treatment by manipulation of the spine, and to treat the patient as a whole to raise basic health levels.

Diagnosis
KL's poor muscle tone was putting increased stress on her spine, and since one cause of poor tone was lack of exercise, treatment should begin there. It was also a constitutional weakness, and therefore amenable to homeopathic treatment. This was indicated by her other symptoms: varicose veins after pregnancy, colds that developed into sinusitis, heavy periods, anaemia, and difficulty in urinating when the back problem was severe. KL's easy-going nature showed her to be relaxed mentally.

Calcarea, Sepia, and *Pulsatilla* would be consi-dered as remedies. *Calcarea* would be chosen as the best fit for KL's constitution. *Pulsatilla* would be given for the acute back pains because it more specifically covers the symptom of back pain originating from prolonged stooping. *Pulsatilla* could also be given for other acute symptoms in a patient with a basically *Calcarea* constitution.

KL's long-term health, however, would need *Calcarea*, which could correct the heavy periods and her rheumatic tendency. Both of these con-ditions were much deeper than the others, and therefore needed a deeper remedy.

This situation illustrates the way in which a homeopath often divides a case. The layered nature of KL's condition revealed itself when it became obvious that a single remedy did not fit the entire symptom picture.

Treatment and prognosis
After chiropractic or osteopathic manipulation, a single dose of *Pulsatilla* 30 might be given to ease the discomfort and promote healing. *Pulsatilla* might be repeated for acute symptoms of pain, as the patient found necessary. After the acute phase had settled, a single high-potency dose of *Calcarea* would be given. Recovery should be quick, and further relapses should be prevented.

Introduction to chiropractic treatment pp. 16–23   Introduction to homeopathy pp. 24–31

TREATMENT BY A
MEDICAL HERBALIST

TREATMENT BY AN
OSTEOPATH AND NATUROPATH

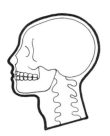

Almost certainly the first advice given to KL would be for her to see an osteopath or a chiropractor to assess what could be done through manipulative therapy. Herbal treatment could be useful in various ways, and there were other aspects of KL's health that needed attention.

Treatment
The relief that KL experienced from the use of hot compresses would be greatly enhanced by the inclusion of essential oil of Lavender in the compress, which would act to provoke increased warmth and muscle relaxation and would have something of an analgesic effect. Her general circulation needed to be improved as shown by her varicose vein problem and the tendency to anaemia. Short-term analgesic and anti-inflammatory agents would be helpful, but in the longer term efforts to improve muscle tone, especially of the abdomen and lower back, and exercises for the legs to assist venous return would be invaluable.

The herbal prescription would include:
● Willow Bark (*Salix nigra*): anti-inflammatory, analgesic, and stimulates digestive function.
● Cramp Bark (*Viburnum opulus*): muscle relaxant, which can also be valuable when used locally.
● Horse Chestnut (*Aesculus hippocastanum*): anti-inflammatory agent, which would act to astringe and tone the walls of the swollen veins.
● Yellow Dock (*Rumex crispus*): improves bowel function and provides iron.
● Black Cohosh (*Cimicifuga racemosa*): relieves muscle spasm and reduces the inflammatory response by increasing blood circulation through the tissues.

The prescription would be adjusted as necessary.

Prognosis and conclusion
With help – probably involving manipulative as well as herbal treatment – KL could improve considerably from her incapacitated state. She would need to take care with her exercise and her posture in the future, and could achieve a greater degree of vitality for many years to come.

KL's history of back injuries had culminated in her "slipped disk", a term which is applied to various back problems, each of which has its own symptoms and an appropriate treatment.

As well as having a flabby abdomen and thighs, KL's history of bleeding during pregnancy, varicose veins, heavy periods and anaemia all suggested a lack of tone in her muscles that was predisposing her to back and disk problems.

Physical examination
The position and mobility of KL's vertebrae were examined, and note was taken of the direction in which she was leaning because of the pain. X-rays would determine the extent of the damage.

Treatment
Deep massage would help drain the areas on either side of the spine. Wedges placed under the pelvis and hips would position the joints in the area, and therefore the lumbar vertebrae also, and help to reduce pain. Positional release techniques would be used rather than high-velocity thrusts wherever KL had structural imbalances. If her lumbar spine was too painful to be touched, initial treatments would concentrate on the upper spine and cranium.

Acute episodes would demand rest – if KL could find a comfortable position and no therapist was available. Heat should not be applied to a painful disk because this would tend to increase the pressure on the nerve; an ice-cold application, however, would encourage the disk material to move back toward its correct position.

A mineral combination of potassium chloride and iron phosphate has some influence on pain caused by inflammation, and could replace analgesic drugs. KL would be instructed in the safe ways of lifting and on the postural use of her body.

Prognosis and conclusion
The prognosis would depend on the extent of the damage, and in severe cases an operation may be essential, but since damage was not too severe in this case KL could expect considerable improvement in her condition with osteopathic help. She would probably, however, have to give up some of her more strenuous activities.

Introduction to medical herbalism pp. 32–39

Introduction to osteopathy with naturopathy pp. 40–47

TREATMENT BY A
FAMILY DOCTOR

This is a condition in which damage of the disks between the lumbar vertebrae causes irritation of the nerve roots that leave the spinal cord between the bones. This can cause referred pain, for instance in the legs, depending on which nerve roots are involved, and nerve damage may result.

Diagnosis involved a combination of clinical assessment and X-rays. Special scans on X-rays can be appropriate in such a case. It would be important to know if her difficulty in urinating was due to the pain of sitting or to interference with the nerve supply to the bladder, in which case urgent investigation by a specialist would be essential.

Treatment

The treatment would involve rest for the acute phase – with or without traction – followed by physiotherapy, exercises and possibly the use of a special corset. Osteopathy would help, provided there was no nerve damage. Surgery was not likely to be necessary, but KL did have a proved disk lesion and the possibility of continued pressure on the nerve roots existed.

KL was not fit and her muscle tone was poor; on top of this she had a job requiring a lot of lifting for which her body was inadequately prepared. A physiotherapist could help her, and taking some exercise could make a great improvement. She might need to consider having extra help in the shop with lifting and packaging.

Although not connected with her back problem, her varicose veins might become a nuisance, and her lack of fitness would contribute to this. Exercises, and possibly the use of special stockings, would be useful. Her fibrositis – which is really a condition of muscle spasm – should benefit from exercise and physiotherapy, or from treatment by an osteopath or chiropractor.

Prognosis and conclusion

A slipped disk is the most important, but not the most common, cause of chronic backache. It is potentially damaging, and although most cases heal with conservative treatment, any worsening symptoms such as numbness and weakness should be referred to a specialist.

CONSULTANT'S COMMENTS

Disruption of the supportive tissue of the lower back is not a matter for superficial judgements. The sheer scale of the human engineering demands in the area, and the vulnerability of the spine and the nerves that come from it, makes this problem a job for the skilled professionals.

All the therapists, even those most qualified to comment, acknowledge the need for caution, but most have approaches they might adopt in reducing contributory factors.

The treatments

The family doctor sets the pace in seeking X-ray and possible specialist diagnosis before going much further. He also gives consideration to treatment by osteopathy, chiropractic therapy or physiotherapy.

The skills of either the chiropractor or the osteopath are an essential part of the possible contribution of the other therapists. Although acupuncture can be very effective in correcting distorting influences in the long term, in China, as elsewhere, it is still secondary to structural manipulation. This is also true for medical herbalism, with its anti-inflammatory and relaxing remedies, and for homeopathy.

Conclusions

This is the sort of case in which the chiropractor's or osteopath's experiences are most useful. For the diagnosis and assessment of this potentially serious form of back injury, the chiropractor with more likely access to X-rays, and closer empathy with the skills of the orthopaedic surgeon, might be the first call. But there are many good osteopaths who would also provide a comprehensive diagnostic service.

Introduction to Western medicine pp. 48–55

TENNIS ELBOW

THE PATIENT

JV is 42 years old and married with two children, aged 13 and 16. He is of medium height and athletic build, with strong features, and a forceful personality. He does not smoke, and drinks wine and beer occasionally.

THE PROBLEM

JV has recently developed the symptoms of "tennis elbow". This condition is caused by minor damage to the tendons of the wrist and the muscles that extend the fingers where they attach to the bone at the outer side of the elbow.

The symptoms started with pain in the outer forearm near the elbow of the right arm – JV is right-handed. The pain is particularly acute when gripping a tennis racket and moving the wrist.

JV plays tennis at least twice a week and once every weekend, and enjoys other racket sports in the winter. He also runs and swims, and plays golf once or twice a month.

Before the tennis elbow symptoms developed, however, the pressures of work (JV is a senior executive in an advertising company) prevented him taking any exercise apart from his summer tennis, although to compensate he tried to play an extra game each weekend.

JV has had regular medical check-ups over the past seven years. Apart from periodic bouts of indigestion, and occasional winter colds, he has been healthy since his youth, although slightly raised blood pressure, probably stress-related, was noted at the last check-up. He also develops mild haemorrhoids occasionally.

TREATMENT BY AN
ACUPUNCTURIST

In traditional Chinese medicine, the condition described as tennis elbow is seen as a problem affecting the *Large Intestine* channel, which traverses the arm at the elbow. The cause is either injury or overuse, although there is often an internal disharmony which acts as a predisposing factor.

The combination of circumstances affecting JV – increased stress from work pressure, reduced regular exercise, and overcompensation – is significant in this case. The increased stress has compromised the *Qi* circulation in his body generally; his slightly raised blood pressure is evidence of this. The impairment of *Qi* circulation also affects the *Blood* circulation, which means that the peripheral parts of the body are insufficiently nourished and protected. They are therefore more susceptible to injury either from the elements or from overuse.

In JV's case, overuse in the extra games of tennis is the specific cause of his problem. Identifying the underlying disharmony is important if local treatment is to have a lasting effect.

Treatment
Needles would be used at or very near to the source of the pain, as well as in the forearm, hand and wrist. This would deal with the local symptoms by improving the circulation of *Qi* in the affected area and in the arm generally.

To correct the internal disharmony, points on the trunk, arms and legs would be needled, so that the general circulation of *Qi* would improve. This would also support the local, symptomatic treatment.

Exercises would be recommended to improve the circulation of *Qi*. JV would have to stop playing tennis during the treatment, or at least until all pain in his arm had disappeared. He would also need to look at the effect of stress on his health and decide how he is going to deal with this.

Prognosis and conclusion
Treatment of tennis elbow with acupuncture is usually effective. Initially treatment would be given two or three times a week. If JV's problem responded normally, a course of about five or six treatments would be expected.

Hypertension pp. 94–97   Haemorrhoids pp. 124–127

Introduction to acupuncture pp. 8–15

TREATMENT BY A
CHIROPRACTOR

JV was asked to strip to the wrist, so that the elbow, neck and upper chest area could be examined freely. The movements of the elbow in bending, straightening and rotating were checked to see if there was any restriction to movement, and to determine which movements aggravated the pain. Palpating all around the elbow enabled specific areas of tenderness to be localized, and any areas of heat or swelling to be identified.

JV's neck was also examined carefully to check for any areas – especially at the base of the neck – where lack of normal spinal mobility might cause nerve irritation and result in referred pain at the elbow.

Treatment and prognosis
The main object, initially, would be to reduce the acute tenderness or inflammation around the elbow. This could be done with the aid of ice packs, cold sprays, or ultrasound therapy. Painful points in the muscles around the elbow, forearm and upper arm would be treated by the application of specific pressure to the tender spots. During treatment, cold spray would be used on these tender points while the elbow was moved in various directions. The purpose of this manipulation is to gradually increase the mobility of the elbow joint.

Any problems revealed by palpation of the spine, especially at the base of the neck, would be treated by specific spinal manipulation, but none was found in JV's case.

Treatment would gradually restore the elbow to normal functioning, but until then JV should not play tennis at all.

To speed the healing process, the elbow and wrist could be immobilized in a sling until the acute, and very painful, phase was over. Ice packs that could be applied at home would also help speed recovery. Once the pain had stopped, exercises would be given to help strengthen the elbow and wrist.

Only if these cautious steps failed would it be necessary, as a last resort, to refer JV for an anti-inflammatory injection of cortisone to the elbow.

TREATMENT BY A
HOMEOPATH

At the first meeting JV's general appearance, manner and posture were assessed for the information they can provide about his character. This had bearing on the context in which his condition had developed, and therefore influenced the choice of treatment. This process is especially important in treating acute complaints because there may not be time to go into the "total symptom picture", and the patient may not be familiar with the detailed investigation required in order to make a homeopathic prescription.

JV's manner indicated a high level of stress in his life, which needs to be borne in mind when treatment is prescribed. He indicated that the stiffness of the injured elbow was worse in the morning and after rest, and lessened as the joint was gently moved, even though doing this was painful at first. The increase of pain when grasping a racket was particularly significant, and indicated the homeopathic remedy *Rhus Tox*.

Treatment and prognosis
Rhus Tox would be prescribed in the 30th potency to treat JV's condition. One dose would be prescribed initially, although this could be repeated at bedtime or in the morning if the symptoms returned after the initial relief. Warm wraps for the elbow would also be recommended, to encourage blood flow in the injured region.

The situation would be reviewed after 48 hours, but normally healing would be well established by this time. Other practical precautions – such as maintaining mobility of the joint without straining it – would be recommended for a period of about ten days, after which time normal activities could be resumed gradually.

Certain factors in the case point to a generalized response to stress as the basic problem. For this reason the constitutional background would also need treatment. JV's general fitness and good health are marred by his lack of relaxation, and he must attend to these if he is to maintain his efficiency. Once the elbow condition had improved he would be treated constitutionally with *Nux Vomica*. This remedy's symptom picture includes digestive symptoms such as indigestion, constipation and haemorrhoids, and also covers raised blood pressure.

Introduction to chiropractic therapy pp. 16–23   Introduction to homeopathy pp. 24–31

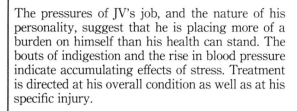
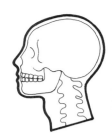

TREATMENT BY A
MEDICAL HERBALIST

The pressures of JV's job, and the nature of his personality, suggest that he is placing more of a burden on himself than his health can stand. The bouts of indigestion and the rise in blood pressure indicate accumulating effects of stress. Treatment is directed at his overall condition as well as at his specific injury.

Treatment and prognosis

The herbal prescription would include:

• Hawthorn (*Crataegus oxyacanthoides*): improves blood supply both to the coronary arteries and the peripheral circulation; helps to return blood pressure to normal.

• Devil's Claw (*Harpagophytum procumbens*): relieves immediate discomfort through its pronounced analgesic and anti-inflammatory properties.

• Gentian (*Gentiana lutea*): a bitter stimulant of digestive and liver function, which decreases the body's toxin build-up.

• Wild Yam (*Dioscorea villosa*): reduces spasm and visceral tension, and has an anti-inflammatory action.

• Lime Flower (*Tilia europea*): acts as a peripheral vasodilator and relaxant, and increases blood flow through the injured tissues.

• Horse Chestnut (*Aesculus hippocastanium*): tones up swollen blood vessels and increases the excretion of toxins through the kidneys.

In addition to the prescription, hot poultices made from fresh Ginger Root would provide extra local stimulation to the blood supply and cleanse the tissues in the injured area. In the course of treatment the prescription would probably be varied to take account of underlying imbalances that would become apparent from JV's specific responses to treatment.

JV would be advised to exercise for a while, primarily by swimming, with only a gradual return to other sports. Yoga would be strongly recommended as a method of combining exercise, particularly of the abdominal muscles, with relaxation. His diet should also be reviewed; his aim should be to eat a greater proportion of wholefoods and to eat his meals more slowly.

TREATMENT BY AN
OSTEOPATH AND NATUROPATH

In taking note of JV's case history, particular attention is paid to the exact circumstances in which the injury occurred. The indications are that the injury occurred suddenly, as a result of weakness from JV's having neglected his accustomed fitness programme, rather than as a consequence of a strain problem that had been building up over a long period.

Physical examination

All joints, muscles, tendons and nerve pathways involved in the elbow's functioning were examined. Questions about the occurrence of pain were also asked – whether it was more noticeable at times of stress in business, for instance – in case this had bearing on his recovery. If healing took a long time, for example, complicating problems such as the effects of stress would have to be considered.

Treatment and prognosis

The first, and most important, requirement would be that JV should avoid any movement that would further stretch the sinew at the point where the tendon inserts into the elbow bone. Inflammation in the elbow joint would be relieved by applying either cold compresses alone or alternating hot and cold packs. Cold is more effective than heat in removing acute pain.

Neuromuscular blocks along the outer side of the forearm were identified by palpation. The tenderness of these blocks would be relieved by deep finger pressure both along and across the muscle fibres. Osteopathic lesions in the vertebrae of the neck that inhibit the blood and nerve supply to the elbow would also be adjusted. Freedom of shoulder movement would be achieved by releasing muscle tension in the back, across the shoulder blades, and in the upper part of the chest.

To assist JV's recovery, specific resistance exercises for the wrists and fingers would be recommended to counteract weaknesses in grasping and lifting or turning the arm, or stretching the fingers. These exercises would be determined by analysis of imbalances in JV's particular case; the same exercises would not necessarily apply to another person.

Introduction to medical herbalism pp. 32–39

Introduction to osteopathy with naturopathy pp. 40–47

TREATMENT BY A
FAMILY DOCTOR

Although the symptoms are commonly described as "tennis elbow", they can also occur as a result of minor strains or injuries to the forearm or elbow at home or at work. A common variation affecting the inside of the elbow, caused by strain of the flexor muscles of the wrist and forearm, is called "golfer's elbow". This is treated in a similar way.

Treatment

The normal treatment for tennis elbow would be simply to rest the damaged muscles and tendons. The application of cold sprays or ice packs to the inflamed area would also help to relieve painful symptoms, although these normally diminish rapidly anyway if the elbow is rested. In JV's case, however, rest would not be entirely practical, because it would be important that he maintained his fitness by continuing to exercise while protecting his injured elbow. Swimming, running and workouts not involving the affected arm would be obvious alternatives to tennis.

Non-steroid anti-inflammatory drugs would be helpful in treating tennis elbow but would not be recommended in JV's case because they can cause stomach irritation, aggravating his indigestion and, at worst, cause gastric bleeding. If JV had time for physiotherapy, a combination of this with ultrasonic treatment would be beneficial. While exercising, a firm arm band strapped around the forearm just below the injured area would allow the strain to be taken a little farther along the muscle, thereby protecting the injured area. If symptoms persisted, an injection of hydrocortisone into the tender area, followed by complete resting of the arm for two days, would help.

Prognosis and conclusion

JV should anticipate spending several weeks without playing tennis, then some more weeks playing carefully, in order to maximize the chances of full recovery. And there is a possibility that the problem may recur. Once recovered JV should try to keep his fitness programme as balanced as possible and should avoid the temptation to over-exercise. It would be advisable for him to use a supporting arm band when playing racket sports.

CONSULTANT'S COMMENTS

The circumstances leading to JV's condition are typical precursors of tennis elbow. It commonly affects people who are fit and active, especially those who tend to push themselves physically, although it is also common among people who exercise to excess in a racket sport after a long period without playing.

The treatments

All the therapies recommend short-term rest followed by a gradual resumption of exercise. They also stress the importance of avoiding the temptation to over-exercise in future.

The homeopath, medical herbalist and acupuncturist emphasize the need for JV to modify certain aspects of his lifestyle and they treat his state of health as a whole. The other therapies focus on local treatment to enable him to return to his habitual activities as quickly as possible. They also offer practical advice about avoiding the problem in future.

It is interesting to note that the chiropractor and family doctor both recommend the application of ice packs to the injured area to reduce both the inflammation and the pain, whereas homeopathy and medical herbalism suggest hot applications, to stimulate the blood supply, cleanse the tissues, and speed up the natural healing process.

Summary

All six therapies seem to be equally successful in treating tennis elbow. Where stress, which is often indirectly associated with the development of such conditions, is a feature of a person's lifestyle, therapies such as acupuncture, homeopathy and medical herbalism can be of additional benefit.

Introduction to Western medicine pp. 48–56

GUIDE TO TREATMENT OF MUSCULO-SKELETAL DISORDERS 1

CONDITION	ACUPUNCTURE	CHIROPRACTIC	HOMEOPATHY
ANKYLOSIS Immobility of a joint	Treatment of a chronic condition may take time but improvement is possible, although it would not reverse changes in bone structure.	Treatment would help maintain mobility of the joints; patient would be referred to a rheumatologist if necessary.	Treatment can be effective. Healing time depends on whether or not the cause is local; manipulation may also be required.
BOW LEG Outward curvature of leg	Would not treat; would refer to a specialist.	Would not treat; would refer to an orthopaedic specialist.	Would not treat; bones still at the formative stage of development may be helped by constitutional treatment.
BURSITIS Inflammation of joint	Treatment can be effective.	Treatment can be effective; referral may be necessary if fluid needs to be withdrawn.	Treatment can be effective, but the time taken will depend on whether the cause is a local injury or more widespread in body.
CARPAL TUNNEL SYNDROME Compression of nerve in wrist	Treatment particularly effective in acute phase.	Treatment can be effective; patient would be referred for surgery if necessary.	Treatment is primarily constitutional, and therefore long-term, but is usually successful.
CLUBFOOT Deformity of foot	Would not treat; would refer to a specialist.	Would not treat, but would refer to an orthopaedic specialist.	Would not treat; constitutional treatment would help stabilize the condition after surgery, and aid recovery.
CRAMP Painful muscular spasm	Treatment would be effective both locally and constitutionally.	Effectiveness of treatment depends on the cause of the condition; referral may be necessary.	Treatment is effective; limitations depend on overall constitutional picture.
DEVIATED NASAL SEPTUM Displacement inside the nose	Treatment could not change any structural problem, but would help clear the nasal passage and improve breathing.	Would not treat; would refer to an orthopaedic specialist.	Would not treat; would refer to a specialist.
DISLOCATION Displacement of a bone	Treatment would help in the relief of pain.	An acute dislocation can be reduced if treated immediately; chronic conditions may need referral for surgery.	Would not treat, although homeopathic remedies provide useful support for other therapies and can help recovery from the physical and emotional trauma.
FIBROSITIS Inflammation around muscle	Treatment can be effective in some cases.	Treatment can be effective.	Localized rheumatism responds well to acute treatment; long-term treatment would be constitutional; some cases would be referred for manipulation.
FLAT FOOT Depression of foot arch	Would not treat; would refer to a specialist.	Would not treat, but would refer to an orthopaedic specialist.	Would not treat; would refer to a chiropractor, osteopath or physiotherapist.
FROZEN SHOULDER Stiffness and pain in shoulder	Treatment of both acute and chronic cases can be effective.	Treatment can be effective.	Treatment is usually successful; the condition needs constitutional treatment for permanent results, and is greatly aided by manipulation.
HERNIA Pushing of gut through wall of abdomen	Treatment could be effective, but hernias are not usually treated by acupuncture.	Would not treat; would refer to a specialist.	Treatment is usually successful; if the hernia has been allowed to degenerate, it may also need physical or surgical treatment.
KYPHOSIS Hunched back	Treatment could help in relief of associated pain.	Treatment can be effective in increasing mobility and reducing any pain or discomfort.	Treatment is often effective, but would also refer to chiropractor or osteopath.
LORDOSIS Backward sway of spine	Treatment could help in relief of associated pain.	Treatment can be effective in increasing mobility and reducing any pain or discomfort.	Treatment is effective if bones are at the formative stage of development; prognosis may also depend on factors such as muscle tone.
LUMBAGO Pain in lower back	Can be very effective in relieving pain; may have long-term benefits, depending on cause.	Treatment is often very effective.	Treatment of acute condition can be effective. Chronic conditions may require osteopathy and chiropractic therapy.

MED HERBALISM	OSTEOPATHY	GEN. MEDICINE	COMMENTS
Treatment could be useful, but success would depend on cause and severity.	Treatment limited by degree of degeneration and patient's willingness to undertake an exercise programme; nutritional regime also required.	Treatment with anti-inflammatory drugs usually effective; long-term specialist follow-up, physiotherapy, and changes in lifestyle also required.	See also **Backache**, pp. 152–155
Treatment could relieve symptoms such as pain or inflammation.	Effectiveness of treatment depends on age of person and stage of tissue degeneration.	Would recommend physiotherapy and exercises.	
Treatment would help to reduce inflammation and effusion of fluid.	Treatment can be effective in both acute and chronic state; chronic treatment might be prolonged.	Rest, alone or combined with anti-inflammatory drugs, can be effective; a change of occupation may also be required.	See also **Tennis elbow**, pp. 168–171
Treatment of limited benefit unless combined with acupuncture or osteopathy.	Treatment can be effective if there is no nerve or tendon damage.	Rest and non-steroid anti-inflammatory drugs usually effective; might refer for local steroid injection, or surgery and post-operative physiotherapy.	
Would not treat; would refer to specialist.	Treatment depends on age. Would not treat if inherited condition.	Would not treat, but would refer to an orthopaedic surgeon; physiotherapy, special appliances, and surgery can also help.	
Treatment effective in most types of muscle cramp.	Prognosis generally excellent if the causes are not irreversible ones, such as circulatory failure.	Treatment difficult; some medications are helpful; exercises and physiotherapy can also help.	
Would not treat; would refer to a specialist.	Treatment can be effective if septum is intact.	Treatment with decongestants is of limited value in acute cases; surgery is the most effective cure.	See also **Sinusitis**, pp. 76–79
Would not treat an acute dislocation; would refer to a manipulative practitioner. Herbalism could help to relieve accompanying symptoms.	Treatment can be effective if immediate and the condition is uncomplicated; homeopathy may be useful for pain relief.	Some cases can be treated easily; others need specialist help; surgical repair is effective for chronic cases.	See also **FIRST AID**, pp. 226–231
Internal and external herbal treatments can be of great value.	Treatment can be effective in both acute and chronic cases.	Counselling helps if stress is a cause; exercise, physiotherapy or osteopathy can treat physical causes; non-steroid anti-inflammatory drugs can also help.	See also **Backache**, pp. 152–155
Would not treat, but would refer for exercises to help correct condition.	Treatment can be effective if general physical tone is good.	Treatment with physiotherapy, exercises and weight-reduction may help; special shoes may also be needed; children would be referred to an orthopaedist.	
Treatment can be effective unless condition is chronic; if tissue degeneration has occurred, however, treatment would be of limited value.	Treatment can be effective if both physical and psychosomatic causes are dealt with.	Rest, heat treatment and physiotherapy are essential; non-steroid anti-inflammatory drugs or injections can help acute cases.	See also **Slipped disk**, pp. 164–167
Would not treat; would refer to a specialist.	Treatment would be primarily naturopathic; it can be effective in the long term if the hernia is reversible by postural changes.	Some hernias require no treatment except physiotherapy or use of appliances; in severe cases, surgery is the definitive treatment.	
Would treat causes such as arthritis; would refer to a manipulative therapist for treatment of body distortion.	Treatment effective if condition is acquired not inherited, and disks are not permanently wedged; primary aim would be to increase mobility.	Would refer to a specialist for physiotherapy, exercises and advice; children must be referred to a paediatrician.	See also **Backache**, pp. 152–155
Would not treat; would refer to a manipulative therapist.	Treatment effective if condition is acquired not inherited, and disks are not permanently wedged; primary aim would be to increase mobility.	Advice on posture, combined with physiotherapy and exercises would be helpful; chiropractic therapy or osteopathy would also be useful.	See also **Backache**, pp. 152–155
Would treat, but if cause was unclear would refer to an osteopath or chiropractor for advice.	Treatment generally very effective.	Condition improved by relaxation, attention to posture, and exercises. Non-steroidal anti-inflammatory drugs may help.	See also **Backache**, pp. 152–155

TREATMENT OF MUSCULO-SKELETAL DISORDERS 2

CONDITION	ACUPUNCTURE	CHIROPRACTIC	HOMEOPATHY
MUSCLE STRAIN Tearing of muscle fibres	Treatment often effective in both acute and chronic conditions.	Acute and chronic conditions can be treated effectively.	Treatment often very effective. It should be accompanied by rest, heat and hydrotherapy where appropriate.
MUSCULAR DYSTROPHY Wasting away of muscles	Treatment may slow down degeneration if condition is treated in its early stages.	Would not treat; but if the patient also suffers with back trouble, that could be treated.	This condition has shown only limited responses to constitutional treatment. Effectiveness would depend on depth of pathology.
OEDEMA Swelling due to fluid accumulation	Treatment can be effective depending on the cause – allergy, disorder of circulation or kidney disorder, or injury – and the general health of the patient.	Treatment may be effective if the problem is due to a circulatory disorder, but if so further medical tests would also be required.	Treatment of oedema due to local trauma is usually successful; treatment of systemic problems depends on seriousness of condition.
OSTEITIS Inflammation of a bone	Treatment may help relieve pain associated with condition.	Would not treat; would refer for specialist treatment.	Treatment can be effective in some cases, but not in isolation from the full constitutional picture.
OSTEOPOROSIS Softening of a bone	Treatment may help; much depends on general health and age of patient.	Would advise on using dietary supplements to help prevent the bones thinning; if there is pain, gentle spinal treatment might be applied.	Response to treatment depends on the stage of the degeneration. If causes are menopausal, there is often a good response.
PARALYSIS Inability to move muscles due to a nerve disorder	If due to stroke, treatment in first six weeks can be effective. Prolonged treatment would be necessary.	Would not treat; would refer to a specialist.	Treatment would depend on cause and degree of pathology. Referral to neurologist would be made.
POLIOMYELITIS Inflammation of grey matter of spinal cord	Would not treat; would refer to a specialist.	Would not treat; would refer to a specialist.	Would not treat; only medical practitioners may treat this disease.
RHEUMATISM Stiff muscles and painful joints	Treatment can be very effective, depending on stage of condition.	Acute and chronic cases can be treated effectively.	A high percentage of success, but treatment may be prolonged if condition is chronic. Referral for physiotherapy may be appropriate.
RICKETS Abnormality of bone development caused by vitamin D or calcium deficiency	Treatment would not reverse structural damage but, with dietary changes, could help restore normal growth in children.	Would not treat; would refer to a specialist.	Treatment can be effective, but cannot repair structural damage. Constitutional treatment with dietary advice would benefit general health.
SPONDYLITIS Inflammation of vertebrae	Treatment can help to relieve pain and increase spinal mobility.	Acute and chronic cases can be treated effectively.	Treatment may relieve acute symptoms and be useful in supporting osteopathic or chiropractic treatment.
SPRAIN Injury to a joint	Treatment is often very effective in aiding the healing process.	Acute and chronic cases can be treated effectively.	First aid treatment is generally very effective.
STIFF NECK Inability to move head freely	Treatment can be effective in relieving discomfort and restoring mobility, depending on cause.	Acute and chronic cases can be treated effectively.	Treatment is often effective as a first aid measure; may refer for physiotherapy, osteopathy or chiropractic therapy.
SYNOVITIS Painful swelling of membranous lining of a joint	Treatment can be very effective.	Acute and chronic cases can be treated effectively.	Treatment can be effective in relieving pain and also preventing recurrence. Massage may be used in addition.
TENDONITIS Inflammation of a tendon	Treatment can be very effective.	Acute and chronic cases can sometimes be treated effectively.	Treatment can be effective in relieving inflammation and pain, and can help constitutionally.
TORN CARTILAGE Cartilage of knee torn away from the supporting ligaments, causing pain	Treatment can be effective but depends on severity of injury. It could not replace surgery if this was necessary. Could help recovery after surgery.	Some cases could be treated; others would be referred to a specialist.	First aid treatment is very effective and can aid speedy recovery. Referral to hospital may be necessary.

MED. HERBALISM	OSTEOPATHY	GEN. MEDICINE	COMMENTS
Treatment would be beneficial in speeding up healing process. Rest and advice on exercises would be essential.	Rest and hydrotherapy, followed by osteopathic treatment, is usually effective.	Rest, physiotherapy and heat treatment are valuable. Non-steroidal anti-inflammatory drugs may help.	See also **Tennis elbow**, pp. 168–171
Treatment unlikely to be effective.	Would not treat.	Specialist supervision required, including physiotherapy, occupational therapy and appliances.	
Treatment of any oedema can be effective; if a structural disorder is involved, herbal therapy could be combined with manipulation.	Treatment by osteopathy and naturopathy can remove cause; would refer to a specialist if heart, lung or kidney problem suspected.	Treatment with antihistamines and steroids helps cases caused by allergy; diuretics are used in cases of cardiac failure.	See also **Hypertension**, pp. 94–97
Treatment would be constitutional; would refer to hospital for tests and diagnosis.	Treatment by naturopathy can be effective, depending on cause.	Would refer to a specialist of bone disorders.	See also **Spondylitis**, pp. 174–175
Treatment would not improve existing condition, but might help to prevent deterioration.	Manipulation is not appropriate. Naturopathic care can prevent the condition worsening.	Can be limited by hormone treatment in post-menopausal women; preventive hormone treatment may be considered in other cases, plus physiotherapy.	
Would not treat, except in acute conditions.	Treatment is effective if a trapped nerve is the cause. If the condition results from a stroke, early treatment can sometimes be effective.	Would refer to neurological specialist.	See also **Stroke**, pp. 206–207
Would not treat acute condition, but constitutional treatment might improve long-term health.	Would not treat acute condition. Naturopathic treatment can help general health. Osteopathy may benefit chronic condition.	Acute attacks require immediate admission to hospital. Inoculation of children is essential to prevent contracting the disease.	
Treatment often effective.	Treatment can be effective, depending on the severity of the condition and cause.	Non-steroidal anti-inflammatory drugs are useful. Physiotherapy, exercises and attention to posture can relieve discomfort.	See also **Rheumatoid arthritis**, pp. 160–163
Could not improve existing condition, but dietary advice and herbal medicines could prevent further deterioration.	Nutritional treatment would prevent further deterioration. Subsequent re-education of posture would be helpful.	If suspected in infancy, would refer to a paediatrician for diagnosis and treatment.	See also **Bow legs**, pp. 172–173
Treatment can be moderately effective over time.	Treatment may relieve pain; would be limited by degree of degeneration and patient's willingness to undertake an exercise and dietary programme.	Difficult to treat; may require X-ray diagnosis, non-steroidal anti-inflammatory drugs and physiotherapy.	See also **Backache**, pp. 152–155
Treatment can be helpful as a first aid measure and to assist the healing process.	Treatment effective in both acute and chronic conditions.	Treatment involves rest and support (such as a bandage). Physiotherapy and ultra-sound treatment may be helpful in severe cases.	See also **FIRST AID**, pp. 226–231
Treatment can be helpful, but if the condition is chronic, it may require manipulative treatment.	Treatment can be effective, depending on the degree of disk and tissue degeneration.	Treatment includes general advice on posture and sleeping arrangements and methods of reducing tension. A surgical collar may be necessary.	See also **Backache**, pp. 152–155
Local external treatment, combined with internal medication, can be effective.	Soft tissue treatment combined with naturopathy can be effective.	Rest and/or anti-inflammatory drugs are effective. Certain types of exercise and sport should be avoided.	See also **Tennis elbow**, pp. 168–171
Local external treatment, combined with internal medication, can be effective.	Soft tissue treatment combined with naturopathy can be effective.	Rest and anti-inflammatory drugs are effective.	See also **Tennis elbow**, pp. 168–171
Treatment promotes healing and reduces inflammation and other tissue damage.	Treatment can be effective, provided the area can be immobilized for a period.	Rest, physiotherapy and avoidance of further trauma are all helpful. Definitive treatment is by surgery after diagnosis by arthroscopy.	See also **FIRST AID**, pp. 226–231

THE SKIN, HAIR AND NAILS

The skin is the covering of the body and one of the five sense organs. Sensory nerve endings embedded in the skin are sensitive to contact. They send nerve impulses to the brain, where sensations of touch, pressure, pain, heat and cold are perceived.

The skin consists of the epidermis, a protective layer of cells, and beneath it a tough, fibrous dermis which contains blood vessels, nerve endings, sweat glands, hair roots and follicles, and sebaceous (oil-secreting) glands. As well as protecting the body through its sensory function, the skin acts as a barrier against invasion of the body by harmful agents and micro-organisms. Its other main function is to regulate body temperature.

The nails are the equivalent of the claws or hoofs of animals. They are made from hard, dead epidermis cells. Their main function is to protect the fingers and toes.

WHAT CAN GO WRONG

The skin can be damaged by heat, cold, chemicals, insects and other organisms, friction and sunlight. Allergies are common causes of skin disorders and typically result in itching rashes or dry scaly skin. Rashes also accompany infectious diseases such as chickenpox and measles. Bacterial infections cause problems such as boils, styes and abscesses. Warts are caused by viruses. Disorders involving impaired skin function include psoriasis, seborrhoea and chilblains. Fungal infections (athlete's foot) and parasites (such as scabies) can also invade the skin.

Complementary and alternative medical approaches sometimes view the skin, hair and nails and their disorders in different ways. A summary of these views follows.

Acupuncture

The skin and body hair are seen, in traditional Chinese medicine, as being under the influence of the *Lung*. The *Lung* supports the defensive *Qi* (*Wei Qi*) which is said to circulate outside the channels, between the muscles and the skin. The *Wei Qi* is said to control the "opening and closing of pores" or temperature regulation. In addition, being the most *Yang Qi* in the body, it protects the surface from external influences – *Heat, Cold, Wind* and *Damp*. The skin is also closely linked with the *Blood*. Many skin disorders are expressions of problems affecting the *Blood*. Skin rashes are seen as the result of *Hot blood*.

The head hair and the nails are both extensions of the *Blood* – they are said to be formed by excess *Blood*. Thus deficiencies in *Blood* may lead to dry, cracked nails, lifeless hair and even loss of hair. The nails are also associated with the *Liver*.

Chiropractic therapy

In general, chiropractic therapy would not aim to treat skin disorders. However, conditions such as psoriasis often accompany arthritis. This might improve with chiropractic therapy for the arthritis. Treatment of spinal problems can improve general circulation and thus the health of the skin.

Homeopathy

Many diseases of the skin are related to its function as an excretory organ. The eruption of boils and spots, as a result of homeopathic treatment, is usually considered beneficial because it indicates that toxins are being removed from within the body to its outermost layer. Measles is an example of this process – the inner disturbance is dispersed and the crisis over when spots appear on the skin.

Rashes and hives can be the result of imbalance of the heat controls of the body. Itching skin and body odour can be caused by the failure of the skin to remove toxins normally, and result in toxin build-up beneath the skin. This, in turn, is the result of a sluggish metabolism, and rather than treat the skin itself directly, a homeopath would aim to improve the liver and digestive functions.

Allergies appear on the skin to protect inner organs. The skin is not therefore treated, but a homeopath looks for the cause of the body's oversensitivity and rectifies this. Eczemas and psoriasis represent deeper disturbances and must be treated constitutionally.

Medical herbalism

Like other complementary and alternative therapies, medical herbalism does not focus on skin disorders in isolation from the patient as a whole. Although local skin problems can arise, and external applications are of value in reducing discomfort, soothing inflammation and combatting infections, it is the herbalist's concern to establish the links between symptoms and their cause.

Skin disorders may be related to the digestive and liver function. Close scrutiny of diet is important to ensure adequate nutrition and elimination of toxins. The skin is one of the body's organs of excretion, and it is important to reduce the load on it by encouraging efficient bowel and kidney function. Hormones, circulation and the nervous system may all be involved in skin problems.

With conditions such as eczema, the complexity of causative factors is clearly evident. Any external irritants and food allergies should be identified and eliminated. A major element in eczema is stress, and counselling or advice on relaxation techniques often form part of treatment. The illness may also be hereditary, and in such cases is difficult to eradicate because it is deeply embedded in the constitution. The aim of a herbalist is to restore overall health rather than suppress symptoms.

Osteopathy with naturopathy

The appearance of the skin, hair and nails reflects a person's state of health. Skin hue (pallor, yellowness, redness), temperature, dryness or moistness, ridged nails or lifeless hair, all provide clues about the health of the patient.

Disorders of the skin must be analysed for their cause rather than treated merely to remove their symptoms. Eating sugar, for example, can promote pimples, and catarrh often precedes dandruff. Factors such as these have to be taken into account before appropriate treatment can be given.

Childhood disorders such as measles are the body's way of shedding inherited toxins, and should not be suppressed, especially once the rash and raised temperature appear.

Chart of disorders

At the end of this section there is a chart listing various disorders of the skin, hair and nails. This is a general, but not definitive, guide to the treatment of such disorders. Complementary and alternative therapies treat the patient as a whole rather than merely the disorder presented. Whether a person can be treated, and the success of treatment, depends on the nature of the condition and the general health of the patient.

ACNE

THE PATIENT

SJ is 20 years old. He is 1.85 metres (6 ft 2 in) tall, slim, and has red hair and a fair complexion. He is a student majoring in pure mathematics and physics. He is well-suited to the pressure at university, and enjoys the social and sporting life associated with being a student. He does not smoke, but drinks several pints of beer most evenings.

THE PROBLEM

SJ developed acne (*Acne vulgaris*) when he was 13 years old. It is a skin condition caused by hormonal changes and often coincides with puberty. His father also suffered from acne in his teens, but none of SJ's siblings do.

The acne covers his face, neck and back, and is in the form of raging pus-filled spots. It is a very unsightly and painful condition. He does not like hot weather and his skin burns quickly if exposed to the sun for long, but the spots tend to dry up in sunny weather and with short periods of sunbathing.

He uses anti-bacterial face washes and commercial acne creams, but they do not make any appreciable difference to his condition.

SJ eats regularly in his college refectory and has conventional tastes in food. He is sociable, although the unsightly condition of his face inhibits his relationships with girls. He is in his college rowing, cricket and rugby teams, and plays tennis during the summer. He is seeking medical advice now because he does not feel that the acne is improving with age and his skin is becoming scarred.

In general, SJ's health has always been good. He had all the usual childhood diseases quite severely, but recovered quickly. His constitution is strong and his only complaint other than the acne is summer hay fever, which he controls effectively with the use of anti-histamine inhalants and tablets.

In traditional Chinese medicine, acne is classified as *Wind* and *Heat* affecting the *Blood*. It is often associated with diet, especially the consumption of spicy or greasy food, or alcohol. These foods cause *Heat* in the *Stomach*, which is transferred via the *Jingluo* to the *Blood*. Because this is a *Yang* condition it mainly affects the most *Yang* parts of the body, which are the face, neck and upper back.

SJ has a hereditary disposition to this condition which means that it is deeply entrenched in his system, and will be difficult to treat. Although his constitution appeared to be strong, he also had seasonal hay fever, which indicated a tendency to *Kidney* and *Lung Qi* weakness. The *Lung* is said to control the defensive *Qi* in the skin, and this was possibly a predisposing factor, especially since his skin was sensitive to the sun. However, in small doses the warming effect of the sun could be said to tonify the *Qi* in his skin, thus helping to improve the condition. In other respects, the symptoms were a typical manifestation of *Wind* and *Heat* as described above.

Treatment
The treatment would be mainly systemic, eliminating the *Wind* and *Heat* from the *Blood* by using points on the *Large Intestine* and *Sanjiao* channels, and strengthening the *Blood* by using points on the *Spleen* channel. A point on the *Du* channel on the upper back would be "bled". This would involve needling the point superficially to cause small drops of blood to appear, a process which is said to draw out *Heat*, and has been shown by research to be very effective. Selected points on the ear might also be "bled".

Prognosis and conclusion
Ten treatments would usually be administered, as frequently as every three days, but less concentrated treatment would also be effective. Controlling the consumption of greasy, spicy foods and alcohol would be important in order to obtain the maximum effect from treatment.

TREATMENT BY A
CHIROPRACTOR

Chiropractic therapy would not be able to treat SJ's acne problem, and he would probably be referred to either a homeopath or a medical herbalist for treatment and dietary advice.

TREATMENT BY A
HOMEOPATH

Acne is a common ailment of puberty, originating from hormonal imbalance. SJ's particular symptoms were the painful and very inflamed spots. The most effective treatment would be constitutional, combined with education about diet and hygiene.

When acne during puberty is prolonged, the tuberculoid "miasm" is most commonly the culprit, since this shows a disturbance in the lymphatic system – indicated also by frequent colds. This, and SJ's other symptoms, indicated a major tuberculoid remedy *Lycopodium*.

Lycopodium would particularly suit SJ because of his academic abilities and his competitive nature. Those who would benefit from this remedy tend to feel inadequate, and thus thrive on situations when they can prove themselves and show off their talents, especially their intellectual skills.

Because of their insecurity, such people do not like being alone and they have low self-esteem. To build this up they need constant reassurance from others. Lack of self-confidence was also demonstrated by SJ's attitude toward girls – because of his unsightly face, he felt less than adequate.

Treatment and prognosis
The constitutional remedy would be *Lycopodium*, given in 1M potency. Initially, it might make his spots worse, and they could take some time to clear. This would be a homeopathic aggravation and a sure sign that healing was in progress. If this occurred, the spots would not be treated, except by thorough cleansing, because treatment would simply suppress the action of the remedy.

The remedy should not need to be repeated for many months because it would work deeply and over a long period.

After a few weeks, when the body's reaction to the remedy has been established, it might be useful to give *Pulsatilla* 6C. This also fits SJ's symptom picture, but is a more specific drainage remedy that would speed up the disappearance of the spots. Acute symptoms of hay fever, during the summer, could be alleviated by *Phosphorus*, a remedy related to SJ's constitutional remedy, *Lycopodium*.

The prognosis is good, but SJ would have to reduce his fat and carbohydrate intake if long-term improvement was to be achieved.

Introduction to chiropractic therapy pp. 16–23

Introduction to homeopathy pp. 24–31

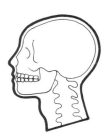

TREATMENT BY A
MEDICAL HERBALIST

The two major factors in creating severe acne are hormonal fluctuations – particularly in male teenagers with high competitive drive – and dietary imbalances. SJ's diet and alcohol intake had placed a considerable burden on his liver, which had affected the amount of toxic waste left in his system and aggravated his skin condition.

Treatment
Attention would focus on reducing the intake, and improving the elimination, of toxins. Dietary reform should be undertaken, with reductions in fatty and fried food, and the virtual elimination of sweet foods. Even when eating in the refectory, SJ would have some choice and should be able to select vegetable and salad dishes. Plenty of fresh fruit should be eaten, rather than sweet snacks.

Slightly more difficult to tackle, given his active social life, would be a reduction in alcohol, but this would be very important.

He should avoid harsh face washes and use mild soaps and cleansers; face packs made freshly from yoghurt, fine oatmeal and powdered slippery elm could be very helpful. To ease the scarring, sparing applications of wheatgerm oil with essential oil of lavender would promote healing.

The herbal prescription would include:
● Burdock (*Arctium lappa*): cleanses the tissues and helps to improve elimination of waste products, especially in the urine.
● Cleavers (*Galium aparine*): improves elimination through the kidneys; also improves the functions of the lymphatic system, thus helping to resist or resolve infections.
● Dandelion (*Taraxacum officinale*): a gentle liver stimulant that encourages the production of bile. It is also a mild laxative and diuretic, encouraging water filtration through the kidneys.

The prescription would be reviewed fortnightly, with remedies added, as required, to improve elimination of toxins.

Prognosis and conclusion
SJ had a pattern of eating and drinking that needed complete revision; unfortunately, university life tends not to favour such changes. His overall health (including his hay fever) would benefit from a cleansing programme.

TREATMENT BY AN
OSTEOPATH and NATUROPATH

Acne is a disorder of the sebaceous (oil secreting) glands of the skin. Each gland is usually associated with a hair follicle, and if these become blocked by sebum, blackheads and whiteheads appear, some of which become pus-filled cysts. It is the ruptured cyst that leaves a scar when healed.

Sebum secretion is hormone controlled, which was why SJ's acne had started at puberty. If there had been insufficient testosterone (male hormone) it could have accounted for inefficient stimulation of the sebaceous glands. It is possible that the hormonal imbalance was tied up with excess growth hormone, resulting in SJ's height.

Investigation, therefore, would take account of SJ's present hormone balance and his eating habits. The pituitary gland, at the base of the brain, controls the hormonal system and depends on an effective sacrocranial mechanism for its correct functioning. Other hormonal glands are influenced by nerves emerging from the spine. SJ's height suggested the possibility of spinal lesions in the thoracic (chest) region – this was confirmed.

Treatment
Neuromuscular massage and structural correction of the spine would aim to improve blood supply (and therefore the removal of waste products) to the skin. Cranial osteopathy would help to balance pituitary activity.

Treatment would require a change of diet to one largely composed of fresh, raw foods (fruits and salads) and the avoidance of white flour and other refined foods, sugar and milk.

Treatment could be augmented at home by daily friction rubs of the whole skin surface with a coarse towel or one wrung out in cold water. Cool baths are always better for the skin than hot baths, and the skin should never be cleansed with soaps that upset the acid-alkali balance of the body surface.

Prognosis and conclusion
SJ would be warned that scarring would take a long time to disperse, even with the avoidance of further acne. Some people remain scarred for life. Vitamin E cream has been found useful in the nourishment of scarred areas.

Introduction to medical herbalism pp. 32–39

Introduction to osteopathy with naturopathy pp. 40–47

TREATMENT BY A
FAMILY DOCTOR

Acne is a seemingly minor, but socially disabling chronic condition which typically, but not necessarily, affects young people. Even when it stops it may leave lifelong scarring. Almost all adolescents have some degree of acne, which is usually worst in the mid-teens. It tends to be more severe in boys, and usually subsides before the twenties.

SJ was fit and taking reasonable measures to control his acne, but could probably benefit from further medical help.

Treatment
A certain amount of ultraviolet light from sunlight would be beneficial, but since he tends to burn SJ may find a filter cream helpful. It is possible that the amount of beer he drinks makes his acne a little worse; he could try reducing his consumption or cutting it out altogether.

It was not likely that his diet was a problem; he was not eating spicy foods which would make him sweat. Medical research gives little support to the notion that acne is affected by diet.

SJ would be prescribed an oral antibiotic – most commonly one of the Tetracycline group of drugs – to be used daily over several months. Astringents and antibacterial agents applied to the skin might also be useful.

If the use of antibiotics was not effective, he would be referred to a dermatologist who could prescribe an anti-androgen either orally or topically. This would be done under hospital supervision.

Prognosis and conclusion
SJ's condition would probably improve as he became older. This common, but usually self-limiting, condition can be greatly helped, and permanent unsightly scarring can therefore be substantially reduced.

CONSULTANT'S COMMENTS

At the age of 20, acne can still be described as a self-limiting condition, which results from the hormonal disturbances that occur in adolescence. Such hormonal effects are very difficult to adjust, and acne would be considered medically unusual only if it lasted much beyond a person's early twenties.

The treatments
The aim of treatment is generally to reduce the effects of the fluctuating levels of androgens (male hormones) on the sebaceous, oil-producing glands. Only extremely rarely does it attempt to interfere with the developing hormonal balance itself. The family doctor acknowledges this, and prefers to concentrate on antibiotic therapy to limit the degree of bacterial infection of the congested sebaceous glands. This strategy is often effective, but there are many who would not choose long-term antibiotic therapy, with its harmful effects on bowel function and on general resistance to infections.

Some practitioners concentrate on reducing the sebaceous activity in other ways, and on cleansing techniques to keep the glands from blocking up. The acupuncturist and homeopath agree on the need to work on a constitutional level. Acne can be a sign of broader disturbances, and these treatments are best able to identify them.

The osteopath and naturopath has a similarly broad approach. This incorporates, as does the advice from the medical herbalist, a useful mixture of dietary and cosmetic approaches. The comments on diet made by the doctor are accurate (dietary factors alone do not appear to provoke acute attacks of acne). Diet can, however, be valuable as part of a broad regime designed to cleanse the whole metabolism.

Herbalism may be the most effective approach because it is specifically geared to "detoxifying" tissues. The "blood-cleansing" herbs are particularly helpful in this type of skin condition.

ECZEMA

THE PATIENT

AB is a 45-year-old married woman, 1.6 metres (5 ft 7 in) tall. She weighs 82 kg (13 stone), but her flesh is firm not flabby. She became grey in her early thirties and has a dry powdery complexion, which flushes red when she is tired or stressed. Her time is devoted to her family (she has two adopted children) and involvement in the local community. She used to work as an art teacher. Her diet is wholefood and vegetarian, but she dislikes exercise and tends to put on weight quickly. She snacks between meals on cakes and biscuits.

THE PROBLEM

During her childhood AB developed eczema (an inflammation of the skin) on her hands, elbows and inner thighs. This has persisted throughout her life, and was treated with the drug hydrocortisone until five years ago, when she learned to avoid irritating substances as far as possible, and live with the condition. The inflamed areas are dry, red, sore to the touch, flaky, and worsen with warmth and in the evenings. Six months ago, the condition deteriorated. This coincided with her son's worries about starting and settling into school.

Although AB is happy as a full-time mother, she misses the stimulation of working and finds the responsibilities of family life overwhelming. Her husband does not devote as much time to the family as she would like.

The eczema developed at about the time AB herself started school, and was accompanied by bouts of asthma. During her teens the eczema disappeared, but her asthma worsened. Both conditions then seemed to clear up, but they returned in her early thirties. She is allergic to dust, feathers, certain fabrics and some detergents. She uses proprietary inhalants to control asthma attacks. During the summer she gets hay fever and has frequent colds. Constipation has been a life-long problem, and she has severe premenstrual tension and period pains. When she was 35 she damaged her back and she still has frequent lower back pain.

TREATMENT BY AN
ACUPUNCTURIST

In traditional Chinese medicine, eczema is associated with the presence of excessive *Damp* and *Heat*. This originates either from the exterior as an invasion of external pathogenic *Damp* and *Heat*, or from the interior.

AB had a serious and complex condition. Eczema and asthma are linked, the *Lung* having a close relationship with the skin. Excessive *Dampness* may be produced by poor *Stomach* function, especially in childhood; children have "hotter" energy than adults and the *Damp* easily transforms to *Damp-Heat*, affecting the skin. The *Damp* also affects the *Lung*, leading to asthma. AB's hay fever indicated a deficiency of *Lung* and *Kidney Qi*, as did colds and bronchitis appearing in the summer.

The eczema itself appeared as *Hot* and *Dry*; the fact that it was worse in the evening suggested *Blood* or *Yin* deficiency. Her grey hair, dry complexion, flushed face when tired, and constipation confirmed this. Her back pains suggested that the *Kidney Yin* was weak. The deficiency undermined the *Liver* function, with stagnation of *Qi* manifesting as painful periods and premenstrual tension; it was also contributing to her tiredness and her sense of being over-burdened, since deficiency of *Blood* would undermine the *Qi* of the body.

At the core of the problem, therefore, was a deficiency of *Blood* and *Kidney Yin*, which had resulted from unresolved *Damp* and *Heat* in the skin and the *Lung*, complicated by stagnation of *Liver Qi*. This was confirmed by AB's choppy pulse. The origins of the disease in the *Stomach* were reflected in the central crack in AB's tongue.

Treatment
AB's treatment would need to be carefully managed, because of the complicated nature of her problem. It would involve achieving a balance between resolving *Damp*, eliminating *Heat*, strengthening the *Blood* and *Yin*, repairing the *Stomach, Lung* and *Kidney* functions, and moving stagnant *Liver Qi*.

Prognosis and conclusion
The prognosis would be good because AB had already stopped using drugs, although treatment would need to be long-term. Exercise and rest would help and she should cut out cakes and biscuits because they exacerbate *Damp* and *Heat*.

Asthma pp. 60–63 Hay fever pp. 72–75 Allergy pp. 86–89   Introduction to acupuncture pp. 8–15

TREATMENT BY A
CHIROPRACTOR

Chiropractic therapy would not normally be chosen for the treatment of eczema. However, AB also suffered with a low back problem, and this was examined so that treatment could be given, if appropriate.

Physical examination
Once the case history details had been taken, a variety of orthopaedic and neurological tests were carried out, which all proved to be negative. AB was then checked for any restriction in spinal movement, and some general restriction in all directions was noted in the lumbar spine, accompanied by considerable muscle spasm. There was also some restriction in the upper thoracic (chest) area of the spine, which could be related to her respiratory problems.

X-rays were then taken of AB's low back to check for any abnormalities. There was some general wear and tear, but no more than would be expected, and otherwise the disks, joints and vertebrae seemed to be in good condition. The conclusion was that the spinal restriction was caused by a lack of normal biomechanical movement in the spine, and chiropractic treatment would be suitable for this.

Treatment
The treatment would begin by easing some of the muscular tension in the low back, before proceeding with chiropractic adjustment in order to restore normal biomechanical movement.

AB would be advised about losing weight and taking more regular exercise. Yoga and relaxation classes might also be of benefit to her. She needed help with stress, which, if controlled, could reduce her attacks of eczema. She might also be recommended to seek help from an acupuncturist, homeopath or medical herbalist.

Prognosis and conclusion
Over a course of four or five treatments AB's back problem could respond well, and she would find that she needed to rest less because of this.

TREATMENT BY A
HOMEOPATH

Eczema is a disease of the skin as an organ, and often runs in families. Very often it is found in association with asthma, the one disappearing as the other increases. Although it is often regarded as an allergy, a homeopath prefers to see it as excessive irritability or dryness in the tissues.

Diagnosis
In AB's case the irritability and dryness came together, and were seen in large inflamed patches that were sore to the touch and worse for heat. She was a tense individual who was not fulfilled in life. The drying heat on her skin was a reflection of her "heated" temperament; as she internalized her anxiety the heat appeared on the skin as further eczema. Tears flowed copiously when she was frustrated and stressed; suppressed anger created heat that remained within.

AB had plenty to keep her occupied, yet without the routine of work she felt a need to be still more occupied, and so she was taking on activities in various community groups, assuming more responsibilities even though she was tired and overwhelmed by those she already had.

The need for stimulation, the dry heat and the suppressed anger pointed to *Nux vomica* as a remedy. This remedy fits a symptom picture of irritability in all tissues of the body, and can thus be used for so-called allergies. In this symptom picture the rhythms of the body are also disturbed, so constipation is common because of uneven contractions in the intestines. Similarly, premenstrual tension and period pains arise because of lack of coordination and irritability, leading in some cases to severe spasms or cramping pains. On the mental level, the symptom picture may take the form of dissatisfaction, restlessness or frustration. A person needing *Nux vomica* is characteristically very independent.

Because her diet was sound, AB's only "bad" habit was her lack of exercise.

Treatment and prognosis
Nux vomica would be given at first in a low potency, and repeated as improvement slowed down. Since there was little to interfere with that improvement, AB's skin would be expected to clear up after an initial worsening over the first week.

Introduction to chiropractic therapy pp. 16–23

Introduction to homeopathy pp. 24–31

TREATMENT BY A
MEDICAL HERBALIST

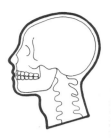

TREATMENT BY AN
OSTEOPATH AND NATUROPATH

Eczema is a complex problem, frequently associated with a variety of factors. In AB's case stress was clearly involved, and a great deal of counselling and support were vital. Careful investigation of possible external irritants should be undertaken. Internal factors needed investigation, particularly diet. The constipation alone indicated the need for careful dietary scrutiny, and the correlation of dairy foods and eczema was significant. The burden placed on her eliminative system by eating sweet snacks was an aggravating factor.

Treatment
Dietary overhaul, and treatment of AB's hormonal imbalance (indicated by premenstrual syndrome), would be important. The lower back pains were probably contributing to pelvic congestion, and manipulative therapy could be valuable.

The herbal prescription would include:
- Nettle (*Urtica dioica*): improves circulation and would provide much-needed minerals to the tissues.
- Chamomile (*Matricaria recutita*): improves digestive function, relaxes pelvic and abdominal muscles, and reduces general tension.
- Dandelion Root (*Taraxacum officinale*): mild liver stimulant and laxative.
- Burdock (*Arctium lappa*): releases toxins from the tissues, and is mildly diuretic.
- Marigold (*Calendula officinalis*): acts as an anti-inflammatory and antispasmodic; helps to reduce tension and irritation; encourages elimination.

The prescription would be reviewed in the light of any changes in health. Also of value would be local creams and ointments to reduce itching and irritation. Long-term cortisone application had made the skin thinner, and AB's dry, inflamed complexion needed to be supplied with nutrient oils to improve its condition.

Prognosis
AB's problems were deeply entrenched but, together with advice and support, herbal treatment could offer significant improvements in her general health and vitality, her eczema symptoms, and related asthma and hay fever problems.

AB's eczema was inseparable from her asthma, hay fever, constipation and allergies. She presented a picture that involved her skin, spine, bowels, chest, ribcage, throat, sinuses and reproductive organs, and was related to her eating habits and to psychological stresses, some of which had been present since childhood.

Physical examination
The examination showed a chronically red, dry skin, hardened by years of inflammation and irritation – skin that was no longer properly benefiting from blood circulation to and from its surface.

Spinal vertebrae were sensitive in areas corresponding to the organs involved in her condition. Low back lesions were also present, accounting for backache and possibly for premenstrual symptoms. The condition of her ribcage and collarbone muscles reflected the difficulty she had in breathing. Carrying excess weight was imposing an additional strain on her breathing and circulation.

Treatment
Spinal and rib imbalances would be treated to ensure an unimpeded nerve and blood supply to the organs and skin. Soft tissue manipulation and vibratory massage would improve drainage of her lymph (fluid that bathes the cells). Attention would be paid to the nerves supplying her bowels, and special techniques would encourage the liver in its function of detoxification.

Naturopathic care would involve avoiding sugary and milky foods, and keeping to her wholefood diet; taking mineral supplements specific to the state of her skin and to chest congestion; and having daily friction rubs to stimulate renewal of skin tissue, with either a dry towel or one wrung out in cold water. She should also find a way to deal harmlessly with stress, and should continue to avoid hydrocortisone, which suppresses inflammation and can perpetuate skin problems.

Prognosis and conclusion
Although this was a complicated condition, there was considerable hope for improvement. Treatment would, however, need to be quite prolonged.

Introduction to medical herbalism pp. 32–39

Introduction to osteopathy with naturopathy pp. 40–47

TREATMENT BY A
FAMILY DOCTOR

AB was suffering from so-called atopic eczema, a condition that usually starts early in life. It is associated with asthma, hay fever and other allergies. Eczema seems to be a disorder of the skin's immunological defences.

Atopic eczema is genetically transmitted, and is a disease that tends to come and go. Attacks can be stimulated by various factors, including superficial infection, irritation from friction (such as scratchy clothing) and psychological stress. It is believed that the worsening from stress is brought about by increased scratching, rather than as a direct effect of stress upon the skin. Atopic eczema usually develops in infancy, but may, as in AB's case, come on later in childhood.

Contact eczema is an allergic response to an external substance, some common examples being biological detergents, nickel in certain jewellery and adhesive plasters.

Treatment

The treatment would concentrate on two areas. First, prevention of the condition's worsening by reducing dryness and flaking with bath oils, with applications which would soften and soothe the skin, and by avoiding irritants and allergy-causing substances. Second, anti-inflammatory medication would be prescribed in the form of corticosteroids, which would be applied to the skin. Sometimes in severe eczema steroid tablets may be necessary, and antihistamines are often given to ease the itching.

AB's stresses and frustrations were certainly aggravating her problem, and family or marital therapy or counselling would probably help her.

She was overweight, unfit and already had a bad back. While this poor physical condition was not directly worsening her eczema, she was failing to look after herself properly, and would need to take measures to improve her general health.

Prognosis and conclusion

AB would have to learn to live with her condition. Eczema is seldom dangerous, but can be so distressing that it requires in-patient hospital treatment. Much, however, can be done to minimize attacks. Self-help groups can be a useful source of advice and assistance.

Introduction to Western medicine pp. 48–55

CONSULTANT'S COMMENTS

The term "eczema" covers a broad range of skin inflammations, and thus sweeping statements about its treatment are unwise. In AB's case the symptoms point to her having one of the most persistent forms of all – atopic eczema. The specialists are correct in being cautious about her prospects, but experience of the benefits of some of the treatments suggests that the conventional verdict of having "to live with it" may err on the side of pessimism.

The treatments

The acupuncturist's account provides a subtle image of the nature of the condition. He recognizes the difficulties indicated by the family doctor, but is justified in being more hopeful about her chance of improvement. The therapy has a good reputation in this area. Homeopathy may also find its ability to affect deep constitutional factors rewarding.

A strong claim for the treatment of eczema comes from herbal remedies with their "blood-cleansing" properties. In this case the medical herbalist correctly takes a cautious view, realizing that the condition's chronic nature brings wide problems. Dietary and hormonal adjustment are thus part of the regime.

Correcting the diet is also the priority for naturopathic treatment, but again other approaches are deemed necessary. Structural work, either by the osteopath or the chiropractor, might have unexpected benefits when accompanied by other treatments.

Conclusions

This is a complicated and entrenched form of a complex condition. AB would be encouraged to follow a number of approaches to correct her slide toward ill-health. There are genuine reasons to hope for more than the palliative treatment offered by conventional medicine.

PSORIASIS

THE PATIENT

HJ is a 14-year-old boy, and is working hard at school. He is bright and intelligent, and used to enjoy sport, but his ill-health has weakened him and he now takes little exercise. He tends to stay indoors and enjoys being on his own, studying, listening to music and playing computer games. He has one brother and two sisters. His family eats a conservative Western diet, with a high proportion of meat and fried food.

THE PROBLEM

HJ has developed a scaly rash on his scalp (rather like an extreme form of dandruff) above the hair line, and a few red patches with silvery scales on his back, elbows and knees. They are not painful and do not itch, but the scales slough off and are unsightly. He has just been sitting school examinations and becomes very tense when he is under pressure. His nails are pitted and his skin is dry. The condition does not result from lack of proper hygiene.

HJ is waiting to have his tonsils removed. He has had tonsillitis about twice a year since he was five years old, but this has recurred monthly over the past year. Both his father and grandfather have suffered from psoriasis, and his grandfather has also developed rheumatoid arthritis. HJ's siblings do not have this skin problem, but his sister also suffers from tonsillitis.

TREATMENT BY AN
ACUPUNCTURIST

In traditional Chinese medicine the skin has a close relationship with the *Lung* and with the *Blood*. The *Lung* is both the source and distributor of defensive *Qi*, which circulates beneath the skin. The *Blood* nourishes and moistens the skin, and disorders of the *Blood* often manifest themselves there.

HJ's psoriasis had appeared at a stressful time in his life and had followed a prolonged period of ill-health, manifesting as tonsillitis. The throat is the "gateway" to the *Lung*; tonsillitis is usually classified as invasion of *Wind* and *Heat*. The attack when he was five years old appeared to have remained unresolved. Repeated attacks had weakened HJ's *Lung Qi*, and he had become generally debilitated. The appearance of psoriasis was a result of this debilitation.

HJ's *Qi* and *Blood* were weak, leading to dry skin and pitted nails. In addition, his diet contributed to the *Heat* appearing in the red, scaly rashes. His thready pulse indicated weakness of *Qi*, while his pale tongue with red points around the tip indicated deficiency of *Qi* and the presence of *Heat*.

Treatment
The tonsillitis problem would need to be resolved before any attempt was made to treat the psoriasis. This would involve strengthening the *Qi* and *Blood* of the whole body – and the *Lung Qi* in particular – using *Lung, Stomach* and *Urinary Bladder* channels. If the swelling and inflammation in the throat continued between attacks, *Qi* and *Blood* in the throat would be moved to eliminate *Heat* and stagnation by using local points. During attacks, the strategy would be to eliminate *Wind* and *Heat*, using *Du, Large Intestine, Stomach* and *Lung* channels. HJ should reduce his intake of meat and eliminate fried foods from his diet. Once this problem had been resolved, and if the psoriasis was still present, treatment to strengthen the *Qi* and *Blood* and eliminate *Heat* would continue.

Prognosis and conclusion
Acupuncture treatment could be used effectively to prevent the necessity for a tonsillectomy, which would simply mask the underlying disharmony. Psoriasis, especially when it has a hereditary basis, can be stubborn to treat. Diet is often an important factor in the success of treatment.

Rheumatoid arthritis pp. 160–163

Introduction to acupuncture pp. 8–15

TREATMENT BY A
CHIROPRACTOR

Psoriasis is not a condition suitable for chiropractic treatment. HJ would be referred to a homeopath, a medical herbalist or an acupuncturist for treatment.

Psoriasis can lead to psoriatic arthritis later in life, as has happened with HJ's grandfather. The chiropractor would again recommend that the psoriasis needed to be brought under control in order to prevent any arthritic conditions.

TREATMENT BY A
HOMEOPATH

Psoriasis is a disease which is known to run in families, and to be exacerbated by stress. It is not caused by poor hygiene, and is often related to a digestive disturbance, so diet should always be investigated. The unsightliness of the condition often causes considerable anguish to the sufferer.

Diagnosis

When dealing with a "disease label" such as psoriasis, the homeopath has to isolate the individual symptoms that lead to an appropriate prescription.

There are seldom symptoms specific to the individual in the eruption itself, but there were several interesting points in HJ's case: there was no itching or pain, most of the eruption was under the hair, and the nails were affected. This pointed to *Mercurius solubilis* as a remedy.

The remedy was confirmed by HJ's episodes of tonsillitis, which fell into a typical *Mercurius* pattern of rawness at the back of the throat, with tiny ulcers in the tonsils themselves. In such attacks the pain – which is worse on the right – shoots up to the ears when the patient swallows.

HJ's withdrawal from society was not surprising, given that most teenagers are self-conscious, but his intellectual pursuits were typical of a *Mercurius* symptom picture.

Treatment and prognosis

The potency would be kept low until the skin regained sufficient strength to function properly. In HJ's case a single dose of *Mercurius solubilis* 30 might be given; then the practitioner would wait, for up to several months, noting the changes that occurred in the skin. When creams such as hydrocortisone are in use it is usual for the eruption to get worse at first, and often the practitioner may withdraw the cream for one or two weeks before the homeopathic medication is given to allow the eruption to come out naturally. The action of the homeopathic remedy would then be clearer. If the skin was in very bad condition, or hydrocortisone had been used for a long time, the cream might be withdrawn very gradually, and the homeopathic treatment started right away, possibly in an even lower potency.

Introduction to chiropractic therapy pp. 16–23

Introduction to homeopathy pp. 24–31

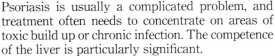

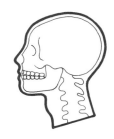

TREATMENT BY A
MEDICAL HERBALIST

Psoriasis is usually a complicated problem, and treatment often needs to concentrate on areas of toxic build up or chronic infection. The competence of the liver is particularly significant.

HJ was no exception to this. The most important areas for attention were his diet (both with respect to its effect on the liver and to strain on the eliminative capacity of the skin), immune activity and how he coped with stress.

Treatment
It would be essential that HJ stopped eating all fried food and reduced meat consumption, dairy produce and sugary foods. Increasing his intake of vegetables and fresh fruits would ensure additional supplies of vitamins, minerals and fibre. There might be a case for short-term dietary supplements, especially of vitamins B, C and E, and of calcium and zinc. Getting some fresh air and exercise would be of value in maintaining heart and lung function and supplying oxygen to the tissues, and in helping to relieve some of the stress from examinations.

The herbal prescription would include:
- Burdock (*Arctium lappa*): powerful cleansing remedy to help remove excess toxins.
- Nettle (*Urtica dioica*): improves circulation and provides minerals.
- Oregon Grape (*Berberis aquifolium*): liver stimulant and mild laxative.
- Chamomile (*Matricaria recutita*): mild relaxant, anti-inflammatory and digestive stimulant.
- Echinacea (*Echinacea angustifolia*): increases resistance to infections; of special benefit to HJ's tonsillitis.

The prescription would be varied as necessary. Local treatment with gargles for the tonsillitis would be of value, and cream for the skin could help with the dry, scaly rash.

Prognosis and conclusion
HJ could expect great improvements in his skin condition. Longer-term factors, notably the recurrent tonsillitis, would require herbal treatment and advice for some time in order to build vitality and restore balance.

TREATMENT BY AN
OSTEOPATH AND NATUROPATH

When a person's skin is in the condition of HJ's, it tells a story of inner disharmony, reflecting an overall lack of health. Persistent tonsillitis is common in those with a catarrhal tendency and inefficient eliminative organs. Recovery would have two phases: disposing of accumulated toxins in his system and strengthening his metabolism.

Physical examination
Examination revealed a general sluggishness of the circulation. A number of neck, cranial and thoracic imbalances were evident. There were sensitive points in his neck, something often associated with sore throats.

Treatment
Osteopathic adjustment of cranial and spinal lesions would first treat nerves supplying the eliminative organs (kidneys, liver, lungs, skin, intestines), then those that govern building-up (anabolic) processes.

No physical treatment would work unless HJ stopped eating all catarrh-forming foods such as dairy produce. A short fast would take the load off the tonsils. If their swelling reduced after three or four days there would be no need for surgery. The skin would take longer because it is often the last to show its disease.

When the temperature and sore throat had disappeared the fast would be broken with fresh fruit. Gradually the diet would be built up to provide nourishment without toxicity. Mineral supplements would be prescribed as required, first to ease pain and inflammation, then to nourish the body as a whole. Hydrotherapy would encourage old skin to slough off and new cells to multiply.

Prognosis and conclusion
Chronic psoriasis is a whole-person disease. It would not benefit for long from fragmentary treatment and might take several courses of constructive therapy before it would finally be disposed of. HJ has good prospects. Older people, who tend to be set in their ways, would be less likely to benefit from treatment.

Introduction to medical herbalism pp. 32–39

Introduction to osteopathy with naturopathy pp. 40–47

TREATMENT BY A
FAMILY DOCTOR

This is a common skin disorder, inherited in families, which occurs in both sexes and at all ages. As with HJ, it is common on the scalp and around the hair line. It prefers extendable surfaces, such as knees and elbows. It may however affect large areas of the body and can be extremely disfiguring and unpleasant. Many patients have characteristically pitted nails.

The cause is not really known, but there is some evidence of an underlying disorder of the immune system. Psoriasis undergoes spontaneous relapses and remissions over the years and in general the disease is more severe the earlier it begins in life. Some patients with psoriasis develop a widespread and destructive joint disease which is very like rheumatoid arthritis.

Diagnosis usually depends on the distribution and character of the attacks, but it can be confused with certain other chronic skin disorders.

Treatment
The two most important remedies are exposure to ultraviolet light and application of tar-like substances to the skin. Steroid ointments are useful, but prolonged heavy use can cause permanent skin damage. Serious widespread attacks are sometimes treated in hospital by a special intensified ultraviolet therapy. Occasionally immuno-suppressive drugs such as Metifotrexate are used, although they have significant side-effects and require strict medical monitoring.

The type of psoriasis associated with tonsillitis follows streptococcal throat infections and spontaneously remits after a number of weeks. It can, as in HJ's case, recur after each throat infection. Swift treatment of acute sore throats would be advisable. Removal of the tonsils might significantly reduce this problem, but it would still be possible to experience the same type of infection after the tonsils had been removed.

Prognosis and conclusion
HJ was unlucky in that he would have to continue to cope with a chronic disease. He might develop an intermittent, but progressive, arthritis. It is likely that his attacks of psoriasis were triggered by stress, and family counselling could well be helpful.

CONSULTANT'S COMMENTS

The mechanism of this condition has been explored medically and shown to be an example of an auto-immune disease, in which the body's immune system attacks its own skin cells, but the causes remain obscure. There is, however, evidence to show that auto-immune destruction can follow previous conditions, such as chronic infections of the lungs, the gut and, as in HJ's case, the throat.

The family doctor points out that the connection between a throat infection and psoriasis is a recognized syndrome. Unfortunately, Western medicine is poorly placed to take advantage of such an observation. Several of the other traditions are, however, extremely well-suited; it is very possible that, in HJ's case at least, a therapy may be measured by its ability to build on the link with tonsillitis.

The treatments
Several practitioners are on promising ground. The acupuncturist, although commendably not expecting too much from clearing the disorder of the tonsils, sees this as central to the wider pathology. The homeopath can be trusted to take all clues into account, and interesting points are made on the practicality of treating such a disorder. The medical herbalist is on firm ground in highlighting the general "toxic" thesis in conditions such as psoriasis, and in having remedies well suited to this.

By contrast, the conventional medical view is limited to containing the condition, removing the tonsils, and pursuing the psychological component of the disorder.

Conclusions
No treatment of psoriasis can be absolutely recommended. The condition is far too complex and individual cases too varied for that. Nevertheless there are many options to try that can genuinely improve on the prospects on offer from conventional medicine.

Introduction to Western medicine pp. 48–55

CONDITION	ACUPUNCTURE	CHIROPRACTIC	HOMEOPATHY
ABSCESS Local accumulation of pus	Treatment can be effective, but depends on the nature, cause and location of the condition.	Would not treat; would refer to a family doctor.	Treatment effective in both acute and chronic cases.
ATHLETE'S FOOT Fungal infection of skin of foot	Treatment can be effective.	Would not treat; would refer to a chiropodist.	Treatment effective when the condition is dealt with constitutionally.
BALDNESS Loss of hair, due to aging or disease (alopecia).	Treatment effective if the cause is alopecia; but would not treat if hereditary.	Would not treat.	Treatment effective for some kinds of baldness, but not hereditary types.
BEDSORE Redness and cracking of skin in areas of continual pressure	Would not treat.	Would not treat; would refer to another practitioner.	Treatment effective, but prevention is better than cure.
BLEPHARITIS Inflammation of eyelids	Treatment can be effective.	Would not treat, but would refer to a family doctor.	Treatment effective.
BLISTER Accumulation of fluid under the skin	Treatment would depend on the cause, type and location of the condition.	Would give first aid treatment only.	Treatment effective as a first aid measure, for example in burns.
BODY ODOUR Caused by breakdown of sweat and dead skin by bacteria	Treatment can be effective, but depends on nature and cause of the condition.	Would not treat; would refer to another practitioner.	When treated constitutionally this condition disappears as general health improves.
BOIL/CARBUNCLE Infection of skin	Treatment is effective in stimulating healing process.	Would not treat; would refer to a family doctor.	Treatment effective in acute stages, and should be followed by constitutional treatment.
BUNION Inflammation of part of big toe joint	Would not treat.	Would not treat; would refer to a specialist.	Treatment effective in acute conditions.
CELLULITIS Spreading of infection beneath skin	Treatment would depend on the condition.	Would not treat; would refer to a dermatologist.	Treatment can be effective, but the whole health pattern should be examined.
CHILBLAIN Cold-induced damage to small blood vessels and nerves in skin	Treatment effective.	Would not treat; would refer to a family doctor.	Treatment effective in both acute and chronic conditions.
CORN/CALLUS Thickening of skin caused by frequent friction or pressure	Would not treat.	Would not treat; would refer to a chiropodist.	Treatment effective when causes such as tight-fitting shoes are eliminated.
CYST Swelling or growth containing fluid or semi-fluid material	Treatment would depend on the nature and location of the condition.	Would not treat; would refer to a family doctor.	Treatment effective in chronic cases.
CYSTIC FIBROSIS Inherited condition; mucous secretions are abnormally thick	Treatment may be effective in the early stages of the disease.	Would not treat; would refer to a family doctor.	Would refer to specialist.
DANDRUFF/ SEBORRHOEA Copious flaking of dead skin on scalp	Treatment can be effective.	Would not treat; would refer to a good hairdresser.	Treatment effective if the condition is dealt with constitutionally.

MED. HERBALISM	OSTEOPATHY	GEN. MEDICINE	COMMENTS
Treatment usually effective.	Treatment can help, especially with the aid of naturopathy.	General treatment is surgical drainage, possibly with antibacterial chemotherapy.	See also **Acne**, pp. 178–181
Treatment effective locally and systemically.	Naturopathic treatment can help the underlying cause.	Treatment with antifungal agents is successful, coupled with care of the skin and footwear.	See also **Ringworm**, pp. 192–193
Treatment can help, especially taken internally.	Would not treat if hereditary.	Not yet treatable unless due to illness, hormone or iron deficiency or psychological cause.	See also **Depression**, pp. 214–217
Treatment reasonably effective.	Would treat only if the patient could be moved.	Would treat; prevent by regular nursing help and avoiding pressure.	See also **FIRST AID**, pp. 226–231
Treatment often helpful.	Treatment can help, especially with the aid of naturopathy.	Treatment usually effective; condtion is generally allergic.	See also **Allergy**, pp. 86–89; **Hay fever**, pp. 72–75
Would treat in a first aid situation; serious condition might be a hospital problem.	Treatment can help, especially with the aid of naturopathy.	Treatment is to keep it clean and dress it if necessary.	See also **FIRST AID**, pp. 226–231
Treatment helpful when the condition is a manifestation of internal imbalance.	Treatment would depend on the cause.	No medical treatment if due to anxiety or poor hygiene, but may indicate underlying disease.	See also **Halitosis**, pp. 80–81
Treatment effective locally and internally.	Treatment can help, especially with the aid of naturopathy.	General treatment is surgical drainage, possibly with antibacterial chemotherapy.	See also **Acne**, pp. 178–181; **Abscess**, pp. 190–191
Treatment may be effective.	Would treat to prevent the condition worsening.	Generally leave condition alone and recommend wide shoes; otherwise refer for orthopaedic surgery.	See also **Corn/Callus**. pp. 190–191
Treatment most effective when combined with massage of oils into affected area.	Treatment would rarely succeed.	Treatment is by antibiotics.	See also **Septicaemia**, pp. 104–105
Treatment effective, and also helpful as prevention.	Treatment can help the underlying cause.	Recommend patient to keep warm and avoid pressure.	See also **FIRST AID**, pp. 226–231
Treatment may help. Often chiropody is valuable.	Would treat to prevent development.	Would treat or refer to a chiropodist.	See also **Bunion**, pp. 190–191
Treatment of limited help.	Treatment would depend on the location of condition and its cause.	Treatment depends on type; would remove or drain if necessary.	See also **Sebaceous cyst**, pp. 190–191
Treatment effective in alleviating symptoms.	Treatment would be based on nutritional advice.	Treatment is supportive, including use of antibiotics and vitamins.	See also **Mouth, throat and respiratory system**, pp. 58–59.
Treatment can be reasonably effective in relieving the problem and improving overall health.	Treatment can help, especially with the aid of naturopathy.	Treatment by scalp medications and special shampoos is helpful.	See also **Acne**, pp. 178–181; **Psoriasis**, pp. 186–189

CONDITION	ACUPUNCTURE	CHIROPRACTIC	HOMEOPATHY
DERMATITIS Disorder of skin caused by allergy or internal factors	Treatment can be effective, depending on the cause of the condition.	Would not treat; would refer to a specialist.	Treatment effective once aggravating factors such as chemicals are excluded.
IMPETIGO Infectious disease of skin	Would not treat.	Would not treat; would refer to a specialist.	Treatment effective.
PEMPHIGUS Large, fluid-filled blisters	Would not treat.	Would not treat; would refer to a specialist.	Treatment effective.
PRURITIS Itching due to disturbance of nerve endings	Treatment can be effective.	Would not treat; would refer to a specialist.	Treatment effective if the condition is dealt with constitutionally.
RASH Eruption or discoloration of skin	Treatment can be effective, but depends on nature and cause of condition.	Would not treat; would refer to a specialist.	Treatment effective.
RINGWORM Fungal infection of skin	Treatment can be effective.	Would not treat.	Treatment effective.
RODENT ULCER Type of skin cancer; spreads only locally	Would not treat.	Would not treat.	Treatment can control the spread of the condition. Would also refer to family doctor.
SCABIES Infestation of skin by, and allergic reaction to, the itch mite	Would not treat.	Would not treat.	Treatment would be aimed at correcting the environmental condition that favoured the parasite; an external preparation would be used in the short term.
SEBACEOUS CYST Swelling in skin due to blocked gland	Might treat this condition.	Would not treat.	Treatment would aim to correct metabolic disorders and raise general health; cure may be slow.
SHINGLES (HERPES ZOSTER) Blisters and pain on skin near nerve endings, caused by nerve infection.	Treatment effective.	Would not treat; would refer to family doctor.	Treatment brings speedy relief from symptoms and helps to prevent recurrence.
SKIN CANCER Abnormal and destructive growth of skin cells	Would not treat.	Would not treat; would refer to a specialist.	Treatment can relieve symptoms, but would refer to a specialist because surgery is usually necessary.
STYE Abscess of an eyelash follicle	Treatment effective.	Would not treat.	Treatment brings speedy relief from symptoms and helps to prevent recurrence.
URTICARIA (HIVES or NETTLE RASH) Itching lumps and eruptions on skin, usually caused by an allergic reaction.	Treatment effective.	Would not treat; would refer to a family doctor.	Treatment effective.
VITILIGO Loss of skin pigment in patches	Treatment is not very effective except in the early stages of the condition.	Would not treat; would refer to a family doctor.	Would refer to skin specialist.
WART/VERRUCA Growth of skin due to viral infection	Would not treat.	Would not treat; but would refer to a family doctor, a chiropodist or another practitioner.	Treatment effective, but may take time.

MED. HERBALISM	OSTEOPATHY	GEN. MEDICINE	COMMENTS
Treatment often helpful.	Treatment can help, especially with the aid of naturopathy.	Treatment by topical steroids is very helpful; it is also necessary to identify the cause (such as an allergy) and remove it.	See also **Allergy**, pp. 86–89; **Eczema**, pp. 182–185; **Hay fever**, pp. 72–75
Treatment reasonably helpful. May need to refer to family doctor because of the infectious nature of the condition.	Would treat if not contagious.	Treatment is by systemic and local antibacterial therapy.	See also **Scabies**, pp. 192–193
Would probably treat, but condition is not commonly seen.	Would treat if not contagious.	Would refer to a dermatologist.	See also **Blister**, pp. 190–191
Treatment often effective, but depends on the cause.	Treatment would depend on the location and cause.	Treatment depends on diagnosis.	See also **Allergy**, pp. 86–89; **Eczema**, pp. 182–185
Treatment often effective, or at least of some value, depending on the cause.	Treatment would depend on the location and cause.	Treatment depends on diagnosis.	See also **Allergy**, pp. 86–89; **Eczema**, pp. 182–185
Treatment often effective.	Would not treat.	Treatment with appropriate antifungal preparation depends on diagnosis.	See also **Baldness**, pp. 190–191
Would treat the whole person. Might refer to a family doctor.	Would not treat.	Would refer to a specialist for diagnosis; treatment by surgery or radiotherapy is effective.	See also **CANCER**, p. 225
Would treat, but would refer to family doctor if treatment did not prove effective.	Would not treat.	Treatment is effective.	See also **Allergy**, pp. 86–89
Treatment of more help for general vitality than locally.	Treatment can help, especially with the aid of naturopathy.	Would treat, or refer for surgery.	See also **Cyst**, pp. 188–189
Treatment very helpful in restoring health and vitality.	Treatment sometimes effective, but success depends on age and general health.	Condition resolves spontaneously; may need antiviral agents for severe lesions.	See also **Pemphigus**, pp. 192–193
Would treat the whole person, but would also refer to a family doctor or specialist.	Would not treat.	Would refer to a specialist for diagnosis; treatment by surgery or radiotherapy is effective.	See also **Cancer**, p. 225
Treatment reasonably helpful, both locally and internally.	Treatment can help, especially with the aid of naturopathy.	General treatment is surgical drainage, possibly with antibacterial chemotherapy.	See also **Abscess**, pp. 190–191
Treatment reasonably helpful.	Treatment can help, especially with the aid of naturopathy.	Treatment is by antihistamines and/or steroids.	See also **Allergy**, pp. 86–89
Treatment limited in its effectiveness.	It is worthwhile trying treatment, but the response is often poor.	Generally no treatment is given; possibly local injections.	
Treatment often effective.	Treatment can help, especially with the aid of naturopathy.	Best treatment is to leave alone to resolve spontaneously; may be removed by surgery, freezing, or burning.	See also **Cold sore**, pp. 80–81

THE SENSES AND NERVOUS SYSTEM

The network of the brain, spinal cord, nerves and sensory cells combine to form the nervous system. It is a system of communication, controlling bodily functions and ensuring its appropriate adjustment to internal and external changes. The brain coordinates all the body's actions, and has the capacity for thought and emotion.

The nervous system gathers information about the condition of the body and the environment outside it. Much of this data is received through the sensory organs – the eyes, ears, nose, tongue and skin. These enable us to see, hear, smell, taste and touch.

WHAT CAN GO WRONG

Disorders of the senses and sense organs have many causes. Degenerative changes may cause progressive loss of vision, hearing, smell and taste. But there are many other specific diseases and infections of the ears, eyes, nose and sinuses that can result in sensory loss. Injury can affect the senses, either through direct organ damage or damage to higher processing centres in the brain.

The nervous system can be drastically affected by selective disorders such as brain or spinal tumours, by chronic conditions such as Parkinson's disease, or by general disorders such as multiple sclerosis. Infections such as poliomyelitis and motor-neuron disease affect the nerves that produce movement. Other conditions may cause only abnormalities of sensation.

Strokes may damage various areas of the brain, whereas both syphilis and multiple sclerosis can devastate any part of the central nervous system.

Inflammation of the brain (encephalitis) may result from some viral conditions. Meningitis is an infection of the membranes covering the brain and is caused by many viruses and some bacteria. The brain degenerates with age but may do so earlier in life, causing dementia – as in Alzheimer's disease.

Complementary and alternative medical approaches sometimes view the senses and nervous system and their disorders in different ways. A summary of these views follows.

Acupuncture

In traditional Chinese medicine, the senses and sense organs are linked with the *Zang* organs – the eyes/sight with the *Liver,* the ears/hearing with the *Kidney,* the nose/smell with the *Lung,* the mouth/taste with the *Spleen,* the tongue/speech with the *Heart.*

Disorders of these senses are often caused by dysfunctions of their related *Zang* organs. Equally, and particularly in the case of the eyes, ears and nose, disorders may arise from invasion by external influences such as *Wind, Cold, Heat* and *Dryness.*

The nervous system, as it is understood in the West, is not recognized by Chinese medicine. Sensation and the normal functioning of all the body systems are part of the function of *Qi* and *Blood.* Loss of sensation and paralysis are the results of *Qi* and *Blood* not reaching the part of the body affected. Loss of voluntary movement is caused by a disorder of *Qi.*

Chiropractic therapy

Diseases of the nervous system often affect the spine and cause back pain. It is important that such conditions are accurately diagnosed, and that patients are referred for specialist treatment as required. Pain related to neurological disorders can sometimes be relieved by chiropractic therapy, but this would only supplement specialist treatment.

Trapped nerves are a common cause of back and referred pain, and can be successfully alleviated by chiropractic therapy.

Homeopathy

Diseases of the nervous system indicate a very deep disturbance within the body and symptoms are ranked high in the hierarchy. The nervous system controls the functioning of all the other systems. People sometimes experience nerve or sensory disturbances during illnesses unrelated to the nervous system. Although a doctor may not be concerned with such minor sensory experiences, these are important symptoms for a homeopath, and aid the selection of remedies.

Medical herbalism

The nervous system is an example of the interactions that take place in the body between mental/emotional and physical factors. The degree of stress in a person's life, whether self-created or external, and his or her reaction to it, is most apparent in the functioning of the nervous system. From these reactions, other systems of the body may be affected.

Environmental and atmospheric factors can lead to incorrect functioning of the nerves, and disturbances in other body systems can, in turn, affect the nervous system. Effective respiratory action and good nutrition are important to ensure normal functioning of the nervous system. Advice and treatment of nervous disorders is aimed not only at reducing stress and emotional tension, but also at improving nutrition, elimination and respiration – essential bodily functions.

Osteopathy with naturopathy

Nerves and sensory organs wither if deprived of nourishment. A fundamental part of naturopathic therapy is to ensure that the patient eats well, and that nutrients are being effectively distributed.

The use of drugs that directly affect the nervous system, whether medically prescribed or self-administered, can affect other systems as well and should be avoided. Rather than depending on tranquillizers to alleviate nervous or emotional problems, counselling or other therapy is preferable and advisable.

Pressure on the cranial and spinal nerves reduces the efficiency of nerve impulses. Such pressure may be the result of injury, disease, spinal lesions or asymmetry of cranial bones. Appropriate osteopathic treatment can alleviate such problems.

Chart of disorders

At the end of this section there is a chart listing various disorders of the sensory and nervous system. This is a general, but not definitive, guide to the treatment of such disorders. Complementary and alternative therapies treat the patient as a whole rather than merely the disorder presented. Whether a person can be treated, and the success of treatment, depends on the nature of the condition and the general health of the patient.

THE PATIENT

MP is 27, single, slim and of medium height. She works in advertising, but devotes most of her energy and free time to developing her own theatre company. She eats whatever food is at hand. She does not take any regular form of exercise, but keeps fit through the intense physical demands of the drama group.

THE PROBLEM

While she was a university student, MP developed intermittent migraine headaches, which she learned to control with proprietary drugs and rest. Over the past year, however, they have become more frequent and now occur every two weeks. Drugs are no longer effective and she is forced to rest for up to two days to combat accompanying symptoms of nausea, vomiting and diarrhoea.

The headaches start with pain over one eye, usually the left, and often develop into neuralgia in the left cheek and the back of her head. Bright light, noise, food smells, movement and reading aggravate the condition, and she is forced to rest – although usually without sleeping – during the day. Hot baths and gentle walks in the fresh air help once the headache has developed. She knows that red wine and chocolate can start an attack, and now consumes neither.

MP is depressed because the headaches are restricting her activities. She is aware that she has recently been too busy, but feels that the headaches are not entirely stress related. She is becoming irritable with her friends, although she was formerly vivacious and easy going. She has tried getting more sleep and staying at home more often but this has not been effective.

MP had her tonsils removed when she was 17 years old. She used to suffer from dysmenorrhoea (period pains), but this has been alleviated by use of the contraceptive pill. She experienced recurrent cystitis and vaginal moniliasis (thrush) while she was a student. She sleeps well but often wakes feeling stiff around her neck and shoulders.

TREATMENT BY AN
ACUPUNCTURIST

Migraine headaches are usually the result of either excessive *Liver Yang Qi* rising to the head and obstructing the channels, or a *Blood* deficiency, causing the channels to be malnourished. The *Liver* syndrome is often caused by stress, bottling up feelings, consuming greasy, spicy food, and too much alcohol. Excessive sexual activity can weaken the *Kidney Yin*, which then fails to control the *Liver Yang*. *Blood* deficiency often results from excessive menstrual bleeding, long-standing illness, or from the health being generally run down.

MP's symptoms suggest that the *Gall Bladder* channel (closely linked to the *Liver* channel) on the head is affected. The origin of disharmony is the *Liver* where the *Qi* is stagnating – indicated by depression, short temper and irritability – which may be caused by stress. Purplish spots on the sides of her tongue, and her "wiry" pulse, confirmed this stagnation.

The *Liver* is a *Yang* organ; the normal movement of its *Qi* is upward and outward. When its *Qi* stagnates, pressure builds up. This must be released, and the excess *Qi* rises up and accumulates in the channels of the head. The sudden explosion of *Yang Qi* also causes the *Qi* of the *Stomach* to react (producing nausea and vomiting) and excessive movement of the *Spleen Qi* (producing diarrhoea).

Dysmenorrhoea often involves the *Liver* if its *Qi* is stagnant. MP uses the contraceptive pill, which masks the dysmenorrhoea, and may contribute to this stagnation.

Treatment
Primarily, treatment would be aimed at reducing the *Yang* of the *Liver*. Points on the *Liver* and *Gall Bladder* channels of the feet, legs and head would be used. MP needs to look carefully at her patterns of diet, exercise, work and relaxation, and might wish to consider finding an alternative to the contraceptive pill. She might also look at the way in which she deals with emotional stress, particularly with regard to bottling up her feelings.

Prognosis
Results are usually good, ten treatments being typical for a course. Administering treatment whilst symptoms are acute is particularly effective.

TREATMENT BY A
CHIROPRACTOR

There is clear evidence that chiropractic treatment is effective in the management and cure of migraine, especially if the migraine is accompanied by pain and stiffness in the neck.

A detailed case history was taken. A number of orthopaedic and neurological tests were then carried out to check bone and nerve function. Particular attention was paid to the neck and thoracic areas, feeling for any parts of the spine that are restricted in movement and accompanied by muscle spasm. In this case the upper part of the neck and the upper part of the thoracic area were found to be affected. An X-ray of the neck was taken to check for any further abnormalities.

The temporomandibular (jaw) joints were also checked, since any problems with these, such as strain, frequent clicking or abnormal movement, can lead to increased soft tissue tension around the joints, which can spread to the facial muscles.

Treatment
MP's treatment would begin with soft tissue manipulation to ease the muscle spasm, which includes any work necessary around the jaw and face, which can be effective in helping cases of headache, migraine and neck pain. This would be followed by chiropractic adjustments to restore normal spinal movement.

Whether or not the contraceptive pill could be a causative factor must be considered, and it may be necessary for her to stop taking it. Because drugs are no longer effective in controlling the migraine she would be advised not to take them.

If MP favours sleeping face down, this can strain the neck and cause headache, neck and migraine problems, and she should change her habit. It may be helpful if, when a migraine starts, she lies on her back with a small towel rolled up under her neck. This allows the neck to relax properly because it is well supported, and will often ease the tension.

Prognosis
It may take three or four treatments before MP feels any benefit or alterations to her migraine patterns. If this treatment does not help, MP will probably be referred to an acupuncturist, a homeopath or a medical herbalist.

TREATMENT BY A
HOMEOPATH

MP has neglected her physical needs for so long that she is now devitalized, and it will take more than rest to restore her health. Diarrhoea and vomiting with the headache indicate a disturbance in the liver, so it is no surprise that the condition is worsened by red wine and chocolate, both of which increase activity in that organ. The contraceptive pill can contribute to congestion caused by this type of disturbance, and it is also often associated with a history of cystitis or thrush.

More specific to this patient is the left-sidedness of the headache which, with the diarrhoea and nausea, may be covered by several remedies – *Spigella, Pulsatilla, Phosphorus, Lachesis* and *Sepia*. These remedies also cover the stiffness of the neck, but *Arsenicum* has all these symptoms and more.

Arsenicum is generally appropriate where the symptom picture includes a positive response to heat sensitivity to food smells. People needing this remedy are often characterized by extreme prostration – MP's need to rest in bed for two days when she gets an attack is typical.

In such cases the use of *Phosphorus* is similar to *Arsenicum* and has to be considered as an option, because the patient is vivacious and artistic – which links to the symptom picture for *Phosphorus*. She is also ambitious and determined, however, with enough confidence and drive to achieve her ideal. *Arsenicum* would therefore be chosen in this case because there is a hint of coldness in her attitude to her job, which she sees as a stepping stone to her true ambition.

Treatment
One dose of *Arsenicum* 10M would be prescribed, but not when the patient has the headache. Because it is possible that there may be one or two attacks after the initial prescription, *Phosphorus* may be used for acute relief. However, it is preferable that the patient perseveres with the treatment and avoids any other medication for a time.

Prognosis
The prognosis in this case is good, but for long term improvement MP also has to look after herself better, eat regularly, and get more sleep.

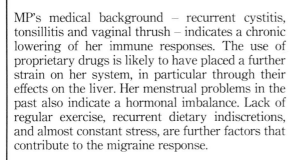

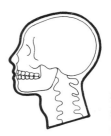

TREATMENT BY A
MEDICAL HERBALIST

MP's medical background – recurrent cystitis, tonsillitis and vaginal thrush – indicates a chronic lowering of her immune responses. The use of proprietary drugs is likely to have placed a further strain on her system, in particular through their effects on the liver. Her menstrual problems in the past also indicate a hormonal imbalance. Lack of regular exercise, recurrent dietary indiscretions, and almost constant stress, are further factors that contribute to the migraine response.

Treatment

Advice concentrates on diet – establishing a more nutritious, varied intake and avoiding excesses of alcohol, coffee, tea, chocolate, dairy produce and refined carbohydrates – and on relaxing exercises. Because her headaches appear to be eased by warmth, using heat packs applied locally to relieve the vasoconstriction (narrowing of the blood vessels), may also be of value.

The herbal prescription would include:
- Feverfew (*Chrysanthemum parthenium*): anti-inflammatory and relaxant to the blood vessels, also a digestive stimulant.
- Rosemary (*Rosmarinus officinalis*): peripheral vasodilator and anti-spasmodic; also acts to restore neuron function (when depression is linked with chronic stress) and to stimulate the liver.
- Chamomile (*Matricaria recutita*): relaxant, helping to calm digestive irritability, with vasodilator and anti-inflammatory properties as well.

The prescription should be reviewed regularly and the advice expanded to include things such as massage for the muscle spasms in the neck.

Prognosis

Improvement in MP's case will take some time, although the prognosis is reasonably good. Some changes in her habits will be necessary to prevent imbalances building up to the point of migraine reaction.

TREATMENT BY AN
OSTEOPATH AND NATUROPATH

MP's shoulder and neck stiffness suggest a structural reason for her persistent headaches. It will be necessary, however, to consider possible nutritional, hormonal and psychological causes.

Nutrition in general is important, with attention to more than the specific items such as red wine and chocolate which directly aggravate her condition.

A healthy blood supply is more likely to nourish the brain and the head than one deficient in nutrients. Digestive organs, such as the liver and gall bladder, are often implicated in the onset of migraine attacks. The contraceptive pill is a hormone, and it is common for its use to coincide with aggravation of such headaches. Cumulative stress is also a common cause of migraine.

Physical examination

A structural examination was carried out to look for possible interference with the nerve and blood supply to the head. Movements of the cervical vertebrae of the neck were studied and restrictions analysed. An X-ray was also taken. Some migraines are related to the bones of the cranium itself. The pathway of MP's headache includes the frontal bone, cheek bone, temporal bone and occiput. Any deviations of these bones must be corrected because each contains small holes through which blood vessels or nerves pass. Any distortion of these vessels and fibres can lead to a migraine attack.

Treatment

MP's treatment would include: neuromuscular soft tissue massage of the shoulders, neck and occipital fibres, and of the abdomen (because the liver and gall bladder are also involved); adjustment of lesions in the spine as a whole, but in the neck in particular; manipulation of the sacrocranial mechanism to ensure healthy flow of cerebrospinal fluid.

During an attack a cold compress may be applied to the abdomen while MP lies down in a darkened room. MP would also be advised to stop using the contraceptive pill, and to examine her diet, which will be reviewed at subsequent visits.

Prognosis

As long as MP takes the advice that she has been given, and is careful about stress, osteopathic treatment may be effective. There is hope for a significant improvement in her condition.

Introduction to medical herbalism pp. 32–39

Introduction to osteopathy/naturopathy pp. 40–47

TREATMENT BY A
FAMILY DOCTOR

Migraine is a common condition in otherwise healthy people. It tends to run in families and is difficult to treat. It is caused by a wide variety of physical and psychological factors.

Treatment
It is extremely important that a patient who is using an oral contraceptive, and who has a history of increasingly severe migraines, should stop taking the pill at once. The importance of this is that there is a risk of a stroke associated with use of the pill even in a young, healthy woman with normal blood pressure. Nevertheless, the pill may not be a major contributor to her immediate problem and stopping its use may bring little change, although her headaches are quite likely to improve significantly.

MP is correct that chcocolate and alcohol are trigger agents, and there may be many others. Most observant adults will, however, have made appropriate connections between food and the onset of headaches, and should not need dietary advice.

There are other factors such as stress – and particularly the sudden release of stress – that provoke attacks. Some sufferers find that it is best just to go to bed, whereas others are helped by more active strategies. Learning to relax her neck and shoulders, and sleeping on a firm, supportive mattress and pillow, will help. Coming to grips with emotional problems and keeping fit are important, but even the most well adjusted migraine sufferers can expect to continue to have headaches.

There is an enormous range of medication, including herbal preparations such as Feverfew, aimed at both prevention and treatment. Drugs such as beta-blockers may have a place in prevention. Simple painkillers such as aspirin, and drugs such as Maxolon (metoclopramide) to prevent sickness can also be helpful. Drugs containing ergotamine are sometimes the only effective medication for the pain, but they increase nausea, and are dangerous if taken frequently.

Prognosis
Assuming that MP's headaches are not related to the pill, it is likely she will have to live with her migraine, but symptoms tend to ease with age and attacks become less frequent. A migraine clinic could advise her, and acupuncture benefits some sufferers.

CONSULTANT'S COMMENTS

The most critical characteristic of migraine is its complexity and volatility. Of all the common conditions, this one is among the most difficult to define, predict and understand. Thus it is hard to recommend any single treatment.

Each of the strategies described could be effective but, equally, none of them may be. In no other condition is it more apposite to suggest that a patient should keep trying until they find a therapy or therapist that can provide positive help.

The treatments
It is unnecessarily pessimistic for the family doctor to say that the patient might have to live with the problem; it would be more helpful to suggest it might be necessary for her to keep trying different treatments until she finds one that works. The thorough examination and X-ray of the neck and cranial structures recommended by the chiropractor and the osteopath is an excellent first step, because skilled manipulation can work wonders. Acupuncture and homeopathy can also sidestep conventional assessments and go right to the heart of the problem.

Herbalism, however, is in a position to have a direct influence on the disorder in conventional terms. The herbalist has correctly opted for a vasodilatory prescription containing herbal remedies of established value in the long term correction of migrainous conditions. If this prescription proved, in fact, to be ineffective, there is a range of others, with quite different action, to choose from. There are also direct measures that might be taken to counter hormonal disturbances and the effects of nervous exhaustion.

Withdrawal from the contraceptive pill is favoured by all practitioners. In most cases it is regarded as suppressing the body's own attempts at achieving hormonal balance. The comments of the family doctor in this case add extra urgency to that recommendation.

SCIATICA

THE PATIENT

SD is 24 years old, 1.5 metres (5 ft 2 in) tall and slim, with a fresh, healthy complexion and clear eyes. She is a journalist and has an erratic lifestyle, eating convenience foods, missing meals, smoking (about 20 cigarettes a day), but rarely drinking alcohol except when eating out. Although she enjoys swimming she rarely has time for it and is thus becoming unfit.

THE PROBLEM

SD has had sciatica (pain in the leg along the course of the sciatic nerve) for seven years. Trouble with her lower back began at age 15 after a holiday job potato-picking. The pain was located in the lower back, and troubled her occasionally if she made unusual movements. However, at 17 years she developed pain down her right leg, which was diagnosed as sciatica. The pain continues to trouble her, especially after doing desk work and when she is particularly tense.

Recently the pain has become worse down the left leg, which she attributes to her posture when typing. At times of extreme stress the pain travels up the spine to the neck and down her arm (on the same side as the affected leg) or more commonly down to her foot. The pain is described as aching rather than shooting, and is best relieved by lying on the floor or applying warm compresses. Sleeping on her front or on a soft bed aggravates the condition. Her back is curved inward below the waist (lower thoracic and lumbar area).

SD is a cheerful, outgoing person, but has a tendency to get over-tense and nervous. She works hard, is self-disciplined, and is eager to make a success of her career.

SD has had no serious illnesses and was a healthy child. She seldom gets colds. Her periods are normal, but she had some pelvic discomfort which, when investigated, revealed a tilted womb. Her father also has sciatica. She wore high heels as a teenager and now has difficulty walking in flat shoes because her calves feel strained.

TREATMENT BY AN
ACUPUNCTURIST

In traditional Chinese medicine three factors are cited as causes of sciatica: invasion of the channels of the back by external pathogenic *Wind*, so that *Cold* and *Damp* may block the flow of *Qi*; the *Qi* of the *Kidney*, controlling the lower back, may be weak, leading to retardation and stagnation of *Qi*; or traumatic injury to the lower back may lead to stagnation of *Qi*. The *Du, Urinary Bladder* and *Gall Bladder* channels are usually affected. If left untreated, stagnation of *Blood* may result, in which case the disease is more' difficult to treat successfully.

This was a chronic problem. The bending and lifting involved in potato-picking suggested injury to the muscles of the lower back, leading to stagnation of *Qi*. There were signs of stagnation of *Qi* and *Blood*, as well as signs of *Cold* caused by the long-term stagnation. The circulation of *Qi* to the *Urinary Bladder* and *Gall Bladder* channels of the legs was restricted, producing the sciatic pain. Stress, because it had weakened her *Qi*, had led to retardation in the *Urinary Bladder* channel, which ascends the back, connecting with the channels of the arm at the nape of the neck. Lack of proper exercise and poor posture were contributing to poor circulation.

Treatment
Her treatment would be concentrated at the source in the lower back. The principle would be to move the stagnant *Qi* in the affected channels and warm the lower back with moxa. Points that were painful on palpation would be needled, as well as points on the *Urinary Bladder* and *Gall Bladder* channels which are specific for this problem.

Prognosis and conclusion
Acupuncture is the most commonly used treatment for sciatica in China. The prognosis would be very good, five to ten treatments usually being effective in the acute stage, although more treatment might be needed in a chronic case such as this. Proper exercise, particularly swimming, would be a prerequisite for prevention in the future. Consultation with an osteopath would be recommended to deal with any contributory structural problems. Lessons in the Alexander technique might also be recommended.

TREATMENT BY A
CHIROPRACTOR

Sciatica is a common condition in people with certain types of low back problem. Some cases are associated with disk abnormalities, but others such as SD's are associated with biomechanical defects causing restricted spinal mobility. This leads to pressure on the sciatic nerve and the resulting pain in the leg. By restoring normal function and mobility to the spine, it is possible to reduce the pressure on the nerve and thus ease the pain and discomfort.

Physical examination
SD had an increased lumbar curve, which was putting tension on the thoraco-lumbar and upper lumbar areas of her spine. Bending to the left and right, and rotation of the spine, showed restriction in the area of the 11th thoracic to 3rd lumbar vertebrae. Forward flexion was slightly restricted, and backward extension increased the back pain. When she was examined lying face up, straight leg raising was painful on the affected side. When lying face down, bringing the heel to the buttock on the bad leg was also painful. All other orthopaedic and neurological tests were negative, and reflexes were normal. Palpation revealed general muscle tension in the lower thoracic and general lumbar area, with spinal joint fixations at the level of 2nd lumbar and in the lumbo-sacral area.

Treatment
The treatment would consist of general loosening techniques to free the tight muscles, followed by specific spinal manipulation at the levels of 2nd and 5th lumbar, and 1st sacral vertebrae.

SD should find time to exercise, and relaxation classes would help her to cope with stress. She would be given advice concerning posture. Because SD worked a great deal at a desk and her sitting posture was aggravating her back, it would be worth considering a special type of chair which would tilt forward while she worked.

Prognosis and conclusion
Due to SD's build, posture and lifestyle it could take 6–8 treatments before she noticed any particular improvement in her condition, and 12–15 before she would be fit enough to be put on routine check-ups about once every three months.

TREATMENT BY A
HOMEOPATH

Sciatica is characterized by severe pain and discomfort when the patient is in particular postures, and often indicates underlying spinal lesions.

Although SD's problem seemed directly related to stooping to pick potatoes, there must already have been a weakness in the lumbar region of the spine for the stooping to have created such a disturbance; the curvature of the spine supported this theory. Thus the prescription would be aimed at strengthening the spine as well as removing the pain and dealing with any lesions.

SD's immediate symptoms were characterized by an aching pain moving up the spine and down into the legs, which was better when she lay on a hard surface or applied heat to the area, and worse when she was sitting. *Rhus toxicodendron* covered the picture well, and often helps when a problem arises from overstraining the back. It might also go some way toward helping SD's strained calf muscles when she wore flat shoes.

Treatment and prognosis
Rhus toxicodendron would be prescribed when the situation was acute, and thus single doses of *Rhus toxicodendron* 30 might be used when the pain occurred. The incidence of sciatica should reduce, because each time *Rhus toxicodendron* was given it would strengthen the muscles. A single dose of a higher potency – *Rhus toxicodendron* 200C or 1M – might be used instead. In a young, healthy person this could be more suitable, and take the patient's body back to its original difficulty in correcting the problem, perhaps causing several days of aggravation in the process, but removing the problem more thoroughly.

After the acute situation had been dealt with, the underlying weakness or constitutional predisposition should be corrected. Although a therapy such as the Alexander technique would help greatly, another homeopathic remedy might be needed to change the metabolism. *Phosphorus* might well help here, because it is indicated for a weak spine, and also in a picture of nervousness and sensitivity coupled with a cheery, outgoing disposition. *Phosphorus* patients can be chaotic about their daily needs and ignore such things as sensible exercise. SD would be given this remedy in a high potency, with advice to reorganize her lifestyle.

TREATMENT BY A
MEDICAL HERBALIST

SD displayed many of the factors which produce and aggravate sciatic pain: a history of strain on the lower spine, inadequate exercise and poor posture. That her symptoms worsened at times of stress was an important feature of her condition.

Treatment

Adequate rest and exercise to relieve tension and strengthen the muscles in the lumbar area would be a vital starting point. Correction of her posture, perhaps with Alexander technique lessons, would also be highly beneficial. Correct support for her lower back when SD was at her desk would be essential. The possibility of osteopathic or chiropractic treatment should be considered.

For overall vitality SD needed to improve her nutrition, with fewer convenience snacks and regular mealtimes. As part of the overall treatment programme, steps to tackle smoking would be important because this would be contributing to generally lowered health. Massage would help to reduce muscle tension and irritability; using essential oils of Lavender, Rosemary, Juniper and Marjoram in this would be particularly helpful.

The herbal prescription would include:
- Black Cohosh (*Cimicifuga racemosa*): relieves inflammation and muscular spasm.
- Scullcap (*Scutellaria laterifolia*): gentle overall relaxant, reducing symptoms of nervous tension and helping to restore normal functioning.
- Rosemary (*Rosmarinus officinalis*): improves circulation to extremities, a nervous restorative, and improves liver and digestive function.
- Chamomile (*Matricaria recutita*): relaxing, anti-inflammatory agent, improving digestion and relieving the build-up of tensions.

The prescription would be varied as necessary; for example, using more strongly analgesic or anti-inflammatory remedies if needed.

Prognosis and conclusion

With changes in exercise, rest patterns and posture, SD could lessen the strain on her lower back considerably, and the herbal medicine combined with local massage treatment would help her to improve her condition and regain greater health.

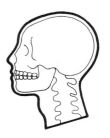

TREATMENT BY AN
OSTEOPATH AND NATUROPATH

SD's sciatica was a result of irritation of the sciatic nerve. The cause could have been toxic, which would mean that the sciatic nerve was inflamed because of ill-health. Eating, smoking, and postural habits could lead to toxic sciatica and perpetuate whatever damage might have occurred at the ages of 15 and 17.

The causes could have been purely structural: pressure on nerve roots caused by misalignment of the vertebrae, arthritic changes or prolapsed (slipped) intervertebral disks. High-heeled shoes disturb pelvic and spinal integrity, but so does a sudden change to low-heeled shoes.

Physical examination

A detailed examination revealed osteopathic lesions in lumbar spinal vertebrae and the sacroiliac joints. There was disk involvement, but X-ray investigation would be needed to confirm whether or not the disk was prolapsed.

Another possible cause of low back and sciatic pain lay in the pelvic cavity from pressure on the nerve from an enlarged organ, a new growth or suchlike. An internal examination would be necessary to find out why SD's womb was tilted and whether the tilt was contributing to any pressure.

Further examination looked for wastage of muscle in either leg, and pain elsewhere in the body that might suggest involvement of the membranes that link the cranium and spine.

Treatment

If a disk had prolapsed there would be more soft tissue massage and positioning than manipulation. Sacroiliac and spinal lesions would be adjusted. Because the cranium interacts with the sacrum, it would be adjusted accordingly. Relaxation techniques and postural awareness would be taught. Smoking should be reduced or eliminated and the diet improved.

SD would be advised to rest on a non-sagging surface. Warmth helped her, but if there was severe pain it might be better to apply a cold, damp cloth to the sacroiliac area – or wherever pain was most obvious. If there was disk involvement, heat could aggravate the pain.

TREATMENT BY A
FAMILY DOCTOR

Sciatica can indicate mechanical interference with the nerve fibres of the lower back, and in this case there is a well-defined area of pain. On the other hand, sciatica often takes the form of a vague diffuse ache and is likely to be a referred pain from a disordered joint or ligament.

Diagnosis can be extremely difficult, although signs from the nerves may precisely indicate a particular disk lesion. It was unlikely that SD had a lesion as high as the 1st or 2nd lumbar vertebrae because involvement of the nerves in this region produces pain in the groin and front of the thigh; lower disk lesions are more common.

X-rays and examination excluded possible causes of the pain such as tumours in the spine, tuberculosis, pelvic tumours and various other conditions. SD was likely to have a mechanical derangement such as a prolapsed intervertebral disk (PID), a congenital abnormality of the spine or chronic ligament strain.

Treatment

PID may be managed operatively or conservatively; surgery would be necessary only if there was an increase in nerve defect. Non-operative treatment is successful in the great majority of cases, and the aim is to reduce strain on the lumbar spine by bed rest – with or without traction – and sometimes by the use of special corsets. Physiotherapy would be essential, and may be supported by special exercises at home. Swimming is particularly therapeutic. Chronic strain also requires physiotherapy or heat treatment. Osteopaths, chiropractors and physiotherapists can all be helpful. For all chronic back problems, posture, work conditions, exercise and suitable beds are important. Some relaxation or Alexander technique classes might be helpful.

Prognosis and conclusion

It is unlikely that SD would require surgery, but if she noticed localized weakness, numbness or difficulty with bowel or bladder function, she should see her doctor and be referred to a specialist. SD was tense and smoked quite heavily, and neither of these things would be doing her overall health much good.

Introduction to Western medicine pp. 48–55

CONSULTANT'S COMMENTS

This severe nerve pain in the leg is in fact a low back problem. Any treatment or care is thus directed to the lower lumbar vertebrae and the sacroiliac joint.

The treatments

As with other back problems, the therapists to turn to first are the chiropractor and osteopath. The family doctor recommends treatment by a physiotherapist, but physiotherapists do not usually have training in spinal adjustment, and they are best seen in a supporting role. However, as with many other back problems, there is also scope for other treatments, especially in preventing recurrence of the attacks.

The claims of acupuncture are supported by research in China, and findings point to relief of local tissue inflammation and swelling as the most tangible benefits. The medical herbalist also has recourse to remedies that will reduce inflammation and, to a certain extent, muscle spasm. It is this latter effect that is the main concern of the homeopath.

Often, sufferers find that susceptibility to attacks is not always directly connected with physical strain, and this suggests that there are likely to be other ways in which non-manipulative therapists could help.

Several specialists suggest that SD learns the Alexander technique. This is a form of postural retraining that has a good record of help in conditions such as this. It highlights, too, the general benefits of looking for ways to correct bad habits of the back. Skilled yoga teaching might also be beneficial.

Conclusions

Sciatica need not be a difficult problem to treat, as long as skilled manipulative techniques are used for specific correction. Other approaches can give long-term benefits. The need for surgery is unlikely.

CONDITION	ACUPUNCTURE	CHIROPRACTIC	HOMEOPATHY
ANOSMIA Absence of sense of smell	Treatment can be effective, depending on cause of condition.	Would not treat; would refer to a specialist.	Effectiveness of treatment depends on the cause. Results are good if cause is catarrh.
ASTIGMATISM Distortion of vision due to irregularities in lens shape	Treatment may be effective.	Would not treat; would refer to an optometrist.	Treatment sometimes effective.
CATARACT Increasing opacity of the lens of the eye	Would not treat; would refer to a specialist.	Would not treat; would refer to a specialist.	Treatment sometimes effective.
CHOREA Disorder of nervous system causing muscle spasm	Treatment can be effective.	Would not treat; would refer to a specialist.	Treatment sometimes effective.
CONJUNCTIVITIS Inflammation of membrane covering the eye	Treatment can be very effective in both acute and chronic cases.	Would not treat; would refer to a family doctor.	Treatment effective in both acute and chronic cases.
CONVULSIONS Brain-induced muscle spasms causing contortions	Treatment can be very effective in chronic cases.	Would not treat; would refer to a specialist.	Treatment effective in both acute and chronic cases, especially in children during fever.
DEAFNESS Loss of hearing	Treatment can be very effective, depending on severity and cause of condition.	Treatment may benefit certain cases, depending on the cause.	Treatment effective in acute cases. In chronic cases results depend on cause.
DIZZINESS Feeling of imbalance and lightheadedness	Treatment can be very effective, depending on cause of condition.	Treatment may benefit certain cases, depending on the cause.	Success of treatment depends on the rest of the constitutional picture.
DOUBLE VISION Sometimes a symptom of a serious condition such as brain damage	Treatment can be very effective, depending on cause of condition.	Would not treat; would refer to a specialist.	Treatment effective after injury; other cases may need further investigation.
EARACHE Pain often caused by infection or catarrah	Treatment can be very effective.	Would not treat; would refer to another practitioner.	Treatment effective in both acute and chronic cases.
ENCEPHALITIS Inflammation of brain	Treatment may be undertaken, depending on circumstances.	Would not treat; would refer to a specialist.	Treatment can be effective.
EPILEPSY Variety of seizure caused by dysfunction of brain	Treatment can be effective in chronic conditions.	Would not treat; would refer to a specialist.	Response to treatment varies in individual cases, depending on any drugs that have been used to control the condition.
FAINTING Temporary loss of consciouness	Treatment can be effective.	First aid treatment may be necessary; treatment depends on the cause.	Treatment usually effective, but depends on the rest of the constitutional picture.
GLAUCOMA Increase in pressure of fluids within eyeball	Treatment can be effective.	Would not treat; would refer to a specialist.	Treatment sometimes effective.
HEADACHE Pain within head or across forehead	Treatment can be very effective, depending on cause of condition.	Treatment frequently effective for this condition.	Treatment effective in both acute and chronic cases.

MED. HERBALISM	OSTEOPATHY	GEN. MEDICINE	COMMENTS
Treatment may help, depending on the cause.	Would treat if the cranial structure is at fault and can be balanced.	Difficult to treat; often psychological and may resolve spontaneously.	See also **Sinusitis**, pp. 76–79
Would not treat; would refer to an optician.	Treatment sometimes possible if cranial structure is at fault.	Would refer to an optometrist.	
Would refer for possible surgery. Treatment may be of value for general health.	Would not treat.	Would refer to an ophthalmic surgeon.	
Treatment likely to be of limited help, depending on nature of problem.	Treatment may be possible, depending on cause.	Would refer to a neurologist.	See also **Tic**, pp. 296–297
Local treatment may be helpful.	Treatment can help, especially with the aid of naturopathy.	Treatment would depend on cause.	
Treatment may be of considerable help; may need to refer to a family doctor.	Treatment would depend on cause.	Treatment would be first aid; might need to refer to neurologist.	See also **Epilepsy**, pp. 204–205; **FIRST AID**, pp. 226–231
Might treat, but referral for further tests is more likely.	Treatment would depend on cause.	Would remove wax from ears, and refer to a specialist if necessary.	See also **Tinnitus**, pp. 206–207
Treatment of some value, but depends on the cause.	Treatment would depend on cause.	Treatment would depend on the cause.	See also **FIRST AID**, pp. 226–231; **Hypertension**, pp. 94–97
Would refer to specialist for tests.	Treatment rarely effective.	Would refer to a neurologist.	
Treatment can be effective.	Naturopathic treatment for acute condition, and osteopathy for chronic condition, can be effective.	Treatment is usually very effective.	See also **Catarrh**, pp. 82–83; **Common cold**, pp. 68–71; **FIRST AID**, pp. 226–231
Would treat if the patient were not in danger; slow but steady improvement is possible.	Would not treat.	Would refer to hospital.	
Treatment can be helpful; severe cases may need orthodox treatment also.	Effectiveness of treatment is variable.	Would refer acute cases to a specialist; can monitor and treat chronic cases.	See also **Convulsions**, pp. 204–205
Treatment is helpful.	Can be treated.	Treatment would depend on cause.	See also **FIRST AID**, pp. 226–231; **Hypertension**, pp. 94–97
Would not treat except to help improve general health.	Would not treat.	Would refer to an ophthalmic surgeon for testing and treatment.	
Treatment can be effective, especially for chronic problems, but depends on the cause.	Treatment frequently effective, but depends on cause.	Treatment would depend on cause. Disorder is difficult to treat.	See also **Migraine**, pp. 196–199

CONDITION	ACUPUNCTURE	CHIROPRACTIC	HOMEOPATHY
LONGSIGHTEDNESS Inability to focus on close objects	Treatment may be effective.	Would not treat; would refer to an optometrist.	Little evidence of effective treatment.
MENINGITIS Inflammation of membranes surrounding brain	Treatment can be very effective in the right circumstances, but requires daily application.	Would not treat; would refer to a specialist for immediate treatment.	Treatment effective; it may be necessary to use antibiotics in such a serious illness.
MULTIPLE SCLEROSIS Damage to nerve cells in brain and spinal cord	Treatment can be very effective, depending on severity of condition.	Would not treat; would refer to a specialist.	Treatment can sometimes help remission.
NEURALGIA Pain located along a nerve	Treatment is effective.	Treatment is frequently effective.	Treatment is effective.
OPHTHALMIA Inflammation of the eye	Treatment is effective.	Would not treat; would refer to a specialist.	Treatment is effective.
OTITIS Inflammation of the ear	Treatment can be very effective.	Would not treat; would refer to a specialist.	Treatment effective in both acute and chronic cases, especially if condition is dealt with constitutionally.
PALSY Paralysis due to stroke, nerve disorder or brain abnormality	Treatment depends on severity of condition and how longstanding it is.	Would not treat; would refer to a specialist.	Treatment can be effective in acute cases. In chronic cases results depend on causes and the degeneration of muscle and nerve tissue.
PARKINSON'S DISEASE Chronic disorder causing shaking, slowness and stiffness	Treatment may be effective.	Would not treat; would refer to a specialist.	Treatment may produce limited results, but allopathic drugs may be more helpful.
SHORTSIGHTEDNESS Inability to focus on distant objects..	Treatment may be effective.	Would not treat; would refer to an optometrist.	Would not treat except constitutionally, when results may be favourable.
SQUINT Failure of eyes to point in the same direction	Would not treat; would refer to a specialist.	Would not treat; would refer to a specialist.	Treatment effective if cause is worms, but even a muscular cause may respond to treatment.
STROKE Disturbance of blood supply to part of the brain	Treatment for this condition and its aftermath is widely used in China; it is not very effective in cases presenting after six months from the onset.	Would not treat; would refer for immediate medical treatment.	Treatment may be effective in an emergency to reduce damage.
TIC Uncontrollable spasm, usually affecting face or head	Treatment can be very effective.	Would not treat; would refer to a specialist.	Treatment may be effective.
TINNITUS Ringing in ears not caused by external sound	Treatment can be very effective.	Treatment effective in certain cases.	Treatment effective if condition is dealt with constitutionally; results vary depending on cause.
TRAVEL SICKNESS Nausea or vomiting caused by motion	Treatment can be very effective.	Would not treat; would recommend homeopathic travel sickness pills.	Treatment is effective.
VERTIGO Sensation that the patient or his/her surroundings are revolving.	Treatment can be very effective.	Treatment effective in certain conditions.	Treatment is effective.

MED. HERBALISM	OSTEOPATHY	GEN. MEDICINE	COMMENTS
Would not treat.	Treatment sometimes helpful.	Would refer to an optometrist or ophthalmic surgeon.	
Would treat mild, viral form of the illness, and can help over a period of time. Would refer for tests.	Would not treat.	Would refer to hospital.	
Treatment can be of value, depending on degree of disorder.	Treatment can often help relieve symptoms.	Would refer initially to a specialist; would provide long-term support.	See also **Musculo-skeletal system**, pp. 150–151
Treatment is often helpful, both locally and in restoring vitality.	Treatment can often be of help.	Treatment would depend on cause; may need to refer to a neurologist.	See also **Migraine**, pp. 196–199; **Sciatica**, pp. 200–203
Local treatment can be helpful in mild cases.	Would not treat as a rule; some problems can be helped.	Treatment would depend on cause. Condition often found in newborn infants.	See also **Conjunctivitis**, pp. 204–205
Treatment depends on cause and site of problem. May need to refer to a family doctor.	Treatment can help, especially with the aid of naturopathy.	Treatment would depend on cause; chronic condition may need surgery.	See also **Earache**, pp. 204–205
Treatment may help over time; would usually refer to specialist.	Treatment can help, but depends on the cause and degree of condition.	Simple traumatic palsies may recover spontaneously; would refer others to a neurologist.	See also **Paralysis**, pp. 174–175
Treatment may have some value.	Would not treat.	Treatment can be helpful for a time.	
Would not treat; would refer to a specialist.	Treatment can help if a cranial fault can be remedied.	Would refer to ophthalmic surgeon.	
Would not treat; would refer to a specialist.	Treatment can help if a cranial fault can be remedied.	Would refer to a specialist.	
Treatment may be valuable in some cases.	Treatment can help rehabilitation.	Minor cases can be treated at home, with the aid of physiotherapy, speech therapy, and occupational therapy.	See also **FIRST AID**, pp. 226–231; **Hypertension**, pp. 94–97
Treatment can be helpful. Counselling or other help may be valuable.	Treatment can often help.	Treatment would depend on the cause.	See also **Anxiety**, pp. 222–223
Treatment of limited help. Might refer to acupuncturist or osteopath.	Treatment can help in some cases.	Not really treatable; medication may help.	See also **Hypertension**, pp. 94–97
Treatment can be effective.	Treatment can often be of help.	Treatment can be helpful, but may cause drowsiness.	See also **FIRST AID**, pp. 226–231
Treatment may be helpful, depending on the cause.	Treatment can help some cases.	Treatment would depend on the cause; recovery may be spontaneous.	See also **Dizziness**, pp. 204–205

THE MIND AND EMOTIONS

Human beings are intelligent and capable of logical thought and expression of emotions. In addition we have the capacity to communicate through speech. These factors, above all, distinguish humans from other animals.

Research has shown that intelligence stems from the brain, but emotions have a complexity that is beyond physiological explanation. The science of psychology has attempted to analyse and understand the mind and its emotions, and there are many different theories about it.

WHAT CAN GO WRONG
Classification of these disorders is very complex. Behavioural and emotional problems may be the result of serious organic diseases such as tumours, infections and degenerative conditions, or of toxic reactions to drugs (illicit and prescribed).

Some doctors believe that disorders such as schizophrenia and manic depression are constitutional problems, whereas others maintain that they arise from patterns of social and psychological problems in the family. It is likely that the familiar states of anxiety and depression are brought about by failure to cope with stresses. These in turn may be caused by emotional conflicts or failure to adapt to social norms in early life.

Mental processes are affected by aging, resulting in memory loss and sometimes dementia. Anxiety and stress have an impact on the general functioning of the body and can precipitate disorders such as migraine, asthma, ulcers and possibly more serious conditions such as heart disease and cancer.

Complementary and alternative medical approaches sometimes view the mind and emotions and their disorders in different ways. A summary of these views follows.

Acupuncture
The mind, in traditional Chinese medicine, is linked to the function of the *Zangfu*, in particular the *Heart* and the *Kidney Jing*. The *Heart* has influence, through the *Shen*, over consciousness. The *Jing* controls the brain matter. Weak *Jing* may occur in elderly people and result in loss of memory or senility. Disturbed *Shen* may lead to disturbed consciousness and mental illness.

The emotions influence the functions of the *Zangfu*. Unexpressed emotion may disturb its function, as may emotions that are expressed too strongly and too frequently. In addition, emotional states and responses may be used as an important source of diagnostic information.

Chiropractic therapy
The onset of up to 70 per cent of back problems can be related to emotional or psychological problems. It is very important for a chiropractor to take this into account when making a diagnosis. Treating the physical problem alone may relieve pain, but this will be only temporary unless the psychological causes are also dealt with.

It is therefore necessary for a chiropractor to build up a rapport with patients so that he or she can investigate deep-seated factors causing the problem. In some cases professional counselling may be required.

Homeopathy

Mental and emotional disorders have a special place in homeopathy because human emotions and states of mind determine personality and individuality. It is on the basis of this that homeopathic remedies are prescribed.

In proving remedies, mental and emotional symptoms were often very noticeable. Through them, the action of a remedy, and the personality and characteristics that it would suit, could be determined.

Mental and emotional symptoms are placed at the top of the homeopathic hierarchy, even though they might seem strange or irrelevant in conventional terms. As a consequence of many serious illnesses, patients are often shocked to find that their personality has changed – they may, for example, be more irritable, angry or tearful than usual. Disturbances on this level are seen as the deepest of all, because a healthy mind is the key to physical health, and a disturbed mind is often the cause of physical disorders.

Homeopathic remedies are aimed at relieving mental and emotional symptoms as well as physical ones. The beginning of recovery from illness is often indicated when a person's emotional state improves.

Medical herbalism

Mental and emotional health are seen as inseparable from the state of physical health. Medical herbalists are familiar with the concept of psychosomatic illness and recognize that emotional stability is crucial to health and recovery from physical symptoms. Emotional stress is now acknowledged as a major cause of illness.

Less well recognized are somatopsychic illnesses, in which physical disorders or dysfunctions create emotional imbalances. Poor liver activity, for example, can contribute significantly to depression, which in turn contributes to a lowering of physical vitality.

Any separation of physical, mental or emotional health is artificial, and medical herbalism takes a holistic view – correcting the causes of disease and not merely relieving symptoms.

Osteopathy with naturopathy

All physical problems are related to the mind and emotions. Either the cause of the physical problem lies partly, or wholly, in the psyche, or the emotions are in some way affected by the physical problems.

Structural problems can be emotionally induced. It is well-known that fear or anger can distort the body, whereas joy can liberate it. Osteopathic adjustments of spinal lesions can be effective in removing long-standing emotional causes.

Bereavement is known to result in a psychic shock that affects the pituitary gland, with consequent hormonal problems. Counselling and naturopathic advice provide more effective therapies than hormone replacement drugs.

Schizophrenics have been helped by programmes of supervised fasting and nutritional adjustment. Hyperactive children and those displaying antisocial behaviour have improved when chemical additives have been removed from their diets. Depressives often have low blood sugar, that can be corrected by avoidance of stimulants such as alcohol, coffee and, paradoxically, sugar itself.

Chart of disorders

At the end of this section there is a chart listing various disorders of the mind and emotions. This is a general, but not definitive, guide to the treatment of such disorders. Complementary and alternative therapies treat the patient as a whole rather than merely the disorder presented. Whether a person can be treated, and the success of treatment, depends on the nature of the condition and the general health of the patient.

ALCOHOLISM

THE PATIENT

NV is a successful, 37-year-old writer, of average height and build. He is married with two young children. Although his work is sedentary, he plays golf most weekends and his weight remains at a constant level. His taste in food is wide-ranging, and he eats a lot of meat and rich sauces. He does not smoke, but drinks with meals and in the evenings.

THE PROBLEM

NV has recently accepted that he is an alcoholic. His alcohol consumption has increased dramatically over the last two years. He usually starts drinking mid-morning or at lunch and continues steadily until evening, when he drinks spirits, then wine with his meal. He believes that his creativity is enhanced by alcohol, and that it helps him to sleep. His work often necessitates business lunches, and his drinking habits originated through these activities. Resolutions to cut down usually happen in the spring, and he drinks less in the summer; he hates the dark, wet winter months.

NV has a moody, erratic temperament, shifting between extremes of high and low spirits. His wife is devoted to him, and he enjoys being with his children, but feels weighed down with responsibility. His drinking is distressing to his wife and he tries to conceal the quantity he consumes.

He drinks a lot socially, but when depressed he drinks alone and keeps bottles in his desk and briefcase. The family have enough money and live well, so there is no real cause for anxiety about practical matters. He takes life very seriously and is a perfectionist.

As a child NV was often ill with minor complaints. He had glandular fever when he was 14, and this left him thin and weak for several years. However, he went to university and was healthy during this period. Constipation troubles him from time to time. He often gets bronchitis during the winter as a result of colds or influenza.

TREATMENT BY AN
ACUPUNCTURIST

Alcohol is said by Chinese medicine to create *Heat* and *Dampness* as well as producing both *Spleen* and *Liver* problems. Alcohol consumption is seen to relate to emotional imbalances associated with these organs, and to the *Heart Shen*, or "spirit".

NV's problems were rooted in his inner emotional turmoil and anxiety. Creative writing, by necessity, involves introspection and a degree of obsessiveness, and this predisposed him to stagnation of *Qi*. The sedentary nature of the work aggravated this. Alcohol stimulated his *Qi*, and thus his creativity, but further impaired the functions of his *Liver* and *Spleen* in circulating *Qi*. Stagnation of *Liver Qi* leads to emotional instability and depression, while poor *Spleen* function promotes an overburdened sense of responsibility. Alcohol had become the cause of his problems and the means by which he was avoiding them.

Treatment
NV's treatment would be aimed at breaking this vicious circle. First, the short-term palliative effect of ear acupuncture would be used to help to break the alcohol habit and deal with withdrawal symptoms. Second, the harmful effects of alcohol would be tackled by using the *Spleen* and *Stomach* channels to disperse *Dampness*, and the *Large Intestine*, *Liver* and *Gall Bladder* channels to move stagnant *Qi* and reduce *Heat* and *Fire*.

Third, acupuncture would encourage changes in the emotional turmoil at the root of NV's addiction, helping to restore his enthusiasm about his life and work. This would involve soothing the *Liver* and pacifying the *Heart Shen* to calm his anxiety and allow his emotions and creativity to flow freely, and strengthening the *Qi* to alleviate his overburdened sense of responsibility and improve his confidence. Lightening his diet by eating more vegetables and less meat would also help, as would taking more vigorous exercise.

Prognosis and conclusion
Acupuncture could not change the life experiences which had brought NV to his present position, but it could help him to make the changes necessary to combat his alcoholism. NV would be advised to seek professional counselling or psychotherapy.

TREATMENT BY A
CHIROPRACTOR

Alcoholism is not a condition a chiropractor would expect to be consulted about. It could be that, during a consultation about something else, the chiropractor would suspect that a patient was an alcoholic. In severe cases there may even be signs that alcoholism is long-standing and may have affected the nerves in such a way as to give the person a certain type of neuritis (nerve pain), particularly in the legs. If such a condition did exist, it would require referral to a neurologist.

In any case, if a person consulted a chiropractor and the evident diagnosis was that of alcoholism, he would be referred to his doctor for appropriate help. He would also be encouraged to contact Alcoholics Anonymous for help and advice.

TREATMENT BY A
HOMEOPATH

Alcoholism is usually a social problem, caused by an inability to cope with life in some way. More rarely it can be an actual craving for alcohol, like a craving for sweet foods. Whatever the cause, once a person is an alcoholic there are problems in withdrawal, and there are often secondary effects that must be dealt with.

Diagnosis
It appeared that NV was not suffering from any secondary effects, although his moodiness might be regarded as being in this category. Two factors stood out in his case: a feeling of being trapped, with a need to avoid responsibility, and his compulsion to set himself high standards. These two feelings were pulling him in different directions, giving rise to inner turmoil and depression. He was making himself feel more isolated by hiding his habit from his wife. The arrival of his second child seemed to have increased his feeling of being trapped, and this was the point at which his alcoholism became a problem.

Lycopodium would be chosen to cover NV's condition, after taking into account his history of constipation and bronchitis, his diet, his swings of mood and his serious attitude to life. A typical *Lycopodium* patient is a young executive who, although successful, is discontented with his achievements because he feels trapped in a safe job when the wild side of his youth has not yet exhausted itself.

Treatment and prognosis
A high potency of *Lycopodium,* 1M or 10M, would be needed to enable NV to come to terms with himself and the dissatisfaction that was unbalancing him. A slight change in diet to food that was more wholesome and rich in nutrients would be recommended to minimize the work done by his liver and relieve some of the stress alcohol was putting upon it. Exercise would be encouraged for the same reason.

Psychotherapy might also help the homeopathic remedy to fulfil its task more thoroughly. If the craving for alcohol continued, a dose of *Lachesis* 30 might end it in this patient. Positive progress would be expected after a few weeks, and this would be monitored regularly – probably every two weeks at first, and then monthly.

Introduction to chiropractic therapy pp. 16–23   Introduction to homeopathy pp. 24–31

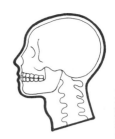

TREATMENT BY A
MEDICAL HERBALIST

As with the great majority of alcoholics and heavy drinkers, NV appeared to be using alcohol as a means of masking deep emotional disturbances. The increase in consumption since the birth of his second child reinforced the link between his feelings of being trapped and his use of alcohol. However, the nature of his personality indicated a predisposition towards alcoholism from a much earlier stage in his life.

Treatment
The main approach to helping NV would involve a great deal of counselling, and support from agencies such as Alcoholics Anonymous could be of great value. His recognition of the problem was a first, vital step towards help and recovery.

His physical condition would need great attention, and a diet lower in fats, rich sauces and the like would be an important change. There might also be scope for winter sunshine holidays to alleviate the depressing effect that lack of sunlight had on his moods. The herbal prescription would include:
- Milk Thistle (*Carduus marianus*): helps to regenerate liver cells and protect the liver against damage from alcohol abuse.
- Dandelion Root (*Taraxacum officinale*): mild liver and digestive stimulant, which also acts as a gentle laxative.
- Centaury (*Centaurium erythraea*): bitter liver stimulant, encourages bile flow.
- Vervain (*Verbena officinalis*): acts as a tonic, improving liver function, and restoring normal nervous function.

The prescription would be varied and reassessed regularly to cope with any change in the physical and emotional picture.

Prognosis and conclusion
The initial change for NV would, of course, be an absolute reduction in his alcohol intake – considering his temperament this might mean complete abstinence – as a prerequisite for any successful treatment programme. Given this change and support, considerable positive alterations in his health are quite possible with herbal treatment.

TREATMENT BY AN
OSTEOPATH AND NATUROPATH

Having accepted that he was an alcoholic, NV would have to be determined to give up drinking. He should join Alcoholics Anonymous or a similar group, and be willing to face an investigation into the reasons for his drinking.

Physical examination
Once these decisions had been made, the first step would be to carry out a detailed examination of NV's health. Alcohol affects the body's ability to absorb nutrients, which leads to malnutrition, harms brain and body cells, and alters blood sugar levels. NV would be tested for muscular coordination, for liver cirrhosis, for damage to stomach and pancreas, and for any mental aberrations.

Treatment
There would be two parallel elements to the treatment. First, NV would be helped through the inevitable withdrawal symptoms which are, in effect, symptoms of alcohol poisoning. Second, he would be helped to restore his mind and body. The treatment would take account of any irreversible changes that had already taken place.

The first aspect of treatment would involve relaxation and advice – probably daily to start with – until he was capable of relaxing on his own at home and at work. In the clinic this would involve, among other things, abdominal and spinal massage and the use of a technique of cranial osteopathy called fourth ventricular compression.

The general health programme would include a dietary regime to restore nourishment to the whole body, involving wholesome eating supplemented by specific minerals and vitamins. Periodically, he would be encouraged to accelerate the elimination of toxins by special diets or supervised fasting.

Osteopathic adjustment of the vertebrae involved in the nerve and blood supply to the metabolic organs such as the liver would be used.

Psychotherapy and counselling would be essential to complement physical care by helping him to avoid despair, depression, impatience, craving and sliding back into alcohol consumption.

Prognosis and conclusion
It is rarely too late to make a change. NV should try to apply his perfectionism to his health and the well-being of his family.

TREATMENT BY A
FAMILY DOCTOR

Alcoholism can be perceived as a disease, and has a basis in physiological and psychological processes. Recognition of alcoholism can be made, for example, by the alcoholic, by family or friends, by workmates, or by doctors or social workers. Biochemical evidence from tests on the blood could be used to estimate the level of damage to his liver.

Treatment
The treatment is a very uncertain business, but alcoholics can often be helped. Areas of treatment include detoxification, psychotherapy (including marital therapy, and groups) and help from organizations such as Alcoholics Anonymous, which can also be invaluable to the alcoholic's partner and family.

Deterrent drugs such as Antabuse (Disulfiram), which make the drinker feel physically sick when he drinks, are sometimes used, but to be effective and safe need considerable supervision. Some patients find it helpful to take these drugs for months or even years.

Prognosis and conclusion
NV had started on the road to recovery by recognizing his alcoholism, but was still deluded that his creativity was enhanced by alcohol, and had not perceived that he had an alcohol-produced, not alcohol-solved, sleeping problem.

He would also need some deeper psychological help and should consider whether he could continue to endure the stress of his writing career. The continuation of his married and family life would clearly be at risk unless he received help.

As a successful, intelligent, young family man, the outlook for NV is good, but there would be difficult times ahead as he and his wife confronted the problem.

This major social malaise causes a great deal of personal suffering and damage, not to mention great expense. Its origins are complex and its treatment can be depressingly difficult. Early recognition is of great importance, before the integrity of a caring family is shattered.

CONSULTANT'S COMMENTS

The effect of alcohol is a complex one, involving physiological and biochemical responses, psychological and emotional effects, and considerable social implications. The condition of alcohol dependence touches all these levels, and any attempt to treat it must do likewise.

Treatments
The family doctor is able to call on a number of resources to help someone in this state, and makes reference – as do some of the other practitioners – to the value of Alcoholics Anonymous. This is the sort of case in which the family doctor, with access to a range of experts and strategies, can often score over those taking a more individual line.

Nevertheless, there are a number of other useful suggestions available here. The acupuncturist is able to draw on a broad and positive assessment of the disorder, and a proven track record for acupuncture in altering dependency cycles. The medical herbalist has remedies that detoxify the liver, and these have been shown to be remarkably successful in a series of trials in the USA. The homeopath can often make considerable headway in addressing the wide constitutional components of the dependent personality.

Conclusions
This is a case in which an individual seriously wanting to break the habit would be advised to follow as many strategies as were available.

THE PATIENT

RY is 40 years old, of average height and of stocky build. He used to weigh a steady 76 kg (12 stones), but he has put on more than 7 kg (15 lb), since he stopped playing football regularly. This he did six months ago, because of his depressed state. He is married with two teenage children and had a successful career as an electrical engineer.

Eight months ago, RY was made redundant, which resulted in total loss of self-esteem. He does not smoke, but now drinks excessively in the evenings. His diet has changed in the last six months to a persistent preference for fatty and sweet foods, and snacks of a similar nature throughout the day.

THE PROBLEM

RY has become despondent about his future. His family is becoming distressed by his condition because he is now irritable and takes no interest in them. He has experienced several attacks of palpitations during the past two months caused by raised blood pressure. He is now anxious about his health and his family, but feels that he has lost control.

RY has always had a tendency to depression but, until his redundancy, lived an active and contented family life. He now does little but watch television, eat, drink and work in the garden. For a few years he has felt burdened with the responsibility of maintaining his standard of living, mortgage, car and teenage children. His wife, who works as a secretary, shares the cost, but RY feels that he should be the breadwinner.

RY has rarely been ill, except with back problems. He injured his neck and lower back playing football ten years ago, and frequently suffers from an acutely stiff neck and aching back. He tends to get constipated and uses laxatives to relieve this. Six years ago he developed slightly raised blood pressure because of weight gain, and took up football and a diet which successfully controlled it.

TREATMENT BY AN
ACUPUNCTURIST

Depression in traditional Chinese medicine is often associated with stagnation of *Qi* of the *Liver*. This, in turn, is seen as resulting from repressed feelings, particularly anger. The stagnation of *Qi* may lead to poor circulation of *Body Fluids* and the accumulation of *Phlegm*, which is said to cloud the mind, producing apathy, muddled thinking and pessimism. Here the mind is equated with the *Shen*, the "spirit", which is associated with the *Heart*. The accumulation of *Phlegm* is said to indicate the involvement of the *Spleen*, which is responsible for transforming and circulating *Body Fluids*.

RY's problems had clearly originated in his redundancy. He was feeling frustrated and angry at his plight and appeared to have no means of adequately expressing his feelings. His irritability, and his withdrawal from a previously active life, indicated that his *Qi* was stagnating, and that the pathology described above had taken hold. His drinking and diet were contributing to an accumulation of *Phlegm*. Constipation was a further sign of *Qi* stagnation. Palpitations showed that the *Heart* was also affected.

Treatment
Moving the stagnant *Liver Qi* would be a basic need in treatment, along with restoring RY's "spirit" and eliminating *Phlegm*. Points selected from the *Liver, Gall Bladder, Pericardium, Heart, Ren, Du, Stomach* and *Spleen* channels would be used.

Prognosis and conclusion
Acupuncture treatment alone might not be enough to bring about long-term change. It would be important for RY to receive counselling about his unemployment, deal with his emotions, and find ways to combat his apathy. Acupuncture would help to stimulate his *Qi* and therefore help him to break out from his depression. Diet and exercise would certainly help. Treatment should continue on a weekly basis while he sorted out his problems.

TREATMENT BY A
CHIROPRACTOR

At the initial consultation, at which RY complained of back pain, it was evident that there was more to this case than just a bad back.

Treatment
It was clear that RY needed genuine help for his depression, probably in the form of guidance and counselling, especially about how to deal with his unemployment problem. He would need to consult a specialist counsellor.

Treatment for RY's neck and back stiffness and tension could be given, but he would be unlikely to respond well to treatment because of his depressed state. Better results might be achieved by a deep relaxing type of massage to ease the muscular tension.

RY would also be given dietary advice to encourage him to eat more nutritious foods and avoid constipation problems. He would be advised to start taking regular exercise again.

Prognosis and conclusion
RY should not be given drugs as a panacea for his condition. Counselling and advice would be the best treatment.

TREATMENT BY A
HOMEOPATH

A blow to the self-esteem – such as redundancy – can cause depression in anyone. But if, like RY, the person needs continuous work and a well-organized environment to justify his self-worth, redundancy can be devastating. Many of his symptoms could be explained by his depression; he ate more and put on weight which, in turn, caused his high blood pressure and palpitations to recur. He then became anxious about his health.

As well as his particular reaction to redundancy, dietary preference for eating fats and sugars pointed to treatment with *Arsenicum*. This is a major remedy for depression caused by loss of self-esteem, associated with irritability and indifference to those one loves and normally cares for.

People suffering from this type of depression tend to be anxious and doubt themselves easily. To cope, they build an enormously well-organized system around themselves to maintain control because they cannot trust others. In many ways, they have a great deal of energy, but when they are sick – either physically or emotionally – they collapse and lose any definition of self that they might have had. RY showed these trends clearly.

Treatment and prognosis
This would involve one dose of *Arsenicum* in a high potency (1M or 10M). The high blood pressure, weight gain and so on would gradually resolve as he gained the confidence and energy to start living more actively again. His confidence should return soon and enable him to go out and look for work again, or create more ambitious projects to satisfy his interests. Further treatment would be necessary only if he relapsed into the same pattern.

The remedy should be sufficient to bring about emotional change, but counselling might be necessary in the short term.

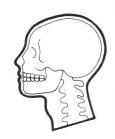

TREATMENT BY A
MEDICAL HERBALIST

In herbal medicine a problem of this kind would be viewed as being much more than simply a depression of the nervous system. Thus work on several aspects of RY's life would be necessary. Apart from clinical advice and treatment, support from family, friends and possibly professional workers would be essential to put a stop to his negative cycle of behaviour.

Treatment
Trying to sort out all his difficulties had become such an insurmountable problem to him that failure and depression were inevitable. The main advice, therefore, would be to tackle problems one at a time, looking initially at those practical things he could achieve, and building up potential success rather than probable failure. Physical and emotional benefits would come from: starting to play football again; planning a programme of activity with his wife, and involvement with his children; a diet plan, moving toward regular meals, and perhaps helping to prepare them; and allowing himself an occasional reward as a stimulus for such efforts.

The herbal prescription would include:
- Wild Oats (*Avena sativa*): nervous restorative that assists the return to normal function over a period of time.
- Hawthorn (*Crataegus oxyacanthoides*): dilates the coronary arteries and tones the heart muscle, slowing and regulating heart rhythm.
- Dandelion Root (*Taraxacum officinale*): gentle laxative and liver stimulant.
- Vervain (*Verbena officinalis*): tonic which improves liver activity and calms nervous irritability and exhaustion.

The prescription would be reviewed frequently, and particular attention would be paid to RY's digestion and defecation.

Prognosis and conclusion
With persistence and support, RY would experience great improvements; the central question of employment, however, would remain the most significant factor.

TREATMENT BY AN
OSTEOPATH AND NATUROPATH

Redundancy can be a severe blow to the pride as well as to the pocket. Different people respond in different ways, and it was obvious that RY had allowed his whole being to deteriorate. As long as he nurtured his misery he would continue to drink and to eat unwisely, and so expand his paunch and reduce his general health. Poor health would aggravate mental problems and increase depression.

However, the fact that RY had sought help would mean that it should be possible to break the cycle of ill health and depression. It would be necessary to look into all aspects of his nutrition, debilitated structure and impaired faculties.

Treatment
The treatment would start with whatever was easiest to alter: it might involve osteopathic correction of his structure, starting with the stiff neck and aching back; it might be helpful to change RY's attitude to drinking and eating, with a gradual return to a balanced intake; or it might involve talking about his feelings of inadequacy, resentment and anger – or whatever was underlying his loss of interest in life.

Chemical, structural and psychological aspects could all be naturopathically helped by temporary dietary supplements of appropriate minerals and vitamins. Homeopathic remedies can also have dramatic effects in restoring harmony.

Prognosis and conclusion
RY would be encouraged to reintegrate all aspects of his life. After a number of treatment sessions he would probably start resuming responsibility for his own welfare and gradually be inspired to find satisfying employment again.

Some depressed people find communication impossible or at best futile. Yet without such communication it is unlikely that an osteopath would be able to provide help.

Introduction to medical herbalism pp. 32–39

Introduction to osteopathy with naturopathy pp. 40–47

TREATMENT BY A
FAMILY DOCTOR

RY was in the familiar plight of a family man facing long-term unemployment. His depression seemed largely due to his feelings of despair and inadequacy in the face of his change of status in his marriage, his family and society. It was worrying that he was expressing his anger and frustration by drinking (there is always a danger of alcoholism), that his eating habits had become poor and that he was using laxatives.

Treatment
Although some doctors may treat this reactive type of depression (so called because it seems to be a reaction to an event in life) with antidepressant medication, a wider view of RY's situation would be helpful. It was probable that he had, or would have, marital difficulties resulting from his loss of self-esteem. He and his wife would gain enormously from talking to a counsellor experienced in marital problems brought about by the loss of employment.

RY would be advised about the importance of diet and exercise, and his blood pressure would need to be checked regularly. His doctor could estimate the seriousness of his drinking by doing special blood tests.

Prognosis and conclusion
A healthy man of 40 who has previously had a successful career would probably recover from an employment crisis, and if his family had the capacity to cope with change this would help him. If RY could be helped to understand and cope with his new situation, he would be able to benefit from opportunities such as retraining schemes or voluntary work.

This is a potentially dangerous situation for RY and his marriage. The impact of loss of employment should never be underestimated.

CONSULTANT'S COMMENTS

Clinical depression places many demands on sufferers, and on those who would help them. The difficulty lies in the fact that it is a deep-seated illness (it is more than just feeling down in the dumps from time to time), and that the depressed person is often even unwilling to see the advantage of doing anything about it.

In earlier times little distinction was drawn between psychological and physical illness. The Greeks saw all human illnesses as disorders of one or more of four "humours" or fluids. For example, excess Yellow Bile led to a choleric disposition, and excessive Black Bile led to a melancholic disorder. Melancholia, the traditional term for depression, was understood as a disorder of bile, or of the liver, and was treated as such.

This appears an unusual approach in modern times, but it warrants consideration. It is the experience of many therapists that metabolic and dietary treatments can have significant effects in helping depression. In this case excessive alcohol and fat consumption must be considered, and several of the practitioners have picked up the connection between this and his "liverish" condition.

The treatments
While antidepressant drugs are often prescribed in modern medicine, the family doctor points out that in cases where the problem arises mainly from external causes these are of limited benefit.

The natural treatments emphasize finding ways to support the sufferer from within. Herbal medicine and acupuncture have long traditions of dealing with such problems, and must be favoured options. Spinal manipulation could be helpful in this case, dietary change can be important, and homeopathy can often reach the very heart of the imbalance.

Homeopathy has the advantage of not demanding too much of the patient. The problem faced by all therapists is maintaining patient cooperation.

INSOMNIA

THE PATIENT

NH is 45 years old, 1.6 metres (5 ft 4 in) tall and has grey hair. She is the mother of two teenage boys. Her husband runs a successful small business. She is artistic, doing pottery and painting when she has time, and sings in a local choral society. She is not interested in cooking, but prepares one meal a day for her family, and otherwise eats little. She keeps fit by being active, but does no systematic exercise.

THE PROBLEM

NH has always suffered from insomnia (inability to sleep), especially if she shares a room, or if there is any noise during the night. She usually has no difficulty in getting to sleep, but often wakes between 1 and 3 am and then cannot get back to sleep again. She finds herself unable to get comfortable and has to get up, have a hot drink and read for a while before she is tired again. After a disturbed night she is irritable and depressed all day. She has a separate room from her husband.

HN is a restless, impatient woman with little tolerance when things go wrong. She often argues with her husband, but then makes up and feels better for a while. She is unfulfilled, but does not know what to do to change this. She finds her family a great burden and responsibility. She has few close friends, but gets on well with people because she can be witty and humorous. Her relationship with her husband is difficult at the moment, but it used to be good.

In general HN is healthy, but she gets colds and coughs in the autumn. The colds are rarely severe, but the coughs often drag on for weeks, and are dry and racking. She often feels tired, but pushes herself to keep going. The best periods of her life were her two pregnancies – although afterward she suffered from postnatal depression – and early in her marriage, when she felt fit and slept well.

ACUPUNCTURIST

In traditional Chinese medicine insomnia is related to disturbance of the *Shen* or "spirit". The *Heart* "houses" the *Shen*, which includes the "mind" and the mental processes. When the *Shen* is not "housed" properly, it "floats", the mind becomes agitated and sleep is disturbed. The *Blood* nourishes the *Heart* and the *Shen*, thus weakness of *Heart Blood* can lead to insomnia. Any condition of emotional or mental turmoil may disturb the *Shen*.

HN was poorly nourished, both physically and emotionally. She was eating sparingly and was unfulfilled in her relationship with her husband. Her insomnia affected her least early in her marriage and during her pregnancies, when she probably felt very fulfilled and received much attention and love from her husband.

Her prematurely grey hair, postnatal depression, chronic insomnia, tiredness, pale tongue and choppy pulse combined to suggest a long-term general *Blood* deficiency affecting the *Heart* and the *Liver*. Deficiency of *Heart Blood* produced insomnia; deficiency of *Liver Blood* produced irritability, depression, restlessness, impatience, poor tolerance and inability to change her situation. Her inability to throw off coughs suggested that the *Lung Yin* had been undermined.

Treatment
The treatment principle would be to calm the *Shen*, and strengthen the *Blood* and *Yin*. Points on the *Heart, Spleen, Ren, Kidney* and *Urinary Bladder* channels would be used. A proprietary Chinese herbal tonic for the *Blood* might also be prescribed because acupuncture alone is sometimes insufficient to strengthen the *Blood*, especially in very chronic conditions. Regular food intake would also be important. Counselling or psychotherapy might also be suggested in order to help HN resolve the emotional difficulties within her marriage.

Prognosis and conclusion
Acupuncture can be very effective in treating insomnia, with results being achieved after as few as ten treatments. In this case, success would to some extent depend on HN's being able to resolve her emotional problems. Acupuncture would help to provide a solid basis on which to undertake changes in her life.

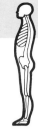

TREATMENT BY A
CHIROPRACTOR

TREATMENT BY A
HOMEOPATH

Chiropractors do not usually treat patients suffering from insomnia. It was interesting that the best periods of HN's life were early in marriage and when she was pregnant, although she suffered with postnatal depression. This could suggest a hormonal imbalance which might be responsible for her various symptoms, but she would need a sympathetic family doctor to refer her to a specialist.

It seemed that she needed to discuss her problems, and perhaps she could be referred to someone appropriate. She might benefit from yoga and relaxation classes, which would also give her the opportunity to meet more people.

Because sleep is the time when the body heals itself, lack of it can give rise to many problems. The causes of insomnia are very varied.

HN showed the irritability and tiredness that often occur with lack of sleep, and the effect this was having on her home life was not surprising. She was impatient, found her family a burden, and argued with her husband. When she went to bed she was still in a state of agitation, being particularly disturbed by noise.

This pattern of insomnia, involving sensitivity to noise and the inability to sleep once awake, pointed to *Sepia* as a treatment. *Sepia* is also notable as a remedy for an active person who is easily run down or tired, and irritable with her family. It is a remedy for women who feel better during pregnancy, but suffer such effects as postnatal depression. It would even cover the dry, racking cough which was one of HN's symptoms. Although *Sepia* is not particularly an autumn remedy, it could be that HN's coughs came on in autumn because of the change of weather at that season.

The remedy fitted all the symptoms, a most important aspect of homeopathic treatment, and no other reason than this is needed for a remedy to be given. However it is necessary to ask how HN got into this state. Despite all that was going for her, she was still dissatisfied, and this gave rise to the nervous agitation which prevented her from relaxing into sleep. The female *Sepia* patient is usually seen as worn down by the load she carries, but often taking on chores and burdens to give her life some firm direction.

Treatment and prognosis
A single tablet of *Sepia* 1M or 10M would work to restore harmony in the whole person, and would calm HN's troubled nerves. Relaxation and counselling might also help, but it is commonly found that *Sepia* restores a patient to herself, so that she finds her direction again. Homeopathy can often cut out years of psychotherapy, or greatly aid that therapy. The most immediate improvement in HN's sleep pattern would be expected to occur in the first few days of treatment.

Introduction to chiropractic therapy pp. 16–23

Introduction to homeopathy pp. 24–31

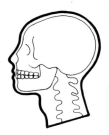

TREATMENT BY A
MEDICAL HERBALIST

For HN, as with most insomniacs, there was clearly an emotional or nervous factor, and counselling would probably be of tremendous value, particularly with regard to her relationships and sense of unfulfillment. It was possible that a significant factor was her hormonal state, which would require investigation. Her resistance to infections, especially of the respiratory tract, needed boosting, and diet, physical exercise and breathing exercises would help.

Treatment
Practical tips for helping sleeping patterns would include warm baths in the evening (especially with the addition of essential oils); the establishment of more regular meal times, including foods rich in calcium and magnesium in the early evening; a walk in the evening; and the use of herbal teas (such as Lime Blossom) to aid relaxation. Dietary supplements might be valuable in the short term. The herbal prescription would include:
- Scullcap (*Scutellaria laterifolia*): relaxant and nervous restorative that helps to calm without being a sedative.
- Wild Oats (*Avena sativa*): gentle but effective nervous tonic that nourishes and restores the nervous system to normal functioning.
- Agnus-Castus (*Vitex agnus-castus*): helps to normalize hormone production; particularly helpful when progesterone output is low.
- Hyssop (*Hyssopus officinalis*): generally calms irritability and restlessness; also a relaxing expectorant for a dry cough.
- Passion flower (*Passiflora incarnata*): relaxant and antispasmodic to induce more restful sleep.

The prescription would be varied as required. Monitoring of her health would be very important and blood tests might be needed to determine any deficiencies, such as anaemia.

Prognosis and conclusion
Counselling would be valuable for HN because her attitude to life and her environment were affecting her sleep patterns, but there were also physical factors contributing to the condition. Combined with advice, herbal treatment can be very helpful indeed in balancing internal functions and restoring more refreshing sleep.

TREATMENT BY AN
OSTEOPATH AND NATUROPATH

HN would not be unique in attributing her distress to sleeplessness when the reverse was the more likely. HN's restlessness was reflected in her insomnia, her eating habits, her irritability and probably her artistic temperament.

Physical examination
The physical examination showed muscle tensions consistent with her tense nature. There were areas of congestion in the soft tissue at the back of her head and neck that were painful to pressure and suggested a barrier to the free exchange of fluids and nerve impulses between the head and trunk. There was rigidity of motion of some of the cranial bones of the skull that could interfere with circulation of fluids in the brain and spinal cord and lead to congestion in brain cavities, and thus possible sleep disturbance.

The sleep centre in the brain could also be affected by poor nutrition, emotional stresses, excessive mental activity and trauma.

Treatment
The first step would be to transfer attention from sleep to health. Healthy people sleep without having to think about it. Next, when in bed, HN should accept that her body and mind would benefit if she pretended to be asleep – that is, lie comfortably with warm feet, let all tight muscles relax, breathe slowly and quietly, let the mind wander and, above all, not actually try to fall asleep.

Cranial and spinal imbalances would be adjusted, and soft-tissue massage would improve circulation.

Foods such as those high in protein which excite brain activity should be avoided close to bedtime. A hot-water bottle at her feet and a cold compress about the abdomen would draw congestion from HN's brain.

Prognosis and conclusion
Psychotherapeutic help could unravel any fears that might account for a subconscious reluctance to drop out of consciousness into sleep. HN should concentrate on improving her general physical and mental health, and allow improvements in her insomnia to follow from this.

TREATMENT BY A
FAMILY DOCTOR

Many people complain of insomnia, and much effort has been made by pharmaceutical companies to manufacture more effective and less addictive sleeping medicines. Research has not shown lack of sleep to be as damaging as is often supposed, although the psychological consequences of long, unhappy, wakeful nights are another matter. Insomnia is usually sleeplessness as a result of stress, although certain illnesses are associated with agitation. Common "drugs" such as caffeine and some asthma medications, can cause sleeplessness.

Treatment
Sleeping medicines would not be recommended. In spite of protestations from the drug industry to the contrary, they tend to be addictive and may not be completely metabolized by the following day. Modern drugs are more quickly metabolized and short-acting, but they are also quite addictive. Hypnotics can be useful in the short term, for example in dealing with jet-lag or travel problems, and short term prescribing at times of severe stress makes reasonable sense.

Some people use a "little tot" of alcohol to help them sleep, but while this can be sensible enough, it must be remembered that alcohol excess is associated with sleeping disorders, not with sleeping well. HN should avoid coffee, strong tea and any other caffeine-containing beverages in the evening. She might sleep better if she did some regular exercises that were healthily exhausting.

Prognosis and conclusion
It was difficult to escape the conclusion that HN's unhappy marriage and general psychological malaise was responsible for her insomnia. She and her husband clearly needed some counselling or therapy. If her husband would not join her in this search for mental help, HN would need something to help her direct herself – not just to the fulfilment that she craved, but to coping with her life in general. She was approaching an age when psychotherapy is less likely to help because of inflexibility in herself, and she would do well to seek help now. Her doctor could direct her to appropriate agencies.

CONSULTANT'S COMMENTS

It is not always appreciated that insomnia can be caused as much by being run-down as by excessive tension. Most commonly, the former kind of insomnia is typified by the sufferer easily going to sleep at bedtime, then waking up in the small hours, as in HN's case. This is a classic symptom of depression.

In such cases, not only are sedative sleeping pills not well suited, they may actually depress the condition further. The aim of treatment should be to nurture and support, to provide tonic rather than sedative treatment.

Even when insomnia is caused by tension, the role of simple sedation is limited. It often brings about sleep, but if attempts are not made to reduce, or come to better terms with, the sources of tension, the insomnia may increasingly come to resemble the depressive type.

Treatments
All the practitioners are in general agreement that support is preferable to sedation. The family doctor shows reluctance to rely on sleeping prescriptions, and provides useful pointers to the correction of wider issues. All the others are concerned in their own ways to identify and treat sources of deficiency in HN. All the treatments have potential validity.

Conclusions
As pointed out by the family doctor and the osteopath and naturopath, the lack of sleep is not itself the main problem. Correction of the wider disease, however, would need concerted action and a measure of good luck, and would probably involve a number of contributions. Prospects for improving the sleeplessness are, nonetheless, quite good.

TREATMENT OF MENTAL AND EMOTIONAL DISORDERS

CONDITION	ACUPUNCTURE	CHIROPRACTIC	HOMEOPATHY
ADDICTION Physical or psychological dependence on a drug or other substance.	Treatment would be in conjunction with counselling.	Would not treat; would refer to a specialist.	Treatment effective in reducing withdrawal symptoms, dealing with underlying cause of the addiction and increasing ability to persevere with cure.
ALZHEIMER'S DISEASE Abnormal brain degeneration in middle age	Treatment would depend on condition.	Would not treat; would refer to a specialist.	Treatment would have very limited effects, because this is a degenerative disease; would refer to a family doctor.
AMNESIA Loss of memory	Treatment would depend on cause.	Would not treat; would refer to a specialist.	Treatment effective if the condition is caused by shock, and may help if the cause is nervous disorder. May refer to a specialist.
ANOREXIA Loss of appetite due to mental disturbance	Treatment would be undertaken only in conjunction with counselling.	Would not treat; would refer to a specialist.	Treatment effective because the problem is dealt with holistically.
ANXIETY Exaggerated fear or worry	Treatment effective, but depends on cause.	Would not treat; would refer for counselling.	Treatment effective because the problem is dealt with constitutionally.
DELIRIUM Disturbance of brain function causing excitement, confusion and hallucination	Treatment can be effective.	Woult not treat; would refer to a specialist.	Treatment effective when condition is part of a fever.
DEMENTIA Form of mental deterioration; most common in old age	Treatment would depend on cause.	Would not treat; would refer to a specialist.	Treatment on a constitutional basis may be effective, depending on the degenerate state of the vital force.
DYSLEXIA Disturbance of reading or writing abilities	Would not treat.	Some chiropractors offer special treatment that can help some sufferers.	Little evidence of treatment being effective.
FATIGUE Chronic tiredness	Treatment effective, but depends on cause.	Would not treat; would refer to another practitioner.	Sleep is the best cure; if the condition is due to weakness, constitutional treatment is effective.
MANIC DEPRESSION Mental disturbance; great depression alternating with normality or mania	Treatment can be effective.	Would not treat; would refer to a specialist.	Treatment is effective because the condition is dealt with holistically; it is hampered if the condition is controlled by drugs.
OBSESSION Mental disturbance in which an idea or object excludes thought of all else	Treatment can be effective.	Would not treat; would refer to a specialist.	Treatment often effective but depends on the cause.
PARANOIA Mental disturbance leading to delusions of persecution	Treatment can be effective; depends on the circumstances and degree of illness.	Would not treat; would refer to a specialist.	Treatment can be effective because the condition is dealt with holistically, but depends on the cause.
SCHIZOPHRENIA Mental disturbance in which thought processes are disrupted	Treatment would depend on circumstances and degree of illness.	Would not treat; would refer to a specialist.	There is little evidence of effective treatment.
SLEEP WALKING Walking or performing other activities while asleep	Might treat, depending on cause.	Would not treat; would offer advice.	Treatment works well because the condition is treated holistically.
STUTTER Speech disorder in which sounds are repeated and speech is hesitant	Treatment can be effective.	Would not treat, would refer to a specialist.	Treatment depends on cause; it can be effective if the condition is dealt with constitutionally.

MED. HERBALISM	OSTEOPATHY	GEN. MEDICINE	COMMENTS
Treatment would depend entirely on individual circumstances.	Treatment can help, especially with the aid of naturopathy.	Would refer for help to specialists or voluntary organizations, depending on type of addiction. Tranquillizers may help.	See also **Alcoholism**, pp. 210–213
Would treat, but results are likely to be limited.	Would not treat.	No treatment is available and prognosis is poor. Would provide care and treat any co-existing disease.	See also **Dementia**, pp. 222–223
Would not treat.	Would not treat as such; the whole person may be helped if patient can communicate.	Treatment is supportive if cause is brain injury; would refer to psychologist if cause is hysteria.	See also **Alcoholism**, pp. 210–213
In addition to treatment, counselling or other psychological aid can be helpful.	Treatment rarely effective.	Family therapy is often quite successful; would provide support for patient and family. Outlook is variable.	See also **Depression**, pp. 214–217
Would treat, but condition may also need psychotherapy.	Treatment can often help this condition.	Treatment is supportive; would refer for counselling and psychotherapy.	See also **Depression**, pp. 214–217
Would be highly unlikely to treat.	Treatment would depend on the cause.	Treatment would depend on cause.	See also **Alcoholism**, pp. 210–213
Would not treat.	Would not treat.	No treatment is available and prognosis is poor. Would provide care and treat any co-existing disease.	See also **Alzheimer's disease**, pp. 222–223
Would not treat.	Would not treat unless a specific cranial osteopathic fault were found.	Would refer to educational psychology or for remedial teaching.	
Treatment can be helpful, depending on the cause.	Treatment can be very effective, but would depend on the cause.	Treatment is rest.	See also **Insomnia**, pp. 218–221
Would treat chronic form only; help would be limited.	Would not treat except to improve general health.	Treatment with medication such as lithium is helpful; urgent, severe cases may need compulsory hospital admission.	See also **Depression**, pp. 214–217
Treatment can help, but condition probably needs counselling or other advice.	Would not treat except to improve general health.	Psychotherapy and behaviour therapy can be helpful.	
Treatment can help, but condition probably needs counselling or other advice.	Would not treat.	Treatment with drugs may be helpful.	
Treatment can help, but condition probably needs counselling or other advice.	Would not treat except to improve general health.	Many sufferers benefit from long-term medication. Some may be admitted to hostels or hospitals. Prognosis is poor.	See also **Depression**, pp. 214–217
Treatment unlikely to help, but may improve other factors producing the problem.	Treatment would be to help the underlying cause.	Treatment is family or individual psychotherapy.	
Would not treat; would probably refer for psychotherapy.	Treatment would be to help the underlying cause, especially if related to the cranial bones.	Would refer for speech therapy, counselling or psychotherapy.	

AIDS

AIDS (Acquired Immunodeficiency Syndrome) is a complex disease. It is associated with infection by a virus known as HIV (Human Immunodeficiency Virus) which attacks, and causes deficiency in, the body's immune system.

Not all people who carry the virus develop the full syndrome (the latest evidence indicates that 50 per cent are likely to remain unaffected after six years), but it is not certain whether they ultimately will or not.

Once the condition starts to develop it takes one of three forms – the diagnosis depends on the presence of various symptoms and, more importantly, secondary conditions. The mildest form involves the continuous swelling of various lymph glands. More serious is Aids Related Complex (ARC), which involves conditions such as diarrhoea, thrush (fungal infection of the mouth), weight loss and exhaustion. Fully developed AIDS involves an unusual form of skin cancer (Kaposi's sarcoma), pneumonia and a wide range of other secondary infections. The first two forms of the disease can both develop into a more serious form.

Although AIDS is associated with HIV, this is almost certainly only part of the story, and other immunological stresses (such as drug and alcohol abuse, environmental toxins, poor diet and stress) are also likely to be implicated.

The short time in which observations of the cycle of the illness have been made means that therapists cannot make many firm assertions about the treatment of AIDS or ARC.

Most complementary and alternative practitioners' experience of the disease has been in large cities in the USA. Practitioners there have been consulted by hundreds of AIDS or ARC sufferers, and their findings are currently the main source of information about the disease.

Treatments

The virulence of the final disease, and its widely fluctuating course in any individual patient, make assessment of any particular treatment difficult. This is compounded by the tendency of AIDS sufferers to use many approaches at once, and their often erratic adherence to treatment regimes. Conventional treatments have had little real success – for example, early hopes for the benefit of the drug zidovudine (formerly known as AZT) seem not to have been borne out – and the experience of complementary practitioners is often discouraging.

An increasing number of reports of research carried out using alternative techniques are emerging. A review of a number of long-term survivors of AIDS showed that almost all of them were using Chinese herbs or acupuncture as a part of their treatment.

Although AIDS is a new disease, its syndrome patterns are not dissimiliar to those of other conditions of immunodeficiency, and several Chinese prescriptions have evolved as possible immunotonics. These, with acupuncture, seem to be especially helpful in containing ARC symptoms and possibly in reducing the risk of the secondary infections that could herald AIDS itself. But the effect of these treatments in sufferers of the full syndrome has been difficult to evaluate.

As further factors that affect the course of the disease are understood, it is likely that more therapies will be able to offer immuno-tonic and other supportive treatments. Certain dietary and food supplement regimes hold promise for the checking of, at least, the early stages of degeneration. Western medical herbalists are looking for herbs comparable to the Chinese species.

Conclusions

AIDS is one of the most serious health problems to afflict mankind since diseases such as smallpox, cholera and plague were brought under control. Claims for its successful treatment must be regarded with extreme caution, not least because of the immense practical difficulties in dealing with sufferers and the serious constitutional debility often present. AIDS is probably not, however, a medical Armageddon. There is room for a little hope that fewer of those who carry the virus will develop any symptoms, and that fewer people who suffer from ARC will develop the full syndrome.

A SAFETY NOTE

Acupuncturists are aware of the apprehensions of the general public about the possibility of the spread of AIDS by acupuncture needles. In the UK and the USA all accredited practitioners adhere to standards of hygiene – involving the use of disposable needles – that eliminate any risk. The involvement of acupuncturists in the frontline of AIDS treatment in the USA should increase the public's faith in their precautions.

CANCER

Cancer is a disorder in which a group of cells in the body multiply out of control and invade healthy tissue. If the cancer cells spread throughout the body, it is usually fatal. Cancer has many aspects and types, and presents a great challenge to any therapy. Conventional treatment has been only partly successful, and any success often involves drastic measures, such as courses of radiotherapy or drugs (both of which can have serious side-effects) or surgery. The diagnosis of cancer usually causes great upheavals in the lives of sufferers and their families.

It is natural that those facing this prospect often want to consider any approach that might be able to help them. The sheer power of modern treatments often provides reassurance to those most fearful of the internal enemy. But others fear the treatment itself and, in seeking to protect their damaged health from further harm, want help to be as gentle as possible.

Alternative approaches

Most complementary health practitioners have experience of patients with cancer asking if there is any alternative available to conventional treatments. Only charlatans are able to give simple assurances. Good practitioners are, however, conscious of the fact that malignant cells do not always multiply unchecked. It has been estimated that of the thousands of billions of cells in the body, on average about ten thousand can be expected to become malignant every day. When a person is healthy, these cells are quickly destroyed by the body's immune system.

For a colony of malignant cells to establish itself, therefore, there has to be a breakdown in normal defences, and a major one at that. Although the fact that cancer has developed points to serious damage to health, which can be very difficult to correct, there are nevertheless powerful forces to the good that might be encouraged.

There can be three approaches to helping cancer victims. The malignancy can be attacked directly; the body's defence and repair functions can be supported; or distress and symptoms can be relieved. Each therapy attempts to contribute in its own way to these ends.

Treatments

Cancers of the inner organs can cause back and shoulder pain. The skills of osteopathy and chiropractic therapy can be directed to the relief of this pain. These can lead to improvements in associated physiological functions, and thus sometimes to the patient's ability to recover. In China, acupuncture is used as part of a broad programme of therapy, which includes modern Western techniques, to alleviate pain and functional disorders associated with the disease (for example, improving the ability to swallow in cancer of the oesophagus). It is also used to treat the side-effects of radiotherapy and chemotherapy.

However, the Chinese are more likely to use herbal prescriptions in their attempts to support immunity and control malignant growth. Early clinical reports point to some success with these therapies, but how they work is often unclear.

Western herbal experience of cancer treatment comes mainly from specialist cancer clinics. There are herbs that are possibly more toxic to the tumour than to healthy cells, and there are indications that some benefit may be derived from these.

The Western medical herbalist, however, like the homeopath and Western acupuncturist, would look primarily for ways to strengthen the patient's constitution and ability to fight back. They would each in their own way apply tonic, supportive measures, usually reserving more dynamic treatment until they saw signs that the patient's underlying strength had been improved. They would seek to combine these approaches with naturopathic techniques of diet management developed at nature-cure cancer clinics. They might also apply some of the counselling, visualization and imagery techniques developed at such centres, both in Europe and the USA.

Conclusions

Alternative treatments for cancer generally aim to support the body rather than attacking the tumour, but there is no easy alternative to drastic conventional treatments. The record of success in treating this disease is sporadic. The best recommendation is to make full use of all available options in a way that most suits the patient's temperament and requirements.

# FIRST AID

This section gives some examples of the ways in which alternative and complementary therapies deal with some relatively simple first aid situations. The standard procedure for each situation is also described. Injuries such as major burns and cuts demand immediate professional attention.

Although acupuncture can only be administered by a qualified practitioner, there are various points that can be massaged using acupressure. These can be learned directly from your acupuncturist, or through special books and courses.

Homeopathy has many remedies that can be used for first aid, but accurate prescribing can be quite complicated. There are, however, many good books on homeopathic self-help, and examples of some of the most common remedies are given here.

Naturopathy and herbalism have a number of useful procedures and remedies that are usually easy to apply.

Chiropractic and osteopathic treatments can generally be undertaken only by .qualified practitioners, but a few practical suggestions are given that arise from their special insights into certain conditions or situations.

BRUISE

Standard first aid
Rest the injured part. Apply a cold compress or a bag filled with ice. If the bruising is severe or seems to spread, this may indicate internal bleeding and medical advice must be sought immediately.

Acupuncture
Apply a moxa stick to the affected area. This has the effect of stimulating the circulation of *Qi* energy and *Blood* to the area, which relieves pain and speeds dispersal of the bruising.

Homeopathy
One dose of *Arnica* 30 taken at the time of injury reduces pain and swelling, and helps to prevent bruising. *Arnica* ointment can be applied directly to the injury if there is no break in the skin.

Medical herbalism
Apply a compress of gauze dressing moistened with two or three drops of essential oil of Lavender diluted in cold water, or a chilled infusion of Comfrey. Remove the compress when it is dry. When the swelling has subsided, apply Comfrey ointment.

BURN, MINOR

A minor (or first degree) burn is defined as one that affects only the outer layers of skin and an area of less than 10 square centimetres (2 square inches).

Standard first aid
Cool the burned area immediately by immersion for several minutes in cold (but not icy) water. If possible, remove any constricting articles (such as watches or rings) before any swelling starts. Apply a clean, dry dressing, but not of a fluffy material. Do not apply greasy or oily dressings. Keep clean to avoid the risk of infection. Do not puncture blisters. If symptoms persist or worsen, seek medical advice.

Homeopathy
An ointment of *Urtica urens* can be applied to stinging burns and sunburned skin. An ointment of *Hypericum* should be used if the burn is throbbing. *Hypericum* 6 may be taken in pill form if pain persists.

Medical herbalism
Apply two or three drops of essential oil of Lavender to prevent blistering. Small areas of sunburn can be treated in the same way.

CRAMP

Standard first aid
The muscles concerned should be gently but firmly stretched. If the cramp is caused by cold, warm the affected part gently. If it occurs in other circumstances, drink large amounts of cool water to which a little salt has been added (about half a teaspoonful to one pint).

Acupuncture
Massage the affected muscle to relieve the spasm and promote the circulation of *Qi* and *Blood*. Moxa can be burned over the affected area to achieve a similar effect.

Homeopathy
Magnesium phosphoricum is useful if the cramp is caused by cold and is relieved by warmth and rubbing. *Nux vomica* is good for cramps associated with menstruation and colic. *Cuprum* is useful for cramps that result from overuse of a muscle.

CUT, MINOR

Standard first aid
Bleeding from minor cuts usually stops quite quickly of its own accord; encourage this by applying local pressure for a few minutes or by raising the injured part. Avoid getting dirt into the wound, and if possible wash it with running water – working outward to avoid infection. Foreign bodies should be removed if this can be done easily and they are not deeply embedded. Cover with a clean dressing, an adhesive one if possible. If the edges are gaping, close them with the fingers and hold them together with the dressing. Seek medical advice about anti-tetanus injections unless recently vaccinated.

Homeopathy
Apply *Calendula* lotion to sterilize and speed up healing. If the cut penetrates beyond the surface layer of skin, use *Hypericum* lotion, which also soothes nerves, so reducing pain. If the cut is blue and numb, use *Ledum* lotion instead. After applying a remedy in lotion form, it should then be given in pill form in the 30th potency.

Medical herbalism
Use Calendula or Comfrey ointment to reduce inflammation and assist healing. Witch Hazel diluted at one tablespoonful to 500 ml (1 pint) of water can be used to wash the cut and to moisten a dressing.

DIARRHOEA

Standard first aid
Anyone suffering from diarrhoea must be careful to drink plenty of fluids to prevent dehydration. If the attack is severe, medical help must be sought. Loss of fluid may cause shock – particularly in children and the elderly.

Homeopathy
There are many remedies for diarrhoea. *Arsenicum album* is used in cases of food poisoning, and when the diarrhoea is watery, burning, very foul in smell and accompanied by vomiting. *Carbo vegetabilis* can be used when there is flatulence and the person feels chilly.

Medical herbalism
Useful teas are Chamomile, Agrimony and Meadowsweet, which should be taken three times a day until the symptoms disappear.

Naturopathy
Grated apple, possibly mixed with live yoghurt, may be helpful. Eating a small quantity of cooked, brown (unpolished) rice can bind the stools. Otherwise, do not eat anything until the symptoms subside.

EARACHE

Standard first aid
Applying dry warmth (but not excessive heat) to the ear may help to relieve pain; a hot water bottle wrapped in a towel is ideal. If the earache is caused by air pressure, which can occur during air travel, hold the nose and swallow or blow out the cheeks. If pain persists after the air pressure has stabilized, seek medical advice.

Homeopathy
There are many homeopathic remedies for earache. *Aconite* is used for earache caused by exposure to cold or dry winds. *Silica* is used for ear problems associated with catarrh. *Mercury* and *Pulsatilla* are both used when the earache develops from a sore throat.

Medical herbalism
Plain steam inhalations, with or without the addition of Eucalyptus, Peppermint or Chamomile oils, may help to relieve catarrh and soothe the ear internally.

Naturopathy
Apply warmth using a hot salt-pack or sand-bag. Heat a small muslin bag filled with salt or sand in an oven. Place it against the affected ear to relieve pain. Fasting for 24 hours may also help.

FAINTING

Standard first aid
A temporarily inadequate supply of blood to the head causes a person to faint. This can be the result of standing up suddenly, but may also be caused by emotional shock. If a person feels faint, he or she should sit with the head between the knees. Sips of water can speed recovery. Smelling salts are sometimes used as a stimulant.

If someone has fainted, raise the legs slightly to restore blood flow to the head. See that there is plenty of fresh air and loosen clothing.

If the person does not regain consciousness within 15 – 20 seconds, or if the faint results from an injury, obtain immediate medical attention. While waiting for attention, place the casualty in the recovery position. The person should be gently turned onto his or her front, with the head turned to one side. On the same side, the arm and leg should be drawn up to a bent position so that the body is supported by them. On the other side, the arm should lie beside the body, and the leg should be straight. The head should be kept on one side so that the airways are kept open and free from obstruction.

Homeopathy
Ignatia is useful for treating people who faint as a result of excitement or shock. *Pulsatilla* may be used if the person is anaemic and has low blood pressure. Both are best if used to improve the constitution rather than merely as a first aid measure.

Medical herbalism
Essential oil of Lavender can be used as a smelling salt.

FROSTBITE

Standard first aid
Shelter and keep the casualty warm, but do not overheat. Give warm liquids, but not alcohol, to drink. Remove any restricting items, such as rings or boots. Thawing of the affected part may be assisted by gently placing a dry, gloved hand on it, or by wrapping it in a blanket, but you must not apply any kind of direct heat or pressure. Do not rub the area because this can damage the skin. Seek medical attention immediately.

Medical herbalism
Herbal drinks, such as Cinnamon, Ginger or Peppermint, may help to warm the body and improve circulation.

HEADACHE, MINOR

Standard first aid
Minor headaches are best helped by rest and relaxation, and avoiding loud noise and bright light. Mild pain-relieving tablets may be taken to alleviate symptoms. Hot or cold compresses can sometimes help. If symptoms persist, recur or are the result of an injury, seek medical advice.

Acupuncture
Points on the head, neck, hands and feet can be massaged once the precise locations of the points have been learned.

Homeopathy
There are many homeopathic remedies for headache. *Nux vomica* is often used when the headache is related to a sluggish liver, which is the case in migraine. *Sepia* may be used in a similar situation if there is any visual disturbance. *Belladonna* may be helpful if the headache is violent and throbbing, comes on suddenly and is accompanied by a temperature.

Medical herbalism
Chamomile, Lime Blossom and Peppermint teas can help. Rubbing a drop of Lavender oil into the temples can also alleviate the pain.

Osteopathy with naturopathy
If the headache is caused by tension, press on the back of the head under the occiput (back of the skull). If caused by food, miss the next meal. If the cause is eyestrain, rest with a cold pad over the eyes.

HICCUPS

Standard first aid
Usual means of obtaining relief involve taking sips of water, holding one's breath or having one's attention distracted. If symptoms continue for more than an hour, seek medical advice.

Acupuncture
Special points on the hands and feet can be massaged to relieve the hiccups.

Homeopathy
Spasm of the diaphragm, which causes hiccups, is most often calmed by *Ignatia*.

Osteopathy with naturopathy
Any painful areas around the vertebrae at the same level as the diaphragm can be gently massaged to relieve symptoms.

INDIGESTION

Standard first aid
Antacids or sodium bicarbonate (bicarbonate of soda) solution normally provide relief. Painkillers, particularly those containing aspirin, should be avoided. If the pain is severe or persists, seek medical advice.

Acupuncture
Special points on the hands and feet can be massaged to relieve pain.

Homeopathy
Simple heartburn responds to *Nux vomica*. Windy colic may be treated with *Argentium nitricum* if it is accompanied by anxiety. A heavy pain in the pit of the stomach can be treated with *Cocculus*.

Medical herbalism
Use Chamomile, Lemon Balm or Meadowsweet tea to relieve symptoms.

Naturopathy
Miss the next meal. Sip lemon juice. Massage the abdomen gently, stroking rather than probing.

INSECT BITE/STING

Standard first aid
Remove the sting, if it is still present, using tweezers or a sterilized needle. Application of cold water, antihistamine creams or tablets, surgical spirit, weak ammonia solution, sodium bicarbonate solution (bicarbonate of soda) or calamine lotion may all provide relief.

If a sting is in the mouth or throat, sluice the area with bicarbonate solution and suck ice to help avoid inflammation, which can be very dangerous if it constricts the airway; if there is any danger of this, seek immediate medical attention. Some people are allergic to stings and this can be extremely dangerous, so if the reaction to the sting is severe, seek medical advice urgently.

Homeopathy
Take *Hypericum* 30 and repeat when the pain returns. *Apis* may be used when there is considerable swelling, especially if the area is hot and shiny red. If the wound generates pus, *Hepar sulphuricum* 6 may be used every few hours until the wound clears up. Should the wound look blue or go numb, *Ledum* may be used instead of *Hypericum*.

Medical herbalism
Apply a dressing saturated with a cooled infusion of Chamomile or diluted essential oil of Lavender (two drops per tablespoonful of cold water).

Naturopathy
Calendula or Pyrethrum may be applied.

MOTION SICKNESS

Standard first aid
Various preventive measures can be taken. Look at things outside rather than inside the vehicle, get plenty of fresh air, avoid twisting the neck, and avoid large, heavy meals before travel. Proprietary anti-sickness tablets may be taken, but these tend to cause drowsiness and should be avoided if driving.

Acupuncture
Special points on the wrist can be massaged to relieve the sense of nausea.

Homeopathy
If the traveller wants to vomit but cannot, and also feels better for fresh air, *Nux vomica* 6 should help. Repeat if necessary after 20 minutes. *Ignatia* may be more effective if it is the smell of tobacco or petrol that causes the problem. *Ipecachuana* is useful where the nausea comes in waves and is not relieved by vomiting.

Medical herbalism
Frequent sips of Ginger, Peppermint or Chamomile tea are often helpful, as is chewing small pieces of fresh Ginger Root.

MUSCLE STRAIN

Standard first aid
Find the most comfortable position for the injured part, then hold it steady and support it. Unless the condition is very mild, seek medical attention.

Chiropractic therapy
Apply gentle heat and then ice alternately, two or three times. Repeat three or four times per day.

Homeopathy
Arnica 30 may help if the strain is in the back. *Rhus tox.* 6 every few hours may be useful if the patient has built up a sweat and been suddenly cooled. In both remedies the affected part stiffens with rest, is very painful when first moved and improves as movement is continued.

Medical herbalism
Gently rub in Comfrey ointment or diluted essential oils of Lavender and Rosemary.

NOSEBLEED

Standard first aid
Find a comfortable position and, with the head tilted slightly forward (not back), pinch the soft part of the nose between finger and thumb for about ten minutes. Do not blow the nose, sniff or do anything else that might dislodge the newly-formed blood clot. If the nosebleed resulted from a blow on the head, or if nosebleeds recur, seek medical attention.

Homeopathy
Arnica 30 may be useful if the bleeding is caused by a hard knock. *Phosphorus* 30 is useful where nosebleeds are a recurrent feature. *Vipera* 30 is recommended if the patient is menopausal.

Naturopathy
Use a cold compress on the abdomen to draw congestion downward.

SPRAIN

Standard first aid
Take any weight off the injured part and make it as comfortable as possible. Support the part with a fairly tight bandage. If a sprained ankle is enclosed in a boot, leave this on because it provides support. Apply a cold compress to reduce pain and relieve swelling. Seek medical advice if the sprain is severe or there is any suspicion of a fracture.

Chiropractic therapy
Support the injury with a bandage, but if this aggravates the pain and swelling, it should be removed immediately.

Homeopathy
Rhus toxicodendron 6 can be used for sprains, especially where there is an inclination to move the joint to stop it stiffening. This may have to be repeated for a day or two at six-hourly intervals, or as the pain recurs. *Arnica* may be more useful if there is much bruising or swelling.

Medical herbalism
Use a cooled Comfrey infusion or diluted essential oil of Lavender (three drops in a tablespoonful of cold water) to make a compress. Comfrey ointment can then be gently rubbed in.

VOMITING CAUSED BY FOOD POISONING

Standard first aid
Lie down and avoid eating or drinking. Start taking sips of iced water after a couple of hours. Once symptoms subside, drink plenty of fluid to replace that lost from the body because of vomiting. Seek medical attention if vomiting persists, if there is sudden, severe pain, a stiff neck or dizziness, or if black or bloody material is produced.

Acupuncture
Special points on the wrists and abdomen can be massaged to relieve symptoms.

Homeopathy
In homeopathy, vomiting is regarded as the body's natural way of getting rid of a swallowed poison. *Arsenicum* is a remedy used to help recovery if the patient is often affected by food poisoning, and is prostrated during the attack.

Medical herbalism
When travelling where food poisoning is common, eat more hot, spicy foods because these encourage gastric secretions and give protection.

GLOSSARY

active movement normal range of voluntary movement of a joint, as performed by the patient.

acute condition disorder in which symptoms develop suddenly and either improve quickly or require immediate treatment.

aetiology investigation of the causes or origins of a disease.

aggravation an initial intensification of symptoms which sometimes results from homeopathic treatment, particularly of chronic disorders.

Alexander technique training in correction of body posture to help alleviate musculo-skeletal problems.

allergen substance that causes an allergic reaction.

allopathy homeopathic term for standard Western medicine; its literal meaning is "other disease".

anabolic steroid type of hormone that promotes repair and growth.

analgesic pain-relieving medicine.

androgen male sex hormone.

antacid substance that reduces excess acidity of the stomach contents, commonly used to relieve indigestion.

antibacterial agent cleansing substance that destroys bacteria.

antibiotic drug used to treat a bacterial infection; examples include Penicillin and Tetracycline.

antibody defensive agent produced by the body in response to the presence of a "foreign" substance, called an antigen, which the body regards as harmful.

antihistamine drug that counteracts some of the symptoms of an allergy (caused by the body's production of histamine).

anti-inflammatory substance that reduces inflammation.

antispasmodic drug or herbal medicine that prevents the spasmodic contraction of muscle.

articulation movement of joints.

astringent substance that constricts blood vessels, ducts in skin or mucous membranes, and therefore often reduces irritation and inflammation; in medical herbalism, astringent herbs are used to treat inflammatory intestinal problems.

autoimmune disease disorder in which the body produces antibodies that act against its own tissues.

benign a tumour in which the cells are not in danger of spreading to other parts of the body, and which are therefore not likely to be life-threatening.

beta-blocker drug that acts on the sympathetic nervous system, suppressing its activity and thus preventing increases in blood pressure and pulse rate.

biomechanical problem alteration of the normal biological functions or mechanics of a joint or joints; common term in chiropractic therapy.

biopsy removal of a small sample of living tissue or fluid for laboratory analysis.

broncho-dilator drug that relieves contractions of the bronchioles (air passages leading from the lungs to the windpipe).

cardiovascular relating to the heart and blood vessels.

cautery burning of tissue using heat, caustics, electricity or lasers to control bleeding and infection or to destroy tumours.

cerebrospinal fluid watery liquid that surrounds the brain and spinal cord, nourishing them and providing protection against physical shocks.

cervical relating to the neck or to the cervix of the womb.

channels in traditional Chinese medicine, invisible pathways of *Qi* both on the surface of, and within, the body.

cholesterol fatty substance found in the body's tissues and blood; excess cholesterol may collect in the walls of the arteries and harden or narrow them.

chronic condition disorder that is deep-seated and long-standing or recurrent.

compress pad of material that is soaked in a hot or cold solution and applied externally.

constitutional relating to a person's physical constitution and specifically to inherited tendencies or underlying patterns of health.

cranial relating to the skull, specifically the bones that enclose the brain.

deficiency disease disorder caused by lack of nutrients, commonly vitamins or minerals.

deficient condition in traditional Chinese medicine, disorder resulting from the body's inability to maintain equilibrium, through deficient functioning of the *Zangfu*.

degenerative condition disorder in which there is a gradual and often irreversible process of decay.

detoxification process of removing toxins from the body.

diuretic substance that reduces body fluids by stimulating the production of urine.

Du in traditional Chinese medicine, channel that runs up the spine, from the coccyx, over the head to the upper lip.

dysfunction abnormal functioning of a system or organ of the body.

eliminative system all organs concerned with elimination and excretion of waste products from the body; including the bowels, kidneys, lungs and skin.

empirical points acupuncture points that are effective for treatment of specific symptoms and conditions.

endocrine relating to glands that produce hormones; examples include the adrenal, pituitary and thyroid glands.

epidermis surface layer of the skin.

essence in traditional Chinese medicine, the pure energy extracted from food that is transformed into *Qi* by the body.

essential oil concentrated, pure aromatic essence extracted from plants.

excess condition in traditional Chinese medicine, a condition in which *Qi*, *Blood* or *Body Fluids* are disordered and accumulate in channels or elsewhere in the body, due to excess functioning of the *Zangfu*.

exciting cause homeopathic term to describe circumstances, such as getting chilled, that influence the onset of a disorder.

expectorant drug or herbal remedy that promotes the expulsion of phlegm from the lungs.

extensor muscle muscle that straightens limbs of the body.

fast in naturopathy, abstention from food, usually for 24 hours and sometimes up to seven days; only water, herbal teas or fruit juices may be consumed during this time.

fungal infection disorder, such as athlete's foot, caused by microscopic fungi.

ganglion a swelling within a tendon or joint.

genito-urinary relating to the genital and urinary systems and their functions.

gynaecology branch of Western medicine that specializes in the treatment of disorders of the female reproductive system.

haemoglobin iron-containing protein in red blood cells, which carries oxygen to the tissues.

haemorrhage bleeding, either internal or external.

healing crisis development of headaches or other symptoms as a response to treatment; it is an indication of the body's struggle to dispel the disease.

high velocity thrust spinal adjustment that involves speed without force, used in chiropractic therapy and osteopathy.

homeostasis the body's natural ability to maintain its state of health and internal balance.

hydrocortisone type of corticosteroid drug.

hydrotherapy treatment of a disorder using water; examples include steam, hot baths or compresses.

hypertension standard medical term for high blood pressure.

immune system the body's natural system of internal defences, based on antibody formation, against harmful organisms or substances.

inflammation redness and swelling of a part of the body resulting from injury or disease.

infusion immersion of herbs in boiling water to make a "tea" or solution for a compress.

inhalant drug that is breathed in through the nose or mouth; used in treating respiratory disorders.

irritant substance that produces an uncomfortable or allergic reaction.

Jingluo Chinese term for channels – the network of invisible pathways of *Qi* in the body.

laxative substance that encourages the evacuation of the bowels.

lesion a wound or area of local tissue damage; an osteopathic lesion is an abnormality (in position or mobility) of vertebrae.

lumbar relating to the lower part of the spine.

lymphatic system network of lymph vessels and glands in the body; the lymphatic system plays an important role in the removal or destruction of bacteria.

malignant relating to cancerous cells that develop and spread, and are therefore potentially life-threatening.

manipulation technique used in chiropractic therapy and osteopathy to adjust the spine, joints or other tissue.

metabolism/metabolic rate combination of biochemical processes in the body and the rate of energy consumption necessary to maintain this.

miasm homeopathic term (literally meaning "taint" or "stain") for underlying physical and mental weaknesses that reduce health and cause chronic illness.

mobilization chiropractic technique that gently increases the range of movement of a joint.

moxa dried leaves of Mugwort; in traditional Chinese medicine, moxa is placed on the end of needles or rolled into a stick, then ignited and held near an acupuncture point to warm and tonify *Qi*; this process is called moxibustion.

mucilage carbohydrate constituent of plants, used in medical herbalism to soothe body tissues.

mucus fluid that lubricates and protects internal membranes.

naturopathy therapy that is concerned with nutritional, psychological and structural aspects of health, regarding each as equally important.

nervous restorative herbal medicine that nourishes and tones the nervous system.

neuralgia severe pain caused by inflammation of nerve fibres.

neurological examination tests to check nerve function.

neuromuscular massage osteopathic massage that influences both nerves and muscles.

occiput bone at the base of the skull.

orthopaedic examination tests to determine whether joint function is normal.

orthopaedics branch of Western medical science that deals with disorders of bones and joints.

palpation physical examination using the hands to feel for abnormalities.

passive movement chiropractic term for movement of joints achieved by gentle pressure, without active participation by the patient.

pathogenic relating to organisms or substances (such as bacteria) that can cause disease; in traditional Chinese medicine, the term refers to either internal or external disease-causing influences.

peristalsis muscle contractions that move substances along a passage; it is peristalsis that pushes food through the intestines.

pharmacology study of drugs.

podiatrist another name for a chiropodist, somebody who treats foot disorders.

polycrest homeopathic remedy with a wide range of action that can be used to treat a variety of illnesses.

potency/potentization dilution and succussion of homeopathic remedies that increases their power and gives them their therapeutic value.

prognosis prediction of the course of an illness.

prolapsed disk (sometimes incorrectly called a "slipped" disk); intervertebral disk (cartilage cushion between the vertebrae) that bulges outward and can press on a nerve, causing pain.

proving homeopathic process for researching and testing the characteristics of a remedy.

psyche combination of mental and emotional processes that characterize the human mind.

psychosomatic physical symptoms that are caused by an emotional or mental state.

Qi (pronounced "chee") in traditional Chinese medicine, the "life-force" or energy of the body, which circulates through the body's channels.

referred pain   pain felt in a part of the body other than its place of origin.

Ren   in traditional Chinese medicine, channel that runs down the front of the body, from the lower lip to the area behind the genitals.

sacrocranial mechanism   in cranial osteopathy, term for the relationship between the pelvis and the head.

sacroiliac joint   joint between the triangular bone at the base of the spine (sacrum) and the iliac bones of the pelvis.

Sanjiao   in traditional Chinese medicine, a *Yang* channel located in the arms; it is the *Zangfu* that maintains the circulation of *Qi* and *Body Fluids*; also known as the *Triple Heater*.

scoliosis   sideways curvature of the spine when viewed from behind.

sebaceous gland   gland that produces sebum, a greasy secretion, from the skin of the scalp, face, neck, shoulders and genitals.

self-limiting condition   disorder that has a limited time-span and clears up without treatment.

septicaemia   standard medical term for blood poisoning due to infection by micro-organisms such as bacteria.

Shen   in traditional Chinese medicine, the "spirit" or consciousness.

soft-tissue   most tissues of the body (muscles, tendons, ligaments and internal organs).

spinal integrity   normal position and function of the vertebrae of the spine.

stagnant Qi   in traditional Chinese medicine, obstruction of the flow of *Qi* in the channels, which causes disease.

stimulation   in traditional Chinese medicine, use of needles to modify or increase the activity of *Qi*.

steroid/corticosteroid   type of hormone; the term is commonly used for certain hormonal drugs with powerful anti-inflammatory properties.

streptococcal   type of bacteria that often cause infections, especially of the throat.

succussion   repeated process of rapid shaking, used in the preparation of homeopathic remedies.

suppressive treatment   use of medicines or other techniques to reduce and control symptoms and thus depress the body's natural healing process.

symptomatic treatment   use of medicines or other techniques to relieve or reduce symptoms.

symptom picture   total pattern of a patient's symptoms that forms the basis of homeopathic diagnosis.

systemic   relating to the body as a whole; in traditional Chinese medicine, disorders affecting the overall balance of bodily energy.

Tai Qi (T'ai Ch'i)   movement-based meditative exercise developed in China as a way of maintaining harmony of both body and mind.

temporal bones   bones that form part of the sides and base of the skull.

thoracic   relating to the chest area and the vertebrae of the upper and middle back.

thrush   fungal infection (also known as candidiasis or moniliasis) of the mucous membranes in the mouth, throat or vagina.

tonification   in traditional Chinese medicine, process that strengthens and supports *Blood* and *Qi* and restores the functions of *Zangfu* organs.

topical application   applying a substance to the surface of the skin.

toxin   substance that is harmful or poisonous to the body; often used to describe the accumulation of waste materials in the bloodstream, which can cause health problems.

trauma   physical injury or emotional shock.

tuberculoid miasm   in homeopathy, type of chronic condition that arises from a family history of tuberculosis.

vascular   relating to the blood vessels.

vasoconstriction   narrowing of blood vessels.

vasodilation   widening of blood vessels.

vertebrae   bones of the spine.

vibratory massage   rhythmic massage used to stimulate healing of soft-tissue.

visualization   meditative therapeutic technique that uses imagined visual images to aid physical or emotional healing.

vital force/vital energy   in acupuncture, herbalism and homeopathy, the "life-force" that sustains natural balance and health; if disrupted it can result in disease.

Yin/Yang   Chinese concept that describes all existence in terms of states or conditions that are different but mutually dependent; traditional Chinese medicine aims to restore balance to these contrasting aspects of the body and mind.

Zangfu   internal organs, as understood by traditional Chinese medicine; they have different functions from the anatomical organs in Western medicine.

ADDRESSES

These addresses are of the main or centralized organizations in each area of therapy. They provide information, and lists of local practitioners or regional offices on request.

GENERAL INFORMATION
The Council for Complementary and Alternative Medicine,
Suite 1,
19a Cavendish Square,
London W1M 9AD
Tel: 01 409 1440
Professional, legal, educational and general information.

The Research Council for Complementary Medicine,
Suite 1,
19a Cavendish Square,
London W1M 9AD
Tel: 01 409 1440
Research information.

Institute of Complementary Medicine,
21 Portland Place,
London W1N 3AF
Tel: 01 636 9543
General information, library, directory of complementary medicine.

The Centre for Complementary Health Studies,
The University of Exeter,
Exeter, Devon EX4 4PU
Tel: 0392 33828
New facility for study in the field of complementary medicine; in future, will provide a major resource of information on the subject.

ACUPUNCTURE
The Council for Acupuncture,
Suite 1,
19a Cavendish Square,
London W1M 9AD
Tel: 01 409 1440
Represents the four main professional associations of acupuncture in Britain; register of practitioners; general and training information.

CHIROPRACTIC
British Chiropractic Association,
Premier House,
10 Graycoat Place,
London SW1P 1SB
Tel: 01 222 8866
General and training information; connected with the Anglo-European College of Chiropractic.

HOMEOPATHY
Society of Homeopaths,
47 Canada Grove,
Bognor Regis,
West Sussex PO21 1DW
Tel: 0243 860 678
Information on homeopathy and homeopathic training; register of qualified homeopaths.

British Homeopathic Association,
27a Devonshire Street,
London W1N 1JR
Tel: 01 935 2163
Associated with the Royal London Homeopathic Hospital; register of physicians with homeopathic training.

Hahnemann Homeopathic Society,
Human Education Centre,
Avenue Lodge,
Bounds Green Road,
London N22 4EU
Tel: 01 889 1595
Promotes homeopathy in Britain; produces the magazine *Homeopathy Today*; general information on homeopathy.

MEDICAL HERBALISM
National Institute of Medical Herbalists,
41 Hatherley Road,
Winchester,
Hampshire SO22 6RR
Tel: 0962 68776
General and training information; register of practitioners; connected with School of Herbal Medicine.

OSTEOPATHY
General Council and Register of Osteopaths,
1–4 Suffolk Street,
London SW1 4HG
Tel: 01 839 2060
General information; register of qualified practitioners; connected to the British School of Osteopathy.

Society of Osteopaths,
12 College Road,
Eastbourne,
Sussex BN21 4HZ
Tel: 0323 638606
General and training information; register of practitioners; associated with European School of Osteopathy.

OSTEOPATHY WITH NATUROPATHY
British College and Association of Naturopathy and Osteopathy,
6 Netherhall Gardens,
London NW3
Tel: 01 435 7830
Information, training and register of qualified practitioners.

College of Osteopaths (and Naturopaths) Practitioners Association,
110 Thorkhill Road,
Thames Ditton,
Surrey KT7 0UW
Tel: 01 398 3308
General and training information; register of practitioners.

WESTERN MEDICINE
British Holistic Medical Association,
179 Gloucester Place,
London NW1 6DX
Tel: 01 262 5299
Information on holistic medicine; multi-disciplinary meetings and conferences.

British Medical Association,
B.M.A. House,
Tavistock Square,
London WC1
Tel: 01 387 4499
Professional association for doctors; enquiries about the NHS and referral (for further information) to other appropriate organizations.

INDEX